W
BLA

A volume in the series

The United States in the World

Edited by Mark Philip Bradley, David C. Engerman, Amy S. Greenberg, and Paul A. Kramer

A list of titles in this series is available at www.cornellpress.cornell.edu.

WHITE WORLD ORDER, BLACK POWER POLITICS

THE BIRTH OF AMERICAN INTERNATIONAL RELATIONS

ROBERT VITALIS

CORNELL UNIVERSITY PRESS
Ithaca and London

First published 2015 by Cornell University Press
First printing, Cornell Paperbacks, 2017

Printed in the United States of America

Library of Congress Cataloging-in-Publication Data

Vitalis, Robert, 1955– author.
    White world order, black power politics : the birth of American international relations / Robert Vitalis.
        pages cm
    Includes bibliographical references and index.
    ISBN 978-0-8014-5397-7 (cloth : alk. paper)
    ISBN 978-0-8014-5669-5 (pbk. : alk. paper)
    1. International relations—Study and teaching (Higher)—United States—History—20th century.
2. United States—Race relations—History—20th century.   3. Racism in higher education—United States—History—20th century.   4. Imperialism—Historiography.   5. Howard University—History—20th century.   I. Title.
    JZ1305.V49 2015
    327.730089'96073—dc23   2015018531

Cornell University Press strives to use environmentally responsible suppliers and materials to the fullest extent possible in the publishing of its books. Such materials include vegetable-based, low-VOC inks and acid-free papers that are recycled, totally chlorine-free, or partly composed of nonwood fibers. For further information, visit our website at www.cornellpress.cornell.edu.

For Chloe and Phoebe
Σὰγαπῶ πάρα πολὺ

Contents

PREFACE

This book has its origins in a cold, gray December afternoon in Worcester, Massachusetts, as I wandered through Clark University's Goddard Library. During its founding decades, Clark was at the forefront of the development of graduate education in the United States, but those days are long gone. I was teaching international relations there in the early 1990s and working hard to avoid my students' final papers when I pulled William Koelsch's history of the school off the stacks. In the section discussing Clark's signal contributions to early twentieth-century social science, Koelsch credited psychologist G. Stanley Hall and historian (and, after 1915, professor of history and international relations) George Hubbard Blakeslee with starting the discipline's first specialized journal, the *Journal of Race Development*, in 1910, which the editors renamed the *Journal of International Relations* in 1919.[1]

This can't be correct, I thought. Everyone in the field understands that the new post-Versailles internationalist think tanks—the Royal Institute of International Affairs in London and the Council on Foreign Relations in New York—rolled out the field's first journals in the mid-1920s. Koelsch, though, was in fact right. My eye-opening reeducation began with the brittle pages of the twelve bound volumes of the forgotten journal and, from there, the Blakeslee Papers at Clark and the Hamilton Fish Armstrong Papers at Princeton University. These records let me piece together the story of the sale of "Blakeslee's magazine" to the Council on Foreign Relations, relaunched with its new, they hoped, punchier title, *Foreign Affairs*.

It took some time for this more accurate story of the origins of the field of international relations to circulate. I began giving papers at conferences on the early history in 1998 and published the first version in 2002.[2] I also contacted the digital repository JSTOR proposing that they make the journal available. I was told that the digitization and dissemination of the *Journal of Race Development* was not in the cards, although I was not told why. Nonetheless, it is available today with a link to its successors. The early volumes can also be downloaded from the Internet Archive. A Wikipedia entry now exists as well. *Foreign Affairs*, though, has not yet amended the brief history on its Web site that William Bundy wrote in 1994.[3] Blakeslee's signal contribution is not referenced there.

Despite this historical amnesia, the journal matters because of what it tells us about the constitutive role of imperialism and racism in bringing an academic discipline in the United States into existence. The evidence of the racist foundations of international relations grew overwhelming as I continued my investigation. My archival research included the private papers of long-forgotten faculty in Cambridge, Chicago, Madison, New York, Princeton, and the Library of Congress in Washington, D.C., and extended to the records of foundations and the many *white* (of course never identified as such) internationalist associations, institutes, research centers, and schools that the Rockefeller Foundation and Carnegie Corporation subsidized in the early decades of the twentieth century. Suffice it to say that the history I uncovered is not how practitioners understand the past of their profession—far from it. It is not the inspiring kind of story that Americans prefer to hear about themselves.

The discovery of the first journal opened my eyes in a second, much more personal and consequential sense. Hall and Blakeslee had invited W. E. B. Du Bois, the giant of twentieth-century thought, or so I came to view him, to join as a founding member of the editorial board. Du Bois published two essays in the *Journal of Race Development*, including most of what became "Souls of White Folk," the most powerful chapter in his incendiary *Darkwater: Voices from within the Veil* (1920). *Foreign Affairs* published him five more times in the next decades before the government began its persecution of the 83-year-old firebrand and alleged subversive.[4] I wondered how had I gone through college and a PhD program in political science and not read him, and I resolved to make up for lost time.

Encountering Du Bois for the first time at age 40—around the time I was promoted to associate professor—influenced the direction of my research but also changed what I would do in the classroom. My retraining began with teaching a course on Du Bois in global perspective with Clark historian Janette Greenwood. Team teaching the undergraduate seminar was a way of learning on the run, which left me wanting to study Du Bois and the thought of other African American thinkers in more depth. So I took a year off from teaching and from research on the Middle East, my ostensible area of specialization, to study African American social and intellectual history with Nell Painter and Kevin Gaines (both then at Princeton) and the history of the "science" of race with Adolph Reed Jr. (then at the New School of Social Research and now a colleague at the University of

Pennsylvania.) Subsequently I began reading the published works and private papers—at UCLA, the Library of Congress, and most crucially at Howard University—of the African Americans who were most engaged, together with the towering Du Bois, in the debates in the field of U.S. international relations in the first half of the twentieth century. Ultimately, that research transformed my understanding of the history and sociology of the discipline.

The African American scholars and the dissections of racism's role in the global imperial order have disappeared from the histories that the vast majority of professors of international relations in the United States tell about themselves and their work today. They view the past the way I once did, with a similar set of blinders. It is thus no surprise that many see and know of no connection between the practices of hierarchy and the field of international relations in the United States. The evidence, on many accounts, is just not there.

In a first-year graduate methods course in the social sciences, students learn to think in terms of a null hypothesis; that is, the default idea that no relationship exists between two phenomena. The central task for the social scientist is to use inferential statistics to establish the grounds for rejecting or disproving the null hypothesis. Multiple times in the course of justifying this project to peers in the profession I was told that black thinkers, beginning with Du Bois, aren't taught in international relations courses because none wrote anything of importance to it. In the chapters that follow, I marshal the archival evidence that forces us to reject that idea—the null hypothesis, in this case—as false, just as it has been rejected in discipline after discipline in the United States in the wake of the black studies revolution that has rewritten the intellectual and social history of the academic professions and of the wider world beyond.

Acknowledgments

Thanks go first to those who subsidized the work: the American Political Science Association, Clark University, the University of Pennsylvania's Christopher H. Browne Center for International Politics and the University Research Foundation, the joint Peace and Security Committee of the Social Science Research Council and the MacArthur Foundation, and the Woodrow Wilson International Center for Scholars. I have never had as much difficulty raising funds as I have had with *White World Order, Black Power Politics*, and I want to express my gratitude in particular to all the reviewers, committee members, and trustees who fought on my behalf (and, incidentally, confirm the validity of the sociological model of academic knowledge production that informs the book). I include the allies I know by name below.

I am grateful to Cambridge University Press for permission to republish (as chapters one and two) my essay "The Noble Science of Imperial Administration and Its Laws of Race Development," which originally appeared in *Comparative Studies in Society and History* in 2010.

The list of advisors, caregivers, critics, and patrons is long, and I am sure I have forgotten a few. Thanks go to Begum Adalet, Hisham Aidi, Raphael Allan, Lisa Anderson, Osman Balkan, Duncan Bell, Tom Bender, Donald Blackmer, Bridget Blagoevski-Trazoff, Jessica Blatt, Cathy Boone, Terry Burke, Zoltan Buzas, Neta Crawford, Victoria de Grazia, David Ekbladh, David Engerman, Cynthia Enloe, Betsy Esch, Joe Feagin, Tom Ferguson, Kevin Gaines, Kim Gilmore, Julian Go, Jane Gordon, Lewis Gordon, Janette Greenwood, David Grondin, Nicholas Guilhot, Charlie Hale, Michael Hanchard, Deborah Harrold, Vicky Hattam, Errol Henderson, John Hobson, Alan Hunter, Amy Kaplan, Persis Karim, Lauren Kientz, Ellen Kennedy, Bruce Kuklick, the late and sorely missed Riki Kuklick, Paul Kramer, Bob Latham, Tilden LeMelle, Daniel Levine, Lily Ling, Zachary Lockman, David Long, Wahneema Lubiano, Ian Lustick, Ed Mansfield, Mark Mazower, Michael McGandy, Gil Merkx, Tim Mitchell, Anthony Monteiro, Dan Monk, Anne Norton, Amy Offner, Nell Painter, Jason Parker, Susan Pedersen, Brenda

Plummer, Vijay Prasad, Adolph Reed Jr., Katharina Rietzler, David Roediger, Dorothy Ross, Kevin Rugamba, Ashley Salisbury, Barbara Savage, Brian Schmidt, George Shepard Jr., Robbie Shilliam, Brad Simpson, Nikhil Singh, Rogers Smith, Steve Smith, Ted Swedenburg, the Tabard Inn, Gaetano Di Tommaso, Evalyn Tennant, Deborah Thomas, Ann Tickner, Peter Trubowitz, Penny Von Eschen, Srdjan Vucetic, Kate Wahl, Alex Weiseger, Stephen Wertheim, Donald Will, Howard Winant, Michael Winston, Kent Worcester, Kevin Yelvington, Marilyn Young, and Tukufu Zuberi.

When Chloe Silverman, my in-house critic and model historian and sociologist of science, gave birth to our daughter, Phoebe Elana Vitalis, in May 2011, my department and dean granted me paternity leave and more over the next two years. That time permitted me to finish this book. Charles and Ray Eames, Bill Hajjar, and Florence Knoll made it comfortable while I did so. It is Chloe and Phoebe though who inspire me. The book is a lilac for them.

Finally, thanks to Beck, Bill Callahan, Andrew Chalfen and Trolleyvox, Susan Cowsill, Miles Davis, Bill Evans, Ferron, Astrid Gilberto, the late Charlie Haden, Jason Isbell, Joni Mitchell, Laura Nyro, Luciana Souza, Jeff Tweedy, Neil Young, Lucinda Williams, Brian Wilson, and Jonathan Wilson.

As my daughter says, "turn it up until the speakers pop."

WHITE WORLD ORDER,
BLACK POWER POLITICS

Introduction
A Mongrel American Social Science

> —Since its inception, American social science has
> been closely bound up with American Negro destiny.
>
> —Ralph Ellison, "American Dilemma"

> —What is this thing called International Relations
> in the "English speaking countries" other than the
> "study" about how to "run the world from positions
> of strength"? In other places, at other times, it might
> be something else, but within those states which had
> the influence—as opposed to those that did not—it
> was little more than a rationalization for the exercise
> of power by the dominant nations over the weak.
> There was no "science of International Relations"
> . . . The subject so-called was an ideology of control
> masking as a proper academic discipline.
>
> —E. H. Carr, "Introduction" to
> *The Twenty Years' Crisis*

In the first decades of the twentieth century in
the United States, international relations meant race relations. This sentence
is bound to strike many readers as both strange and wrong, just as it once
did me. The problem of empire or imperialism, sometimes referred to as
"race subjection," was what preoccupied the first self-identified professors of
international relations. They wrestled with the prospect that a race war might
lead to the end of the world hegemony of whites, a future that appeared to
many to be in the offing. The scholars had also identified the epicenter of
the global biological threat in the three square miles or so at the northern end
of Manhattan borough known as Harlem.

Each of these claims at first presentation seems false because 100 years
later, a new common sense has taken hold. Today, professors teach that international relations is the scientific study of the interaction among "states"
(or "countries" to the uninitiated), with other, lesser "actors" trailing behind.
They also speak more abstractly about study of the "state system."[1] Students
interested in race relations look elsewhere in course catalogs and to other
experts and departments.[2] So too do those wanting to learn about empires,

1

because imperialism is a thing of the past for social scientists. And no one thinks of Harlem as the capital of a country, so it has no standing in any contemporary understanding of international relations.[3]

In African American studies, meanwhile, together with those parts of the humanities and human sciences most impacted by the field's emergence in the 1960s–1970s, scholars study the Harlem Renaissance, which is a shorthand for the remarkable movement of intellectual and cultural self-determination that in the 1920s had white scholars scrambling to head off the end days. Many of the thinkers most closely associated with the movement taught at Howard University in Washington, D.C. The 250-acre campus in the northwest sector of the nation's capital with its Harvard- and Chicago-trained star faculty remains terra incognita in all standard accounts of the discipline of international relations in the United States. This last fact may prove the most discomfiting one in the years ahead.

When we follow the archival record to places beyond Hyde Park, Harvard Square, and Morningside Heights, the central repositories of America's "national" international relations history, to Sugar Hill in Harlem (a mile or so from Columbia University but a world away, judging from our maps of intellectual fields); the District of Columbia's Shaw neighborhood; Port of Spain, Trinidad; Camden, United Kingdom; and Accra, Ghana, it is as if we've left behind one field of study and intellectual disputation and wandered into another that is both wholly separate and intimately related. For convenience, call that field the history of "black internationalism." A central debate in that field concerns the Cold War's impact on the U.S. "long" civil rights movement, with its roots in the Harlem Renaissance, and on the academic enterprise we know as African American studies.[4]

What *White World Order, Black Power Politics* shows is that the intellectual entanglements in Morningside Heights and Sugar Hill are part of a common and complicated history. The project of liberation was from its inception (and by necessity) a world-spanning political and theoretical movement in response to the theory and practice of white supremacy. What is new and important in this book is the discovery that the intellectuals, institutions, and arguments that constituted international relations were shaped by and often directly concerned with advancing strategies to preserve and extend that hegemony against those struggling to end their subjection. The new science emerged as a key supplier of intellectual rationales for the political class long before the Cold War—in fact, for the entirety of the long American imperial century.[5] This discovery upends our commonplace understandings of international relations and U.S. foreign policy.

In this book I trace developments in the history of academic institutions and the politics of academic life not as if they constitute a cloistered world (the "ivory tower"), but as an important part of the history of the United States in the world. It is effectively a sequel to my last book, *America's Kingdom*, about the unbroken past of hierarchy on the world's mining frontiers.[6] There I used company and State Department records to show that the story that the private-owned giant Arabian American Oil Company told about its alleged commitment to developing Saudi Arabia's human capital—one that scholars continued to reproduce unreflectively decades later—was a myth. Similarly, the private papers of professors, journals, research centers, and foundations reveal a story fundamentally at odds with established belief, even if some still consider the oil sector to be orders of magnitude more important to the twentieth century than the knowledge industry. Yes, academics who first defined their subject matter as international relations in the period 1900–1910 were never satisfactorily practical enough to suit the statesmen (and they were all men back then). Policymakers thought the same about most of a later, somewhat better-known, cast of action intellectuals who had occasional walk-on roles in our histories of the Cold War—the George Kennans, Hans Morgenthaus, Walt Rostows, William Kaufmanns, Bernard Brodies, and so on. This tendency on the part of statesmen and politicians to dismiss the value of scholars and their theories continued in the post-1945 era even as the expanding national security state drew increasing numbers of new and rebranded experts on peace and war, defense strategy, and foreign policy into its orbit. Meanwhile, the critics of U.S. Cold War policy considered the various strategic studies institutes, centers, schools, and so forth at the head of the newly commissioned, government-subsidized academic armada to be nothing less than a full-fledged service arm of the empire.[7] The influence of a discipline and its reigning ideas entails more than the extent to which some professor has the ear of the prince or research findings contribute to policy.

Colleges and universities are crucial, obviously, to the continuous reproduction of our everyday ways of thinking, speaking, and writing about world politics, ways that are recognizable not only to the miniscule readership of scholarly journals such as *International Security* and *International Organization* but also to those who read (or write for) the *New York Times* and *Foreign Affairs* or who watch (or appear on) *PBS News Hour* and the *Daily Show*: imagine all those graduates of the Baby Boom– and Cold War–driven years of expansion in American higher education who studied or majored in the subject en route to careers as attorneys, journalists, researchers, writers, teachers, consultants, chief executive officers, department of defense analysts, legislators, staffers, generals, presidential advisors, secretaries of state, and, not least, professors. Henry Kissinger (PhD Harvard 1954), Madeline Albright (PhD Columbia, 1976), and Condoleezza Rice (PhD University of Denver 1981), among many other notables, all studied and taught international relations prior to their years in the White House and leadership positions in the State Department.[8] Fareed Zakaria, the 28-year-old who oversaw a major facelift of the magazine *Foreign Affairs* prior to his star turn at *Newsweek*, *Time*, and CNN, is another PhD (Harvard 1993) in the "realist tradition" as he put it, of "international relations history and theory."[9] The alumni list is almost impossibly long, and their influence, although hard to measure, is real.

Think back to the U.S. invasion of Iraq in 2003 (or for that matter to NATO's intervention in Bosnia in 1993) for evidence of the ways undergraduate lecture and graduate comprehensive exam categories inform debates in the public sphere. Antagonists then routinely identified (or derided their opponents) as Kissengerian "realists" or Wilsonian "idealists." Others claimed that positions on questions of war and peace in the post-9/11 era no longer corresponded to these old ideological constructs (or, as students learn to refer to them, theories, theoretical traditions, or paradigms).[10] Recall, too, the wide play given in the mid-2000s and after to the idea of "soft power." Harvard's Joseph Nye (PhD Harvard 1964), a onetime student of Pan Africanism now judged among the top four or five or six most influential thinkers in the discipline, had coined the term a decade earlier in *Bound to Lead* (1990), and he hit it big after rolling it out a second time in *Soft Power* (2004).[11] Similarly, *Clash of Civilizations* (1996), a book by his late colleague Samuel Huntington (Ph.D. Harvard 1950), Zakaria's dissertation supervisor, sold in greater numbers and presumably earned the author a far greater advance than is typical for a book traded on the academic market.[12] People inside and outside the Washington, D.C., beltway certainly acted as if these books matter.

This is not to begrudge them, by the way. They represent a long tradition of what Bruce Kuklick calls the discipline's "intellectual middlemen" who are skilled at getting ideas across to nonacademic audiences in Washington, New York, and points beyond.[13] Intellectuals played this role long before the Cold War, and it is hardly surprising to find them rediscovering and recycling ideas from earlier years. For example, *Clash of Civilizations* resembles the earlier, arguably more influential, and no less sensational *The Rising Tide of Color: The Threat against White World Supremacy* (1920) by one of Huntington's forebears, T. Lothrop Stoddard (PhD Harvard 1916). Stoddard wrote his dissertation under Archibald Cary Coolidge (PhD Freiburg 1892), the founding editor of *Foreign Affairs*. Stoddard also provided one of the first analyses I know of America's soft power, but his many works on international affairs are all but unknown now. Huntington and Nye (among others) reprise the intellectual middleman's role and also reanimate the arguments of an earlier, not very well known era when biological racism and resource imperialism shaped the discipline and, not coincidentally, the policies of successive U.S. administrations. That history is critical to recovering the ideas of what I call the Howard school of international relations theory, whose leading thinkers alone evinced a commitment to understanding and writing about white world supremacy from the standpoint of its victims.

International Relations 101

The problem, we now know in large part thanks to historians and sociologists of science, is that scholars reliably produce unreliable accounts of the past of their own fields.[14] International relations is no exception.[15] American schoolchildren learn the story of the midnight ride of Paul Revere together with any number of other myths about "the nation's origins, achievements, and destiny."[16] Such myths function to produce a common consciousness and obscure the existence of hierarchy. The practitioner histories of international relations in the United States do roughly the same thing to the same end through the socialization of graduate students in the rituals of PhD programs and through lecture courses that pass on the discipline's invented traditions and escape from knowledge to generations of undergraduates who will become public intellectuals, politicians, and policymakers.

Every year thousands of undergraduates across the United States sign up for a class titled "Introduction to International Relations." In the first week or two they learn that three broad rival theoretical traditions vie for explanatory primacy among specialists. The first (and it is always first) among unequals is "realism." The second is "liberalism" or "liberal internationalism." The third is "constructivism" (thirty years ago it was "neo-Marxism"), a kind of residual category that consists of various persuasions of critics on the discipline's margins, the serious consideration of which is honored more in the breach than in the observance.

For self-identified "realists," the struggle for power among states is a law operating across space and time, one that statesmen in antiquity or their later chroniclers discovered and that their descendants discount at their (and our) peril. Instructors might drive the lesson home for undergraduates by assigning a fragment of the *History of the Peloponnesian War* by Athenian general and historian Thucydides (ca. 460–395 BCE) that is known as the Melian dialogue to demonstrate the timelessness of realism's truth about power politics: "The strong do what they can and the weak suffer what they must."[17]

Who teaches these introductory classes? The professors at the podiums in the large lecture halls are more often than not freshly minted PhDs and new assistant professors, while those who run the small discussion sections—if the undergraduates are lucky enough to have them—are first- and second-year graduate students. An even more reliable generalization is that all those young professors and graduate students in the intro courses will be white. The key point, however, is that these professors and would-be professors have committed vast amounts of their time and energy in an intensive period of immersion in the discipline and its literature. It is any academic profession's primary method for passing on its origin story in the guise of a canon of theories and theorists.

That is, the chains of transmission of the classical beliefs from Thucydides and their transubstantiation into theories by his putative intellectual heirs come to comprise the organizing framework and content of all those intro courses, the undergraduate version a stripped-down version of what is taught to the graduate students. The new professors will design their first stand-alone classes based on the ones for which they served as teaching assistants, which are based on the ones their own professors served as teaching assistants for slightly longer ago at one of the twenty to thirty research universities that reproduce the professoriate (and, increasingly, produce faculty outside the tenure system) across the country. Little wonder, then, that the syllabi all tend to look the same.[18] Identification of and with a tradition helps to make the discipline something more than a collection of professors and graduate students, blogs, journals, annual conventions, PhD qualifying exam reading lists, and anxieties of the moment. Just as inevitably, however, disciplining of this kind shifts one's critical gaze away from the complicated history of the development and transmission of what more often than not are fables of origin.[19]

Consider a heretofore-unrecognized puzzle that emerges from the archive of model syllabi, textbooks, and surveys of teaching and research in international relations that was beginning to be compiled and published in the mid-1920s, which reflected the accumulation of knowledge under the then-new rubric for the previous ten to fifteen years.[20] None of those long-forgotten authors and advocates for recognition of a new interdisciplinary specialization described anything remotely like a continuous tradition traceable to the ancients. To do so would hardly have aided the legitimacy of a claim of autonomy for their new enterprise and its specialized object of knowledge. The pattern is in fact common to academic specializations of all kinds that emerged later in the twentieth century, from art history and literary criticism to cultural anthropology and area studies.[21]

In the case of international relations, conditions changed after World War II. Although international relations professors continued to express anxieties in the 1950s and 1960s about the identity of field as a "real" discipline—presidents of the 50-year-old American Political Science Association (APSA) were still having trouble specifying precisely how their work differed from that of sociologists, psychologists, anthropologists, economists, and even historians—international relations was no longer in need of defense within the postwar university. The Cold War was all the justification the discipline required. It is during this new moment of relative disciplinary security that a new cohort, in the course of seeking to establish its own hegemony, began a process by which they elided "the historical boundary between the era of the research university and the pre-professional era."[22] The professors have not looked back since—at least not without blinders on.

Today, unaware of the history of its early decades, a new generation of specialists in international relations in the United States since the 1950s practice their craft under the sway of two entwined myths of empire. The first is the idea that the United States is not and never was (much of) an imperial power. The second is that the discipline itself has never showed much interest in the study of imperialism. The first idea is, to my thinking, an example of willful ignorance in the face of much devastating argument (and violence) to the contrary across the globe in the last half century. It is basically the academics' version of the flag pin that all politicians now routinely attach to their lapels.[23] We might agree to disagree on this point, although it would take some work to explain the seeming delusion under which an earlier generation labored. There is no disputing the mythical status of the second idea. The authoritative version can be found in the opening pages of Columbia University political scientist Michael Doyle's *Empires* (1986), where he baldly states that "mainstream" international relations showed no scholarly interest in imperialism, a point no reviewer of the book ever challenged him on.[24] Like all myths, its value is not in the facts that it purports to offer but in what it tells us about experts on world affairs such as Doyle who believe it to be a valid argument about the world.

Doyle's disciplinary ancestors knew the opposite to be true about the United States and about imperialism. By "ancestors" I don't mean the fictive ones conjured in today's textbooks and undergraduate lectures. By ancestors I mean (and I use this identifier intentionally) the men at Princeton, Columbia, and elsewhere who founded the first international relations departments, funding committees, memorials, journals, summer institutes, research centers, conferences, and professional associations. I include those who gained the early support of the Carnegie Corporation and the Rockefeller Foundation.

The term "ancestor" includes the textbooks and model syllabi that identified and tried to draw boundaries around the new field for the first time in the years before and after World War I and those who went on the radio and wrote in the mass circulation magazines and newspapers to disseminate its scientific findings.[25] By "ancestor" I mean the whole system of intellectual, professional, and institutional production that has made international relations what it is today, including how international relations is taught in those introductory courses that pass the rudiments of the discipline on to the next generation of scholars, opinion makers, and policy professionals.

Application of a Model of Mixed Institutional Origins

Three well-known phenomena of the last decades of the nineteenth century converged to influence the turn by U.S. universities toward studying the problems that professors and what we now call public intellectuals called supremacy and dependence. A new round of imperial competition and expansion into Africa, Asia, and Latin America was in full swing. The new imperialism coincided with the creation of the flagship institutions of the modern social sciences in America, including departments, schools, endowed professorships, and professional associations.[26] Within many of those departments, evolutionary theory, social Darwinism, and racial anthropology shaped the research orientations of leading scholars and schools.[27]

Various sociologists, political scientists, historians, psychologists, and geographers at Wisconsin, Yale, Chicago, Clark, Johns Hopkins, Harvard, the University of Pennsylvania, and Columbia begin to carve out space for the interdisciplinary study of international relations. They did so even before some of the flagship departments and professional associations of the disciplines were founded.[28] It was insufficient even then, however, to stake a claim for autonomy and resources for the new specialization simply on the ground that the problems produced by increasing contact and conflict across the world's biological borders spilled over the disciplinary ones. Rather, the pioneering specialists offered a unique approach to the better management of colonial administration and race subjection. The theory of "race development" held out the prospect of a more peaceful and prosperous white hegemony while reducing the threat of the race war that preoccupied self-identified white elites in the United States and elsewhere in the 1890s and 1920s and again in the 1950s.

In light of these facts, I propose we do for the history of international relations what others have done for the broader social, cultural, and political history of the United States (of which the academic discipline is a part).

In short, its racism needs to be brought to light and given serious attention. As a case in point and a kind of model of inquiry, we can look to Ann Douglas's 1995 award-winning cultural history of jazz-age New York, *Terrible Honesty: Mongrel Manhattan in the 1920s*. Its key argument is that we can't understand the history of American modernism without understanding the history of Harlem, its "Renaissance," and the African American movement of liberation. Modernism was, she insisted, a thoroughly entangled or, as an international relations professor might say, "complex-interdependent" move-ment of black and white writers, novelists, poets, musicians, playwrights, and philosophers.

What is true about modernism and Manhattan is also true about inter-national relations in the United States in a fundamental respect. That is, we can't understand the history of the early decades of the discipline without understanding the long and globe-spanning freedom movements that are central to its intellectual, social, and institutional development. Consider an-other example to be explored in more detail later, in this case one linking the Harlem Renaissance directly to an important institution of the discipline-in-formation. The publishers of Howard University theorist Alain Locke's famous "Harlem: Mecca of the New Negro" (1925) headed New York's Foreign Policy Association, a more influential group in those years than the city's other private membership organization, the Council on Foreign Re-lations, which at the time functioned more like a club, and a sleepy one at that. To Foreign Policy Association leaders, the Harlem Renaissance was an instance of race development similar to other movements and places where "race contacts" had intensified, notably in settler societies around the globe.

Harlem thus primarily served as a model in the negative sense for the fu-ture of world order as theorized by white scholars in the new modern scien-tific discipline. The Harlem-as-crucible-of-modernism in Douglas's account represented intersecting vectors of artists and thinkers remaking mass culture via engagement with black poets, painters, and playwrights. The opposite was true in the case of international relations theory, where self-identified white professors sought to understand, explain, and improve the world's stock of inferior beings and thus allegedly avert political and biological catastrophe. There, the vision of "interdependence" quickly gave way to the laws, as they described it, of "supremacy and dependency." For the psychologists, geog-raphers, historians, and political scientists pioneering the scientific study of international relations, in other words, Harlem, particularly as the northern migration of African Americans took off in the early 1910s, exemplified the threat to white supremacy posed by "backward" and dependent peoples across the globe.

Harlem represented something distinctly different to the first African American theorists of international relations. As Locke himself wrote, it was the "largest Negro community in the world," the "advance guard of the African peoples in their contact with Twentieth Century civilization," the "home of the Negro's Zionism," and, as "in India, in China, in Egypt, Ireland, Russia, Bohemia, [Jewish] Palestine, and Mexico," the center of a people's "resurgence" and pursuit of "self-determination."[29] It had drawn tens of thousands of migrants from the rural South. It was, not least, a refuge. Locke's Howard University colleagues would frequent the Hotel Theresa (the "Harlem Waldorf") in order to escape the oppressive condition of Jim Crow in the nation's capital city, Washington, D.C.

African Americans might earn PhDs at Harvard, thus demonstrating the validity of the laws of race development. At the same time, they were denied a role in the white profession and university system and were instead forced to create their own journals and associations.[30] In 1963, historian John Hope Franklin described the reality of the conditions under which he and his more senior colleagues still labored within the white academy. "When he is remembered at all he is all too often an afterthought. When his work is recognized it is usually pointed as the work of a Negro. . . . Such recognition is as much the product of the racist mentality as the Negro restrooms in the Montgomery airport are."[31] Even this subordinate form of "recognition" was too much for some white academics. As we will see, the prominence of intellectuals such as W. E. B. Du Bois and Locke in a movement that asserted black people's ineluctable right to equality and liberation led influential whites to denounce higher education for African Americans as a misguided experiment gone horribly wrong.

If we tried to plot a normal distribution (bell) curve of beliefs in black people's capacities for more or less self-determination over the shorter or longer term, we'd fail. The results would skew to the right; that is, against equality. There were white scholars and public intellectuals associated with the new discipline-in-formation who advocated more or less permanent tutelage for darker and inferior people. So T. Lothrop Stoddard, one of the earliest advocates for realism in U.S. foreign relations in the 1920s, proposed the creation of a new representative institution for blacks that would determine policy in matters of exclusive concern to the permanently subordinate race, thus making the House of Representatives and Senate institutions by and for whites alone. Others, including many of the leading race development theorists, could imagine a time a century or two in the future when at least some of the backward peoples would have developed the capacity for self-government. As far as I have been able to determine, however, in the 1920s and 1930s no white international relations scholar argued on either principled or pragmatic grounds for the restoration of black citizenship rights, the dismantling of Jim Crow in the United States, and self-governance, let alone independence, for the colonies. Chicago's Fredrick L. Schuman and other so-called fellow travelers might have taken such a position had they been pressed, but Schuman did not take such a position in his published work. The shape of the curve would approximate a normal distribution only if we added the positions of African American and Afro-Caribbean thinkers.

Princeton-trained Raymond Leslie Buell was the only professor I could find in the 1920s–1930s who actually engaged with African Americans as intellectuals.[32] Buell wrote the discipline's best-selling textbook *International Relations* (1925), in which he analyzed the great problems of world order emerging from the "restless energy of Caucasian people" in their "search for new markets" and "demand for cheap labor." The primary problem was imperialism and the tensions that resulted as white men competed to extend their dominance over inferior races. Whites in settler societies from Canada to New Zealand were also all wrestling with imperialism's mirror image; that is, the tensions that arose as nonwhites sought entrance into the white man's country.

Buell quit his Harvard professorship to run the research program of the Foreign Policy Association because he said he wanted to do something meaningful to improve a world of rising tensions between the races. Yet he based his plans for reform of the southern United States on the system in place in South Africa. His mentor, constitutional scholar Edward S. Corwin, a friend of Woodrow Wilson and editor of the influential series in political science that published *International Relations*, died still waiting to see the Supreme Court's decision in *Brown v. Board* reversed and segregation brought back to schools.[33] Through the World War II years, and as the professors of international relations began to realign history and theory to meet the needs of the new U.S. national security state, too many of them continued to uphold the so-called color line rather than engage critically with the problem of hierarchy and modern world order in the ways that Alain Locke and other renaissance thinkers pioneered.

The Howard School

Explicating the relationship of racism to imperialism was an abiding concern of the scholars that comprised the Howard school of international relations. They include Locke (PhD, Harvard 1918), the Philadelphia-born intellectual powerhouse who won a Rhodes scholarship to Oxford in 1907 (the first and only black awardee for another fifty-six years) and a primary challenger of central tenets of race development theory.[34] The Nobel Prize–winning Ralph Bunche was a onetime radical Marxist thinker (PhD Harvard 1934) who joined the Howard faculty in 1928, a year after graduating from UCLA. His close comrade on the faculty, E. Franklin Frazier (PhD Chicago 1931), studied at Clark and did pioneering work on the black bourgeoisie. They clashed off and on with the pan-Africanist protégé of Du Bois, Rayford Logan (PhD Harvard 1936), who joined the history department in 1938. Bunche, Frazier, and Locke brought the Trinidad-born Eric Williams (DPhil Oxford 1938), whose work upended moralist explanations for the end of the slave trade, to Howard's political science department. He later became first prime minister of independent Trinidad and Tobago. And Logan invited Michigan-born Merze Tate (PhD Radcliffe 1941), the first black woman to receive a doctorate in international relations, to join the history department after Williams and Bunche opposed her hire (and that of a second woman) in political science.

My use of the term *Howard school* harks back the 1990s turn toward speaking about a distinct Italian school of international relations theory inspired by the work of Antonio Gramsci. That label is artificial and complicated: the Italian school scholars did not all use Gramscian ideas in the same way to the same ends, and some identified in this way rejected the label.[35] The same is true about the Howard school theorists and their evolving ideas about racism and imperialism; doubtless they would have rejected the label too. Nonetheless, the Howard school thinkers stand out for their early and relentless critiques of the supposed truths of racial science and the role racism played in sustaining imperialism. They also stand out for the connections they forged—unique among their generation of professors—with the theoreticians of liberation and the future leaders of independent Africa and the island nations of the Caribbean. So despite their intellectual and political differences, they represent a critical counternetwork to the networks dedicated to upgrading the institutions of colonial rule that white professors forged with the so-called Geneva institutions in the era of the League of Nations.

The silence about (that is to say, ignorance of) the Howard school scholars and their work on world politics confirms a central insight of Toni Morrison's "Black Matters." She says that after World War II the American academy took to ignoring racism instead of facing its history and ongoing effects. She calls it "a graceful, even generous liberal gesture" on the part of literary critics who remained silent about practices of exclusion and subordination that are present in the history of letters, the construction of literary canons that entirely excluded African American authors, and the criticisms deemed worth making about the canonical texts, but the point can be generalized, as I demonstrate here.[36] Virtually every history of international relations to date turns out to be about *white* political scientists teaching in *white* departments and publishing in *white* journals. The race blindness is almost certainly unselfconscious. That's Morrison's point. Nor would it surprise her to learn that in the past fifty years the only serious discussions within international relations of Du Bois, Alain Locke, and the handful of other African American theorists of international relations are by the smaller handful of African Americans and Afro Caribbeans who taught international relations beginning in the early 1970s and who teach it today.[37] It turns out that identity matters to the most basic practices of discipline making.[38]

While what I have called the "norm against noticing" explains much of the variance, additional factors are at work that make it harder rather than easier to identify any of the Howard school theorists with the emerging discipline of international relations.[39] One is the unavailability of some critical texts. Bunche's *World View of Race* was not reissued as part of the effort to "restore his reputation," as Arnold Rampersand put it, with the airing on the Public Broadcasting Service of *Ralph Bunche: American Odyssey* (2001, dir. William Greaves).[40] Bunche had disowned his fifteen-year-old study of racism and imperialism in 1950, the year he won his Nobel peace prize and was named a vice president of the American Political Science Association (He served as its president in 1954.). The real revelation is Alain Locke and his controversial 1915 and 1916 Howard lectures on race development, which were not published until 1992. Similarly, the report he wrote in 1928 for the Foreign Policy Association on the League of Nations mandate system was not unearthed from the archives until 2012. Merze Tate's dissections of the failed arms control efforts of the early twentieth century and her histories of imperialist rivalries in the Pacific are also out of print, and four additional completed studies of imperialism in Australasia and Africa languish in her archive.

The more fundamental factor in accounting for the time it has taken to identify, contextualize, and wrestle with the ideas of the Howard school is that a critical mass of African American scholars did not emerge in Cold War international relations in the 1970s and 1980s. This was so despite the significant resources committed to building interdisciplinary African American Studies programs and departments at leading colleges and universities as a way to introduce "non-White subject matter in the curriculum," increase minority enrollment, and create a demand for black faculty.[41] The absence from international relations of all three—black faculty, students, and theory—is a striking difference from disciplines such as English, anthropology (which has since taught us a great deal about the relationship between colonialism and racism), and history (which shares borders with international relations and where nonetheless a virtual barrier has prevented the migration of a two-decade-old scholarship on race and U.S. foreign policy making). In the intervening decades these other fields have produced truer accounts of their own development, reorganized their curricula (at least in part), recognized the force of racism, and, of course, adopted the critiques and once-heretical ideas put forward by black thinkers from outside the segregated white institutions. In the case of international relations, as we will see, a weak challenge from within was contained, preserving the discipline as a white redoubt.

It might have been different. Certainly the divide between African American studies and international relations was not nearly as wide during the first decade of demonstrations, building takeovers, and demands for black and "Third World" studies as it is now. In African American studies today, each of the Howard school thinkers has a biographer and, with the exception of Merze Tate, an important position in the revisionist pantheon of "founders" of the new field.[42] African American studies is now the primary if posthumous home of Du Bois (in the way that sociology often claims Karl Marx as a "founder") and his interlocutors Locke and Frazier, who receive secondary appointments for their signal contributions to the interdisciplinary study of race. The posthumous appointments of Bunche and Logan were delayed for a while. That is because Logan, the onetime pan-Africanist went to his grave opposing black studies (and black identity), while Bunche, who had always rejected racial identification as the basis for organizing in the political arena, had come to be seen as an enemy rather than an ally of worldwide black liberation in the 1960s.

This book recovers some of the lost social scientific context and specifically international relations content of the work of Locke and his colleagues. We are fighting against the tide of the Cold War; the embrace in the African American intellectual community, as elsewhere, of the rewritten past of empire (it never happened); the "Americanist" cast of the departments and centers (to which black internationalism is a reaction), the juggernaut of academic specialization; and, not least, the distorting and flattening effects of all those African American studies lectures, syllabi, qualifying exams, and the like in the intervening decades.

A Minor in African American Studies

African American and Africana Studies departments and programs in U.S. universities emerged out of the demonstrations, takeovers of administration buildings, and so forth on American campuses in the late 1960s, when a student movement arose to demand the inclusion of "black studies" in the curriculum.[43] Some institutions still call the relevant administrative unit the "Department of Black Studies" and the undergraduate course of study the "major in Black Studies." As historian Martha Biondi shows, a fundamental objective in creating black studies was to expose the racism and thus the false claims that underpinned so-called objective and detached scholarship in the disciplines. The critical tool for doing so was to bring black people into history and theory, not just as subjects but also as sources of truer accounts of the world.[44]

Those who founded the first programs, departments, and professional associations emphasized the inescapable interdisciplinary nature of any systematic inquiry into the "development of people of African descent," to quote from the description of the major at Wesleyan University today. Where the exigencies of the Cold War, the needs of the new national security state, and the instrumentalism of foundation officials (from Carnegie to some extent but primarily from the Ford Foundation) drove the building of area studies centers and departments, the demand for Africana studies, in contrast, emerged "from below" and paved the way for women's and ethnic studies.[45] The Ford Foundation spent millions in the 1970s and 1980s on advanced research and teaching capacity, hoping to institutionalize its preferred academic model for what it called Afro-American studies.[46]

According to sociologist Fabio Rojas, who surveyed faculty and universities across the United States, as of the early 2000s, African American studies had survived institutional and intellectual conflicts over legitimacy (and budget lines) to secure a "niche" at "highly prestigious universities." Following Temple University's lead in 1988, the number of PhD programs have increased, albeit slowly. As of 2014 there are a dozen institutions where one can earn a PhD in Africana or black or African American Studies. At the same time, only about 10 percent of four-year colleges and universities offer undergraduate or graduate degrees, and most such programs are small and are often cobbled together through joint appointments. Rojas estimates that a typical department includes seven professors, at least some of whom will have home departments in, for example, history or English. The majority of programs offer bachelor but not master or doctoral degrees.

The boundaries of belonging in African American studies are highly porous in comparison, say, to economics, leading Rojas to call it "a permanent interdiscipline."[47] Nonetheless, in the case of international relations we have a good example of another discipline that until the 1960s or so continued to emphasize (or express anxiety about) both its necessarily "interdisciplinary" character and porous borders with history, political science, area studies, economics, geography, and so forth. Unlike African American studies, no one in the United States thinks of international relations as a permanent interdiscipline. Rather, at most universities international relations now exists formally as a group of specialists (a "subfield" in the profession's argot) within political science departments.

In the course of transmutation from a radical social movement in the 1960s–1970s to academic specialization in the 1980s–1990s, the *American* in African American studies increasingly drove teaching and research in the field. On the one hand, Biondi emphasizes the internationalist (or better) anti-imperialist commitments of the "student generation" and their solidarity with African or Third World liberation movements. On the other hand, Rojas's early 2000s survey reports the relatively low ranking accorded Padmore's *Pan-Africanism or Communism* (1955, reissued in 1972) in a list of would-be canonical texts headed by Du Bois's *Souls of Black Folk*, Toni Morrison's *Beloved*, and Lorraine Hansberry's *A Raisin in the Sun*.[48] Biondi also documents how early leaders of the black studies movement faced serious pushback from foundation officials, university administrations, and hostile white faculty as they tried to combine "the study of continental Africa, the Caribbean, and the United States."[49]

The strongest evidence of the Americanist tilt in the prestige departments—that is, away from the orientation in solidarity with colonial peoples and from the theorizing of the racism/imperialism nexus—is the recent campaign to "internationalize" the study of Aframerica through a renewed emphasis on hemispheric and trans-Atlantic movements of peoples and ideas.[50] This is an instance of a more widespread challenge to "the naturalization" of the American nation-state, or "methodological nationalism," one that is still under way across the more humanistic zones of the human sciences.[51] In 1998, anthropologist Jane Guyer, then at Northwestern University, unearthed the correspondence between her distinguished predecessor and the founder of Northwestern's African studies program, Melville Herskovits, and the Carnegie and Ford Foundations. He had tried to raise funds for a combined, Atlantic Ocean–spanning program in "Negro and African Studies."[52]

Back to the Future

Herskovits's design is a road not taken for Cold War–era Africa "area" studies, African American area studies from below, and, for that matter, for the one area never included on the Social Science Research Council's wartime maps of future "world areas" research, namely, the United States. It is, nonetheless, the model that was used in the 1920s when American race development theorists and their partners in Australia, Canada, China, Hawaii, Korea, Japan, and New Zealand launched the most important research organization in international relations of the interwar years, the Institute of Pacific Relations. Howard's Ralph Bunche attended the institute's Mont-Tremblant conference in 1942 while he was on leave from the university and was working for the Office of Strategic Services. Later he would claim that at the 1942 meeting, the deliberations—which by then had expanded to include Indian nationalists, among others—helped to lay the foundation for the future UN trusteeship system negotiated in San Francisco in 1945.[53]

Tufts political scientist Pearl Robinson, the president of the Association of African Studies in 2007, has done yeoman's work in commemorating Bunche's contribution as pioneering "Africanist," a field that she traces back to the 1880s.[54] Bunche did fieldwork in Togo and Dahomey, but he also did fieldwork in what we now know as Indonesia. Had Secretary of State Cordell Hull not overridden the color line in the State Department to appoint him associate chief of the Division of Dependent Area Affairs (under Alger Hiss), Bunche might be remembered now as a pioneering Asianist, since he had already secured funding to head a two-year study for the Institute of Pacific Relations on the future of the Indonesian independence movement.

What Bunche *was*—and, surely, self- and collective professional identifications then in play trump the ones waiting to be invented—was a specialist in comparative colonial administration, a field in which an ambitious Harvard government department offered the PhD in the 1920s. The field exam, which Raymond Leslie Buell and his colleagues devised, is as good an artifact as any—many more will be found in the pages to follow—of the lost world of the then-new science of international relations in the United States. Du Bois and Locke were engaged with its problems from the start, as second-class citizens to be sure, and things would get worse in the segregated departments and associations before they eventually got better.

Harvard historian William E. Langer (PhD Clark 1923) headed the Research and Analysis Branch of the Office of Strategic Services during World War II. Bunche had joined Langer's team as the British Empire Section's Africa expert, which is what led to his attending the Institute on Pacific Relation's Mont-Tremblant meeting. Langer launched his career as one of the young professors associated with the George Hubbard Blakeslee group at Clark, the founders of the new *Journal of Race Development*, another of those artifacts that we can use to recreate the lost world of the innovators at Harvard, Columbia, and elsewhere who were seeking solutions to the policy dilemmas that "modern" imperialism had produced. The most pressing policy problems arose, the first professors of international relations said, from the extension of the American colonial model in New Mexico and other territories to the new Caribbean and Pacific dependencies. They took great care to emphasize what was "new" about the causes, nature, and consequences of contemporary imperialism, thereby distinguishing the object and defining the boundaries of a new interdisciplinary space separate from the "traditional" concerns of the international lawyers or the antiquarian scholars of ancient Greece and Rome.

Langer also played a role as his teachers and friends oversaw the transition of the *Journal of Race Development/International Relations* to its new owners, the Council on Foreign Relations. He served as editorial assistant to the new editor of *Foreign Affairs*, Archibald Cary Coolidge, who was Blakeslee's teacher and another of the leading figures in the new discipline, and he also later took over the book review section from Clark's Harry Elmer Barnes. What made Langer's reputation and led to his appointment as the inaugural Coolidge Professor of History in 1936, however, was the publication the year before of the highly praised two-volume *Diplomacy of Imperialism*. Although it is virtually impossible to name a leading international relations scholar in the 1920s and 1930s who did not write on the topic of empire, Langer's study stood out for its critical reconsideration of the 30-year-old work by British economist John Hobson, *Imperialism* (1902). Langer repackaged the critique of Hobson as a stand-alone article in *Foreign Affairs*. Thirty years later, Merze Tate's editor had her cut a long first chapter on theories of imperialism from her newest book. Readers wouldn't be interested, he told her. Tate's dissertation supervisor meanwhile had confidentially advised the Rockefeller Foundation against even funding her study. As "far as her field of International Relations is concerned" the history of imperial rivalries in the Pacific was of little significance, he wrote.[55] The book never appeared. That act was a clear harbinger of the world we live in now.

Today a vast gulf divides international relations from Africana studies. It is wider certainly than the walk across Harvard Yard that gets you from the Weatherhead Center for International Affairs to the Hutchins Center for African and African American Research or to and from the high-rises, glass boxes, repurposed American Craftsmen bungalows, Gothic towers, and landmark Minoru Yamasaki buildings that house the two departments on other campuses. We could measure that distance in multiple ways, I suspect. There is little if any overlap in the students in the introductory courses, few if any double majors in an era when double majors are the norm, and the professors in the two disciplines have taken disparate paths to their respective PhDs—English or history or sociology first degrees in the case of Africana studies and political science in the overwhelming majority of cases in international relations. Citation counts would make the division clear as well. Or we can consider a simple anecdote. Du Bois, a giant of American arts, letters, and the social sciences, served on the editorial board of the *Journal of Race Development* and continued to publish on Africa in the successor publications. None of today's premier public intellectuals and leaders in the discipline Du Bois is said to have inspired—Michael Eric Dyson, Henry Louis Gates Jr., Cornel West—writes for *Foreign Affairs*.[56] It is not a criticism. It is an observation that helps explain the large gaps in the posthumously revised curricula vitae of the members of the Howard school.

Meanwhile, in quadrants where *Foreign Affairs* is sometimes mistaken for a peer-reviewed journal, practitioners of international relations unselfconsciously reproduce the views of those in the humanities a generation ago.[57] Political scientists typically understand the tradition of international relations scholarship to be race blind. States, not races, have always been the discipline's basic unit of analysis. The "security dilemma" leaders confront is the timeless problem that constitutes international relations as a discipline, based on ideas the practitioners now routinely trace back to the ancient wisdom of Thucydides and Machiavelli, unaware that the genealogy is an invention of the Cold War years. The specialists contend, further, that if people of color are not read or taught it is because they have not written books and articles that shaped the field or that matter to others working in it now. It cannot be because the hierarchical structures Americans have built, including the discipline itself, using the biologically false idea of race, are to blame.

My study of the Howard school thinkers and their entanglements with the white social scientific world shows how and why these political scientists have gotten it wrong. Consider William Langer's autobiography, *In and Out of the Ivory Tower*, which appeared in 1977, on the eve of his death and in the same year Merze Tate, one of the first political scientists to work on arms control, retired from Howard. Reviewing the start of his long career in Worcester and Cambridge and his role in launching *Foreign Affairs*, Langer thought it important to explain how in those days "international relations meant race relations."[58] Back then the Howard school theorists were the main source of dissent in a rigidly segregated profession regarding the pseudoscientific foundations of the new discipline and the most important center for theorizing the feasible alternatives to continued dependency and domination in the decades before 1960.

Where We Go From Here

I have organized the book chronologically, in four parts, divided into nine chapters. It is a history of the men, overwhelmingly, who argued about race and empire in the course of building institutions inside and outside the white academy in order to advance the new science of international relations. The ideas are known (by some), but not in this context. The institutions themselves are mostly unknown, although they matter a lot, since there is really no other way to define the discipline given, at least through the 1950s, an inability otherwise to distinguish what they did from other social scientists, as those same men routinely admitted. It is also a crowded cast of relatively unknown teachers, researchers, and academic entrepreneurs, so to make the narrative easier to follow, each of the four parts focuses primarily on a distinct pair of scholars: W. E. B. Du Bois and John William Burgess (1898 to World War I), Alain Locke and Raymond Leslie Buell (the interwar era), Ralph Bunche and Edward Mead Earle (World War II), and Rayford Logan and Harold Isaacs (the 1950s). The last chapter is the exception, appropriately, in that it turns to recount the career of Merze Tate.

Part I begins with the responses of the social sciences to America's conquest of Cuba, Guam, Hawaii, and the Philippines in 1898.[59] Imperialism's new era had led to profound divisions across the disciplines, as reflected in the organization of the American Political Science Association in 1903. Chapter 1 discusses the progressives who led the association and their efforts to advance the theory and practice of colonial administration. The imperial turn had multiplied the country's race problems, which, many argued, posed new threats to the continued hegemony or even survival of whites, precisely as the anti-imperialists had warned. John W. Burgess, the giant of late nineteenth-century political science, was one of the most outspoken critics. As a consequence he ended his career as an outcast from rather than leader of the new APSA.[60]

Chapter 2 turns from institutions to ideas. In the new science of international relations, the biological division of the world mattered much more for theory building than a territorial division, but the territorial division that mattered most was that between the so-called tropic and temperate zones of the world economy. These boundaries dictated the path of race development: they had done so in the past through colonization by Anglo-Saxons and would do so in the future through control over and enhancement of the labor power of the semi-civilized races using techniques of uplift. International lawyers might have regarded the boundaries between (the small set of) states (to which the law of nations applied) as essential to their art, but

political scientists defined themselves above all by their difference from lawyers, and in building a science of imperial administration they turned to Herbert Spencer, August Comte, William Graham Sumner, Benjamin Kidd, and
John Wesley Powell, not Hugo Grotius. At the same time, Du Bois and his
heirs in the Howard school would begin to insist that history, not biology, explained hierarchy, specifically the history of colonial and mercantile capitalist
expansion and of the transatlantic slave trade that secured Western people's
dominance and African, Asian, and Caribbean people's subordination.

Part II situates the beginning of the Howard school relative to the other
main developments in the social science of international relations in the
1920s, a decade marked by an increased focus on imperialism, white supremacy, and the prospects of race war. Chapter 3 discusses the rising anxieties
across the so-called Anglosphere as movements of "colored peoples" began
to demand the end of their subjugation. Alain Locke was a leading philosopher of the freedom movements and an indefatigable promoter of the Howard school. Chapter 4 focuses on institution building, including the Institute
of Pacific Relations and the Williamstown Institute of Politics, the Social
Science Research Council's first Committee on International Relations in
1926, and New York's Foreign Policy Association, a progressive counterpart
to the Council on Foreign Relations with a well-funded research program
headed by former Harvard professor Raymond Leslie Buell. Howard's international relations theorists would depend on Buell's brokerage for their entry
to white society, but what defined their opportunities in contrast to denizens
of virtually all other centers of international relations theorizing was Alain
Locke's tireless publishing and networking and, through him, wholly unique
connections to national liberation movement theorists and future leaders of
independent African and Caribbean states.

Part III extends the account through the years of depression and war,
and thus through the shroud of myths that Cold War–era scholars spun
about "idealism" and "isolationism" (and, as one of the converts, William
T. R. Fox, would add, "devil theories of international relations" that cast
"munitions-makers, imperialists, and capitalists" as evildoers).[61] Chapter 5
focuses on the rival Marxisms of Du Bois and his most caustic critic, Ralph
Bunche. Chapter 6 details the efforts by the discipline's would-be grand
strategists to quarantine the Howard school theorists and their dangerous
ideas about the future of black rights at home and in the colonies.

Part IV traces the impact of what MIT's Harold Isaacs (and, later,
Malcolm X) called "the breakdown of the worldwide system of white su-
premacy" on a discipline in the process of its own dramatic reconfiguration.
International relations became the site of study of the relationships among

the "white states" or, as the "biological myth," in Hans Kohn's words, gave way to the "spatial myth," the "great powers." As we will see, among some of the more politically reactionary grand strategists the biological myth still held sway. Younger and more liberal professors in contrast, would insist, just as Raymond Leslie Buell did in 1925, using his exact words in fact, that the new era of complex interdependence was different from some imagined older and obsolete one.

Those who took up the discipline's actual old object of study (what Reinhold Niebuhr, the new prophet of realism, called "the colored continents") did so, it came to be imagined, "for the first time" under an entirely new interdisciplinary specialization called variously "area studies," "development," or "modernization" theory.[62] In other words, hierarchy was now encoded in the architecture of the postwar research university. Accordingly, Chapter 7 shows that the bulk of foundation funds flowed to the proliferating area studies centers and research projects in the 1940s, 1950s and 1960s. One of the unwritten agenda items in the late turn to building African studies and a national African Studies Association—which happened late, since few in the United States imagined the possibility of Africans governing themselves—was keeping governance of the field in the hands of white social scientists and foundation administrators.

Chapter 8 turns to the writing and reception of *The New World of Negro Americans*, the results of a research project at MIT's newly established Center for International Studies that contrasted sharply with the bulk of MIT's contract research, economic development planning for various new states of Asia, and what came to be known as modernization theory. Harold Isaacs used his friend Logan at Howard, among others, to set up dozens of interviews with black writers, researchers, doctors, and lawyers in order to assess the impact of African decolonization on African American identity and the direction of the civil rights struggle.

Howard's political scientists carved out a unique niche for themselves in a still deeply segregated and unequal discipline in part through Buell's patronage, Locke's entrepreneurship, and Bunche's ambition and in part because the white departments and programs were still operating with modest outside funding at best, most of which dried up in the depression years of the 1930s. The tremendous expansion of foundation support for international and area studies centers after the war did not reach the schools and scholars that had pioneered the study of colonialism and liberation movements in Africa. Thus, chapter 9 traces the effects of the Cold War, McCarthyism, and the decision in *Brown v. Board of Education* on a cluster of innovative thinkers in international relations who for a brief period rivaled those at any white institution in the segregated academy.

A brief conclusion reviews the findings and dismisses as a diversion the question that graduate students and professors in international relations, rubbed raw by what they read, will typically fall back on, "How does this matter for theory?" The answer already exists for anyone who really cares. The question they ought to ask instead is this: How does it matter in those domains where what professors do actually makes a difference: the classroom, the department, the campus, and the professional association?

PART I

The Noble Science of Imperial Relations and Its Laws of Race Development

Political scientists in early twentieth-century America who traced the nineteenth-century origins of their field pointed to British theorist and statesman George Cornwall Lewis (1806–1863).[1] His best-known work is *Essay on the Government of Dependencies* (1841). Lewis defined the science of politics as comprised of three parts: the nature of the relation between a sovereign government and its subjects, the relation between the sovereign governments of independent communities, and "the relation of a dominant and a dependent community; or, in other words, the relation of supremacy and dependence."[2] Modern writers, he said, had not yet taken up the nature of the political relation of supremacy and dependency in any systematic way.

Government of Dependencies was first reprinted fifty years later, a moment when modern writers—that is social scientists—were finally taking up Lewis's challenge by founding a new American Political Science Association that would marshal the country's burgeoning intellectual resources in support of the expanded empire. The central challenge that defined the new field called international relations was how to ensure the efficient political administration and race development of subject peoples, from the domestic dependencies and backward races at home to the complex race formations found in the new overseas territories and dependencies. What these generally younger, socialist-leaning, progressive political scientists saw as a bright new dawn for the discipline, the Anglo-Saxon race, and civilization, other social scientists saw instead as a dark and ignoble end of their own 20-year-long effort to bring "the searching light of reason to bear" upon problems of politics.[3]

The early decades of international relations in the United States is a story about empire. We know its outlines mainly due to the work of two historical-oriented specialists in international relations, David Long and Brian Schmidt.[4] The historians of empire and of imperial anthropology have shown us that empire wasn't easily pried apart from race in turn-of-the-century America, so the new disciplinary historians have gotten one important part of the account wrong. The problem is the current under-standing of the place of race in the thought of social scientists of the era. The strand that still resonates in our own time about empire, states, and the like is considered to be the real scientific or theoretical core of the scholars' work, while the strand that involves now-repudiated racial constructs is treated in-stead as mere "language," "metaphors," and "prejudices" of the era. To undo this error and recover in full the ideas of early international relations theorists it is necessary, as John Hobson has shown, to bring the work of historians of conservative and reform Darwinism to bear on the first specialists and foundational texts.

We will also need to loosen the hold a particular idea has over our con-temporary imaginations—that the subject matter of international relations has forever been found on one side of a geographic border between the "do-mestic" and the "foreign"—because the scholars who wrote the first articles, papers, treatises, and textbooks in international relations all included the "Negro problem" in the South within the new field of study. Political scien-tists imagined two fundamentally different logics and processes at work and thus different rules that applied across the boundary dividing Anglo-Saxons or Teutons and the inferior races found in Indian Territory, New Mexico, the Philippines, the Caribbean, Africa, and Oceania. Here was the original and signal contribution of U.S. international relations to the theory and practice of hierarchy, a theory that W. E. B. Du Bois challenged in his continuing arguments about the global color line.

For those who studied fundamental problems of world order at the turn of the century, it was innovations in communications and transportation technologies combined with the unprecedented expansion of capital that had increased contact and thus the potential for conflict between the world's superior and inferior races. Strategies for managing conflict or arresting the natural tendency toward war depended on a correct understanding of the way biology and environment determined and limited the prospects for civi-lizing the child races. Against the varieties of evolutionary theory offered up as explanation and justification for hierarchy, anthropologist Franz Boas and sociologist Du Bois both began in the late 1890s to explain hierarchy instead as the outcome of history, specifically, of colonial and mercantile capitalist expansion and of the transatlantic slave trade that secured the dominance of the West. Boas's role in challenging the idea that hierarchy was natural and biologically rooted is well known. Du Bois's parallel explications are both less well known and misunderstood.

Chapter 1

Empire by Association

In 1906, Alleyne Ireland (1871–1951), the traveler turned expert, read a paper at the third annual meeting of the American Political Science Association in Providence on the growing interest in the theory of colonial administration. The subject was once treated as a "curious by-product rather than as a vital part of Political Science," thus leaving the field to amateurs who had failed "to approach the colonial problem in that scientific spirit which in other departments of study is alone held to justify a public expression of opinion."[1] While not a professor, Ireland was nonetheless seen by many as a pioneer in what he called the "science of imperial administration." He earned this reputation after publishing *Tropical Colonization: An Introduction to the Study of the Topic* (1899). In 1901, the University of Chicago appointed him its colonial commissioner, a post that bought him two years of research for an ambitious eight-volume study on colonialism in all the Asian possessions of the United States, France, Britain, and the Netherlands.[2]

The development in political science Ireland trumpeted is obvious in retrospect. Professors had turned to the question of administration of empire even before founding the American Political Science Association in 1903. The two private eastern university–based political science academies had taken the lead in a series of conferences and in the pages of their respective journals. The American Academy of Political and Social Science, founded in

Philadelphia in 1889, launched a bimonthly journal, *The Annals of the American Academy of Political and Social Science*, in 1890. Harry Huntington Powers, a professor of romance languages turned economist, wrote the lead article in the September 1898 number, "The War as a Suggestion of Manifest Destiny."[3] Powers explained the war as the playing out of an irrepressible struggle for "race supremacy" that was leading rapidly to the necessary subjugation of the world's dependent, weak, and uncivilized nations. Within "two centuries, perhaps in one," only Slavs and Saxons would be left as major powers and would be locked in a struggle to rule the world, Powers predicted.

The academy followed this initial think piece with the first of its special-topics supplements to focus on U.S. foreign policy, a thick volume issued in May 1899 that began with a series of articles on the government of dependencies. By 1901, the academy had added a special department that focused on colonies and colonial government, and at the fifth annual meeting in Philadelphia in April of that year, its best attended to date, the speakers came to grips with the fact that the annexation of new territories had multiplied what were now "America's race problems."

It was hardly necessary for W. E. B. Du Bois, who had come up from Atlanta for the conference, to defend the claim he had made in his address to the American Negro Academy the month before that the color line was "the world problem of the twentieth century."[4] The transnational connections were clear (albeit not in the way Du Bois had envisioned) to those who gave papers on the races in the Pacific, the natives of Hawaii, the races and semi-civilized tribes of the Philippines, the Latin and African races in Cuba and Puerto Rico, and on the Negro question in the U.S. South, where the proven unfitness of African Americans for the ballot was a key reason for believing that all the other less civilized races that were now American dependents would likewise be unable to govern themselves.[5]

As Hilary Herbert, a member of Congress and onetime secretary of the navy lamented, "political science played no part" in the Reconstruction acts, since African Americans were allegedly unfit for participating in government, but Congress had passed them anyway. Herbert, who was there to introduce papers by George Winston, president of North Carolina College of Agriculture and Mechanical Arts, and Du Bois, ended his introduction with a quote as famous in some circles as Du Bois's is about the color line in the twentieth century, "the granting of universal suffrage to the Negro was the mistake of the nineteenth century."[6]

Edward Ross (1866–1951), a sociologist trained in Berlin and at Johns Hopkins who was the best-known scholar at the meeting, gave the keynote address. He used the occasion to elaborate a new theory of the sources of white racial superiority. This work was until recently misrepresented on the American Sociological Association Web site as a critique of racism.[7] There were those, Ross said, under the sway of Darwin who exaggerated the fixed-race element of difference, which was as grave an error as those who believed in the "fallacy of equality" or "the power of intercourse and school instruction to lift up a backward folk to the level of the rest." The sources of difference were subtler. Three factors made the Anglo-Saxon superior: energy, which varied inversely with adaptability to the tropics; self-reliance; and education.

Americans scored high on "tests of superiority" except in the South because of the presence there "of several millions of an inferior race." What would sustain the superiority of Americans was "pride of blood" and "an uncompromising attitude toward the lower races," which secured white men of North America freedom "from the ball and chain of hybridism" that had trapped the Spanish in America and the Portuguese in Brazil and East Africa. "Asiatics" posed the real challenge. They might arrive in the country, enjoy the equal opportunity afforded them, and reproduce at a vastly faster rate than whites, in which case Ross predicted one of three outcomes. Americans might degrade themselves by multiplying more indiscriminately; Asians might adopt the norms of whites, which he judged unlikely; or whites would silently commit "race suicide" as the "farm hand, mechanic, and operative . . . whither away." Much hinged, then, on meeting the challenge immigration posed to white supremacy. Stem the tide and the white man would "play a brilliant and leading role on the stage of history" because of his capacity and efficiency, free institutions, and universal education.

What was left for W. E. B. Du Bois (1868–1963), then still a mostly unknown sociologist but the one true giant at the Philadelphia meeting that weekend, was to cut through all the cant in defense of hierarchy.[8] The world was witnessing a new phase in European civilization's contact with "undeveloped peoples."

> Whatever we may say of the results of such contact in the past, it certainly forms a chapter in human action not pleasant to look back upon. War, murder, slavery, extermination and debauchery—this has again and again been the result of carrying civilization and the blessed gospel to the isles of the sea and the heathen without the law.[9]

Du Bois presented the South as a case of the general phenomenon of race contact in order to challenge the propositions that passed for knowledge in a field "which the average American scientist deems somewhat beneath his dignity, and which the average man who is not a scientist knows all about."[10]

He analyzed Jim Crow's spatial segregation both as a purposeful project and one with a class dimension, similar to most other features of life in the Black Belt. The primary economic problem for African Americans was not how to turn ex-slaves into efficient workers. Rather, the problem was how to overcome slavery's deleterious impact on generations and recognize the structural disadvantages that both black and white workers faced in the post-feudal, unregulated economy. Racism worsened the effects on black working life, leaving little hope of organizing cross-race associations. What was most needed, therefore, was an expanded set of black organizations founded by an expanded cadre of black leaders in defense of community interests. The primary tool in this endeavor was the ballot. Without political power, black people would continue to suffer at the hands of the police and courts and continue to be starved of the public resources necessary for advancement, beginning with decent schools. Over the long term, better education combined with improved political leadership would make his people better citizens.

Thus, there were not just two competing theories of world interracial relations in the United States at the turn of the century, as Cleland Boyd McAfee laid them out in the *Journal of the Royal African Society* just a few years later, but three. One theory insisted that black inferiority was real and ineradicable and thus that equality of any sort was logically impossible. Efforts by blacks to pursue the fantasy of equal rights would lead to increased conflict. The second theory recognized black inferiority as real but not "fundamental." The dominant race would continue, necessarily, to dictate terms to the subordinate one but the fact of subordination need not end in conflict. It was possible to imagine forms of uplift that might over time make possible at least "some points of political, economic, and social equality available for some to-day and for the developed race ultimately." McAfee used the example of Du Bois in fact to show the principle in action: "first-fruits of the new race, now inferior, ultimately not inferior to us though always different from us."[11]

Du Bois challenged both schools with his sustained critique of international hierarchy and of the racialism the West used to buttress it. The key pieces of this antiracist and internationalist perspective were in place in the essay he published in the *Annals* in 1901. He showed that the modern history of civilization building was undeniably brutal and exploitative, however much those who benefited from empire denied it. He linked his argument to the principle that the darker peoples of the world had the same rights of political self-determination as the lighter races. It was the same claim that he had put forward nine months earlier in his speech titled "To the Nations of the World" at the first Pan-African Congress in London.[12] He acknowledged "that it is possible and sometimes best that a partially undeveloped people should be ruled by the best of their stronger and better neighbors for their own good, until such time as the can start and fight the world's battles alone," but this was a frank recognition that sovereignty would be difficult to secure against rival imperial complexes.[13] Du Bois also decoupled strategies of tutelage from a belief in racial inferiority.[14] Above all, Du Bois was pursuing the idea that the world was thinking wrong about race.[15]

Du Bois's arguments gained wider notoriety with the publication of *Souls of Black Folk* in 1903, the "electrifying manifesto" that in the words of Du Bois's biographer "redefined the terms of a three-hundred-year interaction between black and white people and influenced the cultural and political psychology of people throughout the western hemisphere, as well as on the continent of Africa."[16] The review in the *Annals* by Carl Kelsey, the University of Pennsylvania's newly minted expert on the Negro, admitted that there was much to praise in *Souls*, but he instead focused on its purported snarling, overcritical tone and opined that the "chip on his shoulder" would keep Du Bois from gaining the influence he deserved. Du Bois painted too bleak a picture of black-white relations in the South, Kelsey wrote, and seemed obsessed with chronicling "the failures, the injustices, the wrongs." As for the book's most controversial section, the critique of Booker T. Washington and his role in African American disfranchisement, Kelsey said that Du Bois failed to make his case, "although there may be a measure of truth to the charge that [Washington's] educational program is too narrow."[17] Here is a clear illustration of the line social scientists were drawing against advocacy at the beginning of the twentieth century, at least when what was being advocated—black people's rights, say, rather than the advance of U.S. empire—was unpopular. The *Annals* published two more special issues to which Du Bois, the powerhouse Atlanta University professor, *might* have contributed, one on race improvement in the United States (1909) and the other on the New South (1910). Booker T. Washington wrote for both, but Du Bois would not appear again in the journal's pages for a decade.

The Loneliest Political Scientist in New York

The New York Academy of Political Science is the publisher of the oldest political science journal in the country, *Political Science Quarterly*. It responded to the war with Spain with a lead article by Franklin Giddings (1855–1931) titled "Imperialism?" in its December 1898 issue. Giddings played a founding role in and served as a member of the editorial board of *Annals* while he was at Bryn Mawr. In 1894, he accepted a chair at Columbia, where he rose to prominence as a theorist of social evolution with the publication of his *Principles of Sociology* (1896), which others would later describe as a kind of progressive or reformist Darwinism. In it, he argued that even while laws of competition and survival of the fittest operated among higher and lower races and classes, state intervention was often warranted to avoid the kinds of social conflict that were then on the upsurge in the United States. If unchecked, such conflict would end in the decline of the white race instead of its progress, Giddings claimed.[18]

"Imperialism?" begins with an apology "to men whose opinions I have long held in deep respect." Giddings argued that "their ambition to perfect the ethical ideals of the race" had led them to "neglect the humbler task of forecasting social probabilities."[19] He believed that opposition to the war was futile, a conclusion that followed the routine assessments of opponents of the war of the inexorable forces that were propelling it forward (the "jingoes and yellow journals . . . the American population . . . eager to engage in blood-letting . . . the Morgans, the Cabot Lodges . . . war to develop American character, war to afford an outlet to American energies and genius."). The continuing opposition of those opposed to the war to territorial expansion and especially to the retention of the Philippines left them unable to deal realistically with possible outcomes of the war and to the main question they posed: "How can the American people best adapt themselves to their new responsibilities?" Giddings foresaw an eventual expansion of trade with the new tropical possessions "under the more intelligent direction of the white races." The biggest challenge would be to develop methods for governing inferior races from a distance. If this was not done, the civilized world would be forced to abandon all hope of "continuing its economic conquest of the natural resources of the globe." All of these observations led in the same direction: the West's moral evolution and the perfecting of American government through empire building, a necessary step in the continued domination of world politics "by English-speaking people, in the interest of an English civilization."

Giddings's opponents are not named in the essay, but they included Yale's William Graham Sumner (1840–1910), a follower of Spencer, a conservative defender of laissez-faire economics on evolutionary grounds, and the only social scientist to take a leading role in the American Anti-Imperialist League, which was formed in June 1898, just as the United States was in the process of annexing the Philippines. Sumner famously foretold a long war in the Philippines if the United States attempted to replace Spanish rule with one more of those modern conquering states that claimed to be "spreading freedom and truth," which he called "manifestations of national vanity" that every nation laughs at when observing them in others. Sumner also shared the conviction of virtually all other social scientists at the time that the differences between civilized and uncivilized or semi-civilized people made their incorporation as citizens impossible. Nonwhites should instead govern themselves. He suggested a range of outcomes that would follow if this option was pursued, from the dismal conditions in Haiti after a century of freedom to the more promising case of Mexico.[20]

Another of Giddings's unnamed opponents was undoubtedly his colleague, John W. Burgess (1844–1931), the best-known, most influential political scientist in the country, the founding dean of Columbia's School of Political Science, and the founder of *Political Science Quarterly*.[21] Burgess called the war and its aftermath a "great crisis" in his country's history. Two decades later, in his *Reminiscences*, he called the war the "first great shock which I had experienced" in the eighteen years since his move from Northampton to New York.[22] His was a viewpoint sharply at odds with the views of political scientists who were eager to demonstrate the practical value of their expertise. This goes far to explain why *Political Science Quarterly* alone among the professional publications published criticisms of the McKinley administration's imperial turn. Burgess's stature made the dissent all the more significant. His opposition to the imperial adventure also helps explain why, despite his stature in the field, Burgess did not play a leadership role in the American Political Science Association when it was founded a few years later.[23]

What is perhaps most significant about Burgess's opposition is the puzzle it poses. His reputation was built on his magisterial two-volume *Political Science and Comparative Constitutional Law* (1890), which argued that only the Teutonic branch of the Aryan race had mastered the art of political organization in the form of the national state. It was this "fact of Teutonic political genius" that "authorizes them, in the economy of the world, to assume the leadership in the establishment and administration of states."[24] The Teutonic nations ["the English, French, Lombards, Scandinavians, Germans, and North Americans"] had two obligations: to never surrender power to non-Teutonic elements, which meant at times excluding others from participation in political power, and to "carry the political civilization of the modern world into those parts of the world inhabited by unpolitical and barbaric races; *i.e.*, they must have a colonial policy." He added the injunction that Teutonic nations had a responsibility to civilize the uncivilized and semi-civilized "by any means necessary." Three generations of historians of American empire have credited Burgess with an influence second only to Admiral Alfred Mahan for providing the intellectual scaffolding in support of the Spanish-American war on the basis of this 1891 essay while ignoring

Burgess's writings for the rest of the decade and his unequivocal opposition to the new imperialism.[25]

In "The Ideal of the American Commonwealth," Burgess's address at the World's Columbian Exposition in Chicago in 1893, the same series in which Frederick Jackson Turner delivered his famous thesis on the closing of the American frontier and Congress debated the question of annexation of Hawaii, Burgess shifted ground, from an argument about the need for a proactive colonial policy to an argument that the American nation as a "cosmopolitan state" need do nothing more than continue to serve as an example to others. All the other pieces of his argument remained the same: only the Aryan race—the Greeks, the Romans, and the Teutons—had founded and developed

> great states of the world, in a modern sense. . . . We must conclude from these facts that American Indians, Asiatics and Africans cannot properly form any active, directive part of the political population which shall be able to produce modern political institutions and ideals. They have no element of political civilization to contribute. They can only receive, learn, follow Aryan example.

Since the other Aryan stocks had lost their capacities through race mixing, "the prime mission of the ideal American commonwealth [is] to be the perfection of the Aryan genius for political civilization, upon the basis of a predominantly Teutonic nationality," which would become the model "political organization of the world." The key would be to prevent the dilution of the race, "sins against American civilization" that were attempted by some in the past but, "thanks to an all-wise Providence, have failed." With the crime of Reconstruction reversed, the black electorate disfranchised, and immigration restrictions in place, the main threats to realization of the ideal democracy built on principles of liberty and self-government were socialism (in part through the corruption of young American students who studied political economy in Germany) and the growth of the power of the government during the Civil War, hence the importance of the system of checks and balances, especially the judiciary.[26] This fear of unchecked executive power explains his opposition to the course of U.S. foreign policy in the mid-1890s.

Consider in this light his commentary on the Cleveland administration's threat in 1896 to intervene "by every means in its power" in a boundary dispute between Venezuela and the British colony of Guiana if Great Britain did not follow U.S. dictates. Historians have since come to see Britain's bowing to American pressure in the Venezuela dispute as the moment when the United States announced its "arrival as a great power on the diplomatic world stage."[27] Burgess challenged the administration and the jingoists for what he derided as "pseudo-Monroeism." The version of the Monroe doctrine trotted out in the recent conflict was the "slaveholders'" version that was invented in the 1850s during the failed effort to expand the southern plantation system into "Mexico and Central America and even Cuba," an attempt to make "the Gulf the Mediterranean of a slave empire." In the 1890s, there was no longer reason to fear that European states would intervene in the domestic affairs of the Latin American republics. Rather, Burgess believed it was the United States that now seemed poised to extend a protectorate system over the region.[28]

Burgess warned of the responsibilities of establishing a protectorate and of the unreasonable costs of raising the military necessary for it. "Grand prospect! Plenty of offices, plenty of government contracts, large profits, abundance of work, high prices, and endless sensations! But it must all be paid for in the end in mountains of treasure, certainly, and in rivers of blood and centuries of misery probably." Most important, any such "course of conquest" requires an ethical principle for its justification, and the right of self-defense could not be stretched to accommodate empire. The duty of "civilized states to carry civilization into the abodes of barbarism" should not mask other ends nor was it in fact applicable to the countries of the hemisphere, which either were "working out" their "own civilization" or were already governed by other civilized powers. He concluded with a review of the prejudices that lay behind the talk of going to war with Great Britain that originated in badly written school textbooks that offered misguided views on the British Empire and came from those who courted the Irish American vote. As for war talk, once the spirit is excited, "is very difficult for the government to hold its own footing at all against it. It is the most dangerous weapon in all our arsenal of popular prejudices."[29]

The chief jingoist and future chief conspirator in the 1898 war, Theodore Roosevelt, whom Cleveland had made police commissioner of New York, rebutted Burgess's views in the magazine *Bachelor of Arts*: "The Monroe Doctrine should not be considered from any purely academic standpoint . . . but by the needs of the nation and the true interests of Western civilization." Those who attacked the president and his secretary of state and who took the "anti-American side" were not patriots who loved their country but were instead promiscuous lovers of other places, as adulterers are of other women, in the thrall of "a kind of milk-and-water cosmopolitanism," a doctrine that was never attractive to "men of robust character or of imposing personality." The same weak, unmanly, and unpatriotic scholars trembled before a false vision of the future. The United States in fact had no interest in establishing a protectorate over the Americas. Colonies of any kind were "unnatural," and "the only hope for a colony that wishes to attain full moral and mental growth is to become an independent State, or part of an independent State." Most important given the course in 1898 that he is so famously associated with, Roosevelt said that the worst situation from the perspective of development was one in which "the colonizing race has to do its work by means of other inferior races." While there might be some prospect for development in the South American republics, despite "the mean and bloody" recent history, there was little if any chance for race development in the Tropics under the tutelage of a northern European race.[30]

After Giddings's expansive defense of the imperial turn in *Political Science Quarterly*, Burgess offered a careful and narrow-framed critique, "How May the United States Govern Its Extra-Continental Territory?" He began by making his own position clear. He opposed venturing out to seize new lands at the present stage of development of the United States while the home territory remained underpopulated and the country remained divided on key policy issues, from tariffs to "lynch law," and had not yet found solutions to the "Indian problem," the "Mormon problem," and the "negro problem." The pending crisis was thus not about the fact of territorial conquest but how the territories were to be governed, given "the principle of political science, that the same fullness of civil liberty, as well as of political liberty, is not appropriate to all conditions of mankind."[31]

Burgess feared any attempt to govern the recently annexed territories extra-constitutionally, which he said would lead "towards absolutism." No legal precedent existed for doing so. Rather, "all places over which the government of the United States extends constitutes the 'States and territories' or the 'country' of the United States, or the 'American empire,' as the court termed them; and . . . the limitations placed by the constitution on the powers of the government run with the government into all places . . . over which the civil government of the United States extends." The McKinley administration would be wise not to rush to terminate military government, Burgess argued. It would take a while to determine the precise capacity of the people for self-government, and he held out the prospect that Americans might still come to their senses and reverse direction. In that case, and assuming that elements in the Philippines and the Caribbean demonstrated a "fair capacity for self-government," the United States should let the occupied peoples rule themselves and withdraw its military forces. If they did not demonstrate such a capacity and Americans "show in some deliberate and unmistakable way their will to have a colonial empire, we should try territorial rule . . . under the limitations which the constitution imposes upon the government in behalf of civil liberty." If this type of limited government proved impossible, then the constitution would have to be amended "to permit the national government to exercise absolute, or more absolute, civil authority in certain parts of our domain."[32]

It turns out that Burgess got it spectacularly wrong. Americans never did come to their senses. Congress voted to annex Hawaii, where a white oligarchy already ruled, in July 1898, ostensibly as a war measure, although in the famous six-hour naval battle in Manila two months earlier, Admiral Dewey had destroyed every Spanish warship in the Pacific. It was made a territory in 1900. The potential problem posed by white rule over inferior races meant that the transition to statehood would be dragged out indefinitely, similar to the cases of Arizona and New Mexico, which were incorporated in the 1840s and had larger populations than some other recently created states of the union but still ruled along colonial lines. The same was true for Oklahoma, which was carved out of the western half of Indian Territory and incorporated in 1890. As for the new so-called dependencies, Congress had recognized Cuban independence in April 1898, before the beginning of the war, and the Treaty of Paris concluded with Spain in December put Cuba on the path to becoming a U.S. protectorate. The same treaty turned the remaining Spanish colonial possessions over to the United States, and the commissions McKinley dispatched to the Philippines and Puerto Rico resolved the question of fitness for rule of the various nonwhite "alien races" rather quickly, determining that a period of tutelage would be necessary. As for Guam, the absence there of any sign of civilized people, however "friendly" the so-called Chamorros might be, meant that a transition from military to civilian rule might not ever be possible.[33]

Burgess's gravest error, though, turns out to have been his belief that the constitution prevented Americans from ruling any place or people autocratically. The Supreme Court decided otherwise in a series of cases that established the principle of one set of rules for civilized peoples in incorporated territories and another set of rules for the uncivilized in unincorporated territories; that is, a system of political inequality and hierarchy.[34] The court relied heavily on the theorizing of Harvard political scientist Albert Lawrence Lowell (1856–1943), the future president of the university who famously segregated the new Harvard freshman dormitories in 1915.[35] Lowell argued that Congress had the power to decide if the principles outlined in the Constitution ought to determine how territories gained through war or through cession should be ruled. Lowell thus imagined two kinds of territories, incorporated ones that were destined for statehood and unincorporated ones that belonged to the United States but were apparently on a different path.[36] The determining factor was the racial makeup of a territory and thus the capacities of the people inhabiting it.

Elsewhere Lowell showed that a parallel system of hierarchy operated within the continental boundaries of the United States, citing the case of the incorporated territory of New Mexico, where an inferior Spanish race was "not sufficiently trained in habits of self-government." He went further. The "theory of universal political equality does not apply to tribal Indians, to Chinese, or to negroes under all conditions."[37] Lowell's colleague at Harvard, historian Albert Bushnell Hart, who would become president of the American Political Science Association in 1912, analyzed the existing system of hierarchical rule in and outside of the continental boundaries. "In any other country such governments would be called 'colonial.' Indeed, the present government of Oklahoma strikingly resembles the government of New York before the Revolution. . . . In truth, the territories are and ever have been colonies."[38] Self-government proved to be an art few races had mastered, one that required training. Lowell emerged as the country's leading advocate for the creation of a professional school for colonial administration, along the lines of West Point.[39]

Burgess tried futilely to rescue his account of the republic's constitution from the rising imperial tide. After all, the Supreme Court, he wrote in a 1901 critique of the first two of the cases that would later be known as the Insular Cases, had once also appeared to uphold slavery in precisely the same way that it now appeared to uphold "colonial bondage," but the dissenting justices in these cases suggested that reason would ultimately prevail.[40] A year later he opened the pages of *Political Science Quarterly* to none other than John Atkinson Hobson (1858–1940), the British economist and *Manchester Guardian* correspondent during the first year of the Boer War who returned from Africa to publish his critically acclaimed study, *Imperialism* (1902). Hobson's piece, "The Scientific Basis of Imperialism," took aim at the various biological accounts of the necessity for and inevitability of racial conflict and subjugation and at the impoverished ethics that led whites to think they were advancing human progress through their new imperial conquests. Hobson singled out Franklin Giddings numerous times in the article, most crucially for his belief that empire somehow completed a democratic nation's project when it in fact diverted a people from the uncompleted work of developing a rational "national economy." It encouraged militarism and protectionism rather than the spread of "ideas and arts and institutions" or the "empire of the national mind," which he called the only "legitimate expansion." And it stood in the way of a more complex international government that would substitute "rational" for "natural" race selection that might protect "weak but valuable nationalities" and "check the insolent brutality of powerful aggressors."[41]

These criticisms, though, proved to be beside the point. The war gained McKinley and his wildly popular vice presidential running mate, Theodore Roosevelt, a second term in 1900. As the lead article in Walter Hines Page's new quarterly *World's Work*, which was dedicated to the spread of the "evangelical faith" of American democracy across the globe, put it, the reality is "that the mass of men simply do not believe that our liberties are in danger because of our occupation of Porto Rico and the Philippine islands, whatever mistakes we may have committed there."[42] Thus, while his colleagues turned in earnest to building the new science of imperial administration, Burgess shunned—or was shunned by—the new American Political Science Association, home of "self-styled progressives" who seemed committed in fact to "political retrogression" in the direction of "governmental absolutism of earlier times."[43] He retired from Columbia in 1912 but continued to analyze the cataclysmic changes he believed had been ushered in by 1898. It marked the republic's turn toward despotism, bringing about the erosion of civil liberties, the "Democratic Caesarism" of the second Roosevelt administration (1904–1908), and such misguided steps as the Eighteenth Amendment. Above all, the unchecked militarism of the imperialists and of the trusts whose interests they served led the country into war again in 1917.[44] His lifelong efforts to introduce a rational science of politics into the post–Civil War United Sates, he said, had come to nothing.[45]

The Field of Colonial Administration

Burgess might have been the first to imagine the early history of political science as tragedy, but the impact of 1898 looks different when we turn to the professional associations that virtually all professors of political science belonged to at the turn of the century, namely the American Historical Association (AHA) and the American Economic Association (AEA).[46] The report of the 1900 annual meeting of the sixteen-year-old AHA noted that the program was "frankly designed to answer those interests which are at present uppermost in the minds of Americans who care for history."[47] Some of the papers "were not history at all" but instead promoted the idea "that present problems cannot be successfully solved without an attentive study of the experience of the past." The main proof of the anti-antiquarian turn of the association was found in the session on American colonization. A year earlier, at the New Haven meeting, the AHA had organized a new Committee on the History of Colonies and Dependencies, headed by Henry

Bourne, one of the association's unabashed champions of the imperial turn, and Bourne chaired the session in Boston that reported some of the committee's main conclusions.

Bourne's paper, "Some Difficulties of American Colonization," saw two obstacles for an American imperial project, both of which followed from the tight intertwining of race and empire. The first was the abiding, practically "inbred . . . antipathy" of Americans for nonwhites. Bourne contrasted the United States with the colonies governed by England, France, "and even Spain" where races typically intermingled much more freely than in the South under Jim Crow. Thus the extreme hatred was a consequence of the ongoing "race conflicts" that so fundamentally constituted American history and identity. The second obstacle was the difficulty of adapting the century-old American territorial system of expansion to the new possessions.

By way of a necessary if not sufficient step toward securing effective rule over the new dependencies, Harvard professor of government Albert Lawrence Lowell rehearsed the argument of his forthcoming book on comparative colonial civil service and offered recommendations that the Americans emulate the British training of specialists in what we would now call area studies. Alleyne Ireland also attended the Boston meeting's session on colonization, where he said the Americans would inevitably turn to the system of contract or indentured labor the British were using in the West Indies as the most practical solution to governing in the tropics. (When this didn't happen, Ireland emerged as a leading critic of U.S. policy in the Philippines.)

The American Economic Association reacted in similar fashion. In 1899, the association's executive committee appointed a special committee to produce a set of essays on colonial finance. All of the members were close to President Roosevelt—J. W. Jenks of Cornell; E. R. A. Seligman of Columbia; Albert Shaw, a journalist with a PhD from Johns Hopkins; Charles Hamlin, a wealthy lawyer and former treasury secretary; and Edward Strobel, a lawyer, former assistant secretary of state, and financial advisor to modernizing monarchs in various colonies. The studies, which were funded by private businessmen, were published as *Essays in Colonial Finance by Members of the American Economic Association* (1900). The volume "appeared while the U.S. Army was still fighting the insurgent Philippinos."[48]

We can gauge the rapid advance of the science of imperial administration to the commanding heights of the new discipline-in-formation on the eve of the first meeting of the new American Political Science Association by turning to the Universal Exposition in St Louis. The fair's organizers convened a remarkable Congress of Arts and Science that met each day for a week in September 1904, for 250 talks in all, designed to survey each of the branches of twentieth-century knowledge and the relations among them. Politics, jurisprudence, and social science (by which was meant what we today call sociology), were departments of the division of knowledge designated Social Regulation (one of seven such divisions). The Department of Politics was further broken down into five sections: political theory, diplomacy, national administration, colonial administration, and municipal administration, representing the state of the discipline at the time. Papers given at these talks focused on progress in the fields and the most pressing problems of the future.[49]

The sessions on colonial administration elevated two more political scientists into the ranks of leading specialists on empire. The first was Bernard Moses (1846–1930), a Heidelberg-trained professor of history and political science who joined the faculty of the University of California in 1875 (where "he taught every course in history and social science" at the new institution) and founded the separate department of political science in 1903, a year before the St. Louis exposition.[50] Moses is remembered primarily as a pioneer of Latin American studies in the United States, through his work on Spanish colonization of the Americas. It was that expertise that gained him his three-year appointment on the original United States Philippine Commission (1900–1902), which in turn led to his paper at St. Louis, "Control of Dependencies Inhabited by the Less Developed Races."[51]

The second was Paul Reinsch (1869–1923), a professor at the University of Wisconsin who was a founding member and first vice-president of the new American Political Science Association (he later served as the fifteenth president). Reinsch was also the author of the first U.S. textbook on international relations and a future ambassador to China. He established his expertise in the new science of imperial administration by following his path-breaking *World Politics* (1900) with *Colonial Government* (1902). His paper at the congress, "The Problems of Colonial Administration," previewed his volume *Colonial Administration* (1905). In Chicago at the first meeting of APSA three months later, Reinsch delivered another paper based on the book, "Colonial Autonomy, with Special Reference to the Government of the Philippine Islands." These various writings are now well known, thanks to the research of Brian Schmidt. The one key piece that continues to go unnoticed is "The Negro Race and European Civilization," which also appeared in 1905 in the *American Journal of Sociology*.

A third political scientist, William Franklin Willoughby (1867–1960), also made his name at this time and in the same field. Willoughby, who received his PhD from Johns Hopkins, was the twin brother of Westel Willoughby, another Hopkins PhD, the first to teach political science in a separate department, and one of the founders of the American Political Science Association.

(He was later its tenth president.) William Willoughby also eventually served a term as president of the APSA, although he is often described as an economist. Unlike his fellow colonial experts, Reinsch and Rowe, William Willoughby taught mostly as an adjunct while working in a series of administrative positions, first in Washington and then as treasurer and secretary of Puerto Rico (1901–1907) and president of the upper house of the colonial legislature there. His major piece of scholarship in the 1900s was *Territories and Dependencies of the United States* (1905). Willoughby is better known today for the position he accepted in Washington in 1916 as director of the new Institute of Government Relations, which he eventually brought together with the Brookings Graduate School in Economics and Government to create the Brookings Institution.

The agenda of the first annual APSA meeting, held in conjunction with the annual meeting of the AEA, was overwhelmingly given over to problems posed by imperialism, which is hardly surprising given the events of the first years of the century. The United States fought a short war with Spain and a longer one of conquest in the Philippines. Great Britain waged a second war with the Boer Republics in 1898–1902. In 1904, the year of the convention, Russia fought the rival Japanese empire over Manchuria and Korea. Little wonder, therefore, that Alleyne Ireland took note of the rise of the new field of colonial administration in his 1906 APSA address, which he also referred to as the science of "race subjection."[52]

Most work up to that point had been historical rather than practical and most of it had been written by nonspecialists—"lawyers, doctors, soldiers, sailors, politicians, presidential candidates, ministers of the gospel, labor leaders, poets, geologists, engineers and professors of subjects as wide apart as ethics and zoology."[53] Ireland dismissed most of this work as worthless. Instead, dispassionate analysis showed that "the object of colonization" was the establishment of "a profitable commerce" and thus, the proper focus of systematic, comparative investigation was "the degree to which institutions of colonial governance reflected the principle of "exploitation" or that of "development."[54]

Ireland was right, judging from the expanding shelf of books by Reinsch and other political scientists and the growing number of meetings and conference proceedings devoted to problems of dependencies, which included some extremely critical views of the first decade of U.S. rule in the Philippines. The first exuberant accounts of the wholly new course in benevolent empire that was being charted across the Pacific and Caribbean for the economic benefit of native peoples gave way to a precocious critique. Ten years later, it proved impossible to distinguish U.S. policies from the policies of countries with longer records of overseas expansion. And needless to say, by the time of the New Deal the critique had been enshrined as a doctrine of state, in the form of a new "Good Neighbor Policy" that contrasted with the exploitative orders the United States had put in place over the previous three decades. Political scientists were a bit too exuberant in imagining that they had a role to play in designing new and improved political institutions for the tropics; U.S. occupation authorities reached for the same old British-origin "territorial model" of the late eighteenth century to organize center-periphery relations in the newest dependencies at the turn of the twentieth century.

Political scientists were more successful in building new institutions at home, including the world's first journal of international relations, the *Journal of Race Development*, founded at Clark in 1910. The journal and the conferences that supported it in Worcester served as an important node in an ongoing transatlantic debate about the prospects for uplift of backward peoples, from the Sea Islands of Georgia to the Philippine Archipelago.[55]

CHAPTER 2

Race Children

The white social scientists who offered their expertise to the new imperial state and the handful of critics of the new expansionist wave all assumed that hierarchy was natural, that it was biologically rooted, and that it could be made sense of best by drawing on concepts such as higher and lower races, natural and historic races, savagery and civilization, and the like. Consider in this light the late modification of the conventional Spencerian three-stage evolutionary sequence by America's most famous anthropologist and explorer, John Wesley Powell (1834–1902), who helped secure the hegemony of the "Anglo-Saxon branch of the Aryan family" across the continent. He designed the reservation system for the Utes and neighboring peoples in Utah and Nevada and built the U.S. Bureau of Ethnology in Washington, D.C. "to study the tribal peoples [the United States] had defeated." His work had proved, he said, that man passed through four stages: savagery, barbarism, monarchy, and "republikism."[1]

George Stocking argues that if we are to understand the racial ideas of political scientists such as Reinsch, sociologists such as Ross and Giddings, and others involved in discipline building at home and civilization building abroad, it is important to realize that "they were evolutionists almost to a man." Their ideas about evolution reflected the influence of Darwin's *On the Origin of Species* (1859), an older strain of "natural development-theory" that imagined a path from savagery to civilization that Darwin himself drew on, and the influence of American anthropologists working in the 1860s and 1870s. Across those decades older ideas about superior and savage "peoples" and "nations" reemerged as notions of organic and innate differences among the "races" of mankind.[2]

The confluence proved powerfully productive, to judge from the debates, museum exhibits, archeological excavations, and the beginning of Jim Crow the theorizing licensed. Social scientists who began working on problems of world politics or international/interracial relations found grounds for justifying what much later would be called "realism" in arguments about the ceaseless struggle of existence, survival of the fittest, and the aphorism of the era, "might makes right." Those who challenged this stark reading of world order argued that the expansion of civilization would reduce tendencies toward conflict even as it brought the developed and undeveloped races closer together.

However, the shift from discussing biological traits shared by all humans that were evolved from nonhuman species to theorizing about how society evolved and specifically about evolutionary differences among races was problematic. These were wrong roads down which American social scientists rushed headlong. One was a belief that races were so different and so unequal in capacities that they had to have evolved from different origins (polygenesis), an argument that relied on readings of the Bible. It was also one that Darwin himself tried to refute in his second book, *The Descent of Man* (1871), even in the face of his own belief in the reality of racial hierarchy. As Carl Degler explains, Darwin rejected the idea of different species of man. The typical markers of race were impossible to explain using his theory of natural selection—that is, "race was outside evolution."[3]

Through this pathway came one of the first laws of international relations theory, namely that the differences in races made it impossible for whites to acclimate to tropical environments. Stocking considers versions of the theory that were not occasioned by the war of 1898. He includes *Races and People*, the lectures that were published in 1890 by the University of Pennsylvania anthropologist Daniel Brinton, who would soon become president of the American Academy for the Advancement of Science. The boldest or most extreme version of the claim came from MIT economist William Z. Ripley, who argued that no race ever acclimated to a different environment.[4] Thus, colonization of the tropics was impossible. Ripley was a leading figure in the American Economic Association who was famous for his work in both racial taxonomy and railroad regulation. The last article Stocking cites is from 1914, written by Yale's Ellsworth Huntington and published in the *Journal of Race Development*. Huntington, a member of its editorial board, argued that the Negro "would apparently die out in the northern United States were he not replenished from the South."[5] Nonetheless, the theory and its policy implications continued to preoccupy scholars, research programs, and foundations for another twenty-five years.

A second theoretical question with implications for imperial development policy had emerged, namely whether or not it was possible for the different races to "amalgamate," that is, to mate and produce healthy offspring or hybrids. The arguments were more complex and the disputes more serious than in the claim about "acclimation." Ross laid out the basic view in "The Causes of Race Superiority," where he argued that continued white hegemony depended on "pride of blood." Many other examples can be found in the works of others who founded the APSA and published in the *Annals of the American Academy of Political and Social Science* and the *American Journal of Sociology*.[6] Complications arise with characterizing support for the claim, between those, for example, who argued that in fact the offspring of such unions tended to be infertile (thus proving that the races were indeed different species) and those who recognized that such offspring might not be sterile but would produce degenerate offspring. The facts of the case might differ, too, depending on the distance between races. There were possibilities for good "cross-races," and those who rejected polygenesis, for obvious reasons, sought to demonstrate that new and viable mixed races would emerge through intermarriage.[7] The basic point behind all of this social science theorizing was the idea that race mixing between blacks and whites was wrong, a norm that white social scientists clung to long after the scientific scaffolding for it collapsed.

Most social evolutionist thought rested on a second, even more common assumption about the inheritability of acquired characteristics or behaviors (Lamarckism), the main way the races were imagined to have emerged, multiplied, and traveled their different evolutionary pathways, or, for those who imagined a single evolutionary path for all, the way the Anglo-Saxons gained enormous ground as others increasingly lagged behind. Here was the main engine for the creation of hierarchy. Thus one finds descriptions of, for example, "warlike, peaceful, nomadic, maritime, hunting, [and] commercial races" in the writings of these men.[8] One also finds the Jewish nose, which, according to one anthropologist, evolved from its origins as "a habitual expression of indignation."[9] The new social science disciplines were all infected with the idea of the inheritability of acquired characteristics, and in tracing the course of the virus, Stocking refers to virtually every political scientist and sociologist who wrote on "race formation," including Burgess, Giddings, Ross, Kelsey, and Reinsch, in a literature that was spawned, as we have seen, by the new round of imperial expansion.

Consider in this light the pioneering contribution of international relations scholar Paul Reinsch to the *American Journal of Sociology*, "The Negro Race and European Civilization," where he assays the future of an inferior stock in an era of "increasingly intimate contact" among the "peoples that inhabit the globe." The "puzzle," as political scientists say now, was that black people were too vigorous a race to go the way of other races and "fade away." Survival in the face of slavery proved the race's relative fitness, Reinsch claimed. Solving the puzzle, that is correctly assessing the race's prospect for progress, required two things. The first was an expanded case set, to cover "their original state in the forests of central Africa, as a mixed race under . . . Arab and Hamite" race dominance, "living side by side with a white population" and in those "few isolated communities which enjoy rights of self-government based on European models, as in Hayti and the French Antilles." It also required frank recognition that outmoded ideas of "the absolute unity of human beings" and of "the practical equality of human individuals" had been abandoned in conformity with the scientific truth of the essential differences among "types of humanity."[10] Reinsch followed these observations with a long account of his understanding of life in Africa. He contrasted "the marvelous sense for melody" found among blacks in the plantations with the "almost hypnotic effect" of the rhythm of the tom-tom in Africa, the absence of anything like patriotism among those so ready to fight against their neighbors on that continent, and so on.

For Reinsch, these facts confirmed the idea that black brains are physiologically different from white brains even in the face of the accumulating evidence that refuted the idea that the cranial sutures of blacks closed earlier "and [that] organic development of the faculties seem[ed] to cease at puberty." He also argued, however, that physiological differences did not foreclose the possibility for race improvement because an even greater source of difference with the white race than average individual capacities was the burden of the inheritance of social, political, and climatic conditions on the inferior race. In fact, if these conditions were to change it might even lead to changes in the structure of black craniums over time.[11]

Reinsch's main conclusion based on his study of four types of black-inhabited environments (an "original state" of forests in Central Africa, as a mixed-race controlled by Arab and Hamite races in Northern Sudan, living alongside whites in South Africa and North America, and the outlier, that of a self-governing community as in Haiti) is that those outside sub-Saharan Africa had shown some development capacity but only under the tutelage of other races. Reinsch advocated a civilizing policy in Africa that would emphasize economic efficiency, infrastructure development, and the introduction of metallic currency. At the same time, however, native "tribal and social unity" ought to be respected, local institutions kept intact, and property rights preserved. Otherwise, he claimed, Africans would degenerate morally in ways similar to what had happened to blacks in the South after slavery.[12] Reinsch's argument amounts to an early version of what British colonial reformers would come to call the policy of "indirect rule." Reinsch was influenced by accounts of the South's experiments with industrial education and the ascent of Booker T. Washington: "The mass of the negroes cannot pattern primarily upon the whites with whom they come in contact, but should have leaders of their own race to look up to." Yet those "models of leadership" would not emerge unless whites showed "negroes of high character and intelligence" the way. Reinsch assured his readers that nothing in his analysis implied the possibility of "political power over whites" in Africa or of "social equality" anywhere between the two races.[13]

The most important center for research on the psychology and pedagogy of race development was Clark University, which opened in 1889 under the presidency of psychologist G. Stanley Hall (1844–1924). Hall, who was awarded the first PhD in psychology at Harvard and studied under William James, began his career as a professor of psychology and pedagogics at Johns Hopkins in 1882. Like Johns Hopkins, Clark University was dedicated exclusively to graduate education. Hall founded the *Journal of Psychology* in 1887, served as president of the new American Psychological Association in 1892, and, while at Clark, started four more journals, including the *Pedagogical Seminary* (now known as the *Journal of Genetic Psychology*) in 1891 and the *Journal of Race Development* in 1910.

Hall's most famous idea, usually referred to today as the "recapitulation hypothesis," was that the development of the minds of individuals in their early years repeated stages of the mental history of the human race. A child's mind thus was both like that of its own race's earliest ancestors and that of savage adults in the present. Adolescence was a window into evolution, and anthropological studies in the various rain forests and deserts of the world were a window on the world of childhood. Reinsch and others drew on Hall and his many students when they argued that mental development in the lower races stopped at adolescence because the cranial sutures of members of those races fused earlier than they did among white people or insisted that children and savages both acted more out of instinct than intellect. Thus, when Hobson, like many other scholars, journalists, and administrators, used the concept of the child race, the usage reflected the highest stage of social science theorizing rather than inexperience or ignorance. The concept continued to be used for another two decades after Hobson's *Imperialism*. In 1930, John H. Harris, looking forward to the creation of a "World

'Native' Policy" built on the Versailles Treaty, argued that western states had accepted "the principle of 'Sacred Trust' as the basis of relationships between the civilized nations and the backward or child races."[14] A decade later, the once-scientific concept was being denounced as "a patronizing metaphor."[15]

The problem for Hall and all the other race formation and development theorists is that their basic framework was also being dismantled piece by piece in the 1890s and 1900s. Biologists (but not all biologists by any means) were pounding on the edifice from one side, having taken Mendelian principles as the basis for a new field of genetics that could explain an increasingly vast range of hereditary phenomenon.[16] Coming at race theory from the other side was Columbia's Franz Boas (1858–1940), the anthropologist who had once worked for Hall at Clark.

Although the summary statement of Boas's ideas was published in *The Mind of Primitive Man* in 1911, all the key elements of what made up the Boasian revolution could be read in his scientific articles in the 1890s. Among them was the idea that no civilization was "the product of the genius of a single people" but instead that ideas had been widely disseminated through cultural contact. He wrote of the geniuses of peoples rather than of "a people." As Stocking explains, "as a critic of racial thought," Boas sought to define these capacities "in other terms than racial heredity. His answer, ultimately, was the anthropological idea of culture."[17] Degler, writing two decades after Stocking, stresses Boas's underlying "critical method," which was "historical and relativistic." Historical argument substituted for racial determinism. An example is worth quoting at length.

> A skeptic might ask why some modern colored peoples seemed unable to absorb the civilization of white Europe to the same extent as others had done earlier. Boas's response [in 1894] was that disease, competition from European factory-produced goods which drove out native crafts, and the large number of European invaders slowed the assimilation of European culture. In short, history, experience, and circumstances, not race, supplied the answer."[18]

What drove the Boasian revolution ultimately was the anthropologist's ideological opposition to racism.

I draw attention to these points because the same commitment, rare at that time in the American academy, to challenging ideologies of racial hierarchy drove Du Bois. The two shared more than just convictions, however.[19] Du Bois's work in sociology paralleled Boas's investigations in anthropology, and his famous early article on the "Conservation of the Races," when read side by side with Stocking's and Degler's exegeses of Boas, show Du Bois to be another thinker who was pushing on ahead of his time instead of being trapped by it.[20] Du Bois's historical and empirical investigations of the conditions of blacks in the South, including the 1901 *Annals* piece, "The Relation of the Negroes to the Whites in the South," resemble the investigations of Boas. His 1904 essay "The Development of a People," in which he explained conditions in the Black Belt in terms of history rather than evolution, is even more striking because the word race does not even appear in it. Instead, Du Bois spoke of nations, groups, and classes, and, as the title makes clear, of blacks as a people.[21] It bears repeating that this was a time when most other social scientists shared a different set of convictions about equality and about the evolutionary basis of inferiority.

Certainly the growing collection of books and articles by the new specialists in imperial administration of the 1900s confirm that the historicist and culturist turn from biological determinism was slow and piecemeal. None of the imperial theorists ever admitted to a conversion experience similar to that of University of Pennsylvania sociologist Carl Kelsey, the onetime critic of Du Bois's *Souls* who by 1903 had found it impossible to make a precise determination of the collective capacity of black people for progress because of all the blood mixing that had happened in Africa and in the South.[22] By 1907, in pointed commentary on a paper heralding the science of eugenics, Kelsey was challenging its basic precepts. "Heredity . . . should be used to denote those physical characteristics which come to us through the germ cells of the parents. . . . We know pretty definitely today that acquired characteristics are not passed on from generation to generation." Kelsey continued, "This fact . . . is reacting powerfully upon our social theories." Ability could be improved among members of any class. "Here lies an argument for universal education that has as yet been scarcely utilized by our educators." Most important, another "result of our studies is to weaken the belief in superior and inferior races," which meant that it was necessary to rethink many matters, including barriers to immigration and the value of educating women.[23]

The discipline's new experts on colonial administration and race development tended, instead, to cling to the Lamarckian orthodoxy or move on to new projects and new positions during and after World War I, which makes changes in their ideas hard to gauge. The one possible exception is Paul Reinsch, who delivered his last paper on relations between races during his year at the University of Berlin as the Theodore Roosevelt professor, when he traveled to London to attend the First Universal Races Congress in July 1911. The congress was a remarkable (and, until recently, forgotten) event in the shaping of modern ideas about racial equality and the right of national self-determination in the years before the Paris Peace Conference of 1919.[24] The first objective was explicit, the second articulated on the margins and hardly expected by the Londoners who dreamed of rebuilding the empire on a sounder basis.

Dedicated to challenging ideologies of race supremacy and promoting "interracial harmony," over 1000 attended. They represented "fifty races and nations," as Du Bois put it. (In fact, twenty-two states sent representatives.) Mohandas Gandhi; Krishna Gokale, who was one of Gandhi's political mentors; Tengo Jabavu, the founder of South Africa's first Bantu newspaper; the heretical Zionist Israel Zangwill; Haiti's ex-president Francois Legitime; and Filipino nationalist and autonomy advocate Manuel Quezon joined with Mexican, Guatemalan, Japanese, European, and American internationalists; peace movement activists; feminists; and socialists to listen to dozens of papers over four sweltering days inside the University of London's Imperial Institute.[25] A young Alain Locke, who was studying in Berlin, attended the conference, which had an enormous impact on the lectures he would deliver at Howard a few years later. Reinsch wrote one of the papers that was circulated before the conference, although his biography makes no mention of his participation—an irony, given Reinsch's burgeoning interest in what he called international unions.

The organizers sought to avoid signs of discord among participants and urged members to avoid debate on specific political problems in the various colonies and dependencies. Reinsch protested from the floor one day about exaggerated press reports of disharmony at the congress and the prevalence of anti-patriotic views among participants ("internationalism [has] never been anti-national," he insisted).[26]

However, divisions had erupted on some key issues even before the congress was formally convened, during the preliminary meetings of anthropologists and international lawyers. One was the question of the equality of all races and peoples, an organizing principle of the congress that a few participants said could not be true. Another minority view emerged that insisted both on the naturalness of racial antagonism—what we would now call war—as the key means of world progress, again, in the face of the organizers' abiding interest in ameliorating conflict and securing cooperation among peoples. A third dispute dissented from another of the key organizing principles, that the idea of "race" itself was unscientific and in its place terms such as "nations" or even "civilizations" should be used. One point about the contradictory nature of the arguments advanced at the congress still matters today: "If one speaker says that what we must do above all things is to regard other nations as our equals in every way, and leave them respectfully alone to work out their own national ideas, we applaud him warmly. If the next says the purdah system and infant marriages are degrading institutions, and we must crush them out at any cost, we applaud no less."[27]

Reinsch's paper "Influence of Geographic, Economic, and Political Conditions" for the congress's session titled Conditions of Progress, appears to position him closer to the potential "unity of humankind" and farther from the "immutability of hierarchy" end of the spectrum. Certainly he was less interested in explaining differences than in demonstrating the significance of what we now call globalization; that is, the growing unity "of the branches of the human family in all parts of the world" through advances in communication, transportation, and the spread of European and American economic power. He explored differences that hindered or advanced race development and nationalism in Europe, Africa, and Asia, according to the degree to which geography had protected people from climate and from one another. The absence of fixed boundaries and the "eternal shifting back and forth of population elements has retarded African development," he claimed. These rules of geography were coming undone in the twentieth century under the sway of western "scientific mastery." The question was the degree to which the kind of national self-consciousness that had proved critical in the cases of Europe and Japan could emerge elsewhere in an era of interdependence.[28]

Reinsch nonetheless saw powerful regularities operating between the tropic and temperate zones of the world economy, and modern development had made exploitation of tropical industries increasingly easy. He was also convinced that the world distribution of natural resources would work to limit the spread of industry unnaturally by "artificial and political factors." The days of protection were over, he insisted. Neither the west nor the system of civilized states had completed their mission on behalf of humanity, and he repeated a line heard earlier at the conference, that "only the fully national can contribute to the cosmo-national."[29]

The brief 1911 paper, which drew from his new book on *International Unions*, reflected both his rekindled interest in Eastern countries ("the Orient") and the growing force of nationalism in the colonies and semi-colonies, from Persia to India to China. It is also the last piece of scholarship he produced. In it, Reinsch dispensed with explicit arguments about physiology and deemphasized the concept of the immutability of radical differences that just a few years before had made him skeptical of the idea of the equality of the world's peoples. The powerful explanatory force he gave to geography and environment is still hard to separate from ideas about the inheritability of acquired characteristics, as we have seen. And he reiterated the law of the tropics of the new science of international relations. What the paper thus seems to underscore is the degree to which anticolonial nationalism was driving professors to revise and perhaps refine their ideas of hierarchy in ways that would be institutionalized just a few years later at Versailles and in the creation of distinct categories of "mandates," some of which were viewed as moving more or less rapidly toward independence and others of which were destined by their nature to permanent rule by whites.

PART II

Worlds of Color

Raymond Leslie Buell, a 29-year-old instructor in comparative colonial administration at Harvard, wrote to Howard University's Alain Locke on May 23, 1925, at the urging of *Herald Tribune* book critic Lewis Gannett. The ambitious Buell already had two books in print. He published his first one on French party politics when he was just out of the army and before beginning work on his MA. When he published his second book, on the Washington (arms control) Conference, which took aim at Japanese imperialism, Princeton's department of history and politics awarded him a PhD. Henry Holt and Company was about to come out with his third book, the over-700-page *International Relations*.

Buell's advisor at Princeton and friend, Edward S. Corwin, the great legal scholar and associate of Woodrow Wilson, had wanted a textbook on modern colonial politics for his new American political science series, but Buell instead proposed that he write a book that situated problems of colonial administration within a broader framework of nationalism, internationalism, and imperialism. In *International Relations* he turned to the new political science—"where international law leaves off"—to explain the increasing tensions between the world's lighter- and darker-skinned peoples.[1] Harry Elmer Barnes, an apostle of the "new history," called the approach "revolutionary" in his review in the *New Republic*.[2] With the international relations book finished, Buell headed to Africa to deepen his understanding of race contact and conflict in ways that might contribute to solving the so-called Negro problem.

Buell was the first political scientist in the United States to do fieldwork in any of the various African colonies or in South Africa. The trip resulted in *The Native Problem in Africa* (1928), which is still referred to today. He was hoping for Alain Locke's help with contacts among "native leaders." Locke, who had begun teaching and writing on interracial relations after attending the Universal Races Congress in 1911, had just published the work for which he is best known, a special issue of the *Survey Graphic* titled "Harlem: Mecca of the New Negro," which Buell had read and admired.[3]

The Harlem number and the book that followed five months later, *The New Negro*, established Locke's importance not only to what came to be known as the Harlem Renaissance but also to the modern study of the art, literature, and thought of African, Afro-American, and Afro-Caribbean peoples. Reaching out to Locke thus made great sense. The 40-year-old philosophy professor had added the study of African art to his bulging portfolio of projects and had journeyed to Egypt and Sudan in 1923. That trip in turn led to his meeting in 1924 with Ethiopian regent Ras (or prince) Tafari Makonnen (who was crowned king in 1928 and became Emperor Haile Selassie I in 1930).[4] *The New Negro* included images of African sculptures from the new Barnes Foundation in Lower Merion, Pennsylvania, along with Locke's own first essay on the subject.[5]

Locke was then one of the few American intellectuals writing on Africa to have actually set foot on the continent. W. E. B. Du Bois, then 55, traveled there for the first time a few months after Locke. Melville Herskovits, who is routinely described now as "father" of African studies, did the research for his 1923 Columbia PhD on cattle complexes in East Africa in libraries rather than in the field. The new project on cross-race mixtures measured skull sizes of American Negroes, including, famously, students from Howard University, where Locke had helped arrange a visiting position in 1925.[6] Locke was also urging African Americans to pay serious attention to political developments in Africa, especially to the operation of the League of Nations mandate system, an institution of growing interest to Buell for its promise of improved conditions for colored subject peoples.[7]

Buell, who was arguably the most prolific student of international relations in the 1920s and 1930s, has long been forgotten by the many generations of political scientists that followed in his footsteps, although some in Africana studies still discuss him. While a dozen schools, societies, awards, and so forth across the United States were named to honor Locke, he has never been considered as someone who was critically engaged with the ideas that defined the study of international relations in the United States in the 1920s, a decade marked by new theorizing on imperialism, the challenge to white supremacy, and the prospects of race war. Buell's *International Relations*, a popular college textbook, explains the fundamental cause of and most pressing problems of the contemporary world order, namely, the "restless energy of Caucasian people" in their "search for new markets" and "demand for cheap labor." "Complex interdependence," the shorthand phrase he developed to characterize the world order Caucasians constructed and the accelerated extent and pace of interactions among races, is still used by his disciplinary descendants today, although they think of it as something new, different, and more sophisticated than the concept as Buell defined it.

> Two great political problems have arisen out of the contact of the white with the colored races: 1 the problems which have resulted from the extension of the white man's rule to countries inhabited by non-whites—the problems of imperialism; 2 the problem of discrimination against non-whites who have entered or who wish to enter the white man's country.[8]

In other words, the chief *complexity* that underpinned the idea of complex interdependence was the creation of the "racial problem" that led to fierce debates about the causes of war, the future racial balance of power, and the increased likelihood of violent conflict across the color line.[9]

Ultimately, the assumptions that undergirded the discipline-in-formation showed little alteration from the decades of the founding of the American Political Science Association in 1903 and the *Journal of Race Development* in 1910 (after 1919, the *Journal of International Relations*) and the years of World War I through the 1920s.[10] That is, academics continued to think both in terms of territorial and phenotypical units of analysis and of "anthropo-geographical" boundaries.[11] Buell's textbook, which surveyed developments in California and the Pacific coast of Canada and in the settler colonies of Kenya, South Africa, New Zealand, and Australia, included a discussion of the necessity of segregating white and nonwhite peoples. He reduced the "level of analysis" (systemic, domestic, and individual-level variables), as we say now, to focus on the threat interracial marriages posed; they would create "a hybrid population which would have great difficulty in perpetuating the characteristics of either a white or non-white civilization."[12]

If more evidence is needed that the boundaries that defined the professional study of international relations a century ago are not precisely those that preoccupy political scientists today, then consider the founding in 1923 of the Harvard Bureau of International Research. The initial five-year grant of $250,000 (the equivalent of more than $5 million today) from the Laura Spellman Rockefeller Memorial to support research by Harvard faculty "of an international character in the social sciences" paid for Buell's fieldwork in Africa. The funds also supported anthropologist Ernest Hooten's study of prisoners in U.S. jails. Hooten had called for the country to do more "biological housecleaning" after the passage of the 1924 Immigration Restriction Act. The grant also supported a project on mulattos in the United States by Hooten's colleague, Alfred Tozzer.[13]

In American international relations, the epoch-defining world war and the upheavals that followed across Europe, Asia, and the United States basically confirmed the robustness of the imperialism and interracial conflict frameworks of the previous decade and set the terms of debate about precise causes and outcomes. Conservatives explained even the workers' movements of the world as the result of innate differences, of "racial impoverishment," an intellectual feat that amounted to the biologization of class.[14] What appears most distinctive about social scientific identity and practice in the 1920s is the redoubled effort to expose the dangerous "fallacy of equality" that had gained some ground in the previous decade and to extend the ideational scaffolding that supported the concept of international hierarchy.[15] Elazar Barkan concluded that "castigating these racist positions as pseudo-science" would be "anachronistic."[16] Yet Alain Locke did make the argument, the first time I have seen it made in fact, in the opening lecture of his remarkable series on international relations in 1915, *Race Contacts and Interracial Relations*, which he delivered after the Howard University Board of Trustees turned down his proposal to introduce a course on the subject in the regular curriculum.[17] Locke tied the rise of racial science to modern imperialism, again, for the first time to my knowledge, an argument that Du Bois made for the first time in print one month later in the *Atlantic*.[18] It was a turn in theory that white analysts in America appeared unable or unwilling to take.[19]

CHAPTER 3

Storm Centers of Political Theory and Practice

In 1924, Charles Merriam published "Recent Tendencies in Political Thought," an essay on the state of the field. Today Merriam is considered one of the most important political scientists of the early twentieth century. In the essay, he argued that three epoch-making world processes were shaping contemporary political theory. The first was the further development of industrialism, which gave rise both to workers' organizations and the penetration of the "backward states of the world," which he also described as "the invasion of the tropical by the temperate zone." The second was increasing contacts across race. Race problems "continued to be storm centers of political theory and practice." Nationalism was in essence a "modified form of race expression." The "harsh jangle of imperialism" was one important effect of these contacts. The other main consequence of race contact was the revival of the doctrine of self-determination, which "found abundant expression in political-racial propaganda and in military theory" in Europe and Japan and in the "movements for political autonomy" in India, South Africa, Egypt, and Ireland. The third process was the rise of feminism.[1]

A young Raymond Leslie Buell ran headfirst into the maelstrom to preserve the white racial order. The battle in California to block Japanese immigrants from leasing land went back to a 1913 ban on property owning. Buell, then a PhD student in politics who had taken a position at Occidental

College in 1920, wrote to his mentor Edward Corwin at Princeton for advice on teaching constitutional law and to report on his "stumping" in the Imperial Valley *against* the anti-leasing campaign. It turns out that Buell held a relatively moderate position in the debate on the best way to preserve white racial hegemony. So he also spoke "in favor of exclusion, which the Japs didn't like," and regretted being the only white on what was supposed to be a mixed-race committee ("was taken to a hotel and had breakfast, dinner and supper surrounded by the Yellow Peril—and no whites insight [*sic*].”). Yet he said that an evening paper in El Centro branded him a "renegade American" and "the American Legion threatened to tar and feather me."[2]

Buell published articles on West Coast developments in a number of leading journals, although it was touch and go with the editors of the new *Foreign Affairs*.[3] The trustees of financially strapped Clark University sold the *Journal of Race Development / International Relations* to the mix of millionaire lawyers, bankers, and professors who in 1921 had founded New York's Council of Foreign Relations. The new editor, Archibald Cary Coolidge, Harvard's first professor of Russian history and the mentor and close friend of *Journal of Race Development / International Relations* editor George Hubbard Blakeslee, had lobbied to keep the name in order to maintain the connection with "Blakeslee's magazine." When council leaders looked for a more sellable title, Coolidge came up with *American Quarterly Review*. Another Harvard man (the first dean of the Graduate School of Business Administration) and founding member, Edwin Gay, president of the *New York Evening Post*, said that *American Review of Foreign Affairs* was better, and the name was ultimately shortened to *Foreign Affairs*. When it came time to draw up a list of authors for the first issues, Coolidge turned to Blakeslee and others in the Cambridge-Worcester circuit; Harry Elmer Barnes wrote the first book reviews. Later a second Clark professor, William Langer, who had also worked as Coolidge's assistant, took up the reviewer's spot. Blakeslee himself joined the new editorial board. But the early decades of the journal are most closely associated today with another member of the *Evening Post* staff, Balkans expert and dedicated Wilsonian Hamilton Fish Armstrong, who joined as managing editor under Coolidge and then as editor for forty years after Coolidge's death.[4]

Armstrong at first did not think much of Buell, a young colleague of Coolidge at Harvard, where he had started as a tutor in history, government, and economics in 1922. Armstrong voted to turn down Buell's first piece on the new oil imperialism, he told Coolidge, since Buell obviously "was not used to writing." After Coolidge corrected the misperception—Buell "has been turning out books on all sorts of subjects with startling rapidity"— Armstrong tried to reject the next one on the grounds that he wrote too much.[5] But *Foreign Affairs* ran his "Again the Yellow Peril" in 1923, and by the end of that decade Buell had become its most frequent contributor (with the exception of Armstrong himself). Buell wrote on the Opium Conference in 1925, produced two essays on the impact of white rule in Africa in 1927 and 1928, and an essay on the problem of governing mixed-race colonies more generally in 1929.

By then, Buell had abandoned full-time teaching to direct the research program of the New York-based, mass-member, progressive alternative to the Council of Foreign Relations, the Foreign Policy Association. The association had grown out of a small study group, the Committee on American Policy in International Relations, which began meeting in the summer of 1918. Charles Beard (1874–1948) designed the syllabus. Beard, the best-known historian of the first half of the twentieth century and future president of both the American Political Science Association and the American Historical Association, had just resigned his Columbia position in protest of its control by reactionary trustees. The course focused on the nature and extent of future racial antagonisms, control of international waterways, the status of backward countries, control of natural resources, the place of nationality in world organizations, and, finally, the idea of a league of nations.[6] By the end of that year its members had launched the grassroots education campaign as the League of Free Nations Association, and after the debacle over U.S. membership in the League of Nations, it continued its educational efforts as the Foreign Policy Association.[7] By the mid-1920s a research department had been set up and the first of many local branch organizations were built; we now know them as the World Affairs Councils of America. As research director and president of the Foreign Policy Association after 1933, Buell would become one of the most recognized and influential political scientists writing on international affairs during the interwar years.[8]

Buell's controversial 1923 article "Again the Yellow Peril" came out as an increasingly powerful immigration restriction movement launched the campaign that would culminate in the National Origins Act of 1924.[9] Its leaders sought further, permanent cuts in the numbers of "alien" white stocks (Jews, Greeks, Italians, etc.) being admitted into the country and a total ban on admission of nonwhites from "Asiatic countries"; that is, the Japanese.[10] Buell warned that it was dangerous to seek Japanese exclusion by legislative fiat because it would needlessly provoke a foreign power in ways that were likely to harm U.S. interests.

> There is nothing to be said in favor of the immigration of Japanese laborers into the United States. If unrestricted, it would wipe out

American standards of living, eventually reduce us to the economic level of the Oriental, and implant an alien and half-breed race on our soil which might make the negro problem look white. But the best means of enforcing the exclusion of Japanese immigration is not through . . . an exclusion law, but through an exclusion treaty.[11]

His warning proved correct. Anti-American demonstrations, including a rash of suicides, rocked Japan after the 1924 law was passed, and the Japanese government protested the failure to treat Japan equally.[12] Buell would thus be slotted today among those on the losing side of the immigration debate who had taken relatively "egalitarian" and "antidiscriminatory" positions, on "the principle," as Buell put it, "that the segregation of races of different color is necessary, as far as laboring masses are concerned, not because of racial inferiority but because of racial *difference*."[13]

False Prophecies of the White World Order's End

All accounts of the winning side in the scramble to build an impregnable biological fortress around the *native* Americans (meaning the Teutonic or Nordic or Anglo-Saxon "race" or "blood" or "stock," depending on the particular analytical framework used) recognize the influence of Madison Grant, author of the best-selling *Passing of the Great Race* (1916), and his "protégé, T. Lothrop Stoddard. Grant wrote the introduction to Stoddard's own most famous book, *The Rising Tide of Color: The Threat against White World Supremacy* (1920), which made him the leading apostle of Nordic racial supremacy in the United States. Their notoriety was such that F. Scott Fitzgerald created a composite, "this man Goddard," author of *The Rise of the Colored Empire*, who impresses Tom Buchanan early in *The Great Gatsby*. "The idea is if we don't look out the white race will be—will be utterly submerged. It's all scientific stuff; it's been proved."[14]

No one now bothers to note that Stoddard had been the protégé first of Archibald Cary Coolidge, who had come up with Stoddard's dissertation topic on the impact of the French revolution on Santo Domingo and inspired his subsequent turn to writing full-time about international relations.[15] Stoddard's writing career had an impressive start. He published the dissertation in 1914 for general readers, although specialists embraced it as the first scholarly study in English on the topic. Stoddard proposed it as a parable for the race wars to come. The slave revolt on the island was "the first great shock between the ideals of white supremacy and race equality" and culminated in "the tragedy of the annihilation of the white population," when "the black state of Haiti [made] its appearance in the world's history."[16] The course of dollar diplomacy there under President Taft and Secretary of State Philander Knox a century later launched Stoddard's career as commentator on contemporary world affairs, while the occupations of Haiti in 1915 and the Dominican Republic in 1916 boosted sales of his first book. He wrote, "In fine, Santo Domingo's only hope seems to lie in prolonged tutelage to some foreign power which will assure such conditions of order and good government as will permit the development of the country's splendid natural resources and implant the fabric of civilization."[17]

Stoddard started pumping out pieces at an astounding pace, including two more books and half a dozen articles on Europe in the war, and he ranged far beyond the Nordic/Alpine/Mediterranean racial borders. His 1917 article in the *American Political Science Review* introduced the distinction between "blood race" and "thought race" that he derived from the European case, where people believed they were Teutons, Latins, Anglo-Saxons, and Slavs, races that did not in fact exist, fighting a war that was not a true race war but a "domestic struggle between . . . blood-relatives." He then applied his model to the second imagined racial stage of nationalism in the "Mohammedan world," as was seen in the movements that championed pan-Arabism, pan-Islamism, and pan-Turanism.[18] His shining moment came with the publication of a trio of books outlining the dismal prospects for the future of white world supremacy, including the best seller *The Rising Tide of Color* (1920), *The New World of Islam* (1921) and *Revolt against Civilization* (1922). He continued to turn them out, in fact.[19] The controversy surrounding the first, especially in the pages of the liberal journals of opinion *The Nation* and *The New Republic*, was such that respectful reviews of subsequent books began by reassuring readers that there was nothing alarmist about them.[20] The controversy paid handsome dividends, such that by the time his old advisor took up the editorship of *Foreign Affairs*, he couldn't afford the price Stoddard was commanding.[21]

Little wonder. The largest circulation magazine in the country, *The Saturday Evening Post*, had exposed millions to Grant and Stoddard's ideas.[22] Many other influential publications and specialists in world politics lauded *The Rising Tide of Color*.[23]

When newly elected president Warren G. Harding told a crowd of 100,000 "whites and colored people" in Birmingham in October 1921 that "our race problem here in the United States is only a phase of a race issue that the whole world confronts," he cited Stoddard's study. He also evoked a second authority on the world race problem, Lord Lugard, the onetime governor general of Nigeria who was serving as British representative on the

League of Nations Permanent Mandates Commission. Lugard's ideas about Africa held lessons for the South, Harding said, where political and economic rights might gradually be extended but "social equality" was clearly impossible given the "fundamental, eternal, inescapable difference" between the races.[24] Raymond Leslie Buell came to the same conclusion after traveling to South Africa in 1926, where the Herzog government had sought to create a system of black communal councils while preserving white power in the national Parliament.[25]

Stoddard later shifted his views in line with the distinction Buell and many others had started to make between "superiority" and "difference" as the grounds for immigrant exclusion and for what Stoddard called "bi-racialism" as the solution to the "negro problem."[26] His critics unfortunately do not discuss the development of his ideas past 1924 or so, a point that he underscored in his unpublished autobiography. The conventional accounts handed down to us reflect this static view. Elihu Root, Theodore Roosevelt, and several others wrote to Stoddard privately approving the shift.[27] His influence did not depend on his change of view—far from it. After *Rising Tide* was published, Carl Kelsey—the editor of *The Annals of the American Academy of Political and Social Science* who had criticized Du Bois's *Souls of Black Folk* two decades earlier—reached out to Stoddard for his understanding of "the growing significance of race relationships" as he planned the new issue on immigration reform.[28] Stoddard lectured widely and testified before Congress on the necessity of closing the country's borders. The point is that although Stoddard might have been a lightning rod for critics, little really distinguished his views from those of many white scholars, policy makers, and public intellectuals.

Stoddard developed his ideas about biracialism in *Re-Forging America* (1927), a historical account of America's race development that radically revised his notorious view of inevitable Nordic decline. Two critical junctures had shaped the course of American race development, he argued. He dated the first to 1787, the year of the Constitutional Convention that would give Congress the power to outlaw the slave trade twenty years hence and the year the new federal government passed the Northwest Ordinance, which prohibited slavery in the new western dependencies. As a result, America remained "a white man's country," having averted "the ominous shadow from Africa," which might have left the South resembling the West Indies with a "limitless horde of negro slaves," and a total U.S. population that was one-third to one-half black.[29] The threat slavery posed to national race development persisted, however. It led to the "supreme disaster of American history," the Civil War. Stoddard's account underscored the relentless racial impoverishment, political corruption, orgy of materialism, slum building, and radical ideologies that followed Reconstruction in the South and the alien flood in the East and West before the second "great turning point in America's racial destiny," the passage of the 1924 immigration act. The just-in-time closing of the floodgates made it possible to imagine assimilating the high-grade new aliens and, over the longer term, most of the low-grade ones.[30]

Nonwhites, however, constituted a special problem, and defense of "white integrity" or the color line drove Stoddard to propose the "experiment" that he called biracialism. In essence, he wanted to deepen, regularize, ostensibly upgrade, and extend the South's "separate but equal" Jim Crow order to the country as a whole. "Under a perfected bi-racial system, the line separating the races would be straight and logical," he argued. So, for example, all sexual contact across racial groups would be outlawed everywhere instead of in the piecemeal fashion found in the laws of dozens of cities and states. Disfranchisement, the single biggest obstacle to a fair and just segregated order, would be eliminated over time through a "curial system" that assigned blacks a fixed proportion of local offices and legislative seats: "Thereafter, the negroes could divide into parties, enjoy all the thrills of political campaigning, and get as much political experience as their white fellow citizens, without in the least changing the ration of white and colored office-holders and legislators."[31]

Biracialism might work, he said, and thus possibly "exorcise the dread spectre of race-war." Northern black radicals posed the main obstacle to its implementation. They were frequently mulatto and for that reason were particularly susceptible to "doctrines of racial equality and amalgamation." He singled out W. E. B. Du Bois as "a good example. Doctor Dubois [sic] is a light mulatto, and he typifies the intense resentment felt by such persons at the color-line which debars them from full incorporation with the white race." Du Bois's brand of radicalism hadn't mattered very much until the war years, when, because of immigration restrictions, demand for "native labor" had pulled southern blacks into northern cities and factories. Growing frictions in the North and in the military because of the drafting of black men who had tasted freedom in France had led ultimately to "a racial crisis throughout America," marked by urban riots and rural revolts. Foreign-born Afro-Caribbean "firebrands" were a second radical stream that preached violence and hatred, he claimed.[32]

Stoddard ultimately hedged his bets. Biracialism offered a compromise program. If black radicals continued to propagandize unrealistically for the dismantling of the color line, which meant turning "white America" into "mulatto America," then "colonization should . . . be seriously pondered" as another "possible solution."[33]

Private letters of praise for his latest analytical triumph poured in. His sometime critic, Edward A. Ross, the Wisconsin sociologist and past president of the ASA, who more than twenty years earlier had warned of impending white race suicide, wrote to commend Stoddard for the best dissection of "de-Americanization" he had ever seen. Future Supreme Court justice and Alabama Klan member Hugo Black, who had just won a U.S. senate seat, said that every loyal American ought to support Stoddard's white unity program. The University of Oklahoma's Jerome Dowd, who defined his scholarly project as the "sociological study of mankind from the standpoint of race," had just published his *Negro in American Life* (1926). He had stumbled over the issue of how to preserve white domination while securing civil rights for blacks as they slowly developed out of their childlike state.[34] Stoddard had shown the way with his proposed curial model.[35]

The white world's two flagship international affairs quarterlies, *Foreign Affairs* and the *Journal of the Royal Institute of International Affairs*, both reviewed *Re-Forging America*. William Langer, who had just moved from Clark's international relations department to Harvard and turned out hundreds of one-line reviews for *Foreign Affairs*—this one under the heading international relations of the United States—concluded that it presented "a rather lurid picture of present day America, with a suggested solution for our race problem." The editor of the *Journal of the Royal Institute of International Affairs* gave it a longer and more respectable notice that concluded, "An extremely interesting book on what is the most important problem to-day, not only in the United States, but also, indirectly, in Europe." In the longest review in *Economic Geography*, Carleton P. Barnes, who was finishing his PhD at Clark, at the time a citadel of environmental determinism, called its historical account argumentative but convincing and its appraisal of the racial problem excellent.[36] The only serious criticisms of the South-as-South Africa parable came from those whose reasoned arguments for "natural rights" and equality were dismissed as "madness."

New World Negroes

This rising tide of scientific racism in the 1920s that undergirded popular and scholarly accounts of international relations reflected the "apprehension of imminent loss" among the political classes of "white men's countries" in an era of increasing mobility and mobilization of colored peoples. This is the argument that historians Marilyn Lake and Henry Reynolds say Du Bois began to develop in "Souls of White Folk," which was published in 1910, but that claim is not quite correct.[37] They follow the convention of tracing "Souls of White Folk," published in *Darkwater*, back to the short four-page essay with the same title in *The Independent* (August 18, 1910), but the greatly expanded text, including its trenchant analysis of the Great War, explication of the role racism plays in imperialism, and prediction of the coming "fight for freedom" across the colonies and semi-colonies of Asia and Africa, is actually from "The Culture of White Folk," which was published in the *Journal of Race Development* in 1917.

As they also show at great length, by 1924 the governments of the United States, New Zealand, and Canada had followed the "White Australia policy" of implementing or tightening anti-Asian immigration restrictions. Meanwhile, in South Africa, a country that Jan Smuts, its first postwar prime minister, contrasted with the other white dominions—the laws in his country "had never recognized any system of equality"—he and his comrades consolidated the white supremacist order. These are all the same states that "bandwagoned" to defeat the Japanese proposed racial equality clause at Versailles in 1919.

Mark Mazower's brilliant account of the imperial template for the League of Nations recovers the essential role played by South Africa's leader Jan Smuts and, not least, the objective of securing white leadership through its design.[38] Du Bois, for one, had noticed, in his 1925 *Foreign Affairs* article "Worlds of Color," an account of colonialism on the ground in Africa at the dawn of the mandate era. "Jan Smuts is today, in his world aspects, the greatest protagonist of the white race," dedicated to "the continued and eternal subordination of black to white in Africa."[39]

Locke replaced the slighter essay, "The Black Man Brings His Gifts," by Du Bois in the famous "Harlem number" (as the magazine version of *The New Negro* was known) with "Worlds of Color," which appeared as the final chapter in the expanded *New Negro*.[40] This was Locke's response to a postwar order that had grudgingly recognized the "civilized qualities" of some states and dependencies—Poland, Ireland, Egypt, Iraq—while judging black people barbarians incapable of ever governing themselves.[41] These were the "little nations that were weak and white" in Claude McKay's poem, "The Little Peoples," set free by the "big men of the world," while "blacks / less than trampled dust . . . Must still be offered up as sacrifice."[42] Locke wrote, "We are *now* presenting the New Negro in a national and even international scope. . . . As in India, in China, in Egypt, Ireland, Russia, Bohemia, Palestine and Mexico, we are witnessing the resurgence of a people."[43] For Locke, Harlem was a paradigmatic instance of the phenomenon of race development in international relations. His biographers distance themselves from the concept; race development appears in scare quotes all three times they refer to it.[44]

Locke's framing of Harlem as part of a world movement nonetheless draws attention to specific pages in the introductory essay, "The New Negro," which was stitched together from two separate texts in the special number, "Harlem" and "Enter the New Negro." Harlem, with a population of Africans, West Indians, and African Americans that had grown from 2,000 to 200,000 in the space of a single decade, was "the largest Negro community in the world," a "race capital" with "the same role to play for the New Negro as Dublin has had for the New Ireland or Prague for the New Czechoslovakia."[45] Not only was the era of tutelage over for "the Northern centers" of the race, but Harlem was the center of a "new internationalism," the home of the "Negro's 'Zionism.'" It was where the "pulse of the Negro world has begun to beat." The new "enlarged" race consciousness, which had been egregiously misrepresented by the fear-mongering "rising tide of color" school, was a consciousness "of acting as advance guard of the African peoples" and "of a mission of rehabilitating the race in world esteem from that loss of prestige for which the fate and conditions of slavery have so largely been responsible."[46] *The New Negro* circulated widely and established Locke's intellectual reputation across the Black Atlantic.[47]

Both Alain Locke and W. E. B. Du Bois took on Stoddard and his biracialism thesis, multiple times in Du Bois's case.[48] The Locke-Stoddard exchange appeared under the title "Should the Negro Be Encouraged to Cultural Equality?" in the October 1927 issue of The *Forum*, a New York monthly that regularly featured clashing views on the great issues of the day. Locke led off with "The High Cost of Prejudice." Whites in the United States faced a fundamental "social dilemma and self-contradiction" between their commitment to democracy, or what he called their "social creed," and their unremitting oppression of black people. Swedish economist Gunnar Myrdal made the same argument, using many of the same terms, twenty years later in *An American Dilemma: The Negro Problem and American Democracy*.

The white majority's shortsightedness—the "pathetic delusion that it can negate what it denies"—would give way sooner or later. The decision *not* to implement a program of gradual emancipation in the nineteenth century produced a cataclysm that forced the issue. In analogous fashion, whites could still "retard" further change, "but only at general social or net loss." What Locke called "recognition" rather than "denial of equality" and "the scrapping of White Supremacy" might proceed without the waste of talent and diversion of energies, but either way, black "efforts will still go forward almost as fast." Recognition would come in the court of world opinion since ideas are not subject to embargo." The main danger in delay was the likelihood that the next (post–New Negro) generation would turn to violence out of frustration. "Race war? Not exactly. Class war, more likely,—with the Negro group temper profoundly changed from its present patient amiability to social desperation, having in its ultimate disillusionment discovered that it has so little to lose."[49]

If Locke's piece anticipates what Rogers Smith calls the liberal tradition that is associated with Myrdal and with Louis Hartz, with its emphasis on the "American creed," then Stoddard's response in *Forum* is a pitch-perfect performance of the competing ethnonational or "ascriptive American" tradition.[50] What Smith means in plain language is white supremacy. For Stoddard, full "political and social equality" for black people in America was an "illusion" and, thus, by definition, so was the American creed. "We know that *our* America is a *White* America." "White America will not abolish the color-line, will not admit the Negro to social equality, will not open to door to racial amalgamation. . . . If this spells trouble, then trouble there must be." Blacks in the South had accepted biracialism and prospered under it. Locke and other militant northern black intelligentsia who were making "intransigent demands" were "deluding themselves" if they thought they might gain white acceptance by "disproving the charge of racial inferiority," since "White America's attitude and policy toward the Negro is,—not a belief in the Negro's inferiority,—but the *fact* of his *difference*." Yet in the very next sentence Stoddard revealed his late adoption of the difference (not inferiority) idea to be a distinction without a difference. "True[,] most Whites to-day believe the Negro to be their inferior . . . from realization of racial difference and all that that connotes." Stoddard felt compelled to remind Locke of the most "cherished" of Americans' inalienable rights, the "right to their racial heritage."[51]

Du Bois's first engagement with Stoddard had taken place two years earlier in 1925 at the Labor Temple School in Manhattan, which held regular evening lectures organized by its director, Will Durant, who later wrote the multivolume *Story of Civilization*. The two sparred again in a radio debate that was broadcast from New York in September 1927, just before publication of the Locke-Stoddard debate in *Forum*. Du Bois's biographer, David Levering Lewis, says that word of his triumph against the apostle of racism spread far beyond the salons of the "Talented Tenth," or black intellectuals. In private, Madison Grant told his protégé that it was shameful that such a debate had to take place at all. "To have educated such Negroes as Locke and Du Boise [*sic*] was a crime and Harvard and Boston and Massachusetts are all suffering the retribution for their emotional sentimentalism in the last century."[52]

Before a packed crowd at the city's premier boxing arena, the Chicago Coliseum, Du Bois debated Stoddard a third and final time in March 1929. This time his defense of black people's rights to equality against Stoddard's biracial regime led him to pound on the sick heart of white America's fantasy of racial purity and the threat of miscegenation. It was the so-called Nordics whose project had "broken down native family life, desecrated the homes of weaker peoples and spread their bastards to every corner of land and sea." Yet Stoddard and his ilk would now draw the line: "You shall not marry our daughters!" Du Bois hissed in reply, "Who in Hell asked to marry your daughters?" The headline of the next day's Chicago *Defender* read "Du Bois Shattered Stoddard's Cultural Theories."[53]

CHAPTER 4

Imperialism and Internationalism in the 1920s

The long discussion just concluded should make it easier for theorists and historians of African American thought, of Asian American studies, and of colonialism and postcolonial studies to recognize the relevance of the emerging social science of international relations to their own subjects, however insurmountable the distance or unintelligible the reference terms today between them and their colleagues in political science. It really was different once.[1]

I turn now to the three most important institutional developments in advancing research and knowledge about international relations in the United States in the 1920s. They were more important than the rebranding of the *Journal of Race Development* and the monies that the Rockefeller Foundation paid to Harvard to fund its Bureau for International Research. The annual summer Institute of Politics at Williamstown did not survive the economic depression of the 1930s, and the Institute of Pacific Relations was a casualty of the Cold War and McCarthyism. The third, the Social Science Research Council, founded in 1923 to coordinate and support advanced research in a range of disciplines, is still in existence and has had powerful impacts in many areas of the human and behavioral sciences. It created its first committee on international relations in 1926, only three years after its founding.

The directors of the council established its international relations committee, according to its first staff member, James T. Shotwell, Columbia

University's celebrated historian and a member of Wilson's World War I Inquiry, "in order to deal with the projects of research presented to it by the Institute of Pacific Relations. By reason of these requests, the earliest program of the Social Science Research Council in this field had to do with relations with the Orient."[2] The Institute of Pacific Relations was founded during the Conference on Problems of the Pacific Peoples, which the YMCA organized. It was held over two weeks in Hawaii in July 1925. Delegates attended from Australia, Canada, China, Hawaii, Japan, Korea, New Zealand, the Philippines, and the mainland United States. In order to secure funding from the Rockefeller Foundation, the YMCA officials were sidelined and the meeting was given a more disinterested scientific cast.[3] Ray Lyman Wilbur, the president of Stanford, agreed to head it; he had just finished a two-year study of race relations on the Pacific Coast. George Hubbard Blakeslee, the editor of the original *Journal of Race Development* and the country's best-known expert on American foreign policy in the Far East, served as co-chair. As Lyman recalled decades later, mounting "racial tensions . . . between the white and other races of the Pacific" motivated the organizers. "It might be too late to avoid an armed conflict between East and West. But we wanted to appeal to intelligent people in the Pacific countries to make an effort to avert such a catastrophe."[4] Delegates voted to support a permanent organization, comprised originally of six national councils (this was expanded over the next decades to include England, France, the Netherlands, Indonesia, India, Pakistan, and others) and a secretariat that would organize the next conference in Honolulu in 1927 (Thirteen were held in all, the last in Lahore in 1958.).

The founders of the Institute of Pacific Relations viewed a research program, although costly, as vital to the future success of the institute, beginning with the question of the "biological and social effects of race admixture."[5] Thus, the first books produced under the institute's auspices were *Oriental Exclusion*, that is, exclusion as a modern movement by white nations to control biological and economic competition, and *Resident Orientals on the American Pacific Coast.*[6] The creation of an international relations committee within the Social Science Research Council is thus of a piece with the other committees it founded with its earliest partner, the National Research Council: the Committee on Scientific Problems of Human Migration, which was concerned with the postwar "migrational situation" and the "virtual elimination of space as a barrier to racial admixture," a Committee on Racial Problems, and a Committee on Pioneer Belts that focused, in the words of committee head Isaiah Bowman in an agenda-setting *Foreign Affairs* article, a "science of settlement" in aid of white peoples' expansion in northwest Canada, Rhodesia, western Australia, and elsewhere.[7]

The Institute of Politics at Williamstown, which was held each August from 1921 to 1930 on the grounds of Williams College, served as the model for the Institute of Pacific Relations. Contemporaries recognized it as the most influential institutional development in the study of international relations in the United States in the first postwar decade. The *New York Times* called it the country's first "school of foreign affairs."[8] The first funding requests to the General Education Board, one of the philanthropic organizations founded by John D. Rockefeller, described the project as "a conference or institute closely resembling that of the Williamstown Institute of Politics although . . . narrower and more specific in its subject" and stated that its goal was "to solve racial conflict in the Pacific through free and frank discussion." Similarly, the appeal to John D. Rockefeller Jr. for funds named the Institute of Politics at Williamstown as a model for bringing together "men of the East and the West for a thorough discussion of racial problems."[9]

Political scientist Harry Garfield, the president of Williams College, who served as president of the American Political Science Association the year after he founded the Institute of Politics at Williamstown, explained its design: "To aid in the task of bringing home to our people an understanding of international relations in all their aspects—historical, political, social and economic—indeed, every phase in which nations stand to one another."[10] Garfield had obtained the approval of the college's trustees for what was to become the first postgraduate seminar in international relations in 1913, but the outbreak of World War I put the plans on hold. Returning from a stint as U.S. fuel administrator, he obtained the funds to launch the institute in 1921 from Wall Street speculator and Wilson confidante Bernard Baruch, who was not identified in early publicity.[11] The University of Virginia's Bruce Williams, a young assistant professor who reported on the inaugural sessions for the APSA, saw in it a new method for pursuing a "less cloistered and ineffectual" form of "applied political science."[12]

As Garfield explained in a meeting with the group that wanted to organize the Institute of Pacific Relations, the basic format that had emerged in Williamstown was the closed round table or a small group discussion led by an expert in the subject, a set of larger open round tables for all institute members, and public addresses open to the surrounding community. He emphasized the importance of soliciting a wide range of viewpoints and avoiding resolutions of any kind.[13] Each of the institutes combined a focus on world regions and issue areas. Round tables routinely focused on Pacific, Near Eastern, Latin American, and European affairs and in the first years covered subjects such as the League of Nations, disarmament, the Dawes Plan, threats to white supremacy, and the struggle for raw materials.

Senior scholars who ten and twenty years previously had introduced the study of colonial administration and race development in the United States played leadership roles in the Institute of Politics at Williamstown. Blakeslee was responsible for the round tables on Far Eastern affairs. Leo S. Rowe, a University of Pennsylvania PhD who in 1900 had been appointed by William McKinley to the new Puerto Rican Code Commission, was another. He led the institute's annual sessions on inter-American affairs as director general of the Pan-American Union, the precursor to the Organization of American States. The institute also showcased the rising young stars of the field, including Buell and the new University of Chicago professor Quincy Wright; the most highly praised of the young progressives, Edward Mead Earle, who was hired at Columbia after receiving his PhD there for a remarkable dissertation on imperialism in Turkey; and his fellow Columbia PhD, Leland Jenks, who taught first at Amherst and then at Wellesley.[14]

Consider two measures of the institute's impact on the postwar profession. One is the growing shelf of books—twenty-nine volumes in ten years—issued under the institute's auspices, both with the Macmillan Company and Yale University Press. The premier volume collected James Bryce's eight lectures as a book titled *International Relations*, the last book this leading statesman and scholar published before his death in 1923.[15] Professor Achille Viallate of the École Libre des Sciences Politiques (what we now know as Sciences Po) gave the follow-up lectures, issued as *Economic Imperialism and International Relations*.[16] The subjects of his 1922, 1923, and 1924 roundtables served as the foundation of William S. Culbertson's compendium of the "the major economic factors in international relations," *International Economic Policies*. In it he introduced the idea that a new and dangerous form of mercantilism was underpinning the rivalry for "raw materials, energy resources, and the privilege to export capital," which he argued not only fueled tensions among capitalistic nations but also created dangers in the case of nonwhite races.[17]

A second measure of the influence of the Institute of Politics at Williamstown is the proliferation of institutes based on it, some of which were funded by the Rockefeller Foundation's General Education Board. Beyond the Institute of Pacific Relations in Hawaii, there was the Institute of International Relations at Furman University in South Carolina, which moved to the University of Georgia in 1927. Sir Alfred Zimmern copied the model at the University of Geneva, launching the first summer school in international affairs (commonly called the Zimmern School) there in 1924. The University of Chicago launched a smaller, one-round-table version of the institute in 1923 known as the Harris Institute, through the largesse of the heirs of private banker Norman Wait Harris; Quincy Wright was in charge.[18]

According to the American Political Science Review, in 1925, the U.S. colonial commission began the Institute of Inter-American Relations at the University of Puerto Rico, another Williamstown-influenced project.[19] In 1926, "a new star in the constellation of international institutes" arose in Riverside, California, at the Mission Inn, focusing heavily on interracial relations.[20]

Our Legions Are Dollars

The 1928 Williamstown Institute turned more systematically than in previous years to "the growing economic and political interests of the United States in backward countries, the nationalist movements in those countries, and the effect which each of these factors has upon the other."[21] The round tables dealt with economic imperialism more than any other topic, according to the New York Times, including the topics of the continued need for "raw materials in the undeveloped areas" and the consequences of "white nations" sending "their surplus capital and engineering, scientific, commercial and banking experts into the regions peopled by the colored races." The United States was facing the problem of how to avoid "exploitation of colored people," the spread of the kinds of conflicts that it faced in Latin America and Japan faced in China, and the economic rivalries with other imperial powers that had already dragged the world into war. And it faced these problems more acutely "than any other country," having assumed a position of "world leadership," even if today some imagine the time as one of a U.S. return to relative "isolation" and of "withdrawal" from world affairs.[22]

Among the firsts that year, Charles W. Hackett, a historian at the University of Texas and future founder of the university's Institute of Latin-America Studies, led a round table on the Caribbean that was probably the most heated and contested session ever. The New York Times headlined another round table: "First Woman to Lecture." Halidé Edib Hanum, the Turkish writer, feminist, and exiled opponent of Atatürk, led the sessions on problems of Turkey.

However, the other first went wholly unnoticed by the Times. Rayford Logan, a 1917 Williams alumnus, was the first African American to give a paper at Williamstown. The future Howard school mainstay was then at Virginia Union University, where in addition to teaching foreign languages he created the first courses in African American history, African history, and the history of imperialism. At Williamstown he presented a long, carefully crafted critique of the League of Nations mandate system.[23] The "trusteeship" principle enshrined in Article 22 of the covenant, which Wilsonians held up as the answer to the exploitation of subjugated peoples that characterized the past imperial era, was in fact how whites had justified domination over the same "tribal peoples" at least as far back as the Berlin Conference in 1885 and the passage of the Dawes Act in the United States in 1887.[24] The designation of different classes of mandates made tutelage permanent for black people. (Class A mandates were the former Ottoman territories in the Middle East, Class B mandates were the former German colonies in Central Africa, and Class C mandates were the territories in southern Africa and the Pacific that South Africa, Australia, and New Zealand wanted to annex.)

Logan was right, of course. In the original proposal by Smuts, it was the European territories the Russian, Ottoman, and Austrian empires had lost that would require temporary "mandatary" administration. For the "barbarians" in the African and South Pacific territories, "political self-determination in the European sense" was unimaginable.[25] British colonial secretary Lord Milner said that the new African mandates "differ[ed] from colonial possessions possibly only in name."[26] Logan, however, said that ultimately it wouldn't matter. "One need not be too pessimistic about the coming of age of Africa. The best-devised plans of diplomats have vanished as rapidly as their prophecies. Leagues and Covenants to the contrary notwithstanding, the colonies of Africa, it is believed, will one day be independent countries." To that end, Logan's account recognized a positive information-gathering and oversight role for the Permanent Mandates Commission despite the forces of imperialism arrayed against it and despite the commission's inability to force the mandatory powers to accept its authority. Logan ended by reporting on the recommendation from the fourth Pan-African Congress in 1927 that a Negro member be appointed to the commission, which, needless to say, had gone unanswered.

Raymond Leslie Buell ran four open conferences on problems in Africa during the last week. The *New York Times* did take note in his case, and these generated almost as much controversy as the Caribbean discussion. Buell argued in step with Logan and counter to prevailing opinion that African national aspirations were real and the prospect of increasing political mobilization for freedom was likely. Therefore the white race could choose either "a great inter-racial war or a great experiment in inter-racial cooperation and the social control of wealth."[27]

The record to date showed that the continent's people bore more of the costs of "development of its resources" and less of the benefits. However, Buell also discussed recent positive (albeit piecemeal) changes in colonial administration. In the *Foreign Affairs* article from which his talk was drawn, he offered the provisional hypothesis that mandate territories were doing better on various measures than adjoining colonies. This was the question he would guide a young Harvard PhD student, Ralph Bunche, to test just a few years later. (Bunche came to the opposite conclusion.) For Buell, not surprisingly, internationalism in the form of extending the reach of both the mandates commission and the principle of the open door—for capital in all economic sectors and also for missionaries—and encouraging the migration and employment of western doctors, engineers, and teachers was the means by which white governments could shape the inevitable albeit long-term transition ("even if after a hundred years") to self-rule. Buell had concluded his article with the suggestion that the United States and European governments in particular employ African American professionals in African uplift efforts, arguing that this just might head off their turn instead "to supporting anti-racial and revolutionary movements which will be as disastrous to blacks as to whites."[28]

Mordecai Johnson, who two years earlier had become the first African American president of Howard University and whom Locke had recommended for the session, followed Buell with some comments ostensibly on how Africa was viewed by Aframerica.[29] He reinforced Buell's account of the exploitative labor regime on the plantations and in the mines that had decimated communities and lives. The issue, he said, was not between black and white races, but, as in other countries, between "a comparatively small group of capitalists and the great mass of people."[30]

Critics pounded both Johnson and Buell with arguments that might have been novel at the time in the U.S. context but have long since become clichés. Economic historian Charles Ryle Fay, who had trained at the London School of Economics, defended England's honor. It had raised the Gold Coast from "cannibalism to . . . peace and prosperity" while trying to teach Africans self-government, although it was difficult to even get the idea across to them. University of Washington sociologist Roderick D. McKenzie—whom the *New York Times* described as an expert on "race relations," although later histories remember him as a pioneering "human ecologist" and as the person who produced the study *Oriental Exclusion*, disputed Buell's estimates of population decline under European rule and mocked Johnson for believing that the white race was a "great octopus" that went to Africa to "strangle the poor colored people."

Later that night Belgian socialist and Parliament member Louis Piérard gave a speech in rebuttal, reminding critics that whites had "given the natives hospitals, roads, schools, and railways." He called on the audience to deal realistically with the realities of colonialism. Withdrawal would mean either a new world war or a return to barbarism by the natives.

Europe must also think, he added, of the problems of raw materials and migration in the congested and industrial countries of the white world. The development of tropical resources by the white race . . . was therefore proper as long as it went hand in hand with a consideration for the welfare of the natives and with the raising of backward or degenerate populations toward the standards of modern civilization.[31]

Buell was undeterred. The next day he took up the resources issue in a conference on Liberia. His research in Monrovia resulted in a series of highly publicized charges against the Firestone Corporation's one-million-acre rubber concession, which he said was organized as a plantation, unlike the organization of production in the British and French colonies he had visited. One charge he made was that the firm had disguised its role in originating the loan that the Liberian government had been obliged to contract as a condition for Firestone investing there. We know now that Harvey Firestone viewed the loan as an instrument for controlling the Liberian state, precisely as Buell had asserted. The new, higher rate of debt service flowed not to the repaid British and French creditors (thus making interference by the two governments in Liberian affairs less likely), but to the U.S. company, which was overseen by a customs administration that had been reorganized by the U.S. government and was led by Americans.

These terms remained secret until they were exposed in 1931 as an outcome of Buell's second, more explosive charge. He claimed that the firm depended in part on a government-organized system of forced labor—with the rents flowing to officials and their allies—and in part on direct contracts with and payments to rural elites ("tribal chiefs") who pressed villagers into service. Buell went even further. The involvement of former commerce secretary Herbert Hoover (who at the time was running for president) and the U.S. state department demonstrated that the United States was engaged "for the first time in economic imperialism outside of the area covered by the Monroe Doctrine."[32] Buell earned a public rebuke from Phillip Marshal Brown, the former diplomat who was teaching international law at Princeton and was a member of the advisory board of the institute, for injecting partisan politics into a discussion of international affairs, while Harry Garfield challenged Buell's claims. The *Wall Street Journal* reported the state department's criticisms of Buell's numerous "inaccuracies." Nonetheless, three years later a League of Nations investigation confirmed the existence of virtual slave labor in Liberia, which led to the resignation of the Liberian president and others in his circle.[33]

The Institute of Politics at Williamstown also kick-started, ironically enough, the career of the most outspoken critic of the proliferating international relations institutes and of Buell's brand of internationalism in the 1920s. John Franklin Carter was a widely read columnist (who used the pseudonym Jay Franklin) and a confidante of Franklin Delano Roosevelt. He later ran a private intelligence operation for the White House during World War II. In 1922, Garfield hired him to round up speakers in Europe for the next summer's institute. Carter picked up a reporting job while in Rome that opened the door to work for the *New York Times*.[34] His "descent from the heights of Wilsonian idealism" happened early.[35]

In his first of more than thirty books, *Man Is War* (1926), Carter took aim at the peace movement and internationalists who were still seeking to bring the United States into the League of Nations. Efforts to abolish war or scare Americans into joining the league as the means of securing a viable peace rested on a profound misunderstanding (or misrepresentation) of the forces that governed international relations in what he called the Atlantic system. The arguments put forward at the Institute of Politics at Williamstown, the Foreign Policy Association, and kindred groups notwithstanding, "wars are entirely thinkable[,] . . . now in progress, and far from being the downfall of civilization, are being waged in its behalf." The new wars "will take the style of wars of nationalism," which nonetheless needed to be understood as an effect of international forces, imperialism chief among them.[36]

He followed *Man Is War* with a sequel, *Conquest: America's Painless Imperialism* (1928). Attacks on American foreign policy were often wrong-headed because not all empires were alike, he claimed. "American empire is intangible, invulnerable, an influence over the minds and customs of mankind which is confirmed every time the world installs an adding-machine, dances to jazz, buys a bale of cotton, sells a pound of rubber, or borrows an American dollar."[37] This was Carter groping for a strategy to secure what we have since come to describe as domination through consent. In the late 1920s that appeared to him to require accommodation to nationalism in Latin America (anticipating the Good Neighbor Policy of the Roosevelt administration) while resisting interventionist campaigns that promoted democracy in Europe and self-rule in the European dependencies. The United States would lead by example. This position is similar to the one we saw put forward in the 1890s by John W. Burgess and has been revived many times since by conservatives who oppose crusades in the name of decolonization, nation-building, democratization, and the like.

The Origins of the Howard School

One more key institution for the study of international relations in the United States was founded in the 1920s and has gone unrecognized since.

The story of the Howard school, in which Alain Locke played a central role, begins, paradoxically, with his firing in June 1925 by an embattled and, it turns out, last white Howard University president on a campus rocked by rising student ("New Negro") militancy and a faculty fighting for higher salaries. At the height of the crisis with President J. Stanley Durkee and the Howard Board of Trustees, Locke called it "our Bunker Hill days" in a struggle for "the next step of freedom in our Negro colleges."[38] Locke remained institutionally adrift and in ill health while fighting his firing (and editing *The New Negro*). In the spring of 1926 he submitted a proposal to New York's Foreign Policy Association for a study of the African mandates system that would make its operations better known among African Americans in particular. He saw the project as one part of a larger research program on Africa for which he sought funding from the Social Science Research Council. (He did not succeed.)[39] The idea of funding Locke "shook the executive board [of the Foreign Policy Association] to its depths," although he got the grant.[40]

The records I consulted don't spell out the source of the controversy and Locke's biographers don't discuss it. The obvious one is that Locke was a black man and thus his objectivity if not his abilities were suspect. Locke had an ally on the board, however: founding member Paul Kellogg, editor and owner of *The Survey* and *Survey Graphic* magazines. Locke had edited the themed issue "Harlem: Mecca of the New Negro" for the latter. At any rate, the decision came just as Raymond Leslie Buell was taking over from a seriously ill Edward Mead Earle as the Foreign Policy Association's research director. Buell and Locke met for the first time to discuss the project as Locke prepared to set sail for Europe in 1927, and they corresponded periodically over the next months. Mainly Buell sought Locke's help with sources from or about the latter's contacts in Paris, including Senegalese deputy Blaise Diagne and Diagne's most famous antagonist, West Indian writer René Maran.[41] In turn, he provided Locke with an introduction to political scientist (and future American Cyanamid executive) Huntington Gilchrist, a member of the Secretariat of the League of Nations.

It turns out that Buell had doubts about the project ("I am not clear . . . just what Mr. Locke has in mind"). He warned Foreign Policy Association board member Abbe Livingston Warshuis, who had asked Buell for his appraisal, of a potential problem down the road.[42] Locke was unlikely to achieve much in Geneva, particularly during the time that the league's assembly was in session. Buell assumed that the board had fully weighed the "advantages and disadvantages of having a Negro go to Geneva under the FPA name." He worried that Locke would seek additional funds to continue his work in Africa. In that case, the association would doubtless pay a high price in terms of its reputation and future access, since the colonial powers were notoriously suspicious of blacks from the United States working inside the colonies.[43] Were Buell's fears in this case colored by his new employers' decision to fund research that seemed to overlap with his own not-yet-completed study (for which he also depended on Locke's help)?[44] If so, Buell needn't have worried.

It took Locke close to two years to deliver his oft-promised and repeatedly postponed written report on the mandates to the Foreign Policy Association. It was an inordinately long delay, even taking into account the vast array of endeavors Locke was pursuing—writing a grant for a study on African arts and culture; founding a museum in Harlem, where he had relocated; a curatorial project; travel; lectures; book reviewing; and so forth.[45] In addition, Locke had learned on the eve of his Geneva trip that Howard's new president, Mordecai Johnson, was giving him back his job, and Locke returned to the Howard campus full time that fall.

His mandates report frames the issue in terms of the centrality of imperialism in leading to the recent world conflict and the threat that "the imperialistic world powers, America included" continue to pose to world peace. The question for Locke was whether or not the mandates principle, which he said was "a new code of empire," could advance effective internationalist solutions to the problems of race development and reverse the exploitative land, labor, and natural resource regimes that had been in place since the 1800s. Unfortunately, the report never resolved the tension between the workman-like recounting of administrative details and the muted recognition of both the "compromises" involved in the mandates' creation and the continued oppressive conditions under which Africans labored.[46] His biographers call the memorandum "detached," but bloodless may be better, especially in comparison to Buell's and Logan's essays, the latter of which Locke sought in vain to have the Foreign Policy Association publish in his place. In any event, the Foreign Policy Association requested revisions, offered him some extra remuneration for his troubles, and planned to distribute 9,000 free copies, but Locke never submitted a final version.

As he later told his friend Kellogg, it was "an albatross," and he knew both his "role" and his "limitations."[47] The real value of the mandates research, he said, was in inspiring his plan for an "African studies program" at Howard. To be clear, what he meant by the term was an international orientation to "the race problem, not as a special problem but as a phase of world adjustment."[48] The network of race and imperialism scholars he would bring together under this rubric at this juncture rivaled his work as an impresario in African American arts and literature, for which he is most often remembered.

He and his Howard colleagues had already taken the first step by hiring a 25-year-old MA in political theory from Harvard named Ralph Bunche to teach political science.[49] Bunche covered the entire curriculum, from American politics to theories of imperialism and comparative colonial administration. Locke had his eye on Logan, a specialist on Haiti and sharp critic of the U.S. occupation, to head African studies, and he opened the door for Logan at the Foreign Policy Association, where Buell became a great patron. Unfortunately, the Carnegie Corporation turned down the African studies proposal, and Logan did not join the Howard faculty until 1938.[50]

Buell, as president of the Foreign Policy Association after 1933, was the primary promoter of these black international relations scholars to the government, foundations, and the white academy through World War II. It is no discredit to him that his patronage alone was not sufficient to overcome the racism that the Howard school made a central focus of its theorizing. Locke, in turn, was a key intermediary in Buell's and the Foreign Policy Association's efforts to reach out to African American organizations in its various campaigns for the reform of U.S. policies in Cuba, Haiti, Liberia, Puerto Rico, Kenya, and Ethiopia.

The Market Collapse of International Relations

The economic downturn of the 1930s posed an almost insurmountable challenge to institution building in the field of international relations anywhere, let alone at Howard. With the foundations reducing their outlays, the Social Science Research Council closed down its international relations committee and then had to scramble to respond to the outbreak of World War II. James Shotwell, a master internationalist entrepreneur and former head of the Social Science Research Council's international relations committee, sought in vain for funding for two new institutes, one for Central European and the other for Caribbean affairs along the lines of the Institute of Pacific Relations. Princeton launched its School of Public and International Affairs in 1930 to compete with the Walter Hines Page School of International Affairs at Johns Hopkins, which opened the same year, although "school" in Princeton's case was an expression of a more hopeful future. It remained until 1948 (when it was renamed the Woodrow Wilson School) what we would now call a "program" for undergraduate majors built mainly on existing courses. Princeton professor John Whitton told Buell, "A man will be added to the Department of History in order to teach Latin-American problems. Another man, probably a Chinaman, will be added to the Department of Politics to cover the Pacific and the Far East. The course in international law will be lengthened to one year. The same will be done with the course on international relations."[51] Raymond Buell had proposed that he organize an Institute of Interracial Problems at Princeton to anchor advanced study in the discipline, but nothing came of the idea. At Johns Hopkins, the Page School also foundered for most of the decade.

A new and subsequently crucial concept (and identity) for writers and students of international relations—"realism" and "realist"—was introduced in the United States in the 1930s. It was not introduced by one of the "late" repentant Wilsonians of the last half of the 1930s, such as Buell, Edward Mead Earle, Reinhold Niebuhr, or Nicolas Spykman, the latter a specialist on the philosophy of Georg Simmel, who was about to reinvent himself as a student of *geopolitik*. Nor can we credit, as most now do, the former diplomat who occupied the Woodrow Wilson Chair of International Politics at the University of Wales, Edward Hallett Carr, since the book that matters to the conventional lineage, *The Twenty Years Crisis*, did not come out until 1939. It was also not Hans Morgenthau, the German émigré lawyer most associated with the concept who did not come to the United States until 1937 and began teaching the subject during World War II. Rather, the honor belongs to Lothrop Stoddard, whose consistent critique of internationalism and imperialism as the twin threats to Anglo-Saxon hegemony had made him one of the most recognized public intellectuals of the interwar era.

When the market for international relations all but dried up during the worst years of the Great Depression, Stoddard returned to writing on world affairs only in 1932 with two books in one year, *Europe and Our Money* and *Lonely America*. "Realism" was the wholly unfamiliar concept—and was rendered in italics—in both. Harvard's Richard Langer lauded *Europe and Our Money* in *Foreign Affairs* as a "telling attack upon the uncritical investment of American money in Europe." In fact, it was the best review he ever gave Stoddard. *Lonely America*, however, was "like the author's other productions, well-informed, frank, somewhat sensational. . . . As the author sees it, we have gotten ourselves into a pretty mess, and are now alone in a predatory world. He prides himself on being a realist and does not hesitate to lay his color on in gobs in order to get the effects he desires."[52]

Stoddard analyzed the disjuncture between the reality of the dominion the United States exercised—its paramountcy in Latin America and the Caribbean, the swagger of "Gold and Paper" in Europe, and the jostling with other great white powers for influence in the Pacific—and Americans' inability to comprehend the dangers let alone craft a coherent national policy to deal with "the likelihood of armed strife" and "war on a grand scale." Sectional cleavages and the privileged position of banks and other business interests went far to explain the inconsistent and contradictory tendencies in post-Versailles foreign policies that were antagonizing nationalists everywhere and leaving the United States isolated. "We are hated for our tariffs and our immigration laws; for our tourists, our films, and our jazz," Stoddard said. Uncle Sam had been "rechristened "Uncle Shylock.""[53]

Internationalists, he claimed, conjured a phantom world out of "ignorance, sentimentalism, cloudy idealism, bumptious conceit, and smug self-righteousness." He drew on John Carter's *Man Is War* for his critique of the small, unfortunately influential minority of Wilsonians who headed pro-league organizations and comprised the core of both the Council of Foreign Relations and the Foreign Policy Association, which continued to press for deepening U.S. involvement in European affairs. It was sometimes hard to tell, he said, where the honorable if misguided concern for America ended and foreign propaganda and the private projects of bankers and brokers began. The "delusion of international cooperation" was of far greater consequence in the case of the pacifist and disarmament movements, with their lunatic fringe and feminist auxiliary. These disparate currents in support of a misguided internationalist project were propelling the country forward to the surrender of sovereignty, the sharing of resources, the decline of living standards, and, ultimately, the "sacrifice of race."

In the last and most vital matter, he turned to Sir Arthur Keith, the renowned Scottish doctor and anthropologist who warned of the scourge of internationalism: "If all mankind is to sleep under a common tribal blanket, black, yellow, brown, and white must give and take in marriage, and distribute in common progeny the inheritance which each has come by in their uphill struggle."[54] Stoddard also echoed Keith's call to resist. "Head and heart will rise against such a program. . . . Without competition, mankind can never progress; the price of progress is competition—nay, race prejudice and, what is the same thing, national antagonism, have to be purchased not with gold but with life."[55]

Lonely America ended like all the other critiques of the "improvisations" after the accident of "finding ourselves the world Colossus" and of our susceptibility to "the hypnotic power of phrases" with proposals that never quite seem up to the job. Stoddard praised the already impressive upgrades in the U.S. diplomatic machinery and called for more. Similarly, he argued that because of the war, U.S. military capacity had vastly improved to the point where it could protect vital interests in the short term, "but not as strong as they should be in so crucial period of world politics." The real work was to be done in guiding public opinion through an "unremitting campaign of popular education on foreign affairs." Most important, he admonished his readers, "Become clear-sighted realists—or take the consequences."[56]

PART III

The North versus the Black Atlantic

Early in November 1936, Raymond Fosdick, the new president of the Rockefeller Foundation, met for lunch with John Foster Dulles, the managing partner in Sullivan and Cromwell and a foundation trustee. Dulles had recently argued in his article "The Road to Peace" that German rearmament was a positive step toward world order.[1] Fosdick wanted his views on the value of the foundation's current investment in international relations in light of current "chaotic conditions." As we have seen, it would be hard to imagine the advance of the discipline in the United States and elsewhere in the interwar years in the absence of Rockefeller funds, which were then bankrolling the Institute of Pacific Relations, the Council on Foreign Relations, the Foreign Policy Association, the Royal Institute of International Affairs in London, and the International Studies Conference run out of Geneva. Much of this support dated back to the end of World War I, although the foundation had also just agreed to back the creation of a new Institute of International Studies at Yale.[2] Now the foundation's president was asking Dulles to imagine what more practicable course it might take in the future.

Dulles's View of the Discipline

Dulles began by drawing Fosdick out about the foundation's views. Had support for "popular education" on foreign affairs "yielded satisfactory returns?" When Fosdick hesitated, Dulles jumped in. Although he belonged to both the Foreign Policy Association and the Council on Foreign Relations, neither represented "the fundamental type of program which the Foundation was best suited to develop." Dulles thought that "the laboratory approach" would be a better way to go, although he clarified that he did not mean "work carried on in the universities by academic men," since academics did not have a realistic and well-informed view of the "practical aspects of problems" or "the results to be desired from taking practical action."

Dulles said that Chatham House, as the Royal Institute of International Affairs in London was informally referred to, came closest to what he had in mind, but the real problem was that key issues were not being dealt with anywhere. Fosdick agreed and said that the foundation had hoped that the Council on Foreign Relations would evolve in a similar direction and have as much of an impact, but that so far "we have been rather disappointed." He also pushed Dulles for concrete suggestions about the kind of work that needed to be done. The millionaire lawyer answered that while permanent boundaries were key to a peaceful world order, the problem was that, in terms of tariffs and market access, they needed to be "low" so as not to impede "the flow of trade, culture, population" and so forth. And for those who were trying to come up with solutions, the "most profitable point of attack is the colonial possessions." As Dulles's biographer notes about his views more generally in this period, this was an argument that the "great powers" should have access to the colonial possessions, which would still be "locked . . . into a fundamentally exploitative relationship."[3]

This is about as stark a confirmation as exists of the continuing validity of the argument about imperial ambition and the colonial roots of conflict in the twentieth century, two decades after Du Bois first made it. The argument had become a mainstay of theorizing. The transcript of Fosdick's interview with Dulles does more, though, reminding us of the vast gulf between what appeared to matter in the professional study of international relations in 1936—a mere three years before the outbreak of the European war—and the imaginary world that a Cold War cohort of realists would begin to conjure a decade or so later. First and foremost, imperialism remained the central problem for scholars seeking to grasp the nature of and threats to the existing world order. Italy had launched a war of occupation in Ethiopia in 1935, the significance of which Du Bois analyzed in "Inter-Racial Implications of the Ethiopian Crisis: A Negro View" in *Foreign Affairs*.[4] The resurgence of imperialism in Asia—Japan's creation of a puppet state in Manchuria in 1931, its withdrawal from the League of Nations in 1933 following further territorial conquest, and ultimately its full-scale war with China in 1937—made the Institute of Pacific Relations, which had relocated its headquarters to New York, an indispensable information resource as the crisis in Asia unfolded. The Rockefeller Foundation paid for the new research program of the Institute of Pacific Relations on the Sino-Japanese war, and on the eve of that war, the National Broadcasting Company (NBC) covered its 1936 Yosemite conference on the radio.[5]

Most crucial of all, in 1938, the Third Reich launched a project of imperial expansion, not for the recovery of its lost African colonies but for mastery over the territories Hitler deemed vital to a greater Germany, those where hundreds of thousands of German minorities—"racial comrades"—resided. Germany's many foreign policy theorists, specialists in *geopolitik*, and the like, saw "international relations as racial struggle," to quote historian Mark Mazower, although he might as well have been discussing the discipline and its popularizers in the United States.[6] The Nazi campaign confirmed a second key argument of the Howard school about the elective affinity between a by then scientifically unmoored concept of race and empire. For example, a German official wrote from the Ukraine in 1942 that "we are here in the midst of the negroes."[7]

Howard University's Ralph Bunche updated the argument about racism and imperialism in *A World View of Race*, a study of the exploitative economic arrangements around the world that racism helped disguise. *Foreign Affairs* found the time ripe for an extended critique of economic explanations for expansion in the guise of a review by its in-house specialist of John Hobson's 34-year-old *Imperialism: A Study*. Yet it also published *Izvestia* editor Nikolai Bukharin's "Imperialism and Communism," which attacked the pseudosciences of race and *geopolitik* that provided the excuse for fascist expansionism and misled those in the West whose responses to the crisis drew on the same false ideas, for example about the "need" for land or raw materials.[8]

For one more example of what turns out to have been the autumn of imperialism, at least as a critical analytic frame, consider the books that topped leading young international relations scholar Frederick Schuman's list of the field's most vital works in 1937: Grover Clark's twin studies, *The Balance Sheet of Imperialism* and *A Place in the Sun*, for their careful accounting of "the fallacies of imperialist logic."[9] Arguably, the increasing discussions of the reasons for and consequences of imperialism even in *Foreign Affairs* reflected the belief—for the first but not for the last time—that the United States was turning the corner on 1898 and its own decades of crude imperialistic policies, as the new "Good Neighbor Policy" in Latin America and the 1935 declaration of (future) independence for the Philippines demonstrated.[10]

The Shape of Things to Come

Chicago-trained Fred Schuman was the discipline's next Raymond Leslie Buell in terms of his public visibility and prodigious accomplishments.[11] He wrote a dissertation, "American Policy toward Russia since 1917," which appeared in print one year later, in 1928; completed a highly praised follow-up, *War and Diplomacy in the French Republic*, in 1931; and wrote a 750-page textbook, *International Politics: An Introduction to the Western State System*, in 1933 that knocked Buell's *International Relations* off some reading lists. Research in Berlin led to his remarkable *Nazi Dictatorship: A Study in Social Pathology and the Politics of Fascism*, in 1936, which some political scientists criticized for its one-sided negative assessment of Hitler's new order.[12]

Schuman said that what made his international relations textbook different from the traditional approaches—"staggering in volume and overwhelming in complexity"—was his turn to the *"new* political science." The adjective is key, because Buell made the same claim about political science in his own textbook, *International Relations*. What Schuman was bringing to the table was the turn in Chicago political science toward emphasizing the "relations of power in society." In the preface to the second edition, with its now iconic cover of chess pieces arrayed on a board, he says that he based his approach "on the principles of *Realpolitik*" and calls international relations "the game of power politics" played by "members of the Western State System." This is why Schuman sometimes earns a footnote as an example of "classical realism" or a precocious realist thinker. But this way of thinking depended on ignoring a great deal, as is evidenced in his final chapter on "The Passing of Power Politics."[13]

There are two things to note about the change, compared to most of the 1920s, to discussions of or identifications with "realism" and more frequently "power politics" by academics in the mid- to late 1930s. The first is that more often than not these amount to descriptions, using the relevant individuals' own terms, of resurgent tendencies in world politics after Japan and Germany's withdrawal from the League of Nations than to an author's ideological conversion.[14] However, discussions of power politics and realpolitik appear in the journals only a handful of times, at least until the start of World War II.

The second point is the protean nature of mid-1930s American realist discourse and the array of contradictory positions that a proper understanding of power politics somehow produced. There was the defensive (racial) realism of its earliest advocate, Lothrop Stoddard, as we have seen, and the realism of Charles Beard, president of the APSA in 1926 and of the AHA in 1933, who, in two volumes supported by the Social Science Research Council, laid out a blueprint for withdrawal from imperialist rivalries and concentration on national economic reconstruction.[15] The realism of Arnold Wolfers, the Swiss émigré who ran the School of Politics in Berlin until the Nazi takeover, after which he began teaching at Yale, led to his advocacy in 1934 of "moral disarmament" in the face of imperialism, for example curbing the influence of arms makers at the "domestic level," instead of making impossible demands of the League of Nations.[16] Yet the realism of the radical theologian Reinhold Niebuhr led him down the road by late 1937 to "all aid to the allies short of war." It also led him to quit before he could be thrown out of the Socialist Party in 1940 ("an end to illusions"), the year he published *Christianity and Power Politics*. Like a few others then and many others in the decades that followed, Niebuhr had to come up with a work-around, since on the U.S. left neutrality (or anti-interventionism) was the logical course in a conflict between rival imperialisms.[17] This is the reason why some adopted the alternative and hardly hard-headed geopolitical conception of democracies battling dictatorships or totalitarianism or fascism.[18]

Considering Schuman closely in the year or two after he published *International Politics* can tell us more about the complexity of a moment and of a discipline whose history has been flattened by decades of accumulated, hasty, and ultimately unsupportable generalizations. For instance, Schuman was virtually alone in correctly predicting the course of Nazi aggression and by 1935 was arguing that war was inevitable.[19] In his popular writing and frequent public lectures he took the extremely controversial position that the United States and the other great powers needed to combine to reverse the course of Nazi imperialism and check the likely prospect that Japan would join with Germany to force the United States out of the Pacific.[20] Those who are now conventionally associated with the discipline's turn toward interventionism and the promotion of U.S. "grand strategy"—Arnold Wolfers, Edward Mead Earle, Nicholas Spykman, Max Millikan, and many others[21]—were either still solidly in the "isolationist" camp or missing in action, at least in print, so some care is needed in tracing their conversions in 1937, 1938, or later to the cause of Anglo-American alliance or, increasingly, American ascendancy on its own.[22]

Buell's private papers underscore the problem. In the summer of 1944, he wrote to one of the great forgotten analysts of the current scene, the Russian émigré Vera Micheles Dean, about the years before "Ed" Earle and other erstwhile isolationists in the *Nation* and *New Republic* "crowd" had "flopped [that is, "flip-flopped"].[23] Buell's internationalism, in contrast, like his opposition to power politics, never wavered, but as the world moved toward war he came to fear the potential for totalitarianism at home and the complicity of the liberals.[24] He quit the Foreign Policy Association; joined the Republican Party, which he had once denounced for its "moral degeneracy"; and battled isolationism by signing on as a foreign affairs advisor to Roosevelt's opponent, Wendell Willkie, and publisher (*Time, Fortune, Life*) and party stalwart Henry Luce.[25] Like Niebuhr, he hoped to keep the United States out of the fighting while committing to a more resolute internationalism aimed at mediating the conflicts in Europe and the Pacific and reconstructing world organization.

Thus, if, as some believe, the Rockefeller Foundation agreed to fund the Yale Institute of International Studies in 1935 in order to "promote realism and globalism and undermine isolationism," its principals clearly failed to do due diligence.[26] The institute's original proposals emphasized approaches to peace and, more innovatively, the study of U.S. foreign policy. The best-known and most widely read of the publications it subsidized, by Whitney Griswold, a future president of Yale, argued that the United States should pull out of the Pacific (*The Far Eastern Policy of the United States,* 1938). Edwin Borchard, author of the original proposal for the institute, a founding member, and Yale's preeminent professor of international law, was also America's best-known theorist and supporter of neutrality, while its in-house diplomatic historian, Samuel Flagg Bemis, used his new *Diplomatic History of the United States* (1936) to "thump . . . for neutrality and a 'continental policy.'"[27] Raymond Fosdick was impressed enough with institute director Nicholas Spykman to recommend him to Carnegie to head their proposed new project on "the Negro Problem" before Swedish economist Gunnar Myrdal got the job.[28]

Neither the Rockefeller Foundation nor the Carnegie Corporation had conceived (let alone pursued) a project to promote realism and globalism in the mid-1930s. Instead, when Edward Mead Earle sought funds to support a research seminar on U.S. military and defense policy to be run out of his new home at the Institute of Advanced Study in Princeton, Carnegie officials rejected it as tantamount to propaganda. If it were truly necessary, then it ought to be paid for by the government rather than by a private foundation, they argued.[29] The problem is that our histories of the 1930s mostly look back (using documents that do so too) from Pearl Harbor and deftly or not reorder the world to conform to the new line of the day.

Two Disciplines, Separate and Unequal

There is one final thing to consider about the Schuman textbook that introduced undergraduates at Chicago, Yale, Princeton, and elsewhere to the idea of power politics. Schuman was the only white scholar to consider the implications, in print at least, of "the retreat of scientific racism" for international relations theory, at a time when most other historians and political scientists still clung to their belief in the inferiority of black people. So when he analyzed the "dynamic forces" at work in the world, Schuman read remarkably like Buell on nationalism, neomercantilism, and the new and old imperialisms. He even borrowed Buell's trope of an observer looking down "from Mars or the moon." The key difference is that Schuman dismissed the significance of racial identification or racial alliances as somehow displacing nationalism and instead called the racialism that nationalists often deployed "pseudo-scientific rationalizations" and "biological myths." However, the effects of these rationalizations and myths were all too real. Thus, he argued, in the United States, racial science was one element in the oppression of black people who "continued to constitute a degraded and outcast pariah community." Yet the "minority problem" in this case was domestic and not an international one, first, because its resolution was not a matter of self-determination (or irredentism), and second, because the "Negro States of the world—Haiti, Liberia, and formerly Abyssinia—are such feeble midgets compared to the United States that they are in no position to act in a protective capacity, even were they inclined to do so." Certainly no Western state or "international organization" demonstrated a concern for the fate of black people in the United States "save the Communist International."[30]

He was mostly right, although one might have added the Pan-African Congress and even more convincingly the Universal Negro Improvement Association (UNIA), a mass movement of tens of thousands. While Schuman identified himself as a "liberal," others routinely identified him in the 1930s and 1940s as a "fellow traveler" who had defended Stalin's show trials and, as such, would have considered Garvey's UNIA a tragic turn in liberationist thought.[31] He faced numerous campaigns from the Hearst press, wealthy university donors, and the state legislature to have him fired at Chicago and was subjected to multiple federal loyalty investigations after he moved to Williams in 1936, where he became Woodrow Wilson Professor of Government two years later.[32] It appears that fellow travelers mattered—and would continue to matter—to efforts to advance the theory in the white academy and society about the role of racism in sustaining international hierarchy, the theory that Du Bois and Locke had first put forward in the years before World War I.

Twenty years later, on the eve of the next war, the network of professionals and institutions dedicated to teaching, advanced research, and public dissemination of knowledge about world affairs had both widened and deepened. With the foundations scrambling to make up for lost time and respond to the new national emergency, the network would grow denser still, as we will see. New funds flowed to the oldest organizations, the Council on Foreign Relations, the Foreign Policy Association, and the Institute of Pacific Relations. Buell would now have the resources of *Time* and *Fortune* backing him. Princeton's sleepy School of International Affairs suddenly came to life. Many campuses hosted emergency schools of military government for preparing officers to administer foreign occupations and War Department army specialist training programs in, among other key technical fields, "foreign language and area study," which ultimately transformed the organization of knowledge in the discipline.[33] The one downside to the mobilization of academics for the war effort is that it stood in the way of the kind of unfettered "basic" research associated with the advance of knowledge in the social sciences, leading the Social Science Research Council for one to close down its international relations committee for the duration.

The Howard school theorists tried to gain access to this network but failed. They were excluded from the conferences and study groups and their wartime research and institution-building grant applications were turned down, not for what they believed but for who they were. Not even federal government appointments and consultancies made much of a difference. By the end of the war, Buell was virtually their only link to and advocate for them among the new notables in the international relations discipline.

At the same time, the Howard school theorists had become part of a wholly unique counternetwork of leading anti-colonial theorists, public intellectuals, and future prime ministers of Africa and the Caribbean, as we will see, men and women such as Dantes Bellegarde, Nancy Cunard, C. L. R. James, Jomo Kenyatta, Kwame Nkrumah, Nmandi Azikwe, George Padmore (whom Howard professors first knew as Malcolm Nurse), Paul and Essie Robeson, and Eric Williams.[34] These intellectual activists and leaders are all extremely well known today, are read across the global academy, and are frequently the subject of multiple biographies, as are Bunche, Frazier, Locke, and Logan. In contrast, thinkers such as Buell, Earle, Dunn, and their colleagues are all but forgotten.

CHAPTER 5

Making the World Safe for "Minorities"

In 1935, W. E. B. Du Bois published two of the more controversial works of his long career. In June, Harcourt Brace came out with his masterful *Black Reconstruction: A History of the Part which Black Folk Played in the Attempt to Reconstruct Democracy in America, 1860–1880*. In it, Du Bois used a kind of heterodox (or perhaps ad hoc) Marxist framework in order to radically reorient an understanding of the role of slavery in the making of industrial capitalism ("The dark and vast sea of human labor . . . [those] on whose bent and broken backs rest today the founding stones of modern industry") and the historiography of the Civil War ("It was thus the black worker . . . who brought civil war in America. He was its underlying cause.").[1] The brief notice in the June 13, 1935, issue of *The New Yorker* described it as "a scholarly chronicle of the Tragic Era by a noted historian who takes the odd view, in distinction to most previous writers, that the Negro is a human being."

That same month, the New York Times–owned world affairs magazine, *Current History*, ran Du Bois's "A Negro Nation within a Nation." The article is a slightly altered version of a controversial address Du Bois had made the year before at the National Association for the Advancement of Colored People (NAACP) on an issue that had led him to step down as editor of its journal, *The Crisis*, and ultimately resign from the organization.[2] Du Bois said the NAACP's project of integration had failed. He argued that in the face of the Great Depression, the burdens of which had fallen unequally upon the black working class, the only viable solution was recognition of the reality of segregation and its reformation through the building of independent producers' and consumers' cooperatives.

One finds a score of valuable, albeit sharply divided, reviews of *Black Reconstruction* in national dailies and weeklies and in professional social science and history journals. Notably, however, not in the *American Political Science Review* and the *American Historical Review*. The Howard school Marxists all linked their critiques of the book directly to what they saw as Du Bois's disastrous turn toward economic "racialism" and "chauvinism" at a moment when they hoped to turn the NAACP or some successor into an instrument for promotion of a cross-race working-class alliance.[3] Yet a central theme in Du Bois's revisionist history is the success of the southern capitalists' appeal to white racial solidarity that made such a labor movement impossible in the 1860s and after, an argument that the same Marxist critics passed over in silence.[4]

For Ralph Bunche, the future first African American president of the American Political Science Association, Du Bois's "Negro chauvinism" and "racialism" made the "successful crossing with Marxism impossible"—an unfortunate choice of metaphor. Bunche wrote that Du Bois's was a "pseudo-Marxist interpretation" rather than a social scientifically valid application of Marxism-Leninism, hastily applied, as when he appeared to trace U.S. imperialism back to the South without considering the role of "Northern capital in the Caribbean, in Central and South America, and in the Far East."[5] To Bunche's credit, his unpublished 1929 essay, "Marxism and the Negro Question," suggests a certain consistency in his opposition to any strategy of liberation based on an alliance of the black bourgeoisie and working class along the lines of the Third Communist International's "national minority theory" of 1928 and its (brief) call for black self-determination in the South.[6] Bunche also rejected the comparison of African Americans to a colonial people under imperialism, except in the limited sense that the semi-feudal conditions in the South would require "the shattering of the power of Southern landlords through nationalization of the land." Lenin had gotten it right when he described the "Negro people" as "a subject caste on a racial basis," a "remnant of feudalism." Black liberation would come only "as an integral aspect and as inevitable consequence of the revolutionary overthrow of the capitalist system," and the task of communism was to "weld together the masses of the Negro people," tear down "the barriers between the Negro and white workers," and "break the hold of the capitalist political parties" over black people. Much later he testified, "I have never . . .

endorsed the Communist Party, espoused its cause or supported its ends. Its tactics and its revolutionary philosophy and objectives are, and have always been, repugnant to me."[7] It was probably a good thing that his "Marxism and the Negro Question" remained hidden in his archive.

The dismissal of Du Bois's "confused" and "unscientific" pseudo-Marxist theorizing in *Black Reconstruction* by Bunche and his comrades has given way to a dramatically different reading over the past few decades. Cedric Robinson calls it the first real attempt by an American theorist to "sympathetically confront Marxist thought in critical and independent terms" at a time when others (Bunche apparently included) were searching "for ideological orthodoxy" and "cautiously threading an ideological position between Ruthenberg, Lovestone, and Foster in the CPUSA or Trotsky, Bukharin, and Stalin in the Communist International."[8] There has been much less effort until now however to contextualize and historicize Du Bois's program for social reconstruction ("Nation within a Nation") in the 1930s or to move beyond the terms of the debate circa 1970 about "black nationalism."[9] Yet black nationalism by itself, whether or not it was motivated by the Comintern, can't explain a U.S. president's embrace of Lord Lugard and T. Lothrop Stoddard as valued guides in the 1920s for the future of autonomous black political life, as we saw in chapter 2.[10] Nor can it explain Raymond Leslie Buell's appeal to blacks to "set aside their conventional ideas about assimilation long enough to fight for the principle of Negro autonomy and Negro areas" when he appeared at Howard University's extended symposium on Problems, Programs, and Philosophies of Minority Groups in April 1935.[11]

This remarkable event on what then was arguably one of (if not the) most pressing question in international relations is hardly discussed in the histories of the Howard radicals in the 1930s, although Bunche, Frazier, and Locke were all involved in its organization and Du Bois, the bête noir of the scientific Marxists, took part. Rather it seems to have been lost in the shadow cast by a three-day conference at Howard a few weeks later on The Position of the Negro in Our National Economic Crisis. Bunche and others engaged in a debate at his home on the last night of the conference about creating the National Negro Congress as a grassroots, radical alternative to the NAACP. His foundational role in a popular front–era organization with a large presence of Communist Party members would come back to haunt him in the 1950s.[12]

The less well-known Problems, Programs, and Philosophies of Minority Groups conference took place over two weekends in April 1935. They were bookended by an opening address on "The Plight of Minorities in the Present Day World" by Arnold Wolfers, the newly arrived German émigré to Yale and a closing paper, "Making the World Safe for Minorities," by the University of Chicago philosopher T. V. Smith. This was Locke's attempt to establish the global context for the plight of black Americans in the 1930s.[13] He had first tested his ideas in a series of three lectures on "The World of Interracial Relations" at Berea College in Kentucky in 1931.[14] Locke argued that the identification with (or as) a particular subject race in Africa or elsewhere in the late colonial world might have obscured more than it revealed about conditions in the northern or southern United States, in which case the debate about the League of Nations mandate system and the extent to which it masked continued domination offered no real guide for action.

The relevance of the League of Nations did not begin and end with the mandate system, however, since it had also overseen the building of a "minority rights regime" via treaty in the Eastern European states created at Versailles and a few of the other already existing but putatively less civilized polities in the Balkans.[15] The rise of fascism had posed a grave challenge to the idea of securing the collective rights of minorities while pursuing the goal of "assimilation" (and to the idea that what made the states of western Europe "advanced" was that they needed no special protections for their own minorities). One of Hitler's earliest objectives in fact was the overthrow of the minority rights regime; he was aided by the resurgent racism across the continent and, ultimately, by the armies of the Third Reich.

Versailles thus provided Bunche and his interlocutors with a basic piece of their conceptual apparatus. There are no references to *minority* "Negro rights" in scholarly journals until the 1920s. Speakers at the conference addressed minority group tactics, compared Jews and African Americans, and discussed the role of religion, the value of cultural autonomy, and so forth. Bunche led the sessions on imperialism and its treatment of "subject peoples" (hardly "minorities"), but an article he published on the eve of the conferences, "A Critical Analysis of the Tactics and Programs of Minority Groups," explicitly recognized the league's expansive definition as the one that makes it even possible to speak of racial minorities. The paper he would give at the New Deal conference, The Programs of Organizations Devoted to the Improvement of the Status of the American Negro, extended his critique of the warped perspective that minority-group thinking produces. The moment thus might help us understand Bunche's future role in building the human rights regime at the United Nations, which was weaker than and starkly different from the minority rights provisions of the League of Nations. Extension of the latter would have opened the United States to challenge on what Bunche called "jim crowism." The architects in 1945 were explicit about protecting the United States from scrutiny.[16]

"World Aspects of the Race Problem Including the Imperialistic System"[17]

The controversy that swirled around Du Bois's nation-building program led directly to the longest work Bunche published in his lifetime and one that Bunche scholars today value highly.[18] Bunche later disowned it. Locke commissioned *A World View of Race* for an African American adult education pamphlet series he was producing known as the Bronze Booklets. As the inside cover reported, the series, funded by the Carnegie Corporation, aimed at presenting "the Negro's own view of his history." However, Bunche's neo-Marxian analysis of racism as the primary ideological means for legitimizing a hierarchical world order looked nothing like the first three pamphlets in the series on African American adult education, music, and art.

A World View of Race consists of four densely packed but clearly laid out and jargon-free chapters that in essence explain Bunche's appeal to anti-capitalist working-class solidarity as the only means to real freedom for African Americans.

First he showed how all the essential and frequently contradictory claims that made up racial "science," for example, claims about the reality of superior and inferior kinds and the dangers of miscegenation, had been falsified. The puzzle that emerged was the nonetheless increasing visibility of national policies in the name of race.[19] The answer that Bunche offered was that racialism as a "myth" worked as a "perfect stalking-horse for selfish group politics and camouflage for brutal economic exploitation." It naturalized and justified hierarchy in the era of "the rights of man" and the "rights of people." He discussed racism in Germany, and while he recognized the seriousness of racial conflict in the Pacific, India, and the West Indies, all cases where challenges to entrenched systems of subjugation were likely to intensify, he did not attempt anything like a systematic analysis. Instead, he focused primarily on race and imperialism in Africa (as "imperialism's greatest and most characteristic expression") and disputed the significance of the difference between British and French policies, the subject of his 1934 award-winning dissertation. He then turned to the United States and racism's contribution to the domination of the capitalist class.[20]

His biographer, Charles Henry, is right that Bunche's concept of "social race," and his analysis of the conceptual incoherence of all attempts at racial classification and the pernicious effects such attempts produce and sustain, "prefigure" debates that would take place fifty years later (and counting) about race as a social construct.[21] Like some (but not all) who have made the argument since, Bunche thought that racial identification, even as a defensive strategy, made it that much more difficult to confront the problem of class in the United States.[22] Around this time, Buell reported, "I had an interesting talk with Ralph Bunche the other day, who says he is completely an anti-racialist and apparently does not even favor talking about it. His idea is that we should work for an improved social system which will benefit white and black alike."[23] In the book, however, he held out for more: "class will some day supplant race in world affairs. Race war then will be merely a side-show to the gigantic class war which will be waged in the big tent we call the world."[24]

In *A World View of Race*, Bunche took apart a key piece of theorizing by the discipline's founding racial realists. Predictions of world race war "assume that both the white and black peoples of the earth have a common fundamental interest in the color of their skin." Predictions of the rising black or yellow (or later allied black and yellow) races "ignore . . . the class, tribal, religious, cultural, linguistic, nationalistic and other differences among both black and white peoples."[25] It wouldn't be the first time that rational but untrue beliefs proved resistant to debunking by academics, since the "threat" of race war continued to haunt White House advisors and colonial administrators-turned-international race relations experts for decades.

The more important conceptual innovation Bunche made in *A World View of Race* is the insight into the ordering principal that structured the new modern capitalist-imperialist international order. Hierarchy was what mattered most, not "anarchy" or "power politics."

> The vital issues involved in the practices of our contemporary political and economic life more and more imply the inequality of peoples. . . .
> The ruling classes among the dominant peoples of the Western World find it expedient, therefore[,] to hark back beyond Locke, Rousseau and Jefferson to the more limited and comforting philosophy of "equality" advanced by the Greek philosopher Aristotle:—"some men are born to serve and some to rule."
>
> In a world such as ours some such creed of inequality is both inevitable and indispensable. For it furnishes a rational justification for our coveted doctrines of blind nationalism, imperialism and the cruel exploitation of millions of our fellow-men. How else can our treatment of the so-called "inferior races" and "backward peoples" be explained and rationalized?[26]

Ironically, in light of his future career as a UN official who oversaw the process of decolonization, Bunche showed little capacity at this juncture to think creatively about any kind of meaningful strategy for those subjected to economic exploitation, political disfranchisement, and moral debasement in the African dominions, colonies, mandates, and protectorates. The deeper irony is that despite Bunche's analysis of the exceptional conditions of black America, when it came to outlining a strategy for African liberation Bunche's solution remained identical: the violent overthrow of capitalism ("class war") in the West.

Consider in this light his review of George Padmore's brutal dissection of empire, *How Britain Rules Africa*, published the same year. Bunche's criticism follows directly from *A World View of Race*: Padmore's "nationalism" ("the right of self-determination and Africa for the Africans are cardinal points in his thinking") had led him, like Du Bois and other U.S. race leaders, to the false solution of "Pan-Africanism" when the "surest road toward liberation of the African masses" was the overthrow of capitalism in the metropole.[27] It is also true, however, that Bunche had little or no familiarity with the actors and political movements in West Africa, Kenya Colony, and South Africa, and, as he himself admitted, little ability to see colonialism from the standpoint of its victims. In part, it is what drove him to embark on a two-year retraining project in anthropological methods (funded by the Social Science Research Council) with Northwestern's Melville Herskovits, the London School of Economics' Bronislaw Malinowski, and Cape Town's Isaac Shapira). The project included field work in East Africa, and no less important, extended engagements with leading pan-Africanists in London and Paris.[28]

Lymon Bryson, the New York educator who oversaw Locke's series for the Carnegie Corporation, approved Bunche's Leninist-flavored approach to race and imperialism, although he said the Marxism was "wrongheaded." Locke, however, chose not to fight when he received word that that Carnegie would not approve the next booklet in the series, Du Bois's long essay on "The Negro and Social Reconstruction," although Locke had "banked on the demi-Marxian slant of the Bunche point of view to balance the racialist view of Du Bois in a very interesting way." In some way that none of the accounts to date have adequately explained, Du Bois's dissection of the failures of the post-emancipation era and his appeal for black unity for economic and political self-defense troubled the foundation's agent more than Bunche's call for class war.[29]

Black Atlantic Crossings

The history of internationalism in the 1920s and 1930s has conventionally entailed mapping a set of intellectual connections that move in parallel with flows of capital and the maneuvering of diplomats across the Atlantic and Pacific Oceans. The transatlantic or Anglo-American or, as they said then, Anglo-Saxon alliance—for example, the story of the parallel founding of the Royal Institute of International Affairs in London and the Council on Foreign Relations in New York—has so dominated the imaginations of later generations that it was necessary to spend some time tracing the trans-Pacific institution-building efforts (and leading institution builders) of the early postwar period back to the earliest self-defined specialists in international relations. Doing so of course has made it easier to see how empire featured so prominently in the theorizing of academics in the 1910s, 1920s, and 1930s and the racial order to which most critics of imperialism such as Buell remained committed.

Hubert Harrison, a radical journalist and independent intellectual who was born in St. Croix, pinpointed the blind spot in "white capitalist internationalism" when it came to oppressed peoples and in particular those of African descent, and he spent the last years of his life seeking to build an alliance of people of African descent or a "Black International" and, more ambitiously still, a "Colored International" of the world's oppressed peoples.[30] The Pan-African Congresses of 1919 and 1921, which were designed to influence the great powers but were instead opposed by them, was one node of an emerging black internationalist (and increasingly anti-imperialist) counternetwork. Rayford Logan, who joined Howard in 1938, first met Du Bois; established a lasting friendship with Dantes Bellegarde, the Haitian minister to France and its representative to the League of Nations; and forged his deepest political and intellectual commitments at these conferences. E. Franklin Frazier attended the Paris session of the 1921 congress at a time when he was hoping to win a fellowship to study race relations in France and Morocco.[31]

George Padmore, a former Howard student and a Communist Party operative in the period 1927–1933, and his childhood friend, the Trotskyist and outspoken advocate of Caribbean independence, C. L. R. James, were at the center of a second node of individuals and organizations in the mid-1930s. The network included the International African Friends of Ethiopia and the International African Service Bureau, both based in London, but the network stretched across to Paris, the Caribbean, and West Africa.[32] Out of this moment and milieu came *The Black Jacobins*, James's great work about Toussaint L'Ouverture.

Brent Edwards makes the general point about interwar black internationalism that it was "at once inside communism, fiercely engaged with its ideological debates and funneled through its institutions, and at the same time aimed at a race-specific formation" against "the Comintern's universalism, adamantly insisting that racial oppression involves factors and forces that cannot be summed up or submerged in a critique of class exploitation."[33] We have seen a perfect example of this dynamic in Ralph Bunche's dismissal of Du Bois as a racialist (and pseudo-Marxist) who was an obstacle to working-class unity and so objectively served the interests of capital. Like Bunche, Padmore and his comrades attacked Du Bois, other prominent members of the NAACP, and non-Communist black labor leaders on the same grounds, and like Bunche Padmore argued that the path to freedom lay in "the struggle against race chauvinism" and the unity of workers "of all races and nations." Padmore changed his mind after he quit the party in 1933. Word had come down to stop agitating in support of the liberation movements in Africa and Asia. The new Soviet diplomatic offensive sought alliance with the imperialist powers against fascism. Padmore had apparently become one more agent of capitalism and "Betrayer of the Negro Liberation Struggle."[34] The winding path forward as a leading anti-imperialist theorist, pan-Africanist, and brilliant tactician of African liberation would eventually take him to Ghana as an advisor to his protégé, Kwame Nkrumah.

Bunche spent time with Padmore and others in his radical circles in the years before the war, which included Kenyatta, who tutored Bunche in Swahili; Max Yergan, a YMCA missionary who had administered Carnegie Corporation projects in South Africa before his radicalization and move to the United States, where he became head of the National Negro Congress; Paul Robeson, the actor who was arguably the most visible and outspoken advocate of racial equality of his day; Eslanda Robeson, an anthropologist and journalist; and the young Oxford graduate student Eric Williams, who would take over Bunche's classes at Howard during the war years.

The Council on African Affairs

Max Yergan appeared in 1936 at the first National Negro Congress in Chicago. He later moved to Harlem as a National Negro Congress representative, and he was the first African American lecturer to give a course in Negro history at City College of New York. After his arrival, the deteriorating security conditions for black people in the mid-1930s, from Bengazi to Cape Town to the Dominican borderlands, gained increasing prominence on the black internationalist and left-liberal agendas.[35] For instance, Yergan wrote a pamphlet on the toll that producing raw materials took on South African workers (*Gold and Poverty in South Africa*) for Mary van Kleeck of the Russell Sage Foundation.[36] He participated with Bunche and Melville Herskovits, head of the new anthropology department at Northwestern University and the leading figure in "African studies" as it would come to be known in the 1950s, on the Africa panel at the 1938 New York meeting of the Association for the Study of Negro Life. His most important initiative was to found together with Paul Robeson the International Committee on African Affairs in 1937, renamed the Council on African Affairs in 1941, after the war made it impossible to coordinate with comrades in London, Paris, and Cape Town.

The International Committee on African Affairs/Council on African Affairs was what we would now call an activist nongovernmental organization, in this case the first to deal critically with (colonialism in) Africa. It hoped to shape U.S. policy. It was also the only integrated international relations organization of any kind. It mounted a number of large successful conferences, rallies, and speaking tours in its early years. Yergan's ambitions included a research arm and a program for training African students in the United States, but the organization ran on a shoestring budget (Robeson paid the startup costs). Other founding members were Buell, Bunche, Franz Boas, and René Maran, the novelist and great friend of Locke, but it depended on the work and skills of insiders such as Van Kleeck and others associated with the larger, more established Institute of Pacific Relations.

Unlike the latter, however, Yergan had no success with raising funds from the Carnegie Corporation for an organization that was pressing for African liberation. Carnegie had supported programs, as the institution itself later admitted, that made "construction of the apartheid government" possible. Yergan had dim prospects generally of winning over elites with the argument that the oppressed in Africa constituted a vital U.S. interest.[37] As Franz Boas, by then an emeritus professor at Columbia, told him in 1939, "It will not be easy to convince Europeans or Americans that people on lower stages of civilization are not there solely for purposes of exploitation."[38] The views of foundations and state agencies might have shifted marginally after the United States entered the war and prepared to land troops in North Africa, but by that time most of the International Committee on African Affairs/ Council on African Affairs principals were under surveillance and a few, like Bunche, had resigned.[39]

Living Hand to Mouth

Alain Locke was the scholar closest to George Padmore, who had studied with him. Their correspondence tells the story of his and his pacifist comrades' efforts to flee Britain as war threatened in 1938, at least until the signing of the Munich Pact. Up until then, their work had stressed fascism's relationship to other forms of imperialist ideology and practice and pressed the position that the surest path to peace in a world rent by imperialism was for workers to support the liberation of the colonies. In addition, they argued that colonial peoples should seize the opportunity provided by the war to advance one cause only—independence.[40] C. L. R. James was able to reach the United States, but Padmore had been blacklisted. Locke sent him money for a visa and travel costs to Haiti in October 1938, and James sent a copy of the manuscript he had been working on, *The Black Man's Burden in Africa*, to Locke for safekeeping. British publishers wouldn't touch the book after the war began.[41] Padmore ultimately stayed put. He had to close down his journal and struggle to find local outlets for his anti-war views. He wrote regularly for the black press in the United States (the *Chicago Defender*, the *Pittsburgh Courier*, *The Crisis*) throughout the war, but he occasionally had difficulties with U.S. censors in Washington and London.

Eric Williams, who was Padmore and James's protégé, although a much more politically circumspect intellectual, was able to leave for the United States in the summer of 1939 thanks to the efforts of Bunche, economist Abrams Harris, and above all Locke, when he joined the Howard political science faculty. There he began to establish his reputation as one of the two leading scholars of the Caribbean and the modern world economy.[42] In his first year at Howard, the Julius Rosenwald Fund paid for a summer of research in Cuba, Haiti, the Dominican Republic, and Puerto Rico, which he drew on when he produced a long-delayed Bronze Booklet for Locke, *The Negro and the Caribbean* (1942) and when he revised his Oxford D Phil as *Capitalism and Slavery* (1944). He called the former "an out and out attack on colonialism in the Caribbean." He had to resign from the research staff of the Anglo-American Caribbean Commission after Padmore republished the work in London in 1944.[43] *Capitalism and Slavery* ranks with Du Bois's *Black Reconstruction* and James's *Black Jacobins*, and is probably the most well-known among specialists working outside the orbit of Africana studies.[44]

Williams also had to bear much of the teaching burden of a small political science department at Howard that was facing an influx of military trainees at a time when Bunche was on leave from teaching much of the time. Bunche returned to campus in the fall of 1938 with a grant to write a book based on his Africa sojourn, which he never produced. Instead, Raymond Buell tried to arrange a government appointment for Bunche through Cordell Hull, Roosevelt's secretary of state, but Bunche had no luck on this front until 1944.[45] Instead he went on leave from teaching again in 1939 to work with Gunner Myrdal on *An American Dilemma* (1944) while continuing to administer the department, organizing a major conference on Negro studies in 1939 for the American Council on Learned Societies, and seeking, without success, to capture some of the wartime rents for a large research program at Howard.

Bunche produced over 3,000 pages in four long memoranda for Myrdal, but despite encouragement (and unlike other project principals), he never published any of this work. Thus although Northwestern's Melville Herskovits had used Bunche to organize a conference of the American Council on Learned Societies at Howard (any other venue in Washington, D.C., would have run up against the problem of meals and accommodations for the invited African Americans), behind the scenes he had a ready-made excuse for leaving Bunche off the committee-in-formation that would set the agenda for research on blacks during and after the war. He told ACLS Secretary-Treasurer Mortimer Graves that "Bunche has not produced for many years as *we* have hoped he would, and I do not think he ought to be included."[46]

Locke would have to be excluded on different grounds. In 1939, Locke began what turned out to be his last book-length anthology, *When Peoples Meet: A Study in Race and Culture Contacts in the Modern World*, which he put together with Marxist sociologist Bernhard J. Stern. The book presents excerpts from the work of over seventy writers (including Leonard Woolf), biologists, economists, psychologists (including Otto Klineberg), historians (including Jacques Barzun, Hans Kohn, and Arnold Toynbee) anthropologists (including Boas and his students Ruth Benedict, Herskovits, Margaret Mead) sociologists (including W. O. Brown, who was then at Howard but would go on to found the African Studies Center at Boston University; E. Franklin Frazier; and Donald Young, then a key figure at the Social Science Research Council) and political scientists (including G. F. Hudson and Oscar Jaszi).

Locke framed the problem of the book and wrote the introduction to each section. As his biographers stress, these constitute a major restatement of issues that he first wrestled with in his 1915 lectures on international relations. By 1939, he saw racialism as only one mechanism or rationalization in "the struggle for group power and dominance." It was no less a fiction than the idea of "separate, distinctive and ethnically characteristic cultures." He developed taxonomies of cultural conflict—distinguishing, for instance, the operation of power politics in creating minority issues in Europe from imperialism—and analyzed specific techniques or devices of dominance such as racialism and "the tactics of survival and counter-assertion" by "submerged people."[47] The book ends with a survey of contemporary conflict across Europe, the European empires, and the Americas. E. Franklin Frazier was correct in his review to link the analysis in Locke and Stern's *When Peoples Meet* to Lord Bryce's foundational 1902 lecture in international relations, "The Relations of the Advanced and Backward Races of Mankind."

It foretold of the crisis, he said, that was attributable to "the rise of a racial philosophy . . . backed by military power" that now engulfed the world.[48]

Two additional points stand out in Frazier's review, however. He traced the way the "relations between races and its import in world history" had finally emerged as an issue of concern for the wider educated public. "In the United States, the problem of the relations of races has been viewed as a local problem. As the American empire expands into the Caribbean and South America, and finds itself in conflict with Asiatic nationalism and imperialism, the problem of race and culture contact assumes a new meaning."[49] Yet as we have seen, this "new meaning" was the central issue for international relations scholars at Clark and elsewhere in the years before Frazier studied for his MA there. He made the same mistake as Bunche in including Asia and Africa as places where "minorities" confronted "dominant races." The specificity of the American case was apparently still hard to keep straight.

CHAPTER 6

The Philanthropy of Masters

Can we bring together these seemingly dispa-
rate threads of a counter-history of the discipline of international relations in
the United States?[1] The new field of scientific study was concerned not with
the consequences of the anarchical structure of world order, as it is understood today, but with the dynamics of domination and dependency among
the world's superior and inferior races. The first self-identified "realists"
sought the preservation of exclusivist national and Anglo-Saxon prerogatives
in exploiting the raw materials, labor, and material wants of the dependent
races. And the first black scholars (and only them) in a deeply segregated
academy challenged the fundamental premise of international/interracial hierarchy, that different norms applied to different classes of people. Luckily,
the main actors tie these strands together for us.

Rebranding the Anglosphere

Raymond Leslie Buell wrote to Edward Mead Earle on April 15, 1941, about
Earle's upcoming conference on Atlantic relations. After his appointment
to the new Institute of Advanced Study in 1934, Earle, the onetime student of imperialism in the Near East, reinvented himself as a student of
military affairs, a budding grand strategist, and a self-revising historian.[2] The
Carnegie Corporation had finally agreed to fund his new seminar at the

institute on military strategy and a trip to study the new Caribbean bases the United States had obtained from Great Britain in return for the transfer of fifty destroyers to the Royal Navy.[3] The Social Science Research Council had courted him, beginning with an invitation to a November 1940 conference that was ostensibly devoted to "research of practical utility" on relations among the nations of the western hemisphere. But the real agenda was to counter the "totalitarian states' versions of the Monroe Doctrine" and demonstrate how far the U.S. experience in Latin America diverged from the "ruthless imperialist policies of the Axis powers."[4] The Rockefeller Foundation paid to move the Coordinating Committee on International Studies, which was linked to the League of Nations, to Princeton with Earle as research director. The council then voted to designate it the Social Science Research Council's new International Relations Committee. The International Relations Committee's main activity prior to its dissolution was to plan a conference at Prout's Neck, Maine, in August 1941 to discuss the political, economic, and strategic future of the Atlantic area.

Buell wanted to know if Earle had followed up his suggestion "sometime ago" to include "some of the Negro intellectuals," meaning the Howard school theorists, "on any studies connected with international relations." Buell already knew the answer because he met his old friend Rayford Logan for dinner—at Union Station, the only place in Washington where Logan could dine with a white colleague in public. Logan had asked for Buell's help in integrating him and his colleagues in postwar planning efforts. Buell told Earle that Logan, Bunche, and other international relations scholars at Howard deserved invitations: "Confidentially, they feel somewhat offended that they have been overlooked." It was also important to consider the wider political stakes, since in some northern states blacks held the "balance of power" and support for the allies needed some shoring up in this quarter. He quoted from the recent press release by the Alpha Phi Alpha fraternity, the oldest national black intercollegiate association: "however sympathetic whites may be, they cannot know the yearnings in our hearts."[5]

Earle wrote back immediately to reassure Buell: "You are of course quite right that it is outrageous to omit Negro scholars from discussions on the foreign policy of the U.S." Unfortunately, Earle and his colleagues had just held the planning meeting the day before. "Had your letter come a week ago we could have invited one of them." Nonetheless, he and William "Bill" Lockwood, the Institute of Pacific Relations official on leave for two years to help Earle run the Institute of Advanced Study/Social Science Research Council committee, would see that steps were taken thereafter "to include them or others of their race in our discussions." He closed on a slightly defensive note.

"I am sure you know that neither Lockwood nor I has [*sic*] any prejudice whatsoever against Negroes. Overlooking them is a sin of omission which I am afraid we all commit far too often."[6] Lockwood appears from the record to have behaved honorably. But much of what Earle wrote was a lie.

Chicago's Quincy Wright, a recent addition to the Social Science Research Council International Relations Committee, had proposed the conference on the future of the Atlantic area as a possible step toward founding an institute of Atlantic relations. Discussions between him and Edward Carter, secretary-general of the Institute of Pacific Relations, another member, had started even before the committee voted formally to approve it in February 1941. Carter headed the three-man organizing committee.[7] Drawing on the Institute of Pacific Relations model once more, Wright imagined representatives taking part from Scandinavia, the British Commonwealth, the Low Countries, the Iberian states, South America, the United States, France, South Africa, and the Caribbean. One of the topics he wanted covered was "the problem of colonies and backward areas, international controls, [and] mandates."[8]

It was Carter, the chair, who first posed to Earle the possibility of "inviting some South African negro or American negro, or British or American scholar who has recently been in South Africa and is in touch with negro thought as to South Africa's external relations." He was pointed. "It would seem to me that it is of the utmost importance that the point of view of the Africans themselves should be expressed, and that we should refuse simply to rely on a summary of their opinions as reported by their white masters."[9] Carter was basically adopting the convention of the Institute of Pacific Relations regarding conferences. Quincy Wright seconded the proposal. "I think your notion of getting a Negro from West Africa is also good; perhaps someone from Liberia might be invited as well as from one of the British or French colonies."[10] And the committee's secretary, Bill Lockwood, staked out a fallback position.

> I like your proposal of an African negro. If no good candidate turns up I would suggest an American negro scholar, Ralph Bunche of Howard University. Bunche is an able young fellow who has spent several years recently studying problems of native welfare in Africa, especially in South Africa. He has also spent some time in the Dutch East Indies. He is one of a group of scholars at Howard who are particularly interested in colonial problems. I think we might well invite Bunche whether we have an African or not, particularly since intelligent American negroes resent the prevailing assumption that they are not interested in

international relations even at a time when myths of racial superiority play such an important role.[11]

However opponents quashed the idea of inviting Bunche or any other black man from the United States, Africa, or the Caribbean before Buell contacted Earle. Lockwood later wrote discretely about objections that had been raised, complaining it was absurd "to leave out of account the group which almost more than any other has a stake in the present international problem with its racial implications."[12]

Historian and Chatham House insider John Wheeler-Bennett, whose contacts Earle was counting on for assuring a strong British and Commonwealth delegation, killed talk of "inviting negroes" and having them discuss colonial issues. First, he lobbied to narrow the focus of discussion to the "North Atlantic," an idea Carter seconded and one that clearly was attractive to the rest of the group, which quickly began to think in terms of an "Anglo-American sea power bloc" as principal guarantor of the postwar regional order and the nucleus of a new international organization.[13] Wheeler-Bennett questioned the rationale for and the cost of inviting "representatives of the coloured races." South Africans were highly unlikely to attend, in this case, and it "would certainly affect our own people." If it was as vital as others thought, might a Liberian suffice?[14] Earle's promise to Buell to include the Howard group "or others of their race" thereafter was forgotten.

I can't say what factors—distaste or fear of sitting in a room with a black man, an unwillingness to wrestle with the country's most articulate critics of colonialism and racism at a key juncture, an exaggerated sense of the importance of their own project—drove this particular decision. We know however that when Earle returned from his month-long tour of sites for new military bases in Jamaica, Trinidad, St. Thomas, St. Lucia, and Antigua, he underscored the threat to the color line there, in particular the need to send "American young women of fine character to supply an indispensable and altogether legitimate need" in those places where there were too few "white girls" (who were monopolized by the officers). "American soldiers are more than ordinarily dependent upon feminine society. Dancing is, for example, an almost indispensable form of recreation and cannot be provided in any of the West Indian Islands or in the Canal Zone under existing conditions"; that is, because the women in those places were black.[15] Rayford Logan, who gave frequent talks on decolonization and the prospects for black people in the postwar world, found that white audiences—from the American Friends Service Committee, with which he worked closely, to groups on college campuses—still obsessed with and distracted by the issue of miscegenation.[16]

Logan erroneously thought that Buell's backing would make all the difference. "At last it looks as if I am going to make contact with some of the white scholars who are working on the New World Society," he wrote in his diary.[17] His commitment to integrating postwar planning efforts followed naturally from his long held belief that the coming (and then reality of) war could serve the cause of black freedom worldwide. Padmore and others had made the same argument, as Bunche had noted in his journal in 1938, and now he and Abe Harris had joined the black auxiliary of an originally segregated pro-intervention lobby.[18] Logan had already successfully campaigned to press the War Department and other federal agencies to expand opportunities for blacks in the military and the defense industry (they had an "equal right with white men to be shot in the field of battle" is how William "Bill" Riis, a roving editor for *The Reader's Digest* and Logan's friend put it when he lobbied the White House on his behalf).[19]

However, international relations professors and their backers resisted the idea of integrating their inner circles. No African American scholar was invited to join any of the private postwar planning projects at Carnegie, the Council on Foreign Relations, and Princeton. African American intellectuals and organizations, including the National Association for the Advancement of Colored People, would have to pursue the vital questions of the prospect of freedom and the representation of dependent peoples in the future peace conference largely on their own.[20]

"The Atlantic Charter: It Means Dark Races Too"[21]

The one integrated initiative of the early war years, the Committee on Africa, the War, and Peace Aims, involved whites who had long been associated with the interracial cooperation movement, not least its leader, the philanthropist Anson Phelps Stokes.[22] Ralph Bunche was one of the principal authors of its report, *The Atlantic Charter and Africa from an American Standpoint* (1942), an early contribution to the debates launched over whether the Atlantic Charter issued jointly by President Franklin Roosevelt and Prime Minister Winston Churchill in August 1941 applied to the colonial territories and, if so, how to translate its vague terms into concrete policies.[23] Many Black Americans were suspicious, having learned first through George Padmore's reporting that Churchill had assured his own people that the charter's third point concerning the right "of all peoples to choose the form of government under which they will live" and to see "sovereign rights and self-government restored to those who have been forcibly deprived of them" in no way applied to "Colored Races." Presumably the fourth point, which promised "equal access to raw materials of the world," did.[24]

For the Howard school critics of the report, the problem began with the vision that animated it, namely South African prime minister Jan Smuts's updated thinking about "trusteeship"—a putative middle road between equality and naked exploitation that South Africa was charting for the future.[25] For Smuts, the old mandate system may have outlived its usefulness, and the "advanced" states, or "guardians," to use the terms that the committee recommended in place of old and outdated notions of superior and inferior races, would guide the "retarded" ones. To what end? Equality was off the table, apparently. When South Africa's African National Congress demanded full citizenship rights and the dismantling of color bars in accordance with the Atlantic Charter's provisions, Smuts refused to meet with Congress representatives based on such an obviously mistaken understanding of trusteeship.[26]

The Committee on Africa, the War, and Peace Aims outlined four stages, "at least in the colonies with the most advanced native populations," toward effective capacity for self-government or "a steadily increasing share in the determining of government policy" or "autonomy." They didn't offer a timeline but in a footnote referred to a broadly similar plan by W. Bryant Mumford, head of the Colonial Department at the University of London, that envisioned 20-, 40-, and 60-year milestones on the way to dominion status. As an independent state, South Africa was free "to work out its own problem of race adjustment," but the report repeatedly emphasized the signs of positive change there and in the other settler colonies. Apparently, identification with the wartime South African government, a key ally in the struggle against fascism, led to an interpretation similar to the interpretations of those who imagined the Soviet Union evolving "toward something resembling our own and Great Britain's democracy."[27]

Rayford Logan, for one, wasn't fooled. He described the real principles of Jan Smuts's trusteeship policy as "white supremacy, segregation and the continued effective disfranchisement of the native peoples," and he warned of the return of the worst aspects of the old League of Nations mandate system in updated garb.[28] He was also privately critical of Bunche's diffidence.[29] Two recently hired Howard professors, however, pressed the critique of *The Atlantic Charter and Africa* much further. The sarcasm drips from the page of Eric Williams's review in the *Journal of Negro Education*. The committee offered no new rational ground for believing the pieties of British administrators and South African generals about trusteeship. At a moment when "radical changes must be made in the condition of the colonial peoples, the report will seem to those most concerned, the African people, just another in a by now very lengthy list of mild palliatives for a deadly disease."[30] And Merze Tate had just accepted a one-year position in history at Howard, teaching in part for Logan, when she published "The War Aims of World War I and II and Their Relation to the Darker Peoples of the World." The article rehearsed part of the argument of the book that she hoped to write next, tentatively titled "The White Man's Blunders," which would examine the impact of imperialism on the white race.[31] In her reading of the committee's report, the "white man is a century behind the colored man in his thinking on civilization. Long years of imperialism have very nearly deprived him of vision. He still reasons in terms of colonies, colonial development, economic exploitation of "backward regions," and even the most liberal cannot divorce from their minds the idea of "trusteeship" and "international mandate."[32]

Logan, however, thought it absolutely vital to distinguish the idea of "trusteeship," which, however one disguised it, still reflected racist assumptions that undergirded modern imperialism from his preferred vision of a reformed, universally applicable, and internationalized mandate system that represented the best way to secure the rights of colonized people. That is, he rejected the idea that any African colony or protectorate could govern itself, and argued as much on a panel at Howard in early 1943 with the Gold Coast's Frances (later Kwame) Nkrumah, then a graduate student assisting in the army-funded African Institute at the University of Pennsylvania. Nkrumah had "made a fervent plea for the immediate independence of Africa."[33] Logan's rejection stemmed in part from reasons he had specified, however circumspectly, in *The Atlantic Charter and Africa.* He felt that the colonial regimes had not prepared the ground for their own dissolution. Africans thus would need a period of "apprenticeship" during which they would assume increasing responsibility for governance, and since the British, French, Portuguese, South Africans, and whoever might be coveting the former Italian possessions could not be trusted, a reformed and upgraded mandate administration was needed whose authority would supplant that of the colonial powers. As he envisioned his proposed structure, it would consist of trained officials, including Africans and other people of color, and would be headquartered not in Geneva or elsewhere in Europe but in an African city. It would have the authority to hear all petitions from aggrieved subjects.[34]

Logan thought that an internationalized mandate regime was also the best that could be hoped for in light of the power positions of the United States and the other twenty-six signatories to the Atlantic Charter—the "United Nations"—that mattered. Logan's is one of the few explicit assessments I know of this type at this time of the political obstacles to transforming the existing conditions of dependency. The Americans would not support decolonization if it meant opening up Africa to Soviet influence, he insisted, and Great Britain certainly did not intend to give up its colonies. (He was right.) The nascent nationalist movements did not have the ability to dislodge European administrators let alone settlers. (He got this one wrong, at least in part.) And any new state would need European capital investment.[35] Logan could speak with some authority about prospects, since he had worked behind the scenes in 1942–1943 with an American Friends Service Committee contact, Benjamin Gerig, a state department official and Ralph Bunche's future boss, on the international mandate idea.[36] He knew even then that the odds were against such a structure, a reading that later scholarship with access to confidential records shows to have been the case.[37] British officials invested in new mechanisms for maintaining "acquiescence to our rule," including the decision to emphasize "development" as a means of heading off possible American criticisms and, more crucially, meaningful political change.

The future of the colonized areas was entirely ignored at the Dumbarton Oaks discussions that began in August 1944, which prepared the ground for the drawing up of the UN Charter in San Francisco in 1945. Logan also watched the founders of the UN close down debate on the Atlantic Charter's promise of self-determination and seal the fate of colonized people. He became a biting and bitter critic of the betrayal of African aspirations.

However, Logan also became a much more iconoclastic thinker (and gadfly) in the late war and early postwar years as he rethought the basis for his identification with the rapidly evolving African nationalist and pan-Africanist movements. For instance, he had advised the leadership of the NAACP, which had agreed to back Du Bois's proposal to reconvene the Pan-African Congress in Paris in 1945, to instead widen its scope and make it a "Dependent Peoples['] Congress." Bunche, not surprisingly, given both his long-standing antipathy to racialism and his role in building the State Department's new Division of Dependent Area Affairs, argued the same. It didn't matter. George Padmore, Kwame Nkrumah, Joe Appiah (the father of Princeton philosopher Kwame Anthony Appiah), and their comrades had determined to hold a Fifth Pan-African Congress in Manchester, effectively sidelining the Americans, although Du Bois would be welcomed as a "father" of the movement.[38] In his talks Logan had also begun to warn against the danger in the transition to self-government of turning power over to an equally authoritarian faction ("a small group of nationals"), and he began to map the contours of what he called "inter-minority oppression," (what we now call "interethnic conflict" or "intrastate violence"), for example, Serbians exploitation of Croats or Indian prejudice against native Africans in Kenya. The list was long.[39] Thus, he began to find common ground with Bunche when he dismissed the idea of immediate independence for Africa as "nonsense."[40]

Padmore, Bunche's former student, didn't think it nonsense. He was at least as smart as Bunche and Logan, and he later helped engineer what he called the transfer of power in Ghana, so it is worth briefly considering his *The White Man's Duty: An Analysis of the Colonial Question in Light of the Atlantic Charter*, which he wrote with the disowned shipping heiress Nancy Cunard and which appeared soon after *The Atlantic Charter and Africa*. *The White Man's Duty* made three key points.[41] The first was that the empire should be replaced by a federation "evolving toward a socialist commonwealth" on the basis of "economic, political, and social equality in all colonies, protectorates and mandated territories." Cunard's introduction reminded readers that the Dutch government had apparently moved in precisely this direction the previous December, when it committed to constitutional reform in support of racial equality and future dominion status for the East and West Indies; Padmore referred to this as "a partnership of peoples, each autonomous in internal affairs." (The promise was forgotten after the war.) The second point was that institutional capacity was such that in many places, for example the West Indies, Ceylon, and Mauritius, full or what he called "responsible" self-government could be instituted at once, before the war's end, with elected parliaments, the end of the colonial governor's veto power, and so forth. Conditions in parts of West Africa too would allow the building of similar institutions in place of "indirect rule" by the chiefs, since "routine work of administration and the running of daily life are [*sic*] already done by native Africans."[42]

Padmore's third point posed the biggest challenge to all the trusteeship, guardianship, and apprenticeship models of stages toward self-government, of which the American Committee's *Atlantic Charter and Africa* was one example. Regardless of the status of the already existing administrative apparatus or level of educational attainment or communication infrastructure in place in Nigeria or the Gold Coast or in what he called the less-advanced protectorates, where demands for self-government had not yet been made, the best way to "learn the art of government is by practicing it." This is why, he argued, elections for representative councils ought to begin immediately rather than in some (often never-arriving) better tomorrow.[43]

Anson Phelps Stokes reconvened key members of the American Committee along with others, including Melville Herskovits, Edward Carter (secretary-general of the Institute for Pacific Relations in New York), Max Yergan (head of the Council on African Affairs), and Kwame Nkrumah—the latter two at Bunche's instigation—for a meeting at the Brookings Institution in March 1943.[44] Famously, another of the scholars Herskovits routinely denigrated, Carter Woodson, the founder of the *Journal of Negro History*, with whom he fought for control of black studies, turned the invitation down on the ground that he never joined "the oppressor to strengthen his control of the oppressed."[45] They had assembled to plan a follow-up conference on Africa modeled on the recently concluded Mont-Tremblant conference of the Institute of Pacific Relations, and thus discussions naturally segued into the prospects for developing a parallel African institute. A second meeting led to election of Herskovits as acting chair, Du Bois as vice-chair, and Bunche as secretary, but no conference ever took place and the Phelps-Stokes Foundation eventually closed out the account.[46] This was the last time the Institute of Pacific Relations model would be held up as the way to organize an international relations research program. It was long forgotten by the time Diaspora studies unknowingly resurrected the model as Atlantic, Caribbean, Indian Oceans (or Worlds) in the 1980s and 1990s. Funding for Africa area studies lagged in the 1940s-1950s behind Soviet, Asia, and Middle East studies. However, the "world area" study model took over the imaginations of the Cold War–era foundations and their dependencies in the U.S. academy.

Ralph Bunche's Odyssey

By 1940, the outspoken radical who for a short time exhorted the Communist Party to bring about the emancipation of the Negro People and wrote *A World View of Race* had become a more circumspect public intellectual than Logan, the maverick who continued to speak out about racism and colonialism and work with progressive civil society organizations. He had also begun a journey from professor to policymaker. In September 1941, he went on leave from Howard to join the fledgling Office of the Coordinator of Information (after 1942 the Office of Strategic Services) as the British Empire Section's Africa expert under Conyers Read, an English professor at the University of Pennsylvania. Soon after that, he warned Logan that the FBI had Logan, Locke, and other Howard faculty under investigation.[47]

Bunche was one of four Office of Strategic Services officials to attend the Institute of Pacific Relations' December 1942 Mont-Tremblant conference. It was his first international meeting, the high-water mark of the cooperation of the Institute of Pacific Relations with the U.S. state, and the first portent of the coming conflict at San Francisco in 1945 and after over white supremacy and decolonization. With Gandhi and Nehru imprisoned for their role in the "Quit India" demonstrations—where they would remain for the next two years—and the Indians who attended, who were also participating at the Institute of Pacific Relations for the first time, demanded the end of colonial rule. Bunche and other Americans pressed for reforms that would lead to meaningful self-government, and British officials attacked America's double standards in the form of Jim Crow in the South and Japanese internment camps in the West.[48] Bunche returned from Quebec wanting to work on planning instead of writing handbooks for the North Africa invasion. He had notified his superiors in March of his plan to leave Office of Strategic Services "within the next month or so." He had accepted a staff position with the new Ethnogeographic Board, an organization founded jointly by the Social Science Research Council, the American Council on Learned Societies, the National Research Council, and the Smithsonian Institution as an information clearinghouse on the non-European theater of the war.[49] Nonetheless, he then began to negotiate with Carter, the head of the Institute of Pacific Relations, about a position at the Institute. It is good that he did so, because the Ethnogeographic Board would soon be defunded.[50] The institute proposed that he move to New York and lead a multiyear study on the future of colonialism in the Far East. Staff there had begun searching for housing for Bunche and his family, and the head of the Julius Rosenwald fund, Edwin Embree, who had agreed to award a fellowship to Bunche to fund the project, pushed him to take it. "I do think that you have a contribution to make in a definitive report on colonization in the Far East and for the sake of your own career, I should like to see such a scholarly publication behind you."[51] The Institute of Pacific Relations was still expecting him in December 1943, when the announcement came that Bunche would join the State Department at the beginning of 1944.

What happened? Bunche's biographers disagree about details, and none has known about or chosen to report Bunche's plans to join the Institute of Pacific Relations.[52] Salary concerns probably played a role. Bunche had just bought a house in Washington, D.C., and his son was born in September 1943. Bunche also fretted: "Could I be accused of running out on the war effort in order to find a soft spot for myself?"[53] Years later, he gave part of the answer in the form of a homily, "What America Means to Me," for the *American Magazine* (February 1950), which was reprinted in the *Negro Digest* (September 1950) after he won the Nobel Prize. Opponents had blocked his appointment—the State Department was famously one of the last federal departments and agencies to appoint African Americans to high-level positions—until Secretary of State Cordell Hull came to the rescue. The Tennessee native insisted that "a man's color made no difference."[54] Although he remained on the Howard faculty until 1950, Bunche had given his last lectures in the 1940–1941 school year and his career as scholar and theorist was over.

The scholars and theorists of world hierarchy had their work cut out for them. While still in his early days at the Office of Strategic Services, in February 1942, Bunche told his Howard colleague Logan what Colonel Donovan's men were saying about the shape of things to come: "After the war there simply cannot be any of the namby-pamby 19th century liberalism. The United States, in brief, is going to police the world." A few days later Buell basically told Logan the same thing. "Raymond told me that he had just written a one-hundred page memorandum discussing whether the United States would do the job alone or in cooperation with Great Britain. He pointed to the control . . . already established over Ethiopia. All backward countries, whether Poland or Latin American nations, must expect this kind of control, provided the United Nations wins the war."[55] Buell's successor in colonial administration at Harvard, Rupert Emerson, who had been seconded to Washington to manage the transformation of the Bureau of Insular Affairs into the Division of Territories and Island Possessions (or what the Harvard *Crimson* called America's "colonies"), was pessimistic about the chances for blacks anywhere after the war.[56]

Nor would what Henry Luce, Buell's visionary boss, imagined have surprised Logan. "Africa is to be treated as a great corporate treasure-house and play-ground, trusteed for the benefit of all mankind (Egypt, South Africa and *possibly* one or two other parts will be excluded from the Trusteeship). The inhabitants of Africa will be the first charges on the common wealth of Africa. Their health and happiness will be of first concern, but there will be no hurry in working out ideas for self-government."[57] Luce got it only a little wrong.

The Invention of a Tradition

The Rockefeller Foundation's two years of support for the Coordinating Committee on International Studies (the Social Science Research Council's de facto International Relations Committee) ended in December 1941. The committee's secretary, William Lockwood, chose to return to the Institute of Pacific Relations and from there join the Office of Strategic Services in China. The chair, Ed Earle, had too many other obligations to continue; they included serving on the "policy making group" for James Phinny Baxter, the Williams College president who had been appointed coordinator of information for a new civilian agency that would become the Office of Strategic Services. Earle's committee disbanded and the Social Science Research

Council directors halted support for international relations for the duration of the war, probably for good reason.[58]

A new factor had thus been added to the list of obstacles that had long frustrated efforts to advance scientific study in a field that, as Lewis Lorwin, a Social Science Research Council consultant, put it, "requires specialized training not only in most of the social sciences, but also in psychology and biology."[59] The war had triggered a huge movement of scholars from the university sector into government and the military, including the fifty or so who had joined the Office of the Coordinator of Information research staff. Yale professor Whitney Griswold was the Social Science Research Council committee member most worried about the consequences for teaching and scholarship, to judge from the records of the international relations committee final meetings. What was needed, he said, was not another information-clearinghouse committee or policy-relevant research incubator—there were more of those than ever—but a group that would protect the mission of the university against the competing demands of the defense sector and the "general business and research industries." When Earle pressed him on making "academic work" in international relations the main priority, Griswold said that there was "a great need for basic research that is germane to the field of international relations. It will be too bad if we, in our interest in the war, allow that to come to a halt."[60]

Clearly Earle disagreed. He and others instead sought to refashion international relations with their embrace of "European style geopolitics" with the objective of "clarifying the task of statesmen, diplomatists and military planners charged with assuring the survival and future position in the world of the particular state they are serving." It was a dramatic realignment, as William T. R. Fox, one of the new true believers, described it toward the end of his career in the 1980s.[61]

"Bill" Fox was another overworked Temple University instructor who had published on municipal and state government when he accepted a one-year position as instructor and conference director for Princeton's School of International Affairs in 1941. He judged it to be a "better springboard" to a permanent job. Yale hired him two years later.[62] Those years also marked his conversion from student of international law to "power politics." One more "disenchanted realist" is how a laudatory review of his 1944 *The Super-Powers*, the book that coined the term, put it.[63] Fox served as assistant director of Yale's Institute of International Studies under Frederick Sherwood Dunn. The institute is where many of the founding myths of realism first took shape, starting with its own origin story once its principals realized that theorizing a "Universal Policy" for the United States had been its project all along. Peaceful change was out, and "the rise and fall of hegemonies," one of its first research projects in its new funding cycle, was in. Its new journal, *World Politics*, for which Fox served as managing editor, served him and other self-revisers well.

In its second year, 1949, *World Politics* published Fox's "Interwar International Relations Research: The American Experience," the first of his periodic, unabashedly Whiggish accounts of the not-quite-a-discipline. The article includes a brief and dismissive account of the early work of the Social Science Research Council in the field—actually the only account of it until now, although it excludes any mention of the Institute of Pacific Relations. Cramming to fit it into his snapshot of the previous decades' (and generation's) obsessions with the "Geneva institutions" and putative indifference to the nitty-gritty of politics across borders, he skewered the international relations committee for asking mostly wrong questions and doing so with little concern for what we might now call methodological rigor. Luckily, Fox and his friends who were also his patrons at Yale—Dunn and Arnold Wolfers—together with Earle at the Institute for Advanced Studies (whom he misidentified as a political scientist) had rediscovered the central issue of "national security" at just the right time, thus increasing "the relevance of international relations research to the making of public policy."[64]

The critique was probably overdetermined given that the same men were busy reconstituting the Social Science Research Council committee on international relations for a third time, under Dunn's chairmanship, with the hope that the Yale Institute's realist approach to policy relevant strategic studies would gain some traction. There were a few obstacles ahead of them, however. The Social Science Research Council had closed down the first postwar international relations committee after only two years. Dunn had failed miserably at balancing commitments and steering a research program. Fox did better as chair of a new committee on civil-military relations in 1952, renamed the committee on national security policy research four years later.[65] And Whitney Griswold, the opponent of the turn to security studies on the wartime Social Science Research Council's International Relations committee, ended the dream that a Yale group would lead the postwar realist revolution when he took over as university president in 1951. Griswold demanded more scholarship through engagement with the established social sciences (since, he said, neither political science nor international relations were real disciplines) and less "mimeographed reports" and "short books" of the kind usually associated with think tanks and government agencies.[66] Dunn and six others at Yale instead left for Princeton, taking the journal *World Politics* with them and forming the core of the new Center for

International Studies, which the Rockefeller Foundation funded.[67] Bill Fox moved to Columbia to direct the new Institute for War and Peace Studies there. At MIT, Max Milliken, another onetime key associate of the Institute of International Studies at Yale, kick-started the Center for International Studies, another policy-oriented group, the same year, with the CIA's financial support.[68]

As we will see, the institutionalization of the area studies model in the 1940s–1960s, with its professional associations and cognate disciplinary specializations, for example in development studies, modernization theory, and the comparative politics of developing areas, surely aided in the forgetting that was necessary for an invented history of international relations to take hold.[69] The new centers also caused some problems for the empire-building political scientists who were busy seizing exclusive ownership of the international relations brand for their discipline. After the war ended in 1945, U.S. universities resisted more than embraced "national security research." They did not seriously begin offering courses in it until the 1960s. And area studies mattered more to the foundations than security in the first postwar decades.[70]

Still, there are some problems. Decolonization was arguably the single most significant transformation of the twentieth century, yet it is impossible to name a single scholar among those in the contemporary canon who is known primarily for his or her work on the issue. While arguments about imperialism proliferated across the globe after 1945, they completely disappeared from scholarship in a discipline that ten years earlier considered it to be the fundamental problem of world order.[71] Similarly, more United Nations resolutions dealt with racism than with any other issue, according to Paul Gordon Lauren.[72] The threat to "Western white prestige" continued to haunt the men in power in Washington and London (and Australia, New Zealand, and South Africa), yet it is impossible to find the issue discussed in the postwar international relations scholarship. As Toni Morrison argued much later about a different part of the academy, "certain absences are so stressed, so ornate, so planned, they call attention to themselves."[73]

PART IV

"The Dark World Goes Free"

When Kwame Nkrumah traveled to the United States in July 1958 as leader of the new independent state of Ghana, 10,000 African Americans lined the long motorcade's route to New York's 369th Coast Artillery Armory on 143rd street and 5th Avenue. The *New York Times* headline the next day read "Harlem Hails Ghanaian Leader as Returning Hero."[1] Inside a packed hall, 7,000 more jostled for places and struggled to hear the welcome of Ralph Bunche, the 1950 Nobel laureate and undersecretary of the United Nations.

> We salute you, Kwame Nkrumah, not only because you are the Prime Minister of Ghana of Africa, although that is cause enough. We salute you because you are a true and living representation of our best hopes and ideals: of the determination we have to be accepted fully as equal beings, of the pride we have held and nurtured in our African origin, of the achievement of which we know we are capable given only opportunity, of the freedom in which we believe, of the dignity imperative to our stature as men. . . . But above all, Mr. Prime Minister, we embrace you because *you and your people* and *we* are *brothers*—brothers *of* the skin and *beneath* the skin.[2]

Luckily, Harold Isaacs, a research associate from MIT's Center for International Studies was at the armory meeting and taking notes, since none of

Bunche's biographers and interpreters has discussed this public moment of racialism and pan-Africanist pride on the part of someone who had routinely rejected such identifications. In fact, black Muslims in the audience booed him as he took the stage.[3] Isaacs concluded that Bunche was most likely responding to the mood of the crowd, because in a follow-up private interview he responded as we might have expected, by deprecating the idea of any "kinship" with African peoples.[4]

Isaacs, who is all but forgotten now in the many recent studies of the Center for International Studies and the putative origins of "development" and "modernization" theory, was then deep into the research project he had launched at MIT, "World Affairs Impact on U.S. Race Relations," on what he would call "The Break Down of the World-Wide White Supremacy System" after 1945.[5] The study would take him from Little Rock in 1956 to Accra in 1961.[6]

Alain Locke, reliably, had gotten there first. In November 1942, the *Survey Graphic*, which had published his special number on Harlem seventeen years earlier, published "The Unfinished Business of Democracy." In the planning meeting, Locke pressed a roomful of people who were thinking in vague terms about how to overcome the ignorance of whites to zero in on the problem Jim Crow posed for any future American effort at world leadership. His introductory essay returned to the idea of global interconnection ("forces which have all but annihilated longitude and latitude") that had been in eclipse during the world depression. For the United States, the "good neighbor policy," the "practical altruisms of lend-lease aid," and the principles of the 1941 Atlantic Charter suggested that the prospects were good for "leadership in an emancipated new world."

> But against all this, there stands one tragic but not irremedial liability. In the neglected and unresolved problem of the Negro in America, the Achilles of the west has a dangerously vulnerable heel. At any time, in any critical position requiring moral authority before the world, this threatens to impair our influence before the world. . . . It has already done so. . . . The paradox of race has become our democracy's great dilemma.[7]

Locke ended by outlining the consequences for U.S. foreign policy for a state and society in which the balance of forces continued to sustain the "inconsistent half-way democracy which, before this war, conferred freedom for some and subordination for others." Postwar difficulties in the Caribbean, the less-than-whole-hearted cooperation of the Pan-American Union (after 1948 the Organization of American States) with the United States, and continued support for colonial imperialism in Asia and Africa would lay "the groundwork for a global color war."

Locke anticipated Swedish economist Gunnar Myrdal's argument about racism's challenge to the "American creed" in *The American Dilemma*, which appeared in 1944. Myrdal's last chapter, "America Again at the Crossroads in the Negro Problem," sounds a lot like Locke too. He emphasizes the costs that continuing white supremacy would exact on American efforts to lead a postwar world in which the "colored races" were bound to increase in numbers and power. In Myrdal's version, however, the anxiety, similar to the anxieties of the 1890s and 1920s, was palpable, and it is striking that most commentaries then and now fail to note it.[8] Unless ways were found to live "on peaceful terms with colored people," then fueled by their own "race prejudice," they would be "satisfied only by the whites' humiliation and subjugation."[9]

We can trace writings in both sober and apocalyptic registers through the 1950s and 1960s. St. Clair Drake, a sociologist at Roosevelt University, said that the structural position and global ambition of the United States at the time of the Korean War explained the repudiation of racism, similar to what was happening with colonial powers who were conscious of their less-than-secure hold on their dependencies. South Africa, on the other hand, which had no global position to defend, appeared to pursue its apartheid policy with impunity.[10] Drake also recognized the possibility for reversals if the world crisis sharpened. "Whether or not espousal of 'civil rights for Negroes' becomes separated, in the popular mind, from 'Communist agitation' may be a decisive factor."[11] Conflating the two was in fact a basic part of the South's defense of the status quo for the rest of the decade.[12]

Fifteen years later, and in the wake of the brutality unleashed on demonstrators in Selma and Birmingham, C. Eric Lincoln returned to the international system's effects on the fortunes of the civil rights movement in "The Race Problem and International Relations."[13] He traced the impact of World War II and the Cold War on the transformation of what had been a common international system of exploitation of nonwhite peoples ("we were all members of the same club") into a major foreign policy problem for the Truman and Eisenhower administrations. Lincoln suggested that a civil rights movement by itself couldn't explain recent policy changes because African Americans had never stopped struggling for liberation since *Plessy v Ferguson*. Lincoln also underscored the limitations of reforms that were pursued on strategic rather than ethical ("justice") grounds, as was the case with the Truman administration's civil rights commission report, *To Secure These Rights*, that nonetheless were intended to win over the hearts and minds of "the peoples of the world." Such efforts fueled the cynicism about U.S. foreign policy pronouncements in an era of support for the white minority regimes in southern Africa and war in Southeast Asia.[14]

More of the popular, scholarly, and policy writing and pronouncing of the time, however, illustrates the problem of "threat inflation," specifically of the race war that putatively threatened one or more parts of the Anglo-sphere (when it still included South Africa) and thus of "civilization."[15] The argument almost always took the same form. Darker people, who typically although not necessarily were mobilized across colonial and later national boundaries—or in the U.S. case across state lines—would band together in a campaign of cataclysmic violence against whites. Most saw the abnormal psychology of subjugated peoples and the racialism and "rabid" national-ism that feelings of inferiority, alienation, and hatred for whites produced in them as the driving forces behind (or primary causes of) the future war. In addition, communist organizing and propaganda played a part in turning these latent forces into lethal ones.

These ideas appear in the memoranda of countless colonial and state department bureaucrats posted in the Caribbean, the Gold Coast, Burma, and elsewhere.[16] Issues of *Foreign Affairs* in the 1950s and 1960s include matter-of-fact descriptions of the hatred for whites that drives decoloni-zation and the psychological impairments that communists so masterfully exploit. For example, Francis Sayre, a retiring U.S. representative on the UN Trusteeship Council, made the case for providing aid for development in Af-rica even where "feelings of racial inferiority . . . offer serious hindrances to Western attempts to build bulwarks for freedom" lest whites "reap the whirl-wind."[17] In the *New York Times*, foreign affairs columnist C. L. Sulzberger wrote repeatedly about race wars that were allegedly already under way, for example in Algeria, and were on the horizon throughout the 1960s.[18] One problem is that the officials and intellectuals who came to the defense of U.S. policy found themselves rebutting charges that the wartime and Cold War administrations were themselves conducting race wars against Japan in the 1940s and in Korea in the 1950s. Thus, Douglas MacArthur insisted in an interview in the country's influential African-American daily, the *Pittsburgh Courier*, that great efforts by U.S. enemies were under way to provoke "ra-cial war."[19] FDR's former advisor and president of the Twentieth Century Fund Adolph Berle Jr. insisted the same about the Soviet strategy after the 1954 covert U.S. overthrow of the government of Jacabo Arbenz in Gua-temala. Soviet propaganda "sets up the United States as the enemy of the Indian in this hemisphere. This is a plain bid to let loose a race war far wider than Central America . . . to create another Malaya or Indochina in great parts of this hemisphere."[20] A few years later, he wrote in his diary that "we shall have pretty soon, not one Cold War but two or three: Communist against non-Communist; Negro against White; possibly Asian against them all. The mills of the gods of hatred may grind slowly but they grind terribly."[21] If more proof is needed that the concept of race war formed part of the international common sense of the Anglosphere, consider economist and pioneering game theorist Thomas Schelling's seminal 1958 article "The Strategy of Conflict: Prospectus for a Reorientation of Game Theory." His interest was in "the non-zero sum games involved in wars and threats of war, strikes, negotiations, criminal deterrence, class war, *race war*, price war, and blackmail" for which traditional game theory had not yielded much insight or advice.[22]

Unsurprisingly, the versions of race war theory African Americans favored saw the root causes of the impending crisis differently. The long era of imperial exploitation of so-called darker peoples, underpinned by ideologies of master and subject races, had produced the seeds of its own destruction. However, whites placed too much weight on the psychological by-products (resentment, inferiority) among those they had subjugated and not enough on their own largely intact arrogance and sense of superiority. The chief danger was not reverse racialism but the quite natural, albeit tragic, resistance whites exhibited to the notion of relinquishing power.

When African American economist Robert S. Browne published *Race Relations in International Affairs* in 1961, the press added an introduction by Roger Baldwin, a founder of the American Civil Liberties Union and the head of the oldest human rights organization in the United States, the International League for the Rights of Man. Baldwin conceded the point about white supremacy being the crux of the problem but added that "darker peoples, too, are guilty of racial superiority, discrimination and domination among themselves" and suggested that the "world struggle" was not "quite so wholly the white vs black problem."[23]

No one tried harder to anticipate and rebut arguments about the role of imperialism and white supremacy in the new rising tide of color than Sunday *Times* editor H. V. Hodson in his important 1950 address "Race Relations in the Commonwealth" at Chatham House. The onetime editor of the journal of British imperial relations, the *Round Table*, began with the thesis that race conflict threatened the survival of civilization even more than the struggle with communism, and he ended with an appeal for the creation of a new institute of race relations.[24] In between he sought less successfully to salvage, despite the evidence from biologists, his belief in the inherent inequality between the races ("I daresay you cannot tell a greengage chemically from a plum, but they are different, and some may consider the one superior to the other, at least in some respects") and, in disagreement with advocates of "one man, one vote," prospects for a "liberal and enlightened form of apartheid." Although it was true that imperialism's "alinement" with race—which was "to some extent accidental and by no means necessary"—might have amplified the race problem, the days of imperialism were numbered. Something else called "color consciousness," which Hodson distinguished from "race," not least because without it he had no way to explain conflict between the "brown people" of South Asia who were part of the same race as their antagonists the "white people," was another force multiplier, and it mattered more because it was "inescapable," as old as history.[25]

The prospecting for race war intensified in the aftermath of the April 1955 meeting of leaders of twenty-nine North African, Middle Eastern, and Asian states at Bandung, Indonesia, where nationalist forces had fought some of their most bitter battles against the Dutch in the late 1940s. For those primed to see it, the Asian-African Conference, or, as it is more commonly remembered, the Bandung Conference, brought the world's colored peoples together and thus hastened the coming Pan-Asian or Afro-Asian or Black or Brown-Yellow or Third World–wide war against the white man. Thus, according to one memo to Nelson Rockefeller, the U.S. president's special advisor for psychological warfare and Dwight D. Eisenhower's representative in the small group that coordinated clandestine operations, a basic goal was to counter "colored vs. white" movement, which was allegedly led by Red China, and "prevent Africans and Asians from ganging up against the United States."

> The President may wish to name a Negro Ambassador to a large and important country such as France. It seems to me he should avoid sending a Negro to Japan or any other inferiority complex country for subtle but valid reasons of "face." Ralph Bunche would be excellent but perhaps hard to get.[26]

The problem with all the pre- and post-Bandung accounts of the threat (or, for some, hope) of the unity of the colored peoples, the bandwagoning of the yellow, brown, and black races, and so forth, is that it presumed the validity, that is, the universality, of this particular world view. The delegates at Bandung never argued that what united otherwise disparate religions, regions, and commitments was something called race or color. Color was a fact for some and not for others, but for no one was it what united them. On the contrary, many rejected the idea that color mattered. They called it racialism and warned against appealing to it as a dangerous and retrograde step. India's Jawaharlal Nehru, for one, detested such talk.[27]

The Howard school's Merze Tate wrote one of the only two critiques I know of the exaggeration of color consciousness in the decolonization era in the form of a review of the novelist Richard Wright's book on Bandung, *The Color Curtain*.[28] All the race war analyses of the 1950s and 1960s rested on the same exaggerated belief in the significance of racial identification. When Arnold J. Toynbee, one of the most famous historians of the era and the head of studies at Chatham House for two decades, wrote a long and sober assessment of the likelihood of conflict between the white race and a "coalition of all the other races" for the *New York Times Magazine*, a reader wrote in to challenge a key assumption. Toynbee "calls Pakistan and India 'non-white' states, and says their peoples are of the same 'non-white' race. This is absurd. If he differentiates strictly on skin color, then he must also consider the swarthy people of Mediterranean lands as non-white. If it isn't skin color, then what is his criterion?"[29]

As we will see, Isaacs's Center for International Studies study, published as *New World of Negro Americans* (1963), stands out as the most sophisticated—and certainly the most detailed—analysis of the impact of the end of empire and white supremacy. Isaacs is the only instance I know of someone challenging the misleading assumptions (and deep-seated fears) that underpinned the varieties of race war theory on offer, as is evident in his article "Color in World Affairs" in *Foreign Affairs* (1969). The problem is that neither he nor other scholars ever took seriously the degree of threat inflation involved when the case for African American freedom was harnessed to America's hegemonic ambitions, as if the alignment strategies of leaders and the "hearts and minds" of the masses of dozens of new Third World states and states-in-the-making would actually turn on the fate of Jim Crow in the U.S. South. I'm afraid that Orval Faubus, the Arkansas governor who got so much else wrong in the 1950s, was right about the emerging international order.

"Why just this week," Faubus told Isaacs in 1956,

> I had a visitor from India who told me that a million and a half people were killed in India in racial troubles. If we want India as an ally, we're not going to question the Indians about their minority problems. The Communists don't question the Indians about theirs, but they do question ours. I think it's all exaggerated.[30]

That exaggeration or threat that racism at home would somehow act to undermine the hegemonic ambitions of the United States (or, if you prefer, "containment") of course also rested on a false belief about the powerful pull that racial identification or color had on the foreign policy practices of Indians, Pakistanis, Chinese, Saudis, and others. Thus, President Eisenhower opposed the use of military force to "break" the renegade Egyptian ex-client Gamal Abdel Nasser after he nationalized the Suez Canal Company in 1956, fearing that intervention would recoil against the United States, because Nasser "personified the emotional demands of the people in the area . . . for slapping the white man down."[31]

Finally, it is important to emphasize what one of Isaacs's friends and colleagues from the earliest days of the Center for International Studies, Donald Blackmer, told me. No one else at MIT and nearby Harvard thought of Isaacs as a proper international relations scholar. No article or book by any of those more readily identified this way at the time ever discussed let alone spoke so powerfully about racism's role in the post–World War II state system. It was as if department, center, and institute heads had all received the same strategy memos as the Anglo-American diplomats who were charged with depoliticizing the issue.[32] However, the academics operated within the same racial frame. For example, Harvard's Stanley Hoffmann listed race as a primary unifying factor of the North Atlantic zone of peace ("its inhabitants are predominantly white").[33] As we will see, the main exceptions to the informal "see no evil" (save totalitarianism) norm, predictably, were the two new conservative institutes of the era, the Foreign Policy Research Institute founded at the University of Pennsylvania in 1955 and the old Hoover Library and Archives at Stanford, which was given a new profile and a new identity as the Hoover Institution on War, Revolution, and Peace in 1957. Their scholars made the late case for colonialism and, more notoriously, for the biological basis of a world order of racial superiority and inferiority.

CHAPTER 7

The First but Not Last Crisis of a Cold War Profession

Chicago's Quincy Wright was elected the forty-fourth president of the American Political Science Association in 1948 and the inaugural president of the UNESCO-sponsored International Political Science Association in 1949, not least in recognition of his efforts to "bring political science" (back) to U.S.-occupied Germany.[1] The 58-year-old Wright was the most influential of those who began their teaching careers after World War I, although some of his students and his new colleague Hans Morgenthau had fomented the postwar realist "revolution" against Wright's generation of internationalists. With the passage of time, the dulling of memory, and the irresistible tendency to view the Cold War and the expansion of U.S. commitments as a proxy for growth of the profession, Wright's election might appear as if the field of international relations was flourishing.

Princeton's Harold Sprout, an early convert to the cause of geopolitics, didn't think so. Wright was the first international relations specialist in a quarter-century to head the APSA. Sprout identified with a younger cohort of political scientists in "incipient revolt" against the leadership of aging insiders, predominantly American politics specialists, who were seemingly intent on blocking rather than promoting "scholarly talent 'on the make.'"[2] During the war, Bernard Brodie, another rising star of international relations, also complained about being shunted aside in favor of those with no real knowledge; in this case, of military affairs.[3] It was then that the new and outgoing directors of the Yale's Institute of International Studies, Arnold Wolfers and Nicholas Spykman, first began discussing plans to found a separate society exclusively for specialists.[4]

However, the International Studies Association was not created until 1958, and for many years it maintained a precarious existence as a regional grouping of mainly West Coast professors and "practitioners," for example, from the United States Air Force Academy in Colorado Springs. The collective action problem depended on systems theorist Charles McClelland at San Francisco State, who kept the International Studies Association going single-handedly, for its resolution. A small grant from the New World Foundation, which was started from the same fortune that had been used to rescue *The New Republic* a few years earlier, allowed McClelland to take over *Background*, a digest of research findings across the social sciences for teachers of international relations, and make it over as the association's journal.[5] Whatever initial enthusiasm may have existed, the membership had dropped from 200 to 60 by1963, and it took support from the Carnegie Corporation to turn the trend around.[6]

The location of international relations on the "periphery" aside, the problem is that sharp disagreements existed from the start about the reality of, as McClelland put it, an "interdisciplinary emerging discipline" (either ignoring or unaware of the many times in the past half-century the same claim about "emerging" had been made) that could be clearly distinguished from political science. There was also dissension about what constituted the appropriate object of study. McClelland reported to Wright that for dissenters, the view of international relations as "relations among separate entities is now reactionary and obsolete. The preference was expressed for the idea of 'world affairs' in order to recognize the 'unity' of developments and events."[7] Perhaps Wright appreciated the irony that he had joined the same debate about the identity of international relations in the 1920s and, as we have seen, the dissidents' perspective is the one Buell led with in his 1925 textbook, where he described the "complex interdependence of the world."

The irony is deeper still, since Wright, the association's president, doubted that even political science met a strict definition of a discipline that was distinguishable "from other disciplines in the social science field either by its methods or by its objectives." Rather, he offered up what we now call a "constructivist" (and. not least, tautological) understanding in roughly the same way that Du Bois had come to define a Negro as "someone who was made to ride the Jim Crow car," except that political scientists weren't branded or cursed (much) as such by others. "It perhaps has a unity because of a somewhat distinctive bibliography, a history of association and organization, and a group who call themselves political scientists."[8]

Understandably, he finessed the issue a little in his December 1949 presidential address to the APSA: he substituted "science" for "discipline" in the formula.

> Initially we stumble on the insistence by many that a science of politics is impossible. That position can hardly be taken by this Association. We have thousands of members, a half century of activity, a vigorous journal, numerous committees, and an established tradition. These give evidence of a widespread belief that politics can be treated scientifically, that there is a science of politics.[9]

Wright's reference to "thousands of members" should be qualified in two respects. The first is that less than half of those members were university faculty and the second is that the total did not reflect the large number on the books who had failed to pay their membership dues. Why this matters is that by the time Ralph Bunche agreed to serve as president five years later, the APSA faced a serious fiscal crisis due to the decision to staff a new headquarters in Washington, D.C. He spent much of that year seeking additional members from government and the new national security industry, building links to the Eisenhower administration, and searching for an executive director to take the APSA into the new Cold War world.

Keep in mind that Bunche is probably the only APSA president chosen on grounds other than scholarship and likely the only president never to have published in the association's journal, the *American Political Science Review*, or have his work reviewed or cited in it during his lifetime. While the reasons should be clear by now, they went unmentioned in his presidential address at the fiftieth annual meeting. The Supreme Court had decided *Brown v. Board* just a few months earlier, yet Bunche chose to ignore the issue of civil rights entirely. No doubt he had been beaten down by a second, more intense loyalty investigation. He addressed this obliquely toward the end of his talk when discussing three issues that his "personal experiences" suggest should be of concern to the profession. "Thirdly, the striking evidence of fear, suspicion, intolerance, and confusion in the society, providing fertile soil for demagoguery, imperil our traditional freedom, and pose a stern challenge to the political scientist. These are phenomena which surely demand our most urgent concern, on behalf of the nation at large as well as our own professional and personal interest."[10] Eban Miller is right: "The anti-Communist fervor of the postwar years muted—if not entirely silenced—a singular legacy."[11]

Consider in this light Bunche's advice to political scientists to tackle "the problem of colonialism, and more particularly of colonial Africa." He argued, correctly, that the postwar "colleges and universities . . . have been regrettably slow in grasping fully the world significance of this problem. American political science, I fear, has not yet come to grips with it." Then his argument took a remarkably revisionist turn. Political science allegedly had never shown much interest in colonial problems.[12] Bunche's revisionism extended to his own teachers and training and to his longest published work, *A World View of Race*. After the world learned that Bunche would be receiving the Nobel Prize, the national YWCA wrote to him seeking copies, but Bunche sought to dissuade them. "It was a hastily written manuscript and I am not at all proud of it; nor do I recommend it."[13] By coincidence, his longtime colleague Alan Locke had thought to locate and inscribe one of the old Bronze Booklets to commemorate the award. "Dear Ralph: It's a long . . . unforeseen path from this in 1936 to the Nobel Prize award in 1950 but the capacity, the will and the vision was there in 1936, as some of us felt and now know."[14] He never mailed it.

Bunche returned exceptionally good value to the profession during his presidential year when he hired University of Minnesota political scientist and fellow former Office of Strategic Services officer Evron Kirkpatrick as executive director. Kirkpatrick had returned to the intelligence world after the Research and Analysis Branch of the Office of Strategic Services was absorbed by the State Department. He rose to head the CIA's Office of External Research, which was charged with mobilizing academic talent for contract research. He did yeoman's work in turning around the fortunes of the American Political Science Association. Yet as executive director, his continuing relationship with the CIA via the private consulting firm he started and the contracts it obtained from some of the agency's favorite foundations was exposed by young radicals in the late 1960s. These were years of ferment across the U.S. academy and its professional associations. Insurgents in the APSA challenged leadership on multiple fronts, from the ethics of supporting the national security state to the all-but-invisible role of women and blacks in the profession. No group, though, had invested more in its identification with American interventionism than those same young international relations professors on the make, and the only leader to defect was, ironically enough, the 66-year-old crusader for realism, Hans Morgenthau, whom the radical caucus supported in a close contest for the presidency of the APSA in 1970. UN ambassador Jeane Kirkpatrick remembered the defeat of the insurgency as "my husband's finest hour."[15]

The 1950s Ascent of Area Studies

For the postwar professors who had dreams of steering the American Century with their emphasis on national security and theorizing in the new realist style, the increased support of public agencies and private foundations would be crucial, but in the 1950s and 1960s the bulk of private funding went instead to support area and development studies centers. The losers, who increasingly identified themselves against the winners, the newly rechristened "area specialists," as the true "discipline oriented" researchers or "discipline generalists" under the banner of international relations were explicit about it. Columbia's Bill Fox cautioned against assuming that high levels of Cold War funding had meant real "intellectual progress" because "international relations consume only a modest fraction of the resources" compared to area studies.[16] Similarly, in a study conducted under the auspices of the Department of Education, James Rosenau at the University of Southern California calculated the extent of the "disparity": "for every dollar invested in the work of discipline generalists, some five to ten are allocated to other activities in the field of international studies."[17] In the aftermath of serious funding cuts around 1970, the losers pressed the case for the higher valued added from general theorizing and the strengthening of disciplinary identities.

Here again we need to stop and note the irony. A half-century earlier, concern with race development in the tropical zones of the world economy had propelled the identification of the new field of international relations. The postwar realists might have hijacked the brand (or drawn a narrower line around it or obsessed mainly about the "great powers" while leaving the dependencies to others) and "race" would be dropped from all further references to development, but there was nothing less international about the study of "the political cultures of developing areas" and not much that was new either.

> All that was necessary to make the adjustment to the new situation . . . was the substitution of a word. For "race" read "culture" or "civilization," for "racial heredity" read "cultural heritage," and the change had taken place. From implicitly Lamarckian "racial instincts" to an ambiguous "centuries of racial experience" to a purely cultural "centuries of tradition" was a fairly easy transition—especially when the notion of "racial instincts" had in fact been largely based on centuries of experience and tradition.[18]

For proof, consider U.S. president Eisenhower's lament to Charles de Gaulle in 1959 as the two leaders discussed decolonization one night at the latter's summer home, Chateau de Rambouillet. "Many of these people were attempting to make the leap from savagery to the degree of civilization of a country like France in perhaps ten years, without realizing that it took thousands of years to develop the civilization which we know."[19]

In 1947, the Social Science Research Council laid down two putatively scientific ordering principles for building postwar area studies: the "relative power" of a region and its "level of culture." As geographer Robert Hall, chair of the council's Committee on World Regions and founder of Michigan's Center for Japan Studies, put it, "we have more to gain from the study of China or India than we have from, say, the Congo Basin or New Guinea."[20] Not surprisingly, the Social Science Research Council's Carnegie-funded conference on the study of world areas in November brought together over 100 scholars ("the key men," Ruth Benedict and Pearl Buck notwithstanding) on Latin America, the Soviet Union, Southeast Asia, the Near East, Europe, and Far East.[21] Africa was left off the map. The explanation differed just a bit from the one Ed Earle and William Lockwood (who was there, in fact) had used during the war. It was "not through oversight but simply because the study of these areas is so inadequately developed in the United States that it would have been difficult to recruit specialists on them from various disciplines." This was especially true if one left Howard's or other African American specialists off the list of invitees.

Melville Herskovits, the would-be king of African studies, nonetheless protested the omission, arguing that the Social Science Research Council ought to commit to expanding the pool of experts instead of accepting the status quo. Then, having heard that the Carnegie Corporation had begun discussions with the University of Pennsylvania, which had hosted the Army Specialist Training Program, to strengthen its resources in African Studies, Herskovits began a two-year lobbying campaign for his own program at Northwestern as the better bet.[22] The initial modest funding he eventually received in 1948 and the larger grant in 1951 when the African Studies Center was officially founded with Herskovits as director, improved Northwestern's funding position in the 1950s. The Ford Foundation, in its first international initiative, began investing serious money in area studies and Herskovits became a client, although he first had to agree to abandon his decade-long dream of combining African and Negro studies in one center.[23]

Rayford Logan's well-honed instincts about the Truman era, when he served as consultant on UN, Africa, and colonial affairs for NAACP head Walter White, proved correct.[24] The default assumption for white policy-makers, foundation heads, and scholars was that reconsolidated colonial rule would continue in Africa even in the wake of independence for India, Pakistan, Lebanon, and Indonesia. Logan once pressed Deputy Undersecretary of State Dean Rusk in a discussion of the implications of decolonization on the states that were likely to emerge in "Black Africa," and Rusk guessed that Libya ("not black," said Logan), the Rhodesias ("not black either"), and, after prompting, "Nigeria was a possibility."[25] Thus Logan's stock line at the time was "Stop using the expression 'free world.'"[26] Logan also knew that prospects for developing Africa studies were poor as long as such views of and deference to colonial authorities persisted. When the Ford Foundation launched its International Training and Research Program in 1951 (quickly eclipsing Carnegie's area studies investments), Africa was excluded precisely because colonialism still appeared to be a going concern.[27] Finally, Herskovits simply could not be trusted.

When the Ford Foundation tapped him as a consultant in 1952 to organize a small conference on Africa, Herskovits turned primarily to his own former students and friends. He included only one African American, Howard's Rayford Logan, incredibly, leaving Ralph Bunche off the list of invitees in favor of Bunche's staffer (and Herskovits protégé) Jack Harris to represent the UN. At the time, Bunche actually sat on the foundation's board of directors. The black press condemned the "tokenism," and Herskovits did some well-practiced backpedaling. It also turns out that he and two Africa specialists at the state department, William Brown in the Office of Intelligence and Research and Vernon McKay in the Office of Dependent Affairs, had worked out in advance a proposal to fund Northwestern and a second as-yet-unnamed program on the eastern seaboard. Logan lobbied hard for Howard but got nowhere. Meanwhile, Ford officials tried to interest Harvard in building an African Studies Center to be headed by Brown but Harvard declined and Brown instead negotiated with Boston University to start an African Studies Center there. Brown also replaced Herskovits as Ford's primary consultant, and he promised to do what he could to secure funding for the African Studies Program that his friend Frazier had launched at Howard.[28] Ford announced its first grants for universities in African Studies in 1954: five-year commitments to Northwestern ($235,000) and Boston University ($200,000) and a three-year grant—"a pittance," Logan called it—to Howard ($29,000) that was earmarked for the library.[29] The latter figure represents a decrease from the $50,000 that Frazier, after discussions with Ford, determined was the most he might expect.

A reader familiar with the behemoths that the dozens of U.S. area studies centers had become by the 1960s and 1970s, which gave rise to the carping of the less-well-funded international relations theorists, might assume that Northwestern, Boston University, and other early entrants in the competition for foundation and, after 1958, federal dollars had faculty or other assets in place that Howard lacked. Ford, however, commissioned a study in 1958 to assess the strengths and weaknesses of the first batch of African studies programs, and the findings suggest otherwise. For instance, the consultants noted that after receiving grants from Carnegie and Ford, Herskovits's would-be flagship program did not train its students in the political science, history, or economics of Africa. They gave a failing grade to Boston University's graduate program and rejected the pretense that any kind of program really existed at the University of California.[30] This weakness led to their controversial proposal that the United States follow the British (late colonial) model and create a single national center along the lines of London's International African Institute.

Members of the newly founded African Studies Association held a special session on Ford's "State of African Studies" report at its first meeting in August 1958 in Evanston, Illinois, where the consultants defended their call to reverse course.[31] The text of the report, which had been circulated before the conference, included brief surveys of the existing national centers. Unfortunately, the report omitted any negative evaluations, along with any reference to Howard's program.[32]

Logan, who went to Evanston along with Frank Frazier, questioned the omission from the floor. The chairman of the committee, the South Africa–raised president of the University of Rochester, Cornelis W. de Kiewiet, "regretted the omission" as another one of those oversights that had seemed to plague the Howard school over the years. Then why, Logan wondered, had the report also specified that Boston, Chicago, or San Francisco-Los Angeles were appropriate locations for the new center but not Washington? Logan recorded the exchanges from the floor and among conferees after the session in his diary. Frank Frazier believed the writers, he said, but then Frazier was the program's director, the single black insider, and a newly appointed member of the board of the African Studies Association; these factors may have dulled his critical edge a bit. No, another member shot back at him, "Howard would not become part of a national center for the simple reason that it is primarily a Negro institution." Frazier later conceded the point, privately, to Logan.[33]

The report's confidential supplement, which does indeed discuss Howard, confirmed all of Logan's fears. Howard University was an atavism destined to disappear, the supplement said. Its key members, including in this case a future vice-president of both the African Studies Association (Frazier died just before his presidential year would begin) and the American Sociological Association, "did not appear to us to have any very strong drive nor were any particularly concerned with new fields, such as African History." Howard also stood for all "Negro Universities," the report claimed in an attempt to find a work-around for the fact that independent black scholars and faculty at black colleges had pioneered the field, and whites such as Herskovits and Brown had found their first positions at Howard. Blacks had no "prior claims" to the field of African studies, and whatever good work had been done "could equally be done at any other university."[34] In the eyes of the Ford Foundation officials who earlier had approved Frazier's modest funding request, Howard's program would at least exert a moderating influence on "American Negro and native African students who sometimes approach the field with a strong emotional or political bias."[35] Keep in mind too that the reality of segregation meant that Howard still enrolled more African students than any other university in the country in the early 1960s.[36]

The irony in this case did not emerge until a decade or so later. The Eisenhower administration had thrown what amounted to a lifeline to Howard's African Studies Program when it passed the National Defense Education Act in 1958. Among its other provisions, Title VI provided grants to support teaching and research in critical languages and area studies. Howard received its first award in 1959 for its African Language and Area Center. Ten years later, a revolt against its closed, white leadership with their links to the government and the foundations broke out on the floor and shut down the annual meeting of the African Studies Association in Montreal. In the aftermath, Ford did some handwringing that led, among other initiatives, to injecting massive funds into the first U.S. black studies programs.[37] After twenty years of scholarship that was driven by the Cold War and focused on U.S. policy, a post-Herskovits generation of white "Africanist" political scientists, sociologists, and historians could barely comprehend, let alone meet the "demand for an African component in Afro-American studies."[38] Wilbert LeMelle, a Ford Foundation program officer for West Africa who went on to become a U.S. ambassador to Kenya, noted in particular Ford's failure to consider African Americans when developing its programming and its failure to support "a single major African Studies Program among the black colleges."[39]

The highly contested view of the white academy in the 1950s and 1960s by two young leaders of the Montreal insurgency, James Turner and Rukudzo Murapa, seems beyond dispute by now. That is, "black scholars have been continually consigned to a marginal position, and have been forced to languish in the underground of the academic world. This is largely due to a process of white racism that relegates the legitimacy and validity of black scholarship by not providing adequate professional recognition and financial and institutional support."[40]

Fronting

Not only had Rayford Logan seen through the prevarications of his white colleagues (a skill he had perfected through long experience), early on he had also come to suspect that both the intelligence community and U.S. business interests had a role in the emerging African solidarity industry (for lack of a better term), one that seemed resistant to confronting white supremacy in South Africa. These groups entered the field at the same time that the U.S. state indicted the leadership of the older, outspokenly liberation-oriented Council on African Affairs (Du Bois, Robeson, and Alphaeus Hunton, who went to prison for "subversion"). A decade later, revelations would began to appear in *Ramparts*, the *Washington Post*, and the *New York Times* about covert CIA involvement in groups such as the Institute of African American Relations and the American Society for African Culture that helped spur upheavals at the African Studies Association, the APSA, and many other professional associations. Critics then began to construct what they called power-structure analyses of interlocking association directorships and the like. Logan had done the same, although by the 1960s he had become an outspoken critic of student radicalism and especially of the black power movement.

William Leo Hansberry, the historian Frazier sought to exclude from Howard's African Studies Program and who has since come to be recognized as a pioneer in precolonial African and especially Ethiopian history, founded the Institute of African American Relations in 1953 as a way to encourage and support African students in the United States.[41] He brought Lincoln's president, Horace Mann Bond, on board. Its main success in its first years was the opening of a student hostel, Africa House. As Logan later recounted, Hansberry said he had raised the initial funds from Harold Hochschild, the millionaire mining executive (and the father of Adam Hochschild, who wrote for *Ramparts* and later started *Mother Jones*). It is hard to know for sure, since Bond by had already become a thriving middleman for all sorts of U.S. firms seeking concessions in the Gold Coast, Liberia, and Nigeria.[42] As virtually all accounts attest (and unfortunately, these are still fragmentary), control of the Institute of African American Relations, renamed the African American Institute as a condition of support from Carnegie's Alan Pifer, the same official who organized the African Studies Association, slipped away from the founders. Hochschild took over as chair around 1957 and Pifer arranged for the appointment of his clients at the African Studies Association to the board of directors. Logan watched as it happened.

He first encountered principals of the Institute of African American Relations in 1955 in his role as an advisor to the American Friends Service Committee as its new Africa subcommittee considered prospects for its first field sites. The committee held a meeting at Haverford in May out of which emerged plans for what became the United States–South Africa Leaders

Exchange Program, which would bring white South Africans to the United States, to be followed, Logan underscored, by comparable opportunities for "Bantus and coloreds." Logan fought but lost battles at follow-up meetings at the Carnegie Endowment to hold on to the idea of supporting black as well as white South Africans and to keep the project under the umbrella of the Quakers rather than giving it to Institute of African American Relations to operate. When he found that institute board members Edwin "Ned" Munger, a political geographer who had helped establish the American Universities Field Staff, and Hochschild had been brought in, he concluded correctly that the Carnegie and Ford factions had fixed the deal in advance. He was appalled by Munger's repeated tasteless jokes about Ghanaians ("Gonorrheans," "Ghanacologists"), his insistence that Afrikaners were slowly shedding their commitment to white supremacy, and his questionable choice of a South African partner for the leadership exchange project.[43]

The leaders of a second new African solidarity association, the American Society for African Culture, founded in 1957, intended to prevent the white Africanist establishment-in-the-making from adding to its trophy collection by limiting full membership to those of "African descent."[44] The society represented the U.S. support wing (and, it hoped, provided a counter to the left-leaning members) of the anticolonialist Société Africane de Culture of Aime Cesaire, Alioune Diop, and other writers associated with the ten-year-old Paris-based journal *Présence Africane*. U.S. exile Richard Wright, by then another convert to the side of Cold War anticommunism, was also a member. When the editors began planning the First World Congress of Negro Writers and Artists in Paris in 1956 and assigned Wright the task of getting some African Americans to the meeting, Wright contacted, among others, the U.S. embassy in Paris with the intention of putting together a strong U.S. group that could counter the "leftist tendencies" of the organizers and the opening that might provide the Communists.[45] The CIA paid for the five-person U.S. delegation, led by John Aubrey Davis, a CUNY political scientist and civil rights activist, to attend the congress. The funds passed through Davis's American Information Committee on Race and Caste, a group that lobbied for more foreign affairs positions for African Americans. Its main funders to that point had been banking heir Orin Lehman and Walter McCloskey, a Philadelphia-based builder and Democratic Party fund-raiser who was later indicted for corruption.[46]

Following Alioune Diop's opening speech, with Richard Wright sitting on the stage beside him, a message was read to the packed hall from W. E. B. Du Bois. "I am not present at your meeting because the U.S. government will not give me a passport. Any American Negro traveling abroad today must either not care about Negroes or say what the State Department wishes him to say." Du Bois then went on to warn the assembly not to be "betrayed backward by the U.S. into colonialism." As James Baldwin, who was in the packed hall that evening, later wrote, Du Bois had "neatly compromised whatever effectiveness the five-man American delegation then sitting in the hall might have hoped to have."[47] That same American group, which later founded the American Society for African Culture with CIA backing, channeled funds to the Paris group, published its own journal, rented high-end office space and a guest apartment, and ran annual conferences and cultural exchange tours. It attained the height of its influence in the early 1960s when it opened its own cultural center in Lagos.

Logan, an early member of the invitation-only organization, questioned Davis about his exclusion of whites and the mysterious and possibly paradoxical sources of the funding that got him and other founders their junkets to Paris and beyond. "Who was pulling the strings of these organizations [the American Society for African Culture and African American Institute] that are interested in Africa?" He discussed his suspicions at greater length with his confidant Harold Isaacs, unaware that the latter worked at a center that was itself a creation of the CIA. "I asked: How did John A. Davis suddenly become interested in Africa?"[48] Coincidentally, it was around this time that Isaacs interviewed the writer Ralph Ellison, who refused to have anything to do with the American Society for African Culture because its "racial approach to culture" was a form of "fakery and a backward step." Ellison guessed that it was "probably the State Department's idea . . . because of the way they operate."[49]

Waldemar Nielsen, who moved from the Ford Foundation's Overseas Affairs Division to the presidency of the African American Institute in 1961, when he claims that he ended covert funding, came clean after *Ramparts* broke the story of CIA involvement in 1967. Yes, he "was quite aware . . . that the CIA was subsidizing the Institute" and of "the inherent imprudence and impropriety" of it. But the institute was "like a drunk taking the first drink. . . . It is easy to overindulge."[50] In contrast, John A. Davis always publicly denied that the government played any role in supporting the American Society for African Culture, although key staffers had to submit to security clearance investigations and, as one of them later told historian Hugh Wilford, staffers routinely met with CIA case officers.[51]

"In the dazzle of the moment," to appropriate Louis Menand's argument about historical novels set in the 1960s, "people are likely to seem pure reflexes of current conditions." Look harder, however, and the "surface events" reveal themselves as exterior decoration on an unvarying internal structure. That inside space used to be called "human nature," a term with regrettable universalist implications. Now we call it "hardwiring," and we feel much better about ourselves. But it is basically the same thing: the residue of personality that no change can corrode.[52]

In the cascade of crises—Iran, Greece and Turkey, Indonesia, China, Vietnam, Guatemala, Hungary, Egypt, Lebanon, Cuba, the Congo, Berlin, the Dominican Republic—that propelled the American Century forward, social scientists were the volunteer first responders. With revived support from the foundations they began to reengineer some of the wartime institutions and best practices of the prewar era and build the national security and area studies centers, programs, institutes, schools, and so forth that student radicals would protest, picket, and occupy in the late 1960s and early 1970s. I am happy to acknowledge the debt owed the students because it is through the takeover of administration buildings in Columbia and elsewhere that we got the story, at least in part, of scholarship's entanglements with the state and, from there, an understanding of the dubious value of these often-elaborate "feats of ventriloquy."[53] There would even come some slight pushback for a while.

A steady flow of former progressives and communist fellow travelers of one stripe or another crowded to enlist as civilian strategists and would-be nation builders in a global war for freedom. However, McCarthyism also had a remarkable capacity to focus the mind on what really mattered. My colleague, Adolph Reed Jr., says that his father, then a professor of political science at the oldest historically black college in the country, today's University of Arkansas at Pine Bluff, and a future founding member of the APSA's Caucus for a New Political Science during that brief insurgent moment, wrote a blunt letter to Bunche asking what had happened to the onetime radical. Bunche answered as bluntly: he needed to put food on the table.

The unrepentant, like Du Bois, faced the loss of some of the key freedoms worth fighting for, such as the freedom to travel abroad. They went to jail or the state made it impossible for them to continue their research and advocacy work. This is the fate that befell the Institute of Pacific Relations. Others were subjected to ostracism and professional exile, which is what happened to Frederick L. Schuman, author of the book that brought the power politics perspective into international relations. His rehabilitation is long overdue. Alain Locke and Rayford Logan brought Schuman to the Howard campus in 1948 to address early on "The Tyranny of Fear." Logan's consistent opposition to the assault on academic freedom and efforts to expose the state's efforts to influence the African and African American research and advocacy organizations represents his shining hour. There are plenty of other grounds for criticizing him, as we will soon see.

Logan was definitely not dazzled by the moment. Instead, his published analyses and private records from the time point to the ways hierarchy continued to shape the politics and theory about "the colored continents," as Reinhold Niebuhr imagined them in one of the founding documents of the realist revolution in theory.[54] We are also indebted to Logan for showing us how zealous and at times ruthless academics could be in their efforts to exclude or marginalize African Americans scholars and institutions. They operated with an inchoate and entirely fanciful vision of the international sources of domestic politics in the case of so-called colored peoples. For many, the real threat of decolonization in Africa was the prospect of race war at home.

CHAPTER 8

Hands of Ethiopia

This chapter focuses on the writing and reception of *The New World of Negro Americans* (1963) by Harold Isaacs, then a research associate at MIT's Center for International Studies. He was appointed professor of political science soon after, that is, after MIT administrators and trustees sought to end the center's relationship with the Central Intelligence Agency and build a political science department that would provide a recognizable academic home for its faculty.

Isaacs's background, which I discuss below, goes far to explain the unconventional style, research strategy, and concerns of a book that ought to be better known today. *The New World* is the only analysis of the breakdown of the global norm of white supremacy by a white scholar at a leading center, in this case one recognized for its international communications research (the umbrella under which Isaacs did his work) and studies of economic and political development in the new states of Asia. Put slightly differently, he was the sole analyst to register and seek to allay the rising anxieties of leading U.S. officials (among other western elites), about the likelihood of future conflict expressed in the highly charged terms of race war. One of the key conclusions of the book and his subsequent articles on race and international relations is that although decolonization in Africa would not lead African Americans to launch a war of liberation of their own, decolonization was hastening the end of the Jim Crow era and whites should cease the fruit-less and destructive opposition to enormous changes under way around the globe.

No professional political science (let alone international relations) jour-nal in the United States reviewed the book, which is remarkable for several reasons. First, Isaacs shared the Ainsfield-Wolf Award in 1964 with Nathan Glazier and Daniel Patrick Moynihan's *Beyond the Melting Pot* for The *New World's* contribution to the understanding of racism. Second, his previous book, *Scratches on Our Minds: American Views of China and India* (1958) was reviewed in political science, area studies, history journals, and the popular press. In it he explored how negative perceptions of Indians and Chinese mattered to constructions of national identity and, much more tentatively, to foreign policy-making. That is, he admitted the difficulty of weighing these more intangible factors alongside the material considerations that guided the "leadership types" he interviewed.[1] Third, in *The New World* even more than in *Scratches on Our Minds*, Isaacs relied on a model—although he would never have used such a term himself—of the uniquely liberal national character of the United States that political scientists would affirm countless times in the years ahead.

It's not possible to say why American political science and international relations journals ignored *The New World of Negro Americans*. The journal *International Affairs* in London took notice. Staughton Lynd praised it in the standard bearer of the anti-Stalinist left, *Commentary*, which was edited by intellectuals who were close to Isaacs and dreamt of the same pluralist and tolerant America to come. However, Isaacs's study ignited controversy among African American intellectuals even before he finished it, as we will see, and it is only historians of black internationalism who seem to know the book now. His harshest critics were found on the political right; William F. Buckley's review in the *National Review* is a good example. The revelation, however, is the response in the new "scientific" journal, *Mankind Quarterly*, founded in 1960, a place where biological racists in political science, national security studies, anthropology, and kindred quarters kept alive hope that the white Atlantic world order would be restored. The chapter concludes with a discussion of *The Geography of Intellect* (1963), by Isaacs's critic, Nathaniel Weyl, and civilian strategist Stefan Possony, director of the Hoover Institu-tion's research program and a principal of the University of Pennsylvania's new and overtly conservative Foreign Policy Research Institute. Cadres of the institute pressed the case for preserving colonialism intact in Africa, and as events moved in ways contrary to their realist prescriptions, they blamed the Eisenhower administration's alleged anti-colonial biases.[2]

Subsequent generations of scholarship have affirmed Isaacs's reading of the 1950s.[3] His forthright support for African independence; his criticism of the Eisenhower administration's role in aiding colonial and, in the settler colonies, racist orders; and, not least, his withering account in *The New World* of those who quit the United States out of some misplaced identification with (or blindness to) to the various dictatorships emerging in Ghana, Nigeria, and elsewhere all were consistent with his background and enduring political commitments. What requires some explanation is how a comrade of Leon Trotsky and onetime accomplice of the Chinese Communist Party's struggle in Hankow turned up at the Center for International Studies and ultimately became an early member of MIT's political science department.

Idol of the Tribe

In 1930, at age 20, the self-described politically naïve New Yorker set out for Hawaii, Manila, and ultimately Shanghai ("the farthest that it was possible to get away from where I was") to try his hand at journalism. In China, Isaacs soon became friends with a revolutionary named Frank Glass, a Birmingham-born Trotskyist who had helped found and split with the South African Communist Party. Isaacs soon joined the side of the communists in their "struggle against the Kuomintang and the imperialists" by starting an English-language newspaper in Hankow, the *China Forum*. The 1930s was a decade of violent repression of Stalinists and Trotskyists, and Isaacs became a target of Chiang Kai-shek's government, the British authorities, U.S. military intelligence, and the American consul general, although the extraterritoriality provisions then in force afforded him protection that was denied his Chinese comrades. In 1934, he split with his party backers, turned the press over to Glass and the other Trotskyists, and moved to Beijing to research his explosive history of the Stalinist betrayal of the revolutionary forces in the 1920s, *The Tragedy of the Chinese Revolution*, which came out in 1938, with an introduction by Trotsky himself.[4]

Isaacs and his wife Viola returned to the United States in 1935, where he remained active in Trotskyist circles (the U.S. Workers Party, later the Socialist Workers Party), while working in New York for Havas, the French news agency that had employed him in Shanghai. His extracurricular activities included running the party paper, *Socialist Appeal*, and writing for it and other venues using an expanded set of pseudonyms. Perhaps unaware of these details, his longtime MIT colleague Lucian Pye later mischaracterized Isaacs's years in the sectarian trenches as a "period of withdrawal from activism." Then again, having once helped Vietnamese Communist Ho Chi Minh escape from Shanghai, Isaacs's battles with Brooklyn socialists and his assessment of the prospects of proletarian revolution might seem tame by comparison. He told the FBI that he quit the party in 1940. U.S. cultural historian Alan Wald says that until then, Isaacs remained loyal to the Cannon faction, that is, those who followed Trotsky's line on support for the German-allied Soviet Union in wartime in a moment that had split the party.[5]

Isaacs stumbled a bit in his new and presumably unblinkered persona of a writer for CBS radio and, briefly, Lockheed before he joined *Newsweek* in 1943. He headed back to the Pacific in 1944 as a war correspondent and after the war continued to write on Southeast Asia among other assignments, until he resigned from the magazine in December 1949. Although he had passed a wartime U.S. army counterintelligence investigation, his reporting had won him a host of new official enemies. The Kuomintang banned him from China in 1945. And Isaacs got it right (or spoke from experience) about General Patrick Hurley ("a strange old man"), FDR's envoy to the alleged democrat Chiang Kai-shek (a "racketeer, extortionist, and executioner"), in his 1947 book *No Peace in Asia*, where he wrote "All who questioned or criticized his acts were automatically Communists or traitors or, obviously, both."[6]

As Cornell Law School professor and peace activist Harrop Freeman underscored, *No Peace in Asia* stood out both for its unflinching reportage of the brutality through which colonial rule was being reimposed with the aid of the United States and for its "political theorizing."[7] That is—and these are my words not Harrop's—Isaacs sought to expose what was hidden in the turn to "power politics" and "security." So in his discussion of the United States, he challenged the myth of American difference even before postwar academics (e.g., Daniel Bell, Louis Hartz) took Stalin's old idea of "American exceptionalism" and ran with it. Likewise, his spare account of the United States as one more imperial power in Asia undercut much of the tortured logic in émigré Hans Morgenthau's alternative to exceptionalism, namely the even more abstract, internally contradictory idea of the United States as not an imperialist (except when it was) but a "status quo power," which he would unveil in his *Politics among Nations* the next year.

Isaacs's criticism of U.S. policy cost him. The State Department refused him a passport in 1947 on the grounds that he was a "Communist-Defender of Leon Trotsky." He obtained a new passport the following year, and in 1949, on his last trip to Asia for *Newsweek*, Isaacs interviewed Ho Chi Minh via clandestine radio. (He also smuggled funds from a supporter in Singapore to the families of Indonesia's jailed nationalist leaders.) The French refused to allow him to enter to Indochina, but the interview also outraged the U.S. consulate at Hanoi. The State Department subsequently held up his passport again for six months in 1950, upending his planned research for a new book on south Asia that the Guggenheim Foundation had agreed to support.[8] Then, in 1951–1952, as his name repeatedly surfaced in House Un-American Activities Committee hearings on the Institute of Pacific Relations and a Russian spy ring that purportedly was operating in wartime Japan, the FBI launched a new investigation of Isaacs that remained active until 1954.[9]

This background provides much-needed and heretofore missing context for key moments in Isaacs's transition, as he put it, "out of the world of journalism . . . and into . . . a more permissive academic environment."[10] He had resigned from *Newsweek* but didn't write the book for which he had a contract and a Guggenheim grant because it required him to be able to travel abroad. Instead he radically recast his 1938 *Tragedy of the Chinese Revolution* for the Hoover Institution, removing Trotsky's introduction, excising his detailed analysis of the struggles of the "left opposition," and appending a new conclusion titled "The Blind Alley of Totalitarianism" that was thoroughly out of step with the rest of the book. He published the latter as a stand-alone piece in *The Annals of the American Academy of Political and Social Science* for good measure. Was it an act of expediency in the face of McCarthyism? All we know is that he took it out of the 1961 edition and put one of the suppressed chapters back in as an appendix.[11]

A fellow journalist told the FBI that Isaacs had not been able to find much work during his years as a freelancer.[12] An old friend, Edward Morrow, threw him a little business ("it did not amount to much"). So did MIT's new Center for International Studies, which hired him to support the $1 million dollar grant by the Ford Foundation in 1952 that established the international communications program (and provided seed money for the center's better-known turn to economic development), the first of its work that wasn't sponsored by the CIA.[13] Ithiel de Sola Pool, a Chicago-trained political scientist who, like Isaacs, was an ex-Trotskyist, was brought from the Hoover Institution to head the program.[14] Isaacs joined Pool's staff in 1953 where he began his research into the views of American elites about India and China and a second project on African Americans' views of Africa, originally titled "Hands of Ethiopia."

The story Isaacs later told in print of abandoning his work on decolonization in Asia and taking up the study of the "evolution of American society itself" emphasizes his internal intellectual development and renewed commitment to realizing the world promise of America's "open society" at a critical moment. He said that he wrote "copiously" about U.S. policy in China and Korea and about the "McCarthyist spasm," although I have been unable to find any example of the latter.[15] There is plenty of evidence in his archive that he feared the new Eisenhower administration would make the same mistakes in Africa that Truman had in Asia due to its "European-centered myopia." These were studies that Isaacs could do without a passport, and he did not leave the country again until 1957, when he went to Europe, and 1960, when he went to Africa long after the "spasm" had subsided. His views continued to evolve through this period, particularly as colonialism retreated and the Kennedy administration emerged as a champion of development aid to the Third World, for which the MIT center provided much of the brainpower. In 1965, the year he was officially made a member of the new political science department, he signed on to the campaign against "opponents of U.S. policy on the campuses." They failed to grasp what those who were allegedly best positioned at the university—the political scientists, Asian studies scholars, and professors of international relations that Noam Chomsky called the "new mandarins"—knew to be right and necessary, namely launching the ground war and escalating the bombing campaign against the Vietminh and North Vietnam.[16]

Flawed Method, Bad Faith

In June 1961 at the fourth annual conference of the American Friends of African Culture in New York, Roosevelt University's St. Clair Drake and the American Society for African Culture's Harold Mann Bond declared war on Harold Isaacs and a second white reporter, Warren Russell Howe. Isaacs's criticisms of American policy in support of the racist-colonial order went back almost a decade (he wrote that "the most dangerous threat of totalitarianism in Africa is not of Communist but of white European origin" in 1953), but he had just published the results of his meetings with African American expatriates and exiles in Accra and elsewhere in West Africa in a long New Yorker essay, "Back to Africa," the month before. It focused on the shattered illusions of practically all the professionals, teachers, and "seekers" he met, many of whom left to escape racism in the United States only to discover "that he is much more alien in Africa. Whether he likes or not, he is American, and in Africa he becomes an American-in-exile."[17] Even an old friend, the lawyer Pauli Murray, one of the expatriates in Ghana and a key source for his reporting, thought he had gone too far. "You left the picture almost hopeless."[18]

Then, just days before the American Society for African Culture meeting, the influential biweekly Reporter published a short hack job titled "Strangers in Africa" that one-upped Isaacs's *New Yorker* article.[19] It argued that because of the prejudices of Africans, posting African Americans to the newly independent states actually harmed U.S. national interests. The *Reporter's* editor, Philip Horton, an ex-CIA Paris station chief and future professor of public diplomacy at the Fletcher School of Law and Diplomacy, had assembled the brief from the reporting of Russell Warren Howe, a longtime African correspondent who had covered the rise of Kwame Nkrumah from Accra (where he was declared persona non grata despite some early pieces in Nkrumah's defense) and the downfall of Patrice Lumumba from Leopoldville. When Lumumba was murdered and demonstrators in New York had forced their way into a UN Security Council debate on February 15 and fought with police to protest the role of the UN and U.S. in the killing, Horton wanted a piece "as quickly as possible" that would show "the disillusion and setbacks experienced by many American Negroes working or traveling in Africa" and serve as "corrective to the quite vocal sectors of American opinion . . . which tend to romanticize and idealize African nationalism."[20] The critique was overdetermined, given that American Society for African Culture founder St. Clair Drake, who had just returned to the United States after teaching in Ghana for three years, said that Horton had approached him for the same piece, for the same reason.

It wasn't an accident, Drake said, that the pieces appeared when they did. Apparently many middle-class black and ruling-class white Americans feared the "identification of Negroes with Africans," and black Marxists in Paris who denounced African Americans as "agents of imperialism" were just as confused. The history of pan-Africanism; its leading lights, Du Bois, Nkrumah, Garvey, and Padmore; and various phases and tendencies, including the founding of the American Society for African Culture itself, demonstrated the irrationality of the fear of black Americans' identification with Africa easily enough. While Howe's contemptible piece didn't merit discussion, Isaacs's various mistakes, methodological flaws, and overall artless reporting had the same effect of increasing "the fear in America of Negroes' intense interest in Africa." Drake added, "I am hoping that the author will do a *Back to Africa* Part II and make it very clear that he repudiates Russell Howe's position and doesn't like the use to which his article is being put,"[21] For instance, the articles supplied fodder for the racists fighting to keep African Americans out of the United States Foreign Service.

His friend Rayford Logan, who attended the meeting, warned Isaacs about Drake's paper. "The man is diseased. I had not noticed before the strange expression in his eye. . . . [He is] obsessed with a mania to attack you and

Russell Howe."[22] Isaacs though took the high road in his response to Drake and two other critics, Bond, whose paper Isaacs had in hand, and New York state official Anna Hedgeman, whom Isaacs had met in Accra. "I don't think I could quite undertake to meet people like Bond and Hedgeman and Drake at the levels of personalities. They are much too vulnerable. I have neither the interest nor the desire to add to their burdens . . . by indicating how sorry I feel for . . . them." Their reactions confirmed his view of the "new kind of alienation . . . shared in varying ways by many, many others who do not share their particular sentimentalisms about Africa."[23] One of his contacts, writer James Baldwin, made no secret of that despair over the lack of progress toward equality in the United States ("I expect nothing of this country"), neither had Frank Frazier and Kenneth Clark in private interviews. Frazier was considering exile in Africa and Clark was considering going to the West Indies ("You get awfully tired trying to save white folk's souls," Clark said).[24] However, Bond ("a sick old sentimentalist" according to Isaacs) said that blacks would have been primed to tell Isaacs "what that white man wishes to hear," and, like Drake, he challenged Isaacs's sample size. But no one really confronted the alienation argument head on.[25]

The fallout continued as defenders and critics lined up and did battle. Logan's friend, the increasingly conservative red-baiting editor of the *Pittsburgh Courier*, George Schuyler, wrote three consecutive columns supporting Isaacs. Martin Kilson, a young scholar who had trained at Harvard and had just returned from Sierra Leone and Accra, wrote to Frank Frazier, blasting Isaacs's bad faith ("the deepening of whatever differences there are"), distortions, and shoddy scholarship, even as he acknowledged that "all is far from rosy as regards their [the American Society for African Culture's] relations with Africa and Africans."[26] Ironically, Mel Fox, the Ford Foundation program officer who oversaw African studies, compared Isaacs to Frazier for his forthright approach to a subject "that is becoming increasingly enmeshed in a kind of mass self-deception."[27] Isaacs agreed to attend a meeting with his critics organized by the American Society for African Culture. He wrote a withering private postmortem, dismissing as without merit all the charges leveled at him, save "that what I had written was 'destructive of negritude.'"[28] He would spend the rest of his academic career condemning the mysticism and racism that nationalism ("a miserable, leaky, ugly, stinking vessel") everywhere seemed to depend on.[29]

Isaacs published *The New World of Negro Americans* three years later with the *New Yorker* material included without reigniting the controversy. Instead, what engaged most reviewers were the long excerpts ("voices") from the dozens of interviews Isaacs did with Bunche and other "leaders and top achievers." Isaacs's attempt to substantiate the argument about the consequences of decolonization and the transformation under way in African American "group" identity included close readings of black writers (Wright, Baldwin, Hansberry, Hughes, and Ellison) and an eye-opening account of the transatlantic reach of what today is known as the "long civil rights movement." He also included his critique of the aging Du Bois, the intellectual most frequently evoked as an influence by his interviewees even though Isaacs said his books had sat unread on MIT's shelves for decades.

The New World of Negro Americans garnered glowing reviews in major newspapers and leading journals of opinion. The longest and most thoughtful by far was by Amitai Etzioni, who taught sociology at Columbia University. More important for our purposes, Etzioni also was a research associate at Columbia's Institute of War and Peace Studies.[30] Thus, a professor of international relations at the dissident edge of the discipline—he would soon become a founder of the new peace studies movement—engaged Isaacs's account of shifting African American identity in the pages of the *New York Times*. Unsurprisingly, Etzioni focused on Isaacs's argument about the impact of the Cold War on desegregation. Etzioni underscored the problems with Isaacs's underspecified structural account. Isaacs saw fear as the primary factor that was driving change that he understood primarily as a psychological process that would "more or less by itself suffice to undermine the walls of segregation," Etzioni wrote.[31]

Fear was not enough, and factors other than international ones were at work, Etzioni insisted. The industrialization of the South, the migration of Negroes to the North, the reapportionment rule of the Supreme Court, and the actual and potential competition for the Negro vote were are factors that Isaacs underplayed. Obviously they needed to be enhanced before segregation could be weakened.[32]

Racial Realism Redux

The harshest criticism of *The New World of Negro Americans*, in print at least, appeared not in any African American or Pan-African publication but instead in the new *Mankind Quarterly*. Launched in London in 1960, the journal mixed eugenics research and politics. According to its principal editors and writers, the western postwar scientific enterprise had come under the "political domination" of "liberals, Communists, and Jews," who had conspired to suppress the truth about the biological bases of white supremacy.[33] Nathaniel Weyl, a frequent contributor in those years to both *Mankind Quarterly* and William F. Buckley's *National Review*, panned *The New World of Negro*

Americans in his characteristically tendentious style on grounds that were familiar from the era of the *Journal of Race Development*. He argued that the worst of Isaacs's many failings was his incomprehension of the "biogenetic adaptation to specific habitats" (temperate/Caucasoid, hot/Negroid, cold/ Mongoloid) that made any idea of nonwhites collectively opposing white domination impossible. On the plus side, it was probably the case that the kind of tensions between African Americans and Africans Isaacs described had developed because "the Negro intellectual is typically far more Caucasoid in his genetic makeup."[34]

Three years later, Weyl collaborated with Austrian émigré strategic studies scholar Stefan Possony to analyze the implications of the biological inferiority of Africans and African Americans, or "Melanoids," for the Cold War world order. *The Geography of Intellect* used the old arguments on interdependence (except that the terminology had changed to globalization) to ground a defense of eugenics. Intelligence had emerged as a vital strategic resource in short supply that required careful shepherding in accordance with iron laws of climate and mental endowments (lots of geniuses in the temperate zones, none in the tropics). Unfortunately, the policies that were currently in place and were informed by "academic sects," that is, the disciplines of sociology and social psychology, which long ago had abandoned the disinterested search for scientific truth in a campaign to destroy basic American values and institutions, were producing dysgenic outcomes (favoring the "mentally inferior race, ethnic subgroup, class, caste or other division of the social structure" over "its betters") locally and globally.[35]

The attack on integration efforts in the United States was one he had made before, but Possony, doubtless unconsciously, had returned to the roots of American international relations in focusing on the catastrophes unfolding globally as a result of the misguided efforts of the United States to "destroy colonialism" and spend foreign aid dollars on those who were least well-endowed genetically. The "average African Negro functions as does the European after a leucotomy [prefrontal lobotomy] operation," while "we" contribute to "genocide" of the white race there. As for "the Middle East, Latin America and Southeast Asia . . . these regions are genetically unpromising." The key question was what was to be done with "ethnic, national or geographical groups" outside the temperate zone that "*en masse* lack the innate brain power-required for mastery and operation of the tools of modern civilization[.] . . . The accretion of lethal power in the hands of nation states dominated by populations incapable of rational thought could be a harbinger of total disaster."[36]

The same "eugenicists" Weyl and Possony championed in *The Geography of Intellect* hailed the book in *Mankind Quarterly* and the right's two standard bearers, *The National Review* and *Modern Age*. However, the *Political Science Quarterly* assigned the review of the book to the world's best-known scholar of and pioneer in developmental genetics, Leslie Clarence Dunn, who dismissed it as a rehash of the ideas of original *Journal of Race Development* editor Ellsworth Huntington and Gobineau and Galton, characterizing it as racist in its "dealing with African and Islamic peoples," and dedicated not to "critical evaluation of evidence" but to "special pleading." Psychologist Otto Klineberg, who made a career of debunking work of this kind, took it apart in the *Harvard Educational Review*. "The authors do not like the term 'racist,' so I shall refrain from using it . . . although their use of the term 'race' is broad enough to make many geneticists and physical anthropologists squirm."[37]

Fifty years on, there is no reason to be coy. Possony's coming out in print as one of the last two biological racists in the discipline so far—Berkeley's A. James Gregor was the other—deserves some discussion. Possony had traveled far since his wartime association with Edward Mead Earle and the national security seminar at Princeton (and his association with the Office of Naval Intelligence). He deepened his ties to the Pentagon in the early Cold War as a civilian consultant while teaching international relations at Georgetown and joined Robert Strausz-Hupé's new Foreign Policy Research Institute at the University of Pennsylvania. He and Strausz-Hupé coauthored the 1950 textbook *International Relations* in the putatively "infant science" and worked together on virtually all of the institute's early policy studies.[38] Strausz-Hupé praised Possony as a "meticulous scholar . . . Jack-of-all-academic-trades and a man-with-ideas, mostly new." By 1961, Possony had joined Stanford's Hoover Institution of as director of international political studies. He helped align the Hoover Institution with the Foreign Policy Research Institute and the new Center for Strategic and International Studies at Georgetown in stalwart opposition to the seeming accommodation with Third World nationalism by the Kennedy and Johnson administrations.[39]

For Possony and Strausz-Hupé, who wrote *International Relations* in 1950 and then revised it to catch up with the French defeat at Dien Bien Phieu in 1954, "the problem of colonialism" or the rule of "advanced over backward nations" posed the greatest challenge to the west after world communism, although it wasn't really possible to distinguish the two, since Russia and China figured so prominently in and stood to reap the gains of the so-called national independence movements. Western "anti-imperialist groups" played their unwitting role, too, in the "great conflagration in the making" through their "fashionable" albeit tragically flawed arguments about rights of self-determination.[40]

Reprising another of the key arguments of the 1920s, Possony and Strausz-Hupé wrote that colonies were a vital part of the world economy that would have to remain under the control of the west in order to guarantee living standards everywhere. They argued that critics failed in calculating colonialism's costs since exploitation of labor occurs in all lands, not just dependencies, and political domination by the west had led to vast improvements in the lives of most natives through capital investments, infrastructure additions, and so forth. Finally, they wrote, critics evinced a callous disregard for the rights of those most threatened by decolonization, namely white minorities. Critics of colonialism were therefore more wrong than right even if it was true that imperial powers did not always do all they could to advance the welfare of their charges, in large part as a result of the "colonial mentality" of whites "imbued with a feeling of racial superiority."[41]

Possony and Strausz-Hupé's prescriptions followed from their pessimistic (and stunningly wrong) predictions of what would happen if "the old colonial system" gave way to a "system of weak, chaotic, nation-states." Europeans and Jews faced "genocide" in Algeria, and elsewhere "native societies would ring in the grant of independence by resorting to the establishment of home-grown types of oppression such as slavery." Violence against whites and/or alliances with communist countries (for example were the Congo to sell all its uranium to the Soviets) could lead to war with one or more of the erstwhile European colonial powers—so why pull out in the first place? Everywhere "the net result of emancipation would be regressive developments, including a dramatic reduction of health and education standards." Thus, the only reasonable solution (lest "the West, succumbing to suicidal mania, deliberately hastens its own decline") was to upgrade "techniques of colonial administration" while deepening trade with and investment in these sources of vital raw materials and markets for western manufactured goods.[42]

Only the United States could do the heavy lifting in the project of renovating the colonial order along the lines Possony and Strausz-Hupé envisioned, and this increased their pessimism about the future. Successive postwar administrations had instead taken "childish delight" in sabotaging France and Great Britain's imperial ties in such places as India, China, Sudan, and Nigeria. Americans generally believed that "all nations by nature [were] capable of self-government" although the evidence clearly showed that most colonial peoples did not "measure up." Were Americans to overcome their naïveté and take the necessary steps "to forestall a revolutionary assault of unprecedented violence," for instance by increasing foreign aid to "colored and colonial areas," the UN system could play an important subsidiary role.

They tasked the United Nations Education, Social, and Cultural Organization with "improving racial relationships" in the colonial domains, which is noteworthy since Possony would soon declare UNESCO's actual anti-racism campaign a form of "thought control on a global scale."[43]

Possony and Strausz-Hupé stood their ground in the Foreign Policy Research Institute's report *The Idea of Colonialism* (1958), even as Libya, Morocco, Tunisia, Sudan, Ghana, Guinea, and Malaya joined the ranks of "liberated" peoples; as France's Fourth Republic collapsed due to the bloody war with the Algerian National Liberation Front; and as the UN General Assembly stood poised to issue a Declaration on the Granting of Independence to Colonial Countries and Peoples.[44] "A global anticolonial "revolution" would prove disastrous," Possony argued in "Colonial Problems in Perspective." The Soviets would gain immeasurably, while the many peoples who were "incapable of effective self-government" would become fodder for expansionist states. It was still not too late to reform "metropolitan-colonial relationships" in the interests of the free world, but to do so, the "flimsy ideology of extreme anticolonialism" that had gripped too many western thinkers had to be defeated along with "the more stubborn defenders of the status quo" in the French and British colonial administrations. If these things did not happen, then dependent peoples would likely continue to seek their freedom through "strategies of terrorism" since the colonial powers were neither "strong" nor "callous enough to rule by oppression, as do the Communist dictatorships and the racist Union of South Africa."[45] Possony rethought this last point; a few years later he attacked those who "uncritically accept" the idea that the "much maligned" policy of South Africa was either racist or oppressive.[46]

Few were listening, however, and as another thirty new states prepared to take their seats at the UN's General Assembly, the final chapters of Weyl and Possony's *Geography of Intellect* lashed out at the "erroneous policies and self-defeating procedures" of the US in sabotaging the colonial order, deluded by the idea "that men, classes and races are equal in capacity." A "savage race and class war" had already begun, and they prophesied the "subjugation or annihilation of the three millions whites" in South Africa, the rapid decline of the Middle East and Africa into "chaos and barbarism," and the "genetic deterioration in human intelligence" globally. Their research also spoke directly to what we now call "democratization." A decline in brain power corresponded closely with "growing lip service to democracy" or, more precisely, to the "democracy of the unfit," evidence for which could be found everywhere from Kenya to all the misguided local efforts across the United States to "get out the vote."[47]

If we try to plot the Cold War realists and their critics on the hypothetical bell curve I sketched for the 1910s–1920s in the introduction, we run into some difficulties. The obvious one is the lack of data points. That is, very few self-identified professors of international relations wrote about decolonization and its consequences, in contrast to the easy self-identification of such academics when empire or imperialism constituted the primary and nameable object of inquiry. Interestingly, a young Joseph Nye Jr., who studied under Buell's replacement at Harvard, Rupert Emerson, was one of them for a short while. He published his revised 1964 dissertation as *Pan-Africanism and East African Integration* (1967), which sought to explicate the role of ideology as a major policy variable, in this case, in the failed effort by Kenya, Uganda, and its neighbors to form a federation. The irony is just a few years later, after moving on from Africa, Nye's career took off as he and a friend resurrected, doubtless unselfconsciously, the idea of "complex interdependence" that Buell had introduced in his 1925 textbook, *International Relations*. However, Nye's early work positions him far from the tail that defenders of colonialism such as Possony and racist fellow travelers occupy. Nye sits much closer to Isaacs, nearer the middle of the curve, among those who had reconciled themselves to or supported independence and promoted projects of development (what was once "race development") and modernization as the better strategy for securing the mutual if unequal interests of the free world's emerging Third World clients.

Filling out the curve takes some work. One task entails teasing out analytical positions as decolonization unfolded and as many public intellectuals argued, like Possony and Strausz-Hupé, that a properly reformed colonial order remained the primary directive of the white-identified west or North Atlantic community. It also requires distinguishing between biological (that is, classically racist) understandings of the sources and significance of hierarchy and the centuries of "tradition" that explained, as Eisenhower put it, the impossibility of leaping from "savagery to civilization" any time soon. If we could do so, the tail and the right half of the curve would be a little more sharply defined. We would still have to sample outside of or at the edge of the new boundary that I traced in the last chapter between self-identified "discipline generalists" and those with area or regional expertise, leading the original generation of international relations scholars (Blakeslee, Buell, Leo Rowe, Bunche) and others to be posthumously rebaptized as Africanists, Latin Americanists, and so forth. The result would be a better-defined top of the bell and upper part of the left slope, which would be populated by many of Isaacs's MIT colleagues and others in the Social Science Research Council's new Committee on Comparative Politics.

However, the curve would still be missing its left slope and tail; that is, those who saw U.S. hegemony and Third World development efforts as hallmarks of an emerging neocolonial order. As we will see in the next chapter, the Cold War, McCarthyism, and the 1954 Supreme Court decision in *Brown v. Board* all took their toll on the Howard school, and no new theorists of the relationship between racism or other forms of ascriptive hierarchy and imperialism emerged until the end of the 1960s and 1970s, when members of the New Left entered the professoriate and black studies secured a toehold in the elite academy.

CHAPTER 9

The Fate of the Howard School

For those like Stefan Possony, who obsessed about the globally linked Communist and colored conspiracy against Caucasoid civilization, the decade between the *Brown v. Board of Education* decision in 1954 and the March on Washington for Jobs and Freedom in August 1963 was a nightmare. The United States appeared to be headed down the same disastrous road as the European metropoles, Australasia, and the "Third Africa" (the white redoubts and their peripheries arrayed against the Arab north and sub-Saharan black zones), and things would only get worse. They were also unlikely to notice, let alone celebrate, the waning influence of the internationalism that the Howard school theorists had advanced in the 1930s and 1940s. As Penny Von Eschen's pioneering account portrays, intellectuals in the Cold War–era civil rights movement instead increasingly accepted the legitimacy of U.S. hegemony. They argued for desegregation and decolonization on the grounds of meeting the communist challenge. The critique of racism shifted grounds too, from the Du Boisian historical-structural analysis of capitalist slavery and colonialism to a Myrdalian "psychological problem and an aberration in American life," and thus "from an international to a "domestic" problem."[1]

Rayford Logan traded in his pan-Africanist identity to become the Howard school's model Cold War anticommunist liberal. He wrote frequently as a "foreign affairs advisor" to the head of the *Pittsburgh Courier*'s editorial page, George Schuyler, an even more outspoken black anticommunist. Logan's views were now close to those of his friend, Harold Isaacs. The convergence of perspectives also probably helped reduce the wariness between him and Ralph Bunche, who, like E. Franklin Frazier and Abram Harris, once considered him a race man and, as Logan himself believed, "a lightweight." Through all the years of red-baiting and persecution by the U.S. government, Logan remained loyal to Du Bois, the critic Bunche had grown to detest and Isaacs dismissed (together with his "half-digested Marxism") as a failure.[2]

McCarthyism struck the Howard campus hard in 1953–1954. The FBI investigated President Mordecai Johnson and two dozen faculty members for suspected communist ties as a consequence of their entanglements in the postwar civil rights and national liberation struggles. Logan, one of those caught in the dragnet, wrote about his interrogation and the impact of McCarthyism on the campus in his journal and retrospectively in an unpublished autobiography and in his *Howard University: The First Hundred Years* (1969). He called it a blatant effort to sow suspicion and silence him and other "moderate" and "liberal" leaders at Howard, such as Locke and Frazier, in his case because of his outspoken views on the crisis of colonialism in Africa.[3] Logan believed McCarthyist tactics worked, and as proof he pointed to Merze Tate, "the most abjectly intimidated" of all his colleagues. At a tense faculty meeting in May 1953 to discuss the FBI's hunt for communists on campus, she allegedly warned others to steer clear of the NAACP or other suspect organizations.[4] Two years later, he judged her a "craven coward" for her decision to use the term "American *interest* in the Pacific" to describe her emerging research focus "rather than American imperialism because of the danger of criticism."[5] She eventually shook herself free of such fears, but it hardly mattered to Logan. His cordial albeit patronizing relationship with his colleague had turned poisonous. The problem was not simply one of personalities, however; it was a problem of institutional decay and its caustic effects on Logan, Frazier, and many others.

Brown v. Board and its promise of an end—however slow, grudging, and piecemeal—to America's academic apartheid dealt a deathblow to the Howard school. Bunche and Eric Williams were long gone by 1950. Alain Locke died in 1955. Frazier and his colleagues who had been hired just before or during the war carried on in an atmosphere of increasing acrimony and bitterness over the lack of resources and research support. Depending on their age, discipline, and professional networks, they might harbor the "almost impossible" dream of joining a white department as its token minority.[6] The alienation that Harold Isaacs had found in his interviews with black intellectuals was real and was attributable to the precarious positions they occupied in what historian and Logan protégé Michael Winston called an "intellectual periphery" of "isolated Negro colleges and universities which were themselves marginal financially and intellectually." The "token desegregation" of those years proved "sufficient to . . . erode the small but productive clusters of research scholars" and the journals and departments they had built.[7]

When Howard's administration responded to desegregation in 1954 by proposing to begin granting PhD degrees, Logan, Frazier, and other faculty fought against the plan, at great cost to themselves, for nearly a year. They believed it would come at the expense of the struggling undergraduate and masters programs, which were suffering from a reduction in faculty and couldn't possibly succeed when the small pool of talented black PhD applicants in the social and natural sciences gained entry into white private and public universities. Merze Tate renewed her opposition to a doctoral program in 1960 in a way that (consciously or not) was guaranteed to outrage Logan, the department's longtime, increasingly autocratic head. She viewed herself as the one outlier in a post–John Hope Franklin department of narrow ("racially slanted") thinkers that couldn't hope to produce students on a par with other research universities. Yet Logan himself would soon cynically describe Howard's PhD, the first of which was awarded in 1964, as "not the Ph.D. of the type you get from Amherst and Harvard. This is a black Ph.D."[8]

Michael Winston's more measured 1971 assessment states the problem succinctly. There were few if any "recognized scholars" in place to carry on the institution and theory building at Howard after the era of Bunche, Locke, and Frazier, and the most promising young thinkers were "being recruited to white institutions."[9] German Jewish émigré John Herz, Bunche's replacement as chair, left for City College in 1951, the year his *Political Realism and Political Idealism* (1951) won the American Political Science Association's Woodrow Wilson Award.[10] Howard's political science department made one great new hire in international relations in 1957. French national Bernard Fall was on the cusp of recognition as the country's most knowledgeable specialist on Vietnam. He wrote brutal dissections of the failures of the French and later U.S. wars and thus was a target for FBI surveillance. His senior colleague in history, Merze Tate, had helped him secure Rockefeller Foundation support in 1962, which bought him time to finish his *Two Viet-Nams* while living in Phnom Penh (he was persona non grata in South Vietnam by then) and file the first of his many devastating portraits of the Kennedy administration's deceptions.[11] However, Fall died tragically in 1967 when he set off a land mine while accompanying a battalion of marines in South Vietnam.

Tate was easily Herz's and Fall's rival for most accomplished international relations scholar at Howard. She turned her Radcliffe PhD in government into two books published by Harvard University Press: *The Disarmament Illusion* (1942) and the *United States and Armaments* (1948). Hans Morgenthau, the leading realist theorist in international relations in the United States, was one of her early champions. Another was the realist whom Morgenthau had eclipsed, Fred Schuman, who had served on her committee. In the 1950s, Tate launched an entirely new research project on imperialism in the Pacific that resulted in two more highly regarded books on U.S.-Hawaiian relations and dozens of articles, many of which appeared in journals that remained out of bounds to her seniors. Sadly, her papers at Howard's Moorland-Spingarn Research Center contain five unpublished books: another on Hawaii, two on the expansionism of Australia and New Zealand, and two on imperialism in Africa. Like the rest of the Howard school thinkers, she is not recognized in the conventional histories of Anglo-American international theory. The real tragedy is her marginalization at Howard, the discrimination she endured as one of the few women teaching in the social sciences (and one of the only women in the United States teaching international relations in the 1940s, 1950s, and 1960s), and her disappearance from virtually all retrospective accounts of African American intellectual life and internationalist thought.

Missing in Action

Merze Tate began teaching history at Howard in 1942 on a one-year contract, the year her first book, *The Disarmament Illusion*, appeared. A young Eric Williams took over the leadership of the tiny government department when the chair, Bunche, and a second faculty member, Harold Lewis, joined the Office of Strategic Services, and a third, Vincent Browne, entered the U.S. Army officer corps. Even when the department was shorthanded, Williams couldn't bear the thought of hiring Tate or any other woman. "I am exposed, apparently, to a choice between Caroline Ware and Merze Tate. What have I done to deserve that?" he wrote to Locke.[12] Ware, an activist scholar and New Dealer who had written two influential histories, one of New England textile workers and the other of immigrant life in Greenwich Village, had just come out with her call for a new cultural approach to history "from the bottom up," as a later generation of professors referred to it. Logan, the chair of the history department, who was teaching less while serving as interim graduate school dean, considered which of the two to hire in his place. "Tate is colored but a personality problem. Ware is white, lives in Vienna, Virginia, but a more mature scholar and probably less of a personality problem. I incline toward Tate." Tate taught year to year for different programs during the war (for example, the Army Specialized Training Program on campus), but Bunche, who was running his department "by telephone" while relying on Williams and buddy Sam Dorsey, rejected her reapplication, and she contemplated having to leave Howard before she was offered a permanent position in the history department in 1945 or 1946.[13]

Aided by a subvention from Harvard/Radcliffe's Bureau of International Research, Tate published *The Disarmament Illusion*, a project she launched at Oxford under Lord Zimmern, who was routinely if loosely identified as the world's first professor of international relations, and completed at Harvard under Payson Wild. It received strong reviews in both African American and white journals. Elton Atwater, a specialist in arms exports who taught international relations at American University before moving to Penn State in 1950, judged it the "definitive study" of arms control efforts up to the Hague conference of 1907, and others agreed. Logan called the book Tate's passport to "a permanent place among American historians regardless of her color."[14] She combined an exhaustive review of state papers that had never been used before with a pathbreaking, equally detailed (some reviewers maintained it was overdetailed) study of the myriad organizations that constituted "public opinion" on disarmament and the factors that limited the peace movement's influence. Its failure reflects the reality that disarmament was a political and not a moral problem that was driven by the efforts of stronger states to impose and maintain what revisionists later viewed as an unacceptable international status quo.

Little wonder, therefore, that Hans Morgenthau, then still at the University of Kansas, praised it as the definitive history of the movement, written by an author with a "rare gift" for "systematic analysis of political problems." Its main argument was one he said he had tried to make "for almost fifteen years." He was presumably referring to his 1929 Munich PhD thesis and possibly his unpublished "On the Origins of the Political in the Nature of Man," which he wrote the next year in Geneva.[15] Her most thoughtful critic, William Arnold-Forster, a British progressive and advocate of disarmament, said she had failed to analyze sufficiently the underlying forces that fueled increasing arms production in the 1890s, notably the rise of imperialism. Du Bois also criticized her for failing to adopt his own view of economic imperialism as the real cause of the peace movement's failure.[16] Tate was finishing a draft of the highly praised follow-up study, *The United States and Armaments* (1948), which extended her analysis through World War II, when Bunche turned her down for a position in political science.

Her work took a dramatic turn following a 1950–1951 Fulbright year in India, where she taught geopolitics at Nobel Prize winner Rabindranath Tagore's Visva-Bharati ("World") College in West Bengal. The U.S. soft power offensive in Cold War Asia opened up lecture opportunities for her across Southeast Asia, and as Tate would later recall, she "got interested in the Pacific, American imperialism in the Pacific you see, [a] huge topic." Nonetheless the first manuscript she drafted during her 1957 sabbatical year dealt with the expansionism of Australia and New Zealand, especially its legacy of abduction and enslavement of Melanesians. She reworked the study multiple times over the next decade, ultimately turning the one volume into two, but failed to secure a contract from an academic press. C. E. Carrington, the world's leading expert on commonwealth relations at the Royal Institute of International Affairs, who vetted her 1961 Rockefeller Foundation proposal, argued that Tate had identified a question—the partition of the Pacific—of fundamental importance, not least because the consequences were still with us, "comparable with . . . the much more familiar partition of Africa." Her analytical lens was wider than that employed by most experts in Australia and New Zealand. Likewise the anonymous New Zealand specialist who reviewed a late version of the manuscript emphasized the "prodigious amount of work" that Tate had done and her unique conceptualization of the topic. However, her own thesis advisor, Payson Wild, who had moved from Harvard to become the vice-president of Northwestern, thought a historical work on imperialism in the Pacific had little value for the field of international relations in the United States in the 1960s.[17]

A tenacious researcher and indefatigable writer, by 1960, Tate had produced large parts of another massive draft manuscript on America's imperial turn in Hawaii, together with a score of articles on great power diplomacy in the Pacific, missionaries and their role in the U.S. eclipse of Great Britain in Hawaii, the relationship between slavery and the debate on U.S. annexation, and the effects of nuclear weapons testing in the South Pacific. She relied on the research assistance of her graduate student Fadela Foy and grants from Howard's president, the Rockefeller Foundation, the American Council of Learned Societies, and the *Washington Evening Star*. By 1959, she had broken out of the confines of Howard's *Journal of Negro Education* to place the first of a number of articles in *Political Science Quarterly* and (in 1960) the *Pacific Historical Review*. She was also asked to join the programming committee for the 1963 meeting of the American Historical Association; at the annual meeting that year, she chaired a session on diplomatic history. Tate's editor worked with her to pare down her manuscript, which was published as *The United States and the Hawaiian Kingdom*, a surprise best-selling book of 1965–1966 for Yale University Press (along with *The Papers of Benjamin Franklin*, she liked to brag). She reworked the excised chapters for *Hawaii: Reciprocity or Annexation* (1968), in which she engaged critically with economic determinist explanations of the crisis leading to the 1893 "revolution."[18]

Considering Tate's outpouring of scholarship from the mid-1950s through the 1960s as a whole, we see her working simultaneously in two analytical styles that scholars today treat as successive, somewhat antagonistic historiographical movements (or moments). First, her accounts of the clash of rival great and subimperial powers in the Pacific place her among the few scholars of the 1950s who studied empire and the United States as an imperial power (Wisconsin's William Appleman Williams is the most famous example). Tate drew on her training at Oxford and at Harvard, where she studied international relations with Fred Schuman. As we have seen, imperialism remained the central problem of world order for her colleagues at Howard too, and for the Indian and other South Asian intellectuals she engaged with in the 1950s.

Second, Tate's work presaged what a later generation offered up as a corrective, under the rubrics of "internationalism" or "transculturalism" or "cosmopolitanism," to histories of great power rivalries over one or another region.[19] Those calling for studies of missionaries and mining firms in the 1980s had no idea that Tate had worked this vein decades earlier. She produced two more manuscripts on railways and the mining sector (what she called "the sinews and arteries of empire") in Africa based on research trips in the 1970s. She drafted them during her last years at Howard and after her retirement in 1977. They were never published.

Tate's time in India influenced her research program, obviously, but it also reshaped her understanding of race as a universally valid analytical category. Her work thus departed from the essentialism that substituted for knowledge of (let alone empathy with) diverse peoples and regions. This shift can be gauged, for example, by her critique in the *Journal of Negro Education* of Richard Wright's exaggerated color consciousness in his reports of the Asian African conference at Bandung, although, as we have seen, he was hardly alone in imagining that Egyptians, Iranians, Indians, and Chinese identified themselves as fellow "colored" or "darker" races. The difference can also be gauged by comparing her work in the late 1950s and 1960s with her early 1942 essay on the war's impact on the "darker peoples of the world," which predicted a future world race war; the book she proposed to write on the "white man's blunders"; or her first review in the *Journal of Negro Education* of Krishnalal Shridharani's *Warning to the West* (1943), which Shridharani wrote to shatter the illusion of white supremacy. Decades later Tate recalled her time in Santiniketan the way Locke remembered Paris: "That period that I spent in India, I felt more like a human being, valued for my worth than any time in my life."[20]

After reading her papers and, more crucially, those of her longtime department chair, Rayford Logan, one can't help but think that Tate was reflecting not only on her experiences as a black person living in the United States and England but also as a woman teaching at Howard. Her outspokenness about gender discrimination at the university helped earn her a reputation as a "personality problem."[21] As one of Howard's most productive scholars in the arts and sciences and a recipient of honorary degrees from Western Michigan (1952), Morgan State (1968), Bowie State (1977), and Lincoln University (1978), she never believed that she was paid what she deserved.

More than that, she also had to endure working under an increasingly hostile, vindictive, even paranoid Logan. From the time she was hired in the 1940s through her return from India in 1951, Logan had signaled his support and respect for her scholarship, organizing abilities, and "meticulous" fulfillment of obligations in many ways. He and his wife had even hosted her bon voyage party, but their cordial, first-name-basis relationship turned poisonous in 1955 (the reasons remain unclear). He began to catalogue her seemingly unreasonable requests for course relief, better teaching times, and the like in his diary. She might have hoarded office supplies or complained that the administration treated the history department worse than the physics department. This is all the routine business of an academic department and the source of headaches for department heads anywhere. Yet in Logan's mind Tate had turned "insufferable." She was a "damn bitch."[22]

The squabbling and Logan's petty requitals continued for years. He interrogated graduate students about her behavior. The epithets grew uglier. Sympathy for Tate was unconscionable, he claimed. Didn't those who considered him to be unjustly "persecuting" Tate (although doing little to stop him) realize that it reinforced her "behaving like a goddamn fool"?[23] This downward spiral in dignity reached its depressing nadir in 1964 when Tate was attacked and stabbed by a teenager in the yard of her Perry Street home. In his diary, Logan called Tate a "pathological liar," believing she had made up the incident (the "alleged" and "miraculous" attack, the "fantastic" story) to grab the headlines. He ignored her letter for help in organizing Howard students for a blood drive. Instead, local Radcliffe alumnae stepped in. It was far from Logan's shining hour, and he resigned as chair soon after (which at least rid him temporarily of the "monster.").[24]

Her relations inside the department doubtless improved during her last ten years, particularly after Lorraine A. Williams moved from head of the social sciences department to chair of history in 1970.[25] Williams committed some of the department's resources to assembling a volume of Tate's essays, which was published as *Diplomacy in the Pacific* (1973). Tate agreed to donate her papers to Howard in 1974 and created the Merze Tate Fund in history in 1977, having already endowed scholarships at Radcliffe and programs, including a center, at Western Michigan, where she had studied as an undergraduate.[26] She retired still believing that she had not gotten the recognition and the salary she deserved, and in 1990 she gave $1 million not to Howard but to Western Michigan. The effects of her outlier status there—a woman, decidedly not a radical, who joined the faculty as the era of Locke, Bunche, Logan, and Frazier was coming to an end, whose cosmopolitanism was out of step with developments in black thought, who did not write about her own "race," and who played no role in "the movement"—linger. Accounts of pioneering black PhDs in the political science profession omit her name.[27] Forty years after the Moorland-Spingarn Research Center began to receive her papers and fifteen years after her death, her archive, including all her unpublished manuscripts, was still unprocessed when I consulted it, a jumble of papers in a mass of boxes stored off site. At least one scholar had been denied access to them shortly before I visited Howard in 2009. I was luckier.

Fables of the Reconstruction

In 1969, McGeorge Bundy, the head of the Ford Foundation who had served as John F. Kennedy's national security advisor, announced the first of a total of $15 million in grants to support black studies in the United States, which he heralded as a means to diversify curricula, faculties, and students on the nation's campuses. It was a response to a student movement that had gone beyond protests over the war and was demanding the transformation of the racist university order in the name of self-determination or black power. Some departments, disciplines, and professional associations experienced tremendous change in the next decades, both in terms of the subjects worthy of investigation and the closely correlated rise in the numbers of African Americans entering the ranks of graduate students and faculty. Other disciplines, including international relations, remained largely insulated from the battle for black studies or successfully headed off the insurgency.

For a few years, George Shepherd Jr., the onetime executive secretary of the American Committee on Africa who founded *Africa Today*, headed a Ford-funded Center for International Race Relations at the University of Denver's new Graduate School of International Studies. Founded in

1969, the center focused on "the role of race in comparative and international systems." Race and ethnic conflicts were on the rise globally, while the handful of works addressing the issues, for example by Harold Isaacs, were by "scholarly observers of international relations" rather than by "the pacesetters in the field." Shepherd partnered with a recent Denver PhD in international relations, Tilden LeMelle, one of the leaders of the insurgency in African studies, and the two men promised to "apply analytical tools to the study of race in world affairs" and thus bring it into a mainstream of "modelbuilders, theoreticians, and textbook writers" *for the first time*, a claim that could only be made out of ignorance of the history we have reconstructed at great length here. The highly praised, agenda-setting volume included essays by two of the discipline's newest "standard bearers," James Rosenau and Karl Deutsch. Deutsch's essay was a tour de force. He outlined how racism might work to buttress monopoly privilege at local, national, and global scales. He chided his colleagues for failing to investigate the myriad dimensions of the problem and designing credible remedies—for example, by identifying and nurturing African American genius (instead of denying its possibility) and paying reparations to the victims of apartheid.[28] While producing a flurry of conference proceedings, working papers, and books between 1969 and 1973, the center served as a locus for Shepherd's longtime, continuing work on apartheid in South Africa.[29] LeMelle, though, quit within two years and returned east as a professor of black and Puerto Rican studies at Hunter College. Shepherd stepped down as director of the center in 1972, after only three years. Jamaica-born Locksley Edmondson, a theorist of racism and world politics, who was teaching Africana studies at Cornell, took over for a year. He was followed by Denver sociologist John Grove, but the school's dean closed the center in 1976. This was an unusually short life span for an institution of this kind.[30]

Now imagine a young scholar two decades later trying to make sense of her discipline's silence about race and racism. By the 1990s, black enrollments in PhD programs in all branches of political science had declined, African Americans were all but invisible in international relations, and they were missing entirely from "the literature" as it was taught at the leading East and West Coast institutions.[31] Roxanne Lynn Doty turned to the work of Denver's center, when the academic ancestors seemingly first considered the role of race in world politics, to ground her own analysis.[32] Others have followed in her wake, seeking to bring racism and hierarchy back into focus, but their work isn't taught in the graduate field seminars at Harvard, Princeton, Columbia, Stanford, Chicago, Yale, Berkeley, Michigan, and MIT.

In the early 2000s, in contrast, in the run up to and in the wake of the U.S. "unilateral intervention" in Iraq, many of the leading names in international relations at those very institutions began to consider the question of empire and imperialism once more, in the pages of *Foreign Affairs*, the successor to the *Journal of Race Development* and in *Orbis*, the journal that Strausz-Hupé founded, among other places. Two young and ambitious theorists, Daniel H. Nexon and Thomas Wright, seized the opportunity in "What's at Stake in the Empire Debate" to elevate the discourse and think more generally about hierarchy in international relations. Surprisingly, "mainstream international relations analysts" had done little, they said, since Michael Doyle published *Empires* in 1986.[33] Doyle, a leader of the discipline, teaches at Columbia now, the school that Burgess built, where Parker Moon, who inspired the young Harold Isaacs, wrote *Imperialism and World Politics*, which was reprinted multiple times through the 1960s. Doyle trained at Harvard in a department that had pioneered in the study of colonial administration, the same one that trained Du Bois, Bunche, and Tate. He was at Princeton for years, where Buell finished the first of his many works on imperialism and tried to build the first center for interracial relations. Yet Doyle wrote as if he had stumbled upon a vast undeveloped land that was waiting for his theory building to begin.

He took his lead from Lord Hailey, the British colonial official whom Buell had known personally and whose ideas about preservation of empire were the foil for the Howard school theorists during World War II. "Imperialism is not a word for scholars," Hailey said as one way of delegitimizing such critics as Ralph Bunche and George Padmore in the debate about the future of the colonies. Doyle repeated the claim uncritically, if not blindly: "Imperialism was not in the mainstream of scholarly literature on world politics" in 1940, he wrote.[34] He never said what precisely the mainstream was when Fred Schuman's 1933 textbook was being read by undergraduates enrolling in ever larger numbers as the war began or when Klaus Knorr arrived at Princeton with others from Yale and took over the directorship of the transplanted Center for International Studies, which Doyle headed for a while in the 1990s. Knorr had completed his dissertation on comparative colonial policy at Chicago in 1941. A great deal of intellectual, cultural, and ideological work would have to be done to construct an identity for the discipline that Knorr's successor and many others in American international relations take for granted now.

Conclusion
The High Plane of Dignity and Discipline

> The theorists may not have been very good but they were certainly no worse than anyone else.
>
> —Carl Kaysen quoted in Kuklick, *Blind Oracles*.

The amnesia about a discipline's (and thus a society's) long entanglement with race and empire extends beyond the work of the Howard school theorists, obviously. To dismiss the scholarship of whites as a catalog of errors and wrong turns on the way to our illustrious present is to succumb to one more illusion. As Charles Lindblom, a former president of the American Political Science Association, concluded, while some political scientists believe themselves to be engaged in "scientific inquiry" the enterprise is better understood as an "endless debate."[1]

A Better Tomorrow, Tomorrow

Consider the case of Leonard Woolf, the influential member of the Bloomsbury group, founder of the Hogarth Press, and husband of Virginia. He also mattered to the course of international relations theory in the 1920s through his works on war, international government, the mandates, and imperialism. Writing in the *Journal of International Relations* in 1921, Harry Elmer Barnes judged Woolf's *Empire and Commerce in Africa: A Study of Economic Imperialism* (1920) as "a contribution to the literature of cardinal importance."[2] Woolf's sharp questioning of the mercantilist underpinnings of imperialism and of the high-minded, self-denying principles in which such policies came wrapped has lost none of its force. "The State, enthroned in its impersonality and a glamour of patriotism, can always make a wilderness and call it peace, or make a conquest and call it civilization."

Another of his important contributions has gone unrecognized until now. Decades before the post–World War II realists began to identify the ancient Greek historian Thucydides as one of their own, Woolf introduced a discussion of the Melian dialogue in Thucydides's *History of the Peloponnesian War* ("the strong do what they can") for the first time in an international relations journal in order to lay bare the struts and bolts of hierarchy. That is, the Athenians described a world divided in two. In one, principles, rights, and ethics applied. In the other, people were ruled through coercion. The full quotation matters:

> For ourselves, we shall not trouble you with specious pretenses—either of how we have a right to our empire because we overthrew the Mede, or are now attacking you because of wrong that you have done us—and make a long speech which would not be believed; and in return we hope that you, instead of thinking to influence us by saying that you did not join the Spartans, although their colonists, or that you have done us no wrong, will aim at what is feasible, holding in view the real sentiments of us both; since you know as well as we do that right, as the world goes, is only in question between equals in power, while the strong do what they can and the weak suffer what they must.[3]

In *Empire and Commerce*, Woolf advanced the idea that trusteeship was a means by which the right and law that governed one-quarter of the world might be extended in the face of the weakness of subject races and the relentless press of investors competing to control raw materials, utilities, and so forth in the colonies and dependencies. The "European state," he hoped, would be "changed from an instrument of economic exploitation into an instrument of good government and progress, not for a few hundred white men but for the millions of Africans."[4]

The rhetorical power of that dream of a "better tomorrow, tomorrow" (in Stephen Colbert's words) has lost none of its force a century later. Barack Obama insisted on as much to those assembled for the first U.S.-Africa Leaders Summit in the summer of 2014:

> As President, I've made it clear that the United States is determined to be a partner in Africa's success—a good partner, an equal partner, and a partner for the long term. We don't look to Africa simply for its natural resources; we recognize Africa for its greatest resource, which is its people and its talents and their potential. We don't simply want to extract minerals from the ground for our growth; we want to build

genuine partnerships that create jobs and opportunity for all our peoples and that unleash the next era of African growth. That's the kind of partnership America offers.[5]

While Woolf had high hopes 100 years ago for the new League of Nations' mandate system, historian Rayford Logan posed some sharp questions, as we saw. The vaunted new thinking about "sacred trusts" at Versailles in 1919 and all such institutions intended to redress the wrongs of colonialism reflected the same principles that were advanced while European powers were carving up Africa at the Berlin Conference in 1884–1885.[6] Evictions, forced labor, peonage, and political disfranchisement continued in the African (and Pacific) mandates, as Logan, Buell, and others showed, with only slight differences (if any) from what was happening in other colonies.[7] In 1929, a British Labour government passed a Colonial Development Act, with much fanfare, to end the exploitation and neglect of so-called colored races after a first postwar decade fixated on the increased exploitation of raw materials. Unfortunately, the 1929 act served primarily to encourage increased British exports and reduce unemployment at home.[8] "Reform" turned out to mean "more of the same."

Widespread labor unrest in the Caribbean on the eve of World War II led to the addition of "Welfare" to the title of the old act and the creation of a joint Anglo-American Caribbean Commission for which Howard's Eric Williams served as consultant and, later, director of research. With each emendation and extension beyond Trinidad in 1945, 1950, and after, there was, as we saw, an intellectual middle*woman*, in this case, Margery Perham, who was ready to work up an article for *Foreign Affairs* that acknowledged past failures. Despite such missteps, the postwar Labour Party government would guide the empire's "partners" safely on their long, steep climb toward self-government and away from the cliff edge the "doctrinaire emancipator" would lead the colonized to.[9]

Logan's solution to the problem of the ever receding horizon of self-determination entailed mobilizing the NAACP and kindred organizations behind the transfer of authority over all existing colonies and dependencies to a new, upgraded mandate administration. He also insisted that commission members include actual subject peoples. Instead, the UN Trusteeship Council created at San Francisco in 1945, where Ralph Bunche relaunched his career, would "supervise" only eleven B class and C class mandates-turned-trusts out of the eighty or so colonies and dependencies around the world. The members of the council were the administering powers—the UK, France, Belgium, New Zealand, Australia, and the United States (the occupying power in Micronesia and a few other Pacific islands)—and an equal number of nonadministering UN members. Logan concluded that the darker races had been betrayed once more.

Did the new trusteeship administration make a difference? We can't say with any certainty. The reality is that Somaliland, Togoland, Tanganyika, Ruanda-Urundi, Samoa, and other trusts opted for "premature" independence around 1960 in lock step with national liberation movements and other agents of what Harold Isaacs called "the great continental rearrangement" and the "end of white supremacy in the world."[10] To my knowledge, no one has since gone back to compare the administration of trust and nontrust territories in the decade or so before the passage of UN's Declaration on the Granting of Independence to Colonial Countries and Peoples in December 1960.

The precise date matters because with the rush to decolonize thereafter and the passage of time, not to mention the kinds of prejudices we have been exploring throughout this book, it is conventional now to imagine the Trusteeship Council's mission as that of guiding the "transition to independence." Yet as we have seen, the council's founding officials considered such a future extremely unlikely.[11] The debate, to the extent that there was one, was still between those who explained the unfolding catastrophe as a result of the limited capacities of black peoples and those who emphasized empire's raison d'être: maximum exploitation at minimal cost.

If anything, Bunche, who headed the UN's Trusteeship Division that was the precursor to the UN Trusteeship Council, grew more, not less, pessimistic about the prospects for independence for much of Africa. The trustee powers themselves, with the exception of New Zealand, all abstained from the 1960 declaration with South Africa, which had refused to transfer its own mandate over what is now Namibia. Fifty years later, a handful of scholars began to agitate for the resurrection of the only recently mothballed UN trusteeship apparatus. Palau gained its independence in 1994 although the U.S. Department of Interior still oversees federal programs there. For some, refitting the trusteeship system is the answer to the problem of "rogue states" and "state failures" in Cambodia, East Timor, Kosovo, Sierra Leone, and elsewhere. For others, it is a humane alternative to the destruction the United States wrought in Iraq in 2003. All these advocates of "neotrusteeship," though, conjure a past that never actually existed.[12]

The subsequent waves of Cold War and post–Cold War history writing, theory building, and identity crafting have contributed to making that imagined past seem plausible to otherwise smart people today. We saw Ed Earle, the Institute of Advanced Studies' resident "re-imagineer," make the case for Wilson as a true balance-of-power realist, although his revisionism never gained traction. Instead, today, Wilson is cast as the dreamer of self-determination and inspirer of independence movements in Africa and Asia.[13] These "liberal internationalist" fables assume that the meaning of the concept of self-determination between then and now is fixed. They exaggerate its place at the Paris Peace Conference. They ignore the fundamentals of the political science of the day that were advanced by Wilson himself, Princeton's most famous political scientist, concerning the differing capacity of races to comprehend or move toward "self-government." Today's liberal internationalists plug in a ready-made story instead of seriously interrogating indigenous ideas of freedom circulating in Cairo, Delhi, Shanghai, and Mecca. That tale always assumes faith in the transparent and honest sentiments of one or another U.S. visionary (Wilson in 1919, Roosevelt in 1942 with the Atlantic Charter, Truman in 1948 during the run-up to the partitioning of Palestine, Eisenhower in 1956 after the Suez Crisis, Kennedy in 1961 with his "embrace" of "non-alignment," and so on). The tale inevitably ends with disenchantment. That story reflects deeply held prejudices in western international relations theory about what John Hobson calls the "derivative" or defective agency of so-called nonwhite or nonwestern peoples.[14]

When U.S. identity was "recoded" in international relations theory during World War II, the discipline turned its back on the analyses of the "new imperialism" of the 1920s. The turn was akin to the hastened recoding of Germany during World War I from exemplary "Teutonic constitutional" democracy to corrupt autocracy at home and from reformist liberal imperial power to brutish exploiters abroad, in Africa. Scholarship on imperialism in the interwar years propelled the careers of young white international relations scholars, including Harry Barnes, Leslie Buell, Ed Earle, Leland Jenks, Parker Moon, and Quincy Wright.[15] By the 1940s, the study of American imperialism had been abandoned and the Cold War's leading international relations theorist, Hans Morgenthau, limited his discussion of the Caribbean in *Politics among Nations* (1948) to a paragraph or two on the U.S. acquisition of the Virgin Islands from Denmark in 1917.[16]

The record since that time affords many opportunities to gauge the seeming impossibility of reconciling the theory with the practice of the civilizing mission or of its cognate, race development that J. A. Hobson, the advocate for enlightened imperialism, first identified in 1902. I have discussed two such cases. (In any such effort, it's important to keep in mind that after 1950 or so, the modifier "race" was dropped in favor of "economic" or "political" development and that "development" has since given way to "modern nation-building."[17]) The first case is that of Harold Isaacs, who compared the lofty ideals of the Truman administration and Point IV aid with the brutal record of U.S. imperialism in Asia. This was the last time Isaacs deployed the imperialism concept. After that, he began a political twelve-step program at the Hoover Institution and from there, he joined MIT's Center for International Studies. The incoming Kennedy administration tacitly acknowledged the reactionary nature of U.S. foreign policy in the 1950s. The new president called for recalibrating relationships, recognizing nationalism and not confusing it with communism, and embracing guided independence in Africa.

The second case is the brutal escalation of the war in Vietnam that key Center for International Studies mandarins and Harvard Kennedy School builders championed. As Bruce Kuklick shows in *Blind Oracles*, even those who began to rethink their support for the war kept their doubts to themselves, particularly with the growth of the New Left on campuses across the country. Kuklick details how Ernest May and others identified the radical revisionist historians and sociologists of the Cold War and their studies of economic imperialism as a threat to the "professional authority" of mainstream international relations scholars and argued that the danger needed to be contained.[18] Leaders of the stillborn insurgency in political science have a hard time recalling a single young international relations scholar in the forefront of their movement that backed the failed bid of the 66-year-old Hans Morgenthau for the presidency of the American Political Science Association in 1970. International relations scholars are conspicuous by their absence, too, from the compendia and other artifacts of the era, such as *The End of Political Science* (1970), the San Francisco Marxist collectivist journal *Kapitalstate*, and so on.

The decades since the early 1970s are littered with the promises by one U.S. administration (and its scholarly auxiliaries) after another that American policy would empower democrats and indigenous entrepreneurs instead of the dictators, oligarchs, and crony capitalist allies of the preceding administration.[19] In the region I know best, the Middle East, the George W. Bush administration spoke of the failures of his forerunners to advance the democratic nation building that was finally under way in Iraq under U.S. tutelage after 2003.[20] Nonetheless, in Cairo in May 2011, President Obama ostensibly opened a "new chapter" in U.S. diplomacy in support of "self-determination" after "decades of accepting the world as it is in the region."[21] You get the picture.

Across the White Meridian

It is hard for readers today to accept the idea that race or the color line is where academic ancestors located the "international" in international relations.

It shouldn't be. After all, the first U.S. Christian missionary association, the American Board of Commissioners of *Foreign* Missions, sent its agents to India, Hawaii, China, and Tennessee, among the Cherokee in the 1820s and 1830s. However, missionaries couldn't settle in the Black Belt; it was illegal for slaves to read and write.[22] Nonetheless, as we saw, Aframerica was in essence just one more "case" for assessing the laws of race development and their limits in an era when white supremacy began to encounter sustained challenges to its preferred world order in the 1920s. Thus I suggested some grounds for rethinking the genealogy of the idea of the "internal colony," a mainstay of 1960s and 1970s theory that critics of black separatist thought blamed on a misguided despair and problematic readings of Lenin.[23]

Ralph Bunche opposed Garvyism and its "back to Africa" call. He also rejected the so-called Black Belt thesis, including the chimera of pursuing independence in some southern territory (where white international relations theorists and statesmen nonetheless proposed to apply lessons learned in the study of colonial rule in Africa). Let's not confuse the Bunche of the "American Creed" and recipient of a Boy Scouts of America Silver Buffalo Award (1951) with the agitator and small "c" communist who joined the Howard faculty in 1929. For him and the other Howard radicals, world-wide black liberation would come only through a working-class alliance and anti-capitalist revolution. They got that one wrong. We should also acknowledge that Marcus Garvey, leader of the trans-Atlantic black mass movement that seemingly confirmed political scientists in their beliefs about races and world politics, got at least one argument right about what we might now call the "international decolonization regime" in U.S. domestic politics. African Americans would not be free unless and until Africans were free. Garvey first made this argument in the 1920s.[24] In the 1950s and 1960s it became a mainstay of policy analysis, by Isaacs most notably, and, two decades later, it was rediscovered by students of "Cold War civil rights."

One of Bunche's arguments in *A World View of Race* stands the test of time. He argued that racism served as a remarkably productive device for the imperialist. I have traced the idea back to Locke and Du Bois, identifying it as a central tenet of Howard school theory when most white international relations theorists clung to the seeming truths of the science of dominance and subjugation. At the same time, I was unable to find any white international relations scholar other than Fred Schuman who confronted this uncomfortable truth head on in his writings in the 1930s. The story is different after World War II, when the "biological myth" that races are real came under attack and, as we saw, scientific racists in the discipline took to conspiracy theories to explain the seeming eclipse of reason among liberals.

I also traced the lingering effects of the previous decades of theorizing about race and international relations in the renewed predictions of race war in the 1960s by politicians and pundits. We can also turn to memoirs, diaries, and biographies of the policymakers and grand strategists with which international relations theory is centrally concerned, to gauge the persistence of the belief in the biological basis of hierarchy through the last half of the twentieth century.[25] As President Richard Nixon reportedly told his chief of staff, the inferiority of the black race was real, and he and staff needed to keep abreast of the research that linked race and intelligence. But he felt that he would also have to "do everything possible to deny" these truths publicly lest he stir up "latent prejudice."[26] Meanwhile, those who would trace the rationally deliberative character of the retreat of racism from international relations scholarship (or who believe in the "internal discursive" approach to the history of international relations theory) have their work cut out for them. The debate never happened.

The debate about the applicability of models of empire to the United States after World War II never happened either. What awaits sustained study is the conversion of a Cold War discipline to ideological anticommunism and to the vision of the U.S. state as a "liberal leviathan." Racism and imperialism were among the chief sins committed by both the vanquished German and still-to-be-defeated Soviet totalitarian rivals (although conditions in the American South were a problem for the theory). The few holdouts such as Schuman were denounced and embargoed, suffering a repetition of John Burgess's fate in 1898, when the discipline first took up the cause of U.S. imperialism.

The Resource Curse

The University of Sheffield's John M. Hobson, the great-grandson of one of those progressive imperialists of the 1890s, has done crucial work in demonstrating not just ruptures but, more crucially, continuities in arguments in defense of hierarchy that were in play in the 1920s and remain in play today. One argument that Hobson doesn't spend much time on is the right to secure the resources western civilization needs. We saw Robert Strausz-Hupé and Stefan Possony call for the United States to restore the colonial order in Africa and Asia to ensure western control over "strategic" raw materials. This is precisely the kind of "crackpot realism" that sociologist C, Wright Mills said in 1958 was the stock in trade of the new national security scholars.

The 1973 oil crisis spurred the creation of an entirely new field of alleged expertise in "energy and security," represented by such stalwarts as Daniel

Yergin, a Cambridge University PhD and the founder of Cambridge (Massachusetts) Energy Research Associates; Melvin Conant, who went from studying race in the 1950s to working for Exxon and then teaching at the National War College; and Stephen Krasner, a Stanford professor and a senior fellow at the Hoover Institution. The Foreign Policy Research Institute in Philadelphia keeps alive the memory of Possony's chief patron, Robert Strausz-Hupé, who did more than anyone else to make geopolitics a respectable part of the Cold War intellectual arsenal. Self-taught "geostrategist" Robert Kaplan serves as one of its advisory board members now. As Hobson shows, the arguments in Kaplan's *The Coming Anarchy: Shattering the Dreams of the Post Cold War* (2000) and *The Revenge of Geography: What the Map Tells Us about Coming Conflicts and the Battle against Fate* (2012) are unselfconscious updates of the ideas of the *Journal of Race Development*'s Ellsworth Huntington and others. Arguments about hierarchy and fears about resource scarcity remain difficult if not impossible to pry apart.

In the wake of the September 11, 2001, attacks on the Twin Towers and the Pentagon, Kaplan held up Samuel Philips Huntington as a visionary of the world "as it really looks."[27] Critiques of Huntington's prophecy in his *The Clash of Civilizations and the Remaking of World Order* (1996) are legion. It is sufficient to note three points. Each generation of believers in the truth of the immutability of races (then) or civilizations (now) appear to think it is enough to repeat the mantra that racists such as Jan Smuts and T. Lothrop Stoddard taught their disciples in the 1920s. The mantras say that we aren't talking "superiority and inferiority"; we are only talking "difference." Here Huntington, who launched his career with the support of the Social Science Research Council's successor committee, closely resembles both Stefan Possony and T. Lothrop Stoddard and is as unconvincing as they were. We saw Alain Locke take on these fictive ideas about races, cultures, and civilizations back in the 1920s, although no one appears to remember that now. Huntington would have appeared quite familiar to Locke in another respect: Locke dedicated much of his work to debunking the taken-for-granted idea that Africa had no real civilization. After divining the identity of the world's seven civilizations (western, Confucian, Japanese, Islamic, Hindu, Slavic, and Latin American), Huntington famously hedged his bets by positing an eighth, "possibly African" one.[28]

Beyond Ikenberry and toward the End of Hierarchy

Although he anticipated Gunnar Myrdal's interpretation of the American creed by a decade or two, Locke would have a harder time with its recent, wholly unconvincing extension to the U.S.-dominated world order. Princeton's G. John Ikenberry argues that the particular liberal characteristics of American hegemony best explain its durability. He describes the American Century as a restrained and penetrated order, in the senses that other states (Great Britain, France) have an unusual degree of voice in American domestic politics and that over time institutions (NATO, GATT) came to lock in the partners. He contrasts this liberal settlement—that is, the creation of a new order after World War II—with the containment order (or settlement) vis-à-vis the Soviet Union.

What is remarkable in this account of world politics is the complete disappearance of what were once known as the inferior races. Thinkers such as Mahan, Bryce, and Adams, whom Ikenberry describes as the original intellectual sources of American liberal hegemony, were, as we saw, among the country's great racial supremacists, and his account rehabilitates—doubtless unselfconsciously—an ex-Herrenvolk U.S. democracy's ruling ideas. It is probably unselfconscious too about its embrace of international inequality, the missing third "postcolonial" settlement. One has to read these works carefully to realize that the rules of liberal hegemony apply to industrialized states only. True, Ikenberry writes,

> the United States has pursued imperial policies, especially toward weak countries in the periphery. *But U.S. relations with Europe, Japan, China, and Russia cannot be described as imperial, even when "neo" or "liberal" modifies the term.* The advanced democracies operate within a "security community" in which the use or threat of force is unthinkable. Their economies are deeply interwoven. Together, they form a political order built on bargains, diffuse reciprocity, and an array of intergovernmental institutions and ad hoc working relationships.[29]

What is a paradox for Ikenberry, as it was for Louis Hartz before him when he surveyed the American liberal tradition to the "water's edge," is better understood as a constitutive feature of the contemporary world order. The fact of hierarchy doesn't trouble a current generation that, like the ones before, sees it as natural or is unable or unwilling to see it at all. The more one emphasizes the essentially consensual dimensions of U.S. hegemony, the easier it is to see some of the basic and contrasting institutions and norms that apply outside what Karl Deutsch called the North Atlantic security community, which was bound, nonetheless, according to Stanley Hoffman, by its white racial identity. Decades later, others began to describe the league of alleged freedom-loving, English-speaking peoples without irony as the Anglosphere.[30]

As we have seen, the archives reveal what amounts to a lost world of international relations scholarship buried under the "schools of strategy" built in the 1950s and 1960s. That history bears scant resemblance to the stories told in field seminars in seminar rooms every semester, where professional identities are continuously remade. These myths have a strong hold over the U.S. profession, and the U.S. profession was and arguably still is hegemonic across the Anglosphere.[31]

Drawing on the typology of intellectual fields produced in the 1980s by organizational sociologist Richard Whitley, Ido Oren says that for decades international relations typified a "polycentric oligarchy" in which leaders of the two competing schools, realist and liberal, exerted market power over scarce reputation-making resources. (He also believes that it is moving—funeral by funeral, retirement by retirement—in the direction of a less rigid, "fragmented adhocracy.")[32] Yet some of the characteristic forms of exclusion that mark the discipline in the United States today have little if anything to do with the so-called paradigm war. So, even if the so-called war is winding down, a more open and cosmopolitan profession is unlikely. Radical or Marxist thinkers, journals, and debates disappeared from reading lists and practitioner histories decades ago. The intellectual nationalism as revealed in survey courses, author lists, journal article rosters, and the birthplaces of the research faculty of the major departments reinforces the effect. I lack Oren's confidence about the gradual process of generational change.

Indeed, international relations research faculty across the United States are not likely to introduce graduate students to the arguments and thinkers of what MIT professor Lincoln Bloomfield once referred to as the "militant right" in foreign policy, political economy, and national security studies, and its historical influence within and beyond the discipline goes unrecognized.[33] *Orbis*, originally the militant right's answer to *Foreign Affairs* and *World Politics*, has little standing today, if the routinely cited surveys of the profession are to be believed. Ideological blinders of this kind, together with the effects of time on memory generally, might lead someone reading my discussion of Possony's *The Geography of Intellect* to respond that this particular Washington and specifically Pentagon insider and director of research at the Hoover Institution "was not a major figure in the discipline." Think again. It is also important to note that the militant right leveled a double critique at a discipline-in-reformation: that it was insufficiently aggressive in the face of the communist threat and that the scientists' self-styled "behavioral revolution" in international relations theory was intellectually irresponsible. That attack ultimately led to the creation of rival networks of think tanks, strategic studies associations, and the like. That history also has yet to be written.

The lingering effects of the racism in America that the profession of international relations both reflected and helped advance in the decades when empire was still "a word for scholars" can be gauged in today's departments and schools of international relations. No critical mass of intellectuals of color exists in this sector of the U.S. academy. The work of the Howard school thinkers are not taught. Prejudice can continue to operate unopposed; when a faculty member proposes a next project on regional economic organizations in Africa and the Caribbean, his colleagues will criticize it for a lack of theoretical ambition in comparison to the study of "important places or problems."

The condition is quite possibly permanent. The 1960s, when the black studies revolution broke out on college campuses, was a "critical juncture." Although the insurgency resulted in the partial decolonization of some regions of the humanities and human sciences, international relations today remains a white, mainly male rampart that exhibits routine anxieties about the various threats beyond the walls.

This book is a brief for deepening engagement across the paradoxical interdisciplinary divides in the humanities and social sciences. If I have identified a weak point or two in the intellectual bulwark of the practitioners, exploiting that weakness will depend on the cooperative efforts of critics on the periphery of the discipline and potential allies among scholars within the humanities. The hope is that historians, historical sociologists, and professors of literature, culture, and theory will engage with critical international relations scholarship, beginning with John Hobson's brilliant post-Said genealogy of the varieties of Eurocentrism that haunt international thought in the twenty-first century. His work applies, for instance, to the histories of Anglophone internationalism that nonetheless tend to stop at the edge of the Black Atlantic (and the Black Pacific).[34] Similarly, international theorists in American studies and beyond have much to teach dissidents.[35] Critical scholars in all these fields are well positioned to continue the kind of analysis begun here. The boundaries of international relations theory and in particular work in security studies, "grand strategy," and the study of U.S. foreign policy remain open and ripe for infiltration. Colleagues there should lead their students across the borders of inquiry and, as Louis Menand advises, "take no hostages."[36]

There is no mystery about why the barbarians of cultural studies and the critics of scientific expertise are seen as threats to disciplinary order and subject to embargo as far as possible. Some may accept the revisionist account of the discipline's past presented here but argue that it is an anomaly or exception, as Americans often do about the nation's less-than-perfect past.

The founders have been forgotten for good reason. They seemingly had not yet discovered how to inoculate themselves against the ravages of culture. Needless to say, no such vaccine exists. The history of ideas, institutions, and practices has a constitutive role in their present forms and functions. Just so, critics have exposed the many ways in which deep-rooted commitments to hierarchy continue to inform the discipline and its allied intellectual networks even now.[37] Meanwhile, in the "real world," the subjection continues through new-old policies of intervention, tutelage, and targeted killings in new-old zones of anarchy and civilization deficit. It leads one to ask what other unselfconscious factors of the day distort scholars' understandings, given that so many in the American academy were hypnotized so long by the seeming truths of racism.

NOTES

Preface

1. Koelsch, *Clark University*, 70.

2. Vitalis, "International Studies in America"; and Vitalis, "Birth of a Discipline." For circulation of the journal's origin since then, see, for example, Anderson, *Pursuing Truth, Exercising Power*; Blatt, "'To Bring Out the Best That Is in Their Blood'"; Norton, "Political Science as a Vocation," 69; Lederman, "Anthropological Regionalism," 313; Lowndes, Novkov, and Warren, *Race and American Political Development;* and Tickner, *A Feminist Voyage through International Relations*, 121.

3. William Bundy, "The History of Foreign Affairs," *Foreign Affairs*, 1994, http://www.foreignaffairs.com/about-us/history, accessed October 4, 2014. I presented a short version of the story on a panel on which managing editor (and now editor) of *Foreign Affairs* Gideon Rose also appeared.

4. See Peter Kihss, "Dr. W. E. B. Du Bois Joins Communist Party at 93," *New York Times*, November 23, 1961.

Introduction: A Mongrel American Social Science

1. There are, nonetheless, scholars in international relations in the United States, Canada, Great Britain, Australia, and elsewhere that are critical of the mainstream's ongoing, pervasive preferential option for the powerful and more generally for "the West." See Barkawi and Laffey, "The Postcolonial Moment in Security Studies"; Hobson, "Is Critical Theory Always for the White West and for Western Imperialism?"; and Hobson, *The Eurocentric Conception of World Politics*. For the relationship between Hobson's work and mine, see Vitalis, "A Great-Grandson Breaks New Ground in Critical IR Thought."

2. Around 1998, as I launched this project on recovering the history of black scholars in international relations in an era of segregation, racism, and imperialism, other political scientists were taking up the issue of race in the contemporary era and the discipline's silence about it. They include Roxanne Doty, Siba Grovogui, Errol Henderson, Sankaran Krishna, James Mittleman, Randy Persaud, Robbie Shilliam, Srdjan Vucetic, Rob Walker, and Hilborne Watson. For a comprehensive bibliography and representative example of the state of the art, see Buzas, "Race and International Politics." For the present range of views, see "Confronting the Global Colour Line: Space, Race and Imperial Hierarchy in World Politics," a special issue of the *Cambridge Review of International Affairs* (26, no. 1 [2013]). I intend this and subsequent citations to the secondary literature to be suggestive rather than exhaustive. Interested readers are always one click or one book or article away from the expanded set of references, and we have a lot of ground to cover across the humanities and social sciences.

3. See, however, Singh, *Black Is a Country*.

4. Those who aren't familiar with the signal contributions of Carol Anderson, Brent Edwards, Kevin Gaines, Paul Gilroy, Robin Kelley, Winston James, Susan Pennybacker, Brenda Plummer, Nikhil Singh, and Penny Von Eschen, among others, will find the references and get up to speed on the state of the art in Gore, *Radicalism at the Crossroads*; McDuffie, *Sojourning for Freedom*; Makalani, *In the Cause of Freedom*; and James, *George Padmore and Decolonization from Below*.

5. See Go, *Patterns of Empire*, for a recent standout in the long analytical tradition that international relations has for the most part ignored; Hobson, *The Eurocentric Conception of World Politics*, part II, for the varieties of positions on offer; and Kramer, *Blood of Government*, for an exemplary analysis of the role social scientists played in the occupation of the Philippines.

6. Vitalis, *America's Kingdom*. For a brief discussion of the relationship between *America's Kingdom* and this book, see my "Writing America's Kingdom," http://abuaardvark.typepad.com/qahwa_sada/files/americaskingdom.pdf, accessed July 25, 2014.

7. See, for example, Mills, "Crackpot Realism"; Chomsky, *American Power and the New Mandarins*; and Oren, "The Enduring Relationship between the American (National Security) State and the State of the Discipline," 51–55 for just three of the many influential dissections of the university's relationship to empire. One might also follow Chomsky's many exchanges with political scientists in the 1960s and 1970s in the *New York Review of Books*. For policymakers' views of new model of international relations professors and a likening of their role to that of "shamans," see Kuklick, *Blind Oracles*.

8. Rice studied with Albright's father, Josef Korbel, the founding director of the Center for International Studies at the University of Denver.

9. Zakaria, "The Rise of a Great Power," 1, 3.

10. See, for example, James Traub's review, "'The Right War?' and 'A Matter of Principle': Everybody Is a Realist Now," *New York Times*, October 30, 2005, http://www.nytimes.com/2005/10/30/books/review/30traub.html?pagewanted=all, accessed July 16, 2014. In addition, see Oren, "The Unrealism of Contemporary Realism."

11. Nye, *Bound to Lead*; and Nye, *Soft Power*, which has gone through multiple editions. For the reputational rankings, see Maliniak, Peterson, and Tierney, "Trip around the World." For a dismissal of the consensus view, see Anderson, "Consilium," 119. The *New Left Review* devoted an entire issue to Anderson's two-part analysis of "nonconformist" and "mainstream" foreign policy analysis.

12. Huntington, *The Clash of Civilizations and the Remaking of World Order*.

13. Kuklick, *Blind Oracles*, 40, describes George Kennan, the culturally conservative career diplomat and later "guru of foreign affairs" as the "first intellectual middleman of postwar national security studies."

14. The critique in Waever, "The Sociology of a Not So International Discipline," applied to virtually the entire contents of the 50th-anniversary issue of the journal. Kuklick calls the genre "practitioner histories."

15. I began this project at the same time that Carleton University's Brian Schmidt (PhD State University of New York, Albany, 1995) was completing a dissertation that would become *The Political Discourse of Anarchy*. Twenty years later he leads a small group of exceptional professors of international relations who prove the rule. That is, they have made the history of the discipline and its leading ideas a primary focus of their scholarship (a "subfield"), attending to the problem of historical validity in ways that historians do and moonlighting insiders do not. They include Luke Ashworth, Duncan Bell, John Hobson, David Long, Nicolas Guilhot (the one non–international

relations outlier), and Ido Oren. Their work has been of tremendous value, and this book succeeds in part to the extent that its findings are surprising and yet convincing even to them. Nonetheless, the imagined audience for this book extends beyond them and kindred dissident international relations theorists to diplomatic and intellectual historians, historical sociologists of race and empire, students of interwar internationalism, historians of the social sciences and area studies, humanists in American studies, African American studies, and specialists in black internationalism.

16. Thomas, "'We're Saying the Same Thing,'" 40–41.

17. On the uses and abuses of Thucydides, see Garst, "Thucydides and Neorealism"; Bagby, "The Use and Abuse of Thucydides in International Relations"; and Welch, "Why International Relations Theorists Should Stop Reading Thucydides."

18. To test this claim, browse one of the online syllabus repositories in international relations.

19. Schmidt, *The Political Discourse of Anarchy*, for example, demonstrates that the "first great debate" from which the discipline is said to have emerged never actually occurred. His critic, Ole Waever, is right that the idea nonetheless "has become socially real if historically false"; Waever, "The Sociology of a Not So International Discipline," 692. The idea of "race" is another, even more immutable, biologically false social fact, although there is no convincing those leading what Troy Duster calls "the current march toward a biological reinscription of the concept." Duster, "Race and Reification in Science," 1050–1051.

20. See Moon, *Syllabus on International Relations*; and Ware, *Study of International Relations in the United States*. Both the new International Institute of Education (est. 1919) and the Social Science Research Council (est. 1923) sought to advance the new science in the United States, the latter through its Committee on International Relations. World War I led to increased enrollments in courses devoted to what the post-1898 pioneers at Wisconsin, Chicago, Clark, Harvard, and, above all, Columbia, offered up as a "new" interdisciplinary science, and the objective was to advance teaching and research in the peacetime context of the founding decade of the League of Nations and growing tensions across the color line.

21. Menand, *The Marketplace of Ideas*, 107–117.

22. Ibid., 115. For the effort to secure hegemony, see Guilhot, *The Invention of International Relations Theory*; and the H-Diplo/ISSF Roundtable on Nicolas Guilhot, ed. *The Invention of International Relations Theory: Realism, the Rockefeller Foundation, and the 1954 Conference on Theory* (2011), 3, 5 (November 9, 2011), available as a PDF file at http://h-diplo.org/roundtables/index.html#2011.

23. Since some will consider this an overstatement, let me note, first, that it is a claim about a central tendency and not a report of the result of a polling of the professoriate. I have nonetheless been told more than once that the discipline has resolved the question definitively in the negative. I was told this, second, even as a few card-carrying U.S. members of the American Political Science and International Studies Associations used the occasion of accounts in the press and journals of opinion for and against America's "new" imperial turn in Iraq to weigh in. The rough result was two qualified no answers. One is in Lake, *Hierarchy in International Relations*, which draws in part on earlier formulations and rediscovers what an entire generation took for granted; namely that hierarchy and not anarchy characterizes the world we live in. The other is in Ikenberry, "Illusions of Empire," which affirms the liberal or exceptional nature of U.S. rule. There was one yes response, in Nexon and Wright, "What's at Stake in the American Empire Debate." Motivated readers might further test the claim by examining syllabi repositories to see if these works are included in the syllabi of courses that prepare graduate students for their exams in

the field. They didn't in my department. They are less rather than more likely to do so as Americans imagine the end of such episodes and the pundits turn to debating U.S. "retreat" and "retrenchment."

24. Doyle, *Empires*, 11. See, however, Vitalis, "Birth of a Discipline"; and Barkawi, "Empire and Order in International Relations and Security Studies."

25. I use the Carnegie Corporation grant programs and the Rockefeller Foundation here for convenience while recognizing that the latter in particular emerged out of the amalgamation of a number of different "memorials" during the period with which we are concerned. For background by the sociologist most concerned with the relationship of foundations to international relations as an academic discipline in an era of the rise of global U.S. power, see Parmar, *Foundations of the American Century*.

26. One problem is that until very recently studies of the history of the emerging social science disciplines have failed to consider the new imperialism as a phenomenon that shapes these institutions. See Kramer, "The Pragmatic Empire," 380–383 (revision published as *Blood of Government*), together with my own and other contributions to Long and Schmidt, *Imperialism and Internationalism in the Discipline of International Relations*; and Steinmetz, *Sociology and Empire*, notably the introduction by Steinmetz and Go, "Sociology's Imperial Unconscious," 83–105. Calls for recovering and overcoming the imperialist predisposition of international relations are common abroad. See e.g., Jones, *Decolonizing International Relations*.

27. Stocking's pathbreaking account of neo-Lamarckism in the social sciences, *Race, Culture, and Evolution*, discussed a number of scholars in international relations and articles from the field's *Journal of Race Development*, but Stocking's work on racial science was not linked to theory building in political science and international relations until Hattam, *In the Shadow of Race*; Vitalis, "The Noble American Science of Imperial Relations and Its Laws of Race Development"; and Hobson, *The Eurocentric Conception of World Politics*. Hattam and I are both indebted to Adolph Reed Jr.

28. Compare with the idea that international relations "emerged as a social science relatively late," in the 1930s, at the University of Chicago in Frieden and Lake, "International Relations as a Social Science." Among other ironies, the essay appears in the journal *Annals of the American Academy of Political and Social Science*, where early international relations theorists (not international lawyers) started publishing at the turn of the century.

29. For references to self-determination, see Locke, "Enter the New Negro," 631–634; and "Harlem: Mecca of the New Negro," 629–630.

30. These institutions and publications in turn have not been recognized in histories of international relations until now.

31. Franklin, "Dilemma of the American Negro Scholar," 71. I found the essay by first reading Howard historian Michael Winston's influential "Through the Back Door."

32. If Nancy Cunard, the disowned shipping heiress, anthologist extraordinaire (Locke's copy of her *Negro: An Anthology* (1934) sits in the University of Pennsylvania's rare books room), and George Padmore's collaborator, represents the model race traitor of her time, then interwar-era international relations represents an empty set. However, Locke's papers include correspondence in 1923 with Carl Joachim Friedrich, a future president of both the American Political Science Association and the International Political Science Association. Friedrich was then on a kind of student goodwill tour, had not yet finished his Heidelberg PhD, and was three years away from his original appointment as lecturer at Harvard. Locke had been teaching for over a decade. Yet Friedrich calls the diminutive Locke "my little philosopher" in

recalling a night, I think, at the theater (meanwhile typing "J" for "I" throughout). "You cannot imagine how glad J am about the last evening with You, and J am always carrying around with me the problems of racial sex arisen there. J was surprised to find verified my assertion that a slawic [Slavic?] joung man wouldn't accept the second play at all in hearing the judgment of Palacek about it. Whatever it may be, J am too stupid to understand it, what constitutes these metaphysical differences. Why can't the one people make wonderful music when the other makes beautiful dramas? Why can the one peo[p]le produce merely efficient businessmen when the other produces victorious generals? Are those facts all accidental?" Friedrich to Locke, January 12, 1923, box 30, folder 29, Papers of Alain Leroy Locke, Moorland Spingarn Research Center, Howard University, Washington, D.C. (hereafter Locke Papers).

33. See Frances Buell's unpublished memoir of Corwin, April 1959, box 40, folder 15, Misc., Buell, Frances, 1946–1959, Raymond Leslie Buell Papers, Library of Congress, Washington, D.C. (hereafter Buell Papers LC). Both the *New Yorker* and the *University of Michigan Law Review* turned down the memoir for publication.

34. See Francis Stead Sellers, "The 60-Year Journey of the Ashes of Alain Locke, Father of the Harlem Renaissance," *Washington Post Magazine*, September 12, 2014, http://www.washingtonpost.com/lifestyle/magazine/the-60-year-journey-of-the-ashes-of-alain-locke-father-of-the-harlem-renaissance/2014/09/11/2ea31ccc-2878-11e4-86ca-6f03cbd15c1a_story.html, accessed September 30, 2014.

35. See Gill, "Gramsci and Global Politics," 1; and Gill, "Epistemology, Ontology, and the 'Italian School,'" for the first uses of "Italian school." For its dissemination, see Germain and Kenny, "Engaging Gramsci." For a different and narrower application of the concept to Howard's leading thinkers, see Henry, "Abram Harris, E. Franklin Frazier, and Ralph Bunche."

36. See Toni Morrison's "Black Matters," the first of her three Massey Lectures, in *Playing in the Dark*, 9–10.

37. I am including Tilden LeMelle, who taught at Denver and the City University of New York; Lockesley Edmundson at Cornell; Martin Kilson in the years since his retirement from teaching at Harvard; Neta Crawford at Boston University; Hilbourne Watson, recently retired from Bucknell; and Errol Henderson at Penn State. In addition, see "ISP Forum: Diversity in the International Studies Profession," notably the briefs by Christian Davenport, Brandon Valeriano, Wendy Theodore, and Minion K. C. Morrison.

38. On the parochialism of the U.S. professors in these matters generally, see Alker and Biersteker, "The Dialectics of World Order."

39. Vitalis, "The Graceful and Generous Liberal Gesture."

40. Arnold Rampersad quote from the distributor's publicity materials for the documentary. http://newsreel.org/video/RALPH-BUNCHE.

41. Huggins, "Afro-American Studies: A Report to the Ford Foundation," 29.

42. Tate's research program can hardly be fitted to either tendency or moment—methodological nationalist or global imaginary—in the story black or Africana studies tells about itself, and she has been completely overlooked until recently. Sexism has played a role as well, as we will see.

43. To simplify a little, the first signals a more expansive focus on the reasons for and contemporary conditions of the larger African diaspora, of which African Americans form a part.

44. Biondi, *The Black Revolution on Campus*, 174–180.

45. Wallerstein, "The Unintended Consequences of Cold War Area Studies."

46. Rooks, *White Money/Black Power*.

47. Rojas, *From Black Power to Black Studies*, 3, 21.

48. Biondi, *The Black Revolution on Campus*, 249–253; Rojas, *From Black Power to Black Studies*, 202.

49. Biondi, *The Black Revolution on Campus*, 251.

50. Kelley, "'But a Local Phase of a World Problem.'" Among other signposts and programmatic statements of the shift, this key piece by Kelley appeared in a special issue of the *Journal of American History* titled "The Nation and Beyond: Transnational Perspectives on American History," which is itself evidence that other quadrants of the humanities or human science were busy taking the transnational turn as well.

51. Steinmetz, *Sociology and Empire*, x; Wimmer and Schiller, "Methodological Nationalism and Beyond."

52. Guyer, "Perspectives on the Beginning"; Gershenhorn, *Melville J. Herskovits and the Racial Politics of Knowledge*, 182–187.

53. See Ralph Bunche to Joseph Willits, [Head of the Social Sciences Division,] Rockefeller Foundation, September 15, 1950, box 112, folder Institute of Pacific Relations, Ralph J. Bunche Papers, Charles E. Young Research Library, University of California at Los Angeles (hereafter Bunche Papers). Bunche pressed Willits to aid the Institute of Pacific Relations as it faced charges of abetting the communist takeover of China and/or serving as a communist front. If the latter were remotely true, Bunche would have dissociated himself from it, as he had the Committee on African Affairs. Instead, he was working quietly to save it.

54. Robinson, "Area Studies in Search of Africa"; Robinson, "Ralph Bunche and African Studies"; and Robinson, "Ralph Bunche the Africanist."

55. Payson Wild to Gerald Freund, March 24, 1961, Record Group 1.2, Series 200S, box 522, folder 4459, Rockefeller Foundation Archives, Rockefeller Archive Center, Tarrytown, N.Y. (hereafter Rockefeller Foundation Archives).

56. Other intellectuals, particularly those in African studies and Caribbean studies, those who campaigned against apartheid, and those who founded organizations such as Transafrica, did write cogent analyses of contemporary world affairs for scholarly and movement journals. A good place to start is Minter, Hovey, and Cobb, *No Easy Victories*.

57. *Foreign Affairs* is conventionally categorized and ranked with the discipline's peer-reviewed journals without noting the key difference. In addition it is usually the only non-peer-reviewed journal included on such lists. See, for example, Yoder and Bramlett, "What Happens at the Journal Office Stays at the Journal Office." The authors were unaware of this key difference with the rest of the list (e-mail communication with me), as was I until recently. EBSCO Information Services meanwhile distinguishes between "academic" (that is, those with footnotes) and "scholarly" (peer-reviewed) journals.

58. Langer, *In and Out of the Ivory Tower*, 81.

59. For a complementary account of a moment that deserves more extensive study, see Go, "Sociology's Imperial Unconscious."

60. Gunnell, "Founding of the American Political Science Association," discusses Burgess's eclipse without reference to the imperial adventures that played a key role in provoking the split. For Burgess as a public intellectual, see Nicols, *Promise and Peril.*

61. Fox, "Interwar International Relations Research."

62. Gilman calls "the postwar comparativists" associated with the Social Science Research Council in the early 1950s "the first group of American political scientists to consider non-Western countries worthy of systematic empirical inquiry"; Gilman, *Mandarins of the Future*, 118.

**Part I: The Noble Science of Imperial Relations and
Its Laws of Race Development**

1. See Fairlie, "Politics and Science," 24.

2. Lewis, *Essay on the Government of Dependencies*, v. Lewis was a parliamentarian and prolific writer, friend of John Stuart Mill, among others, who in 1836 began two years of service in Malta on a commission designed to reform the government there. The *Essay* may thus have been influenced by this experience. Under Palmerston he served as chancellor of the exchequer, home secretary, and, finally, war secretary.

3. Quoting from a tribute paid to Burgess by W. Randolph Burgess of the Federal Reserve Bank of New York in an address ostensibly about the Young Plan. He had delivered it at Columbia's Academy of Political Science, which Burgess had founded. See Burgess, "Introductory Remarks," 213.

4. See Long, "Paternalism and the Internationalization of Imperialism"; and Hobson, *The Eurocentric Conception of World Politics*.

Chapter 1: Empire by Association

1. Ireland, "On the Need for a Scientific Study of Colonial Administration," 210.

2. The eight-volume study was never published. Ireland produced two books, *The Far Eastern Tropics* in 1905 and *Province of Burma* in 1907, then reemerged, after a hiatus, in 1914 as the biographer of Joseph Pulitzer.

3. Powers originally trained in and taught romance languages at Wisconsin and then at Oberlin. He returned to Wisconsin to do a year's work in economics and was appointed to a professorship of economics and social science at Smith. He was next hired at Stanford, went abroad again to study economics and social science in Germany, and accepted a chair in economics and social science at Cornell in 1899. As far as I can tell, he never published any work in economics. He resigned his chair in 1902 to found the country's first organization dedicated to study abroad for undergraduates, the Bureau of University Travel, and wrote extensively in the next decades on U.S. history and politics. For background, see *Cornell Alumni News* 6, no. 26 (April 16, 1902), 190.

4. Du Bois, "The Present Outlook for the Dark Races of Mankind." Du Bois used the revised phrase "the problem of the twentieth century is the problem of the color line" in his "Address to the Nations of the World" at the Pan-African Conference in London in July 1900 and again *The Souls of Black Folk* (1903), in the introduction and again in chapter 2.

5. In addition to the papers in volume 18 of *Annals of the American Academy of Political and Social Science*, titled *America's Race Problems*, see Kelsey, "The Negro Farmer." Kelsey, who took up a teaching position at Penn and served as the academy's main expert on African Americans, evoked the Philippines in the introduction to this study of rural sociology, where he wrote that the Republicans were not about to repeat the mistakes made in the South, 5.

6. Herbert, "The Race Problem of the South," 97, 99.

7. Ross, "The Causes of Race Superiority." See http://www.asanet.org/page. ww?name=Edward+A.+Ross&section=Presidents, accessed June 27, 2007. The American Sociological Association biography of Ross was edited following my initial circulation of these materials. It now says that Ross "explored the dimensions of racism" in "Causes of Race Superiority"; see "Edward Alsworth Ross," American Sociological Association, http://www.asanet.org/about/presidents/Edward_Ross. cfm.

8. Du Bois was known to the group around the *Annals* as a result of the year he spent at the University of Pennsylvania working on the project that resulted in the *Philadelphia Negro* (1900). He had already published two pieces in the journal. The record of the 1899 annual meeting noted that Du Bois's paper was regarded by "many present . . . as the feature of the whole program." See *Annals* 17 (May 1901), p. 87. Booker T. Washington was also scheduled to address the group, but he never showed up, and his paper, which was to be published in the *Annals*, apparently never arrived.

9. Du Bois, "The Relation of the Negroes to the Whites in the South." The paper became "Of the Sons of Masters and Men," chapter 9 of *The Souls of Black Folk*.

10. Ibid., 122.

11. McAfee, "Studies in the American Race Problem." The piece is a measured criticism of Alfred Holt Stone's *Studies in the American Race Problem* (1908). Stone believed that U.S. race problems were relevant to race problems in the African colonies and argued that it was important to encourage pride of race instead of training blacks to be white men. McAfee was then a faculty member at Park College in Missouri. Later he would lead the Presbyterian Board of Foreign Missions.

12. For Du Bois at the congress, see Lewis, *W. E. B. Du Bois*, 251.

13. Du Bois, "Relation of the Negroes to the Whites," 131.

14. In contrast, the liberal anti-imperialist theorist John Hobson, writing at roughly the same time, argued for an international regime—a "federation"—that would prevent the exploitation of dependencies and instead rationally guide processes of "racial or national selection" in a more efficient and progressive direction. Hobson, "The Scientific Basis of Imperialism."

15. See Du Bois, *Autobiography*, 197. I am following the unconventional but to my mind correct interpretations of Du Bois's rapidly evolving ideas at this time as developed in Bay, "'The World Was Thinking Wrong about Race.'"

16. Lewis, *W. E. B. Du Bois*, 277. The critical method and analyses of *The Souls of Black Folk* demonstrate that Du Bois was repeatedly ahead of his time. After it was published, Du Bois took his first fateful step away from the academy (no great university would even consider hiring him), toward building a political movement to combat racism and reverse black disempowerment, first through the Niagara Movement in 1905 and soon after that through the founding of the NAACP.

17. Kelsey, Review of *Souls of Black Folk*.

18. Ross, *Origins of American Social Science*, 128–130. On reform Darwinism, see Bannister, *Social Darwinism*, especially 137–162.

19. Giddings, "Imperialism?," 585–586. The remaining quotes in this paragraph are found on 587, 595–99, 600, and 602–604. Giddings capitalized on events in Asia and the Caribbean and in 1900 published a disparate set of essays under the title *Democracy and Empire*, which included "Imperialism?" But all reviews noted that the book had little to do with the topic and that Giddings's effort to knit together his work on regulation, socialism, industrial democracy and other matters with the topic of empire did not really hold together.

20. Sumner, *The Conquest of the United States by Spain*, 9, 15.

21. The School of Political Science was the core of what is now known as the Graduate School of Arts and Sciences. For Columbia under Burgess's influence, see Ross, *Origins of American Social Science*, 259. For Burgess's politics, see Oren, *Our Enemies and US*.

22. Burgess, "How May the United States Govern Its Extra-Continental Territory?," 1; Burgess, *Reminiscences of an American Scholar*, 312.

23. Somit and Tanenhaus note Burgess's opposition to the war was an instance of the widely shared expectation that members of the emerging discipline would involve

themselves in the great issues of the day, but they don't make any connection between empire (nor do they use the word) and the founding of the association. See Somit and Tanenhaus, *The Development of American Political Science*, 44. They also observe that Burgess's memory in *Reminiscences of an American Scholar* is "faulty because in it he writes that he and others at Columbia were so alarmed by developments that they 'at once began publishing articles in the *Political Science Quarterly* against any steps being taken by our government which would lead to war with Spain.'" Although Somit and Tanenhaus say that "no articles were run along the line indicated" (44), Burgess was no doubt thinking of his own January 1899 lead article, which Somit and Tanenhaus missed, perhaps because of their choice of sample years.

24. For the follow-up quotation, see Burgess, *Political Science and Comparative Constitutional Law*, 1:39 and 46. Reviews of the book drew attention to his pronouncements on Teutonism and empire (see, e.g., the unsigned review, "Burgess's Political Science," *The Nation* 53, no. 1369 [September 24, 1891], 240–241). Woodrow Wilson, whose harsh review of the work is well known, was conspicuously silent about these matters. See Woodrow Wilson, "A System of Political Science and Constitutional Law," *Atlantic Monthly* 67 [May 1891]: 694–699. On Burgess and Teutonism generally, see Farr, "The Historical Science(s) of Politics," especially 79–86.

25. Pratt, "The 'Large Policy' of 1898," 239, is a good place to start.

26. Burgess, "The Ideal of the American Commonwealth," 405–407, 410–411. He is also famous for advising the white oligarchy in Hawaii about how to effect the disfranchisement of the nonwhite elements on the islands. A few years later Burgess would describe black enfranchisement as a sin and Reconstruction as a punishment in gross excess of the crime. See Benjamin Shambaugh's review of *Reconstruction and the Constitution*. Shambaugh, a political scientist at the University of Iowa, concluded his review with an amazing commentary: "Some argue that it was the fact of the Spanish-American war that ended the sectional divisions, but the two peoples had [marched together in battle] before and that had not prevented the dissolution of the Union." The real significance of the War was "that the Republican party, in its work of imposing the sovereignty of the United States upon eight millions of Asiatics, has changed its views in regard to the political relations of races, and has at last virtually accepted the ideas of the South upon the subject. The white men of the South need now have no further fear that the Republican party, or Republican administrations, will ever again give themselves over to the vain imagination of the political equality of man" (130).

27. See Gibb, "Unmasterly Inactivity?," 24; Vucetic, *The Anglosphere*, 22–53.

28. Burgess, "The Recent Pseudo-Monroeism," 45.

29. Ibid., 52, 55, 66.

30. Roosevelt, "The Monroe Doctrine," 220, 223, 227, and 228. Roosevelt dedicated the book to Henry Cabot Lodge. I am quoting from a 1900 edition that was printed after Roosevelt was elected governor of New York.

31. Burgess, "How May the United States Govern Its Extra-Continental Territory?" 2, 14.

32. Ibid., 3, 11, 17–18.

33. Thompson, "Imperial Republic."

34. For the rulings known collectively as the Insular Cases, see Smith, *Civic Ideals*, 433–439.

35. On the color ban in Harvard's dormitories, see Painter, "Jim Crow at Harvard: 1923."

36. Lowell, "Status of Our New Possessions."

37. Lowell, "Colonial Expansion of the United States."

38. Hart, *Actual Government as Applied under American Conditions*, 368–369.

39. A. Lawrence Lowell, *Colonial Civil Service.*

40. Burgess, "The Decision of the Supreme Court in the Insular Cases."

41. Hobson, "The Scientific Basis of Imperialism," 487–488.

42. "The March of Events," in Page and Page, *The World's Work, A History of Our Time,* 1, no. 1 (November 1900), 4, 17.

43. For this characterization of progressives, see his "What Is Real Progress in Political Civilization?" October 12, 1921, Box Labeled Burgess, John W, Manuscripts: Addresses and Articles # 1, John William Burgess (1844–1931) Papers, Special Collections, Low Library, Columbia University, New York.

44. See Burgess, *Recent Changes in American Constitutional Theory,* chapter 3, "Constitutional Development or Transformation from 1898 to 1914," unpaginated (unfortunately). Also see Burgess, *Reconciliation of Government with Liberty,* 358–383; and Burgess, *Foundations of Political Science,* 134–140. The latter extracted his arguments about nation and state from his two-volume 1890 treatise, *Political Science and Comparative Constitutional Law,* which he prepared for publication in 1917 at the urging of Columbia's president, Nicholas Murray Butler, for use by those who were determining the fate of the former German colonies.

45. Burgess, *Reminiscences of an American Scholar,* 312–341. He ended his memoir in 1907 with his year in Berlin, but it was not published until the year after his death, in 1934. The delay in publication has never been explained, but in his unpublished and uncatalogued papers he reported that his publisher had broken their contract. Typed memorandum on the fate of his books, n.d., in box labeled Burgess, John W, Manuscripts: Addresses and Articles # 1, Burgess Papers.

46. This focus of political scientists and economists on efficient administration of empire was first discussed in the 1970s in Furner, *Advocacy and Objectivity,* 285, but has not been cited since.

47. Andrews, "Boston Meeting of the American Historical Association," 424. The rapporteur noted, just as frankly, that the "medievalist found little to interest him professionally; the student of ancient history . . . would have found still less. Instead Modern American problems had the foremost place."

48. See Silva and Slaughter, "Prometheus Bound," 791–792.

49. See Willoughby, "Report of the Secretary for the Year 1904," 30. Reinsch was appointed head of the section of dependencies, Rowe, who was then a colonial administrator himself, of was appointed the head of the section on municipal government. The division of the association into sections continues; today there are over sixty.

50. Watson, "Bernard Moses: Pioneer in Latin American Scholarship," 212. Moses sat on the original executive committee of the APSA along with other figures discussed here. He retired from Berkeley in 1911.

51. Rogers, *Congress of Arts and Sciences,* 387–398.

52. Ireland, "On the Need for a Scientific Study of Colonial Administration," 212

53. Ibid., 210.

54. Ibid., 215–216.

55. For the Atlantic crossings of these ideas, see Hobson, *The Eurocentric Conception of World Politics.*

Chapter 2: Race Children

1. See Worcester, *A River Running West,* 96, for "Anglo-Saxon," and 398 for the paraphrase of Powell's vision for the bureau. See Stocking, *Race, Culture, and Evolution,* 128–129, for Powell's late anthropology. One of the less-heralded feats of Worcester's beautiful biography is the detour he takes to avoid addressing Stocking's superior analysis of Powell's contribution to race theory.

2. Stocking, *Race, Culture, and Evolution*, 112, 121.

3. Degler, *In Search of Human Nature*, 15. See, however, a slightly contrasting reading of Darwin in Stocking, *Race, Culture, and Evolution*, 46–47.

4. William Z. Ripley, "Acclimatization," *Popular Science Monthly* 48 (March 1896): 662–675.

5. Ellsworth Huntington, "The Adaptability of the White Man to Tropical America." I am quoting the discussion in Stocking, *Race, Culture, and Evolution*, 54–55.

6. See, for instance, the treatise by James Bryce, the British ambassador to the United States and fifth president of APSA, *The Relations of the Advanced and the Backward Races*.

7. Stocking, *Race, Culture, and Evolution*, 48–49.

8. Ibid. 240.

9. Robert Bennett Bean, "The Nose of the Jew and the Quadratus Labil Superioris Muscle." Bean (1874–1944) was an anthropologist and anatomist who did work on the brain of the Negro at Michigan before joining the Philippine Medical School in 1907. His main work in this period is *The Racial Anatomy of the Philippine Islanders: Introducing New Methods of Anthropology and Showing Their Application to the Filipinos with a Classification of Human Ears and a Scheme for the Heredity of Anatomical Characters in Man* (Philadelphia: J. B Lippincott 1910). Quoted in Stocking, *Race, Culture, and Evolution*, 244.

10. Reinsch, "The Negro Race and European Civilization," 145–148, 150–152. The essay later formed part of chapter 2 of his *Colonial Administration*.

11. Reinsch, "The Negro Race and European Civilization," 154–155.

12. Ibid., 164–166.

13. Ibid., 166–167.

14. Commenting on the Simon Report for India and as reported in *Pacific Affairs* 3, no. 9 (1930): 897.

15. Smith, "The Book of the Quarter," 75, quoting W. M. Macmillan in a review of Macmillan's *Africa Emergent*.

16. "Across about twenty years, Lemarkianism in biology ended 'not with a bang but a whimper . . . as its older defenders passed away and younger biologists directed their research along Mendelian lines." Stocking, *Race, Culture, and Evolution*, 254.

17. Ibid., 214.

18. Degler, *In Search of Human Nature*, 67.

19. Baker, *From Savage to Negro*, 99–126.

20. Put another way, Stocking's work offers additional support for the revisionist readings of Bay and Holt, referenced above. See in addition Liss, "Diasporic Identities."

21. Du Bois, "The Development of a People."

22. See Kelsey, "Evolution of Negro Labor."

23. Carl Kelsey, "Comments on D. Collin Wells, 'Social Darwinism,'" 711. Wells was a sociologist at Dartmouth and a member of the founding executive committee of the ASA. His paper confounded the other commentator, Frank Ward. He had come with a pre-written response, but despite the title Wells's paper was not about the growing European critique of ideologies of economic and race struggles, to which the concept "Social Darwinism" conventionally referred; instead, it was about the importance of pursuing the new science of eugenics.

24. For the historiography, see Sluga, *Internationalism in the Age of Nationalism*, in particular her references to foundational work by Mansour Bonakdarian, Marilyn Lake and Henry Reynolds, Susan Pennybacker, and Paul Rich.

25. As the organizer, Gustav Spiller, wrote in his original notice in *The Times* (London) a year earlier (September 6, 1910, 6), the conference would "discuss general relations between peoples of the West and those of the East" and would include

speakers from "China, Japan, India, Turkey, Persia, and Egypt, beside the negro race in America and Africa." For the papers, see Spiller, *Papers on Inter-Racial Problems*.

26. "Science and the Millennium," *Times* (London), July 28, 1911, 8.

27. Ibid.

28. Paul Reinsch, "Influence of Geographic, Economic and Political Conditions," in Spiller, Papers on Inter-Racial Problems, 49–52.

29. Ibid., 53, 55.

Part II: Worlds of Color

1. See Raymond Leslie Buell to Edward Corwin, March 18, 1923, box 36, folder 36, Writings, International Relations 1923–1924, Raymond Leslie Buell Papers, Library of Congress, Washington, D.C. (hereafter Buell Papers LOC).

2. Harrly Elmer Barnes, review of *International Relations*. Remembered now chiefly as a Holocaust denier, Barnes was regarded at the time as a brilliant historian or history-oriented social scientist. Trained by Dunning at Columbia and recruited to Clark by its president, G. Stanley Hall, he became a full professor at age 30. Barnes served as co-editor of the *Journal of Race Development/Journal of International Relations* in its last years.

3. Raymond Leslie Buell to Alain Locke, May 23, 1925, box 18, folder 2, Correspondence, Buell, Raymond L, Alain Locke Papers, Moorland-Spingarn Research Library, Howard University, Washington, D.C. (hereafter Locke Papers).

4. Harris and Molesworth, *Alain L. Locke*, 147–148. Locke's friendship with Pixley Seme, a founding member and future president of South Africa's African National Congress, dated back to his Oxford years. The two helped found Oxford's African Union Society in 1908. He traveled with Seme in 1923 (67–68).

5. For Locke as the "father of the so-called Harlem Renaissance," see Huggins, *Harlem Renaissance*, 57. For the controversies that surrounded *The New Negro* and his editorship of it, see Rampersad, "Introduction." On Locke's involvement with millionaire Albert Barnes and his new art education project promoting Negro art, see Helbling, "Albert C. Barnes and Alain Locke"; and Helbling, "African Art and the Harlem Renaissance." The Barnes Foundation was incorporated in 1922.

6. No anthropologist in the United States had done fieldwork in Africa, according to a 1925 assessment by Clark Wissler for the Laura Spelman Rockefeller Memorial. See Stanfield, *Philanthropy and Jim Crow in American Social Science*, 78. Herskovits did his first field work in Africa in 1931 after completing a third major research project in Surinam. His 1931 research marks the beginning of his influential (and self-revisionist) ideas about African survivals in the New World. Chronological details are found in the biography included in the finding aid to Melville J. Herskovits Papers at the Northwestern University Archives in Evanston, Illinois, http://findingaids.library.northwestern.edu/catalog/inu-ead-nua-archon-1230. www.library.northwestern.edu/archives/findingaids/herskovits. pdf. See also Gershenhorn, *Melville J. Herskovits and the Racial Politics of Knowledge*.

7. For Locke's first discussion of the mandates, see "Apropos of Africa." This particular article has eluded most analysts and bibliographers, but Edwards includes it in his discussion of Locke in *Practice of Diaspora*, 108–109. Buell's first piece, "'Backward' Peoples under the Mandate System," appeared four months later. He gave a paper on the same topic, "The Mandate System as an Antidote to Imperialism," on the panel Colonies, Mandates and the Far East at the nineteenth annual meeting of the American Political Science Association in December. It was one of eight panels

for the meeting, six of which were about various aspects of administration. The topic of a second international relations panel was the League of Nations.

8. Buell, *International Relations*, 5, 59.

9. For an early version of the argument, see Bryce, *The Relations of the Advanced and the Backward Races*.

10. The name change followed the retirement of Clark University's president and the journal's founder, G. Stanley Hall, when Hall's original co-editor, George Hubbard Blakeslee, brought on the young Columbia-trained Harry Elmer Barnes as co-editor. I could find no documentation about the reason for the name change.

11. On "anthropogeography," of which Yale's Ellsworth Huntington is the most influential American practitioner, see Merriam, "Recent Tendencies in Political Thought," 19; and Thomas, "Some Representative Contributions of Anthropogeography," 457–507.

12. Buell, *International Relations*, 59.

13. See Ada Comstock (president of Radcliffe) to the trustees of the Laura Spelman Rockefeller Memorial, n.d., 1928, box 54, folder 573, Series 3.6, Laura Spelman Rockefeller Memorial, Rockefeller Archive Center, Tarrytown, New York. The bureau was a significantly scaled-down version of a proposal that originally envisioned a foundation for instruction in international affairs that would fund fellowships and seminars in addition to research. The original award (for five years) and the $500,000 renewal (for ten years) made it the best-funded university international relations institute through the interwar years. Compare, for example, the Wait Harris Memorial Foundation at the University of Chicago, which was founded the same year with a total endowment of $150,000, revenue from which would be used to fund foreign lecturers (*Survey Graphic*, April 1923, 51). Barkan's *Retreat of Scientific Racism* includes a frank appraisal that Hooten's research on the biological basis of criminality was "a dead end" (105). See Spiro, *Defending the Master Race*, 235, for Hooten's quote.

14. Most notoriously, Stoddard, *Revolt against Civilization*. "More and more we are coming to see that hatred of civilization is mainly a matter of heredity; that Bolsheviks are mostly born and not made." (224). William McDougall, the British-born Harvard psychologist and holder of the William James Chair of Psychology wrote a long laudatory review "Stoddard's The Revolt against Civilization," in the *Quarterly Journal of Economics*. This is not surprising; Stoddard took the basic argument from William McDougall's lectures in *Is America Safe for Democracy?*, an account of imminent American decline unless enlightened opinion embraced eugenics. In a subsequent volume, *The Indestructible Union*, McDougall proposed as an "act of justice" that would solve the "negro problem" that the federal government purchase land either in some part of the southern states or abroad and that white America assist in building an independent negro nation. In his review, William Yale Elliott, then at the University of California, absolved McDougall for his self-professed sin of writing as a foreigner on American nationality. "Professor McDougall may claim to pass a sufficiently high test to satisfy the Ku Klux Klan—from whom he professedly differs chiefly in the possession of a sense of humor." Elliott, Review of *The Indestructible Union*, 197.

15. Retrospective accounts recount the science wars between the Boasians and their critics in physical anthropology and biology or between them and "scientific racists." See Barkan, *Retreat of Scientific Racism*; and Foley, *Spectres of 1919*. The *Survey Graphic* instead referred to the "culture historians" and the "biological sociologists"; see "The Gist of It," *Survey Graphic*, June 1, 1924, 267. As we have seen, however, there were three, not two, camps on world interracial relations. The more one includes the work of black intellectuals, the easier it is to discern this.

16. Barkan, *Retreat of Scientific Racism*, 111.

17. The rejection followed his effort to make the course appear less controversial by changing it from interracial relations to interracial history. Logan, *Howard University*, 171. The Howard chapter of the NAACP and the Social Science Club sponsored the series, which Locke gave again in 1916. They remained unpublished until Jeffrey Stewart assembled them from Locke's papers. See Locke, *Race Contacts and International Relations*.

18. Du Bois, "The African Roots of War." It appeared in revised form as "Hands of Ethiopia" in *Darkwater*. As his biographer David Levering Lewis notes, the essay, "one of the analytical triumphs of the early twentieth century," appeared two years before Lenin's *Imperialism: The Highest Stage of Capitalism*. See Stewart's introduction to Locke, *Race Contacts and International Relations* for evidence of Locke's first talks emphasizing the relationship of scientific racism to imperialism; Stewart, "Introduction," xl.

19. Leonard Woolf, a former colonial administrator and a supporter of the mandate system, nonetheless also argued that "nine-tenths of what is said and written about race and racial conflicts, about the inferiority and superiority of races, and about their inherent antipathies, is unmitigated nonsense"; Woolf, *Imperialism and Civilization*, 19.

Chapter 3: Storm Centers of Political Theory and Practice

1. His *tour d'horizon* is included in Merriam and Barnes, *History of Political Theories*, quotes from 1–4.

2. "The Americanization movement asked me to go down and talk against them." Buell to Corwin, November 30, 1920, box 3, folder 2, Edward S. Corwin Papers, Department of Rare Books and Special Collections, Princeton University, Princeton, New Jersey. Corwin wrote back with advice on pairing a casebook with one of his own briefer texts, "to fill in the chinks between the cases," before turning to Buell's extracurricular activities. He added, "Speaking of 'chinks,' your adventures as a pro-Japanese propagandist were quite exciting." Corwin to Buell, December 16, 1920, box 36, folder 5, Buell Papers LC.

3. See Buell, "The Development of the Anti-Japanese Agitation"; and Buell, "Some Legal Aspects of the Japanese Question."

4. For the history detailed here I have relied on the correspondence between Hamilton Fish Armstrong and Blakeslee, box 8, and between Armstrong and Coolidge, box 2, Hamilton Fish Armstrong Papers, 1893–1973, Seeley Mudd Library, Princeton University, Princeton, New Jersey (hereafter Armstrong Papers). On Armstrong, see Roberts, "'The Council Has Been Your Creation.'"

5. See Coolidge to Armstrong, December 9 and 11, 1922, box 17, and June 13 and 14, 1923, box 18, Armstrong Papers; and Buell to Coolidge, November 15, 1922, and April 12, 1923, box 21, Armstrong Papers.

6. Edwin Bjorkman, "The League of Free Nations Association of the United States," ms., Board Minutes and Other Official Records of the Executive Committee, Foreign Policy Association, New York, microfilm reel 1, Foreign Policy Association Papers, Seeley Mudd Library, Princeton University, Princeton New Jersey.

7. Dennis, *Foreign Policy in a Democracy*.

8. Nonetheless, during his years as research director he taught colonial government at Columbia (1929–1930), as a visiting professor of international relations at Yale (1930–1931), as a lecturer at the School of Public and International Affairs at

Princeton (1931–1932), as a lecturer at the New School (1932), and as a visiting lecturer in international relations at Harvard (1933–1934).

9. Buell, "Again the Yellow Peril."

10. The key sources include Higham, *Strangers in the Land*; Daniels, *The Politics of Prejudice*; King, *Making Americans*; Ngai, *Impossible Subjects*; Spiro, *Defending the Master Race*; Painter, *The History of White People*; and Ly and Weil, "Antiracist Origin of the Quota System."

11. Buell, "Again the Yellow Peril," 307.

12. Stalker, "Suicide, Boycotts, and Embracing Tagore."

13. Buell, "Again the Yellow Peril," 309, my emphasis. Ly and Weil, "Anti-Racist Origin of the Quota System" thus distinguishes between "racialist" and "racist" camps on these questions. For Buell's later stumping, see the clipping "Raymond Buell in Address Opposes Anti-Jap Measure," *Los Angeles Telegram*, August 24, 1924, box 40, folder 14, Buell Papers LC.

14. Fitzgerald, *The Great Gatsby*, 12–13.

15. For Coolidge as a mentor, see the excerpt of the interview with Stoddard in the *Boston Transcript*, April 4, 1931, in Coolidge and Lord, *Archibald Cary Coolidge*, 70–71. See also Bachman, "Theodore Lothrop Stoddard," 43–45, which draws on an unpublished and quite possibly lost autobiography by Stoddard. Coolidge's biographer denied that the two even had ties.

16. Stoddard, *Revolution in San Domingo*, vii–viii.

17. Stoddard, "Santo Domingo: Our Unruly Ward," 731. The glowing review of it by Columbia's professor of international law and diplomacy John Bassett Moore, who had just come out with his own lectures on American imperialism and expansion (*Four Phases of American Development*, 1912) drew the parallel to Reconstruction after abolition. He noted that the success of revolution in Haiti led to "massacre of the whites."

18. Stoddard, "Pan-Turanism." The term then connoted the idea of the racial unity of peoples originating in Central Asia, including Maygars, Turks, and other members of the putative "Turanid" race.

19. *Racial Realities in Europe* (1924); *Social Class in Post-War Europe* (1925); and *Re-Forging America: The Story of Our Nationhood* (1927), all published by Scribner's.

20. "There is nothing in the present volume to bear out the charge which has been brought against some of his other writings of alarmist intentions"; Lybyer, Review of *The New World of Islam*, 324. Harold Lasswell began his brief review of *Social Class in Post-War Europe* with the warning" "those who shriek at the name of Stoddard would be ill-advised to flee" (701). In his unpublished autobiography, Stoddard conceded that he had written *The Rising Tide of Color* to "shock" the general public "awake." Bachman, "Theodore Lothrop Stoddard," 99.

21. "Lothrop Stoddard called in on me yesterday pretty well satisfied with the world in general and with his own fortunes in particular. He referred with good-natured tolerance to Barnes's criticism on his book. He is going to Europe and is to write twelve articles for the *Saturday Evening Post* for which he will received $1,000 a piece. That shows the financial competition that we are up against." Coolidge to Armstrong, November 2, 1922, box 17, Armstrong Papers; Bachman, "Theodore Lothrop Stoddard," 152–153.

22. Painter, *The History of White People*, 302–304, 321–324.

23. Ellsworth Huntington praised *The Rising Tide of Color* for its frank prediction of the "end of white political control from Anatolia to the Philippines"; Huntington, Review of *Rising Tide of Color*, 146.

24. "Harding Says Negro Must Have Equality in Political Life," *New York Times*, October 27, 1921, 1. Du Bois, who had raised the fundamental issue of social equal-

ity in the pages of *Crisis*, took the speech apart in "President Harding and Social Equality." Marcus Garvey, on the other hand, embraced Harding as an ally. See Lewis, *W. E. B. Du Bois*, 70–71. For one of the first historical analyses of the speech in the context of the Republican Party's efforts to rebuild alliances in the South, see Sherman, "The Harding Administration and the Negro."

25. See Buell's account in *The Native Problem in Africa*, 1:136–149. See also his retrospective account of its influence in shaping proposals he began to put forward in the 1930s (and was clinging to) as an alternative to equality in the South; Buell to Francis E. Rivers, February 14, 1944, box 12, folder 18, Buell Papers LC.

26. Stoddard first discussed a system of hardened segregation, the banning of mixed marriages, limited political rights in communal matters, and the encouragement of separate development for blacks in the south in an interview in 1922. See Bachman, "Theodore Lothrop Stoddard," 145.

27. Ibid, 217.

28. Ibid., 101.

29. Stoddard, *Re-Forging of America*, 46–50, 191.

30. Ibid., 236–248. The "local alienisms" that might persist in various cities of the Northeast would serve to "prevent the American people from being lulled into false security that would result in fresh misfortunes." (251)

31. Stoddard, *Re-Forging of America*, 312, 321.

32. Ibid., 276–280. For proof of this "furious rage," Stoddard quoted the first half of Claude McKay's poem "White Houses" that Locke published in the *New Negro*, but he omitted the poem's final lines: Oh, I must search for wisdom every hour, / Deep in my wrathful bosom sore and raw, / And find in it the superhuman power, / To hold me to the letter of your law! / Oh, I must keep my heart inviolate, / Against the potent poison of your hate.

33. Stoddard, *Re-Forging of America*, 324.

34. Quoted in Levy, *University of Oklahoma*, 138. Dowd is crediting with founding the departments of sociology, anthropology, and economics and helping found the School of Journalism, the College of Business Administration, and the School of Social Work at the University of Oklahoma. It is little wonder that he never managed to complete the masterwork. See also McKee, *Sociology and the Race Problem*, 82.

35. Dowd went on to praise his exposé of anti-Americanism in the universities where men were being stamped with "the Doctor Kallen philosophy." See Bachman, "Theodore Lothrop Stoddard," 214–217, for Stoddard's correspondence with Ross, Black, and Dowd.

36. William Langer, review of *Re-Forging America* by T. Lothrop Stoddard, C. A. M. review of *Re-Forging America*, and Carleton P. Barnes, review of *Re-Forging America*.

37. Lake and Reynolds, *Drawing the Global Colour Line*, 2.

38. Mazower, *No Enchanted Palace*.

39. Du Bois, "Worlds of Color," 437.

40. To be precise, he created a final section of the book titled "Worlds of Color" comprising solely Du Bois's *Foreign Affairs* article, which Locke retitled "The Negro Mind Reaches Out."

41. Mazower, "Paved Intentions," 78.

42. From *The Liberator* (July 1919), as reprinted in Van Wienan, *Rendezvous with Death*, 262.

43. Locke, "Foreword," xxvi, my emphasis.

44. See Harris and Molesworth, *Alain L. Locke*, 192, 195, 207. For evidence of Locke's familiarity with the *Journal of Race Development*, see the syllabus that accompanied his 1915 lectures in Stewart, *Critical Temper of Alain Locke*, 407–414.

45. Locke, *The New Negro*, 6–7. The figure for population growth comes from Douglas, *Terrible Honesty*, 73.

46. Ibid., 8, 14–15.

47. See the discussion of Locke's legacy in Africa in Harris and Molesworth, *Alain L. Locke*, 386–387.

48. Guterl discusses the exchanges in *The Color of Race in America*, 42–144. The earliest reconstruction of Locke's round is in Mason, "Alain Locke on Race and Race Relations."

49. Locke, "The High Cost of Prejudice."

50. Smith, "Beyond Tocqueville, Myrdal, and Hartz." Smith and Samuel Huntington, one of his critical foils, both trace the concept of the "American Creed" or its popularization to Myrdal, while giving the "tradition" it is said to represent a more illustrious set of eighteenth- and nineteenth-century ancestors. See, e.g., Huntington, *Who Are We?*, 66–67. In fact, the "The American's Creed" was the winning entry in a wartime patriotism contest by William Tyler Page, which the House of Representatives adopted in 1918. See Page, *The American's Creed*. Schools used it to transmit the faith and support Americanization. See, for instance, Rice, "What Shall We Do for Armistice Day?" One can chart its revival in school materials issued at the start of World War II, including its adaptation into patriotic songs for children. It was thus a well-known phrase by the time historian Arthur Schlesinger used it in 1943 and Myrdal in 1944.

51. Stoddard, "The Impasse at the Color-Line."

52. Grant said Stoddard's proposals about biracialism would not solve the problem and that exile or amalgamation were the only real solutions. Grant to Stoddard, September 28, 1927, as quoted in Bachman, "Theodore Lothrop Stoddard," 231. See also Lewis, *W. E. B. Du Bois*, 2: 235.

53. Lewis, *W. E. B. Du Bois*, 2: 237. It is impossible to top Lewis for drama.

Chapter 4: Imperialism and Internationalism in the 1920s

1. Jane Gordon makes the point more formally: the discipline of political science was historically heavily creolized. Drawing on the full range of resources relevant to understanding the political world, its early participants forced a shared field language through which those working on divergent questions could communicate findings (even if incompletely) to one another. Many constitutive works in this area of inquiry could as easily be considered studies in history, psychology, or sociology as in theory. They could be defined multiply precisely because their authors were less concerned with demonstrating subfield mastery or loyalty than with grasping problems larger than any single, historically contingent scholarly niche. Gordon, *Creolizing Political Theory*, 16.

2. See "A Preliminary Draft of a Survey of the Study of International Relations in the United States," prepared in connection with the Program of Research in International Relations of the Social Science Research Council under the direction of Dr. James T. Shotwell," 20, June 1933, box 133, folder 7, Charles E. Merriam Papers, Regenstein Library, University of Chicago.

3. Akami, *Internationalizing the Pacific*, 51–52.

4. Anderson, "Pacific Dreams," 29–39; Wilbur, *The Memoirs of Ray Lyman Wilbur*, 315–320, quote on 318. Lyman gives key credit to co-chair Blakeslee, who is not given sufficient recognition in the secondary literature on the Institute of Pacific Relations.

5. Hooper, "A Brief History of the Institute of Pacific Relations," 112.

6. McKenzie, *Oriental Exclusion*. McKenzie was a human ecologist who studied under Park at Chicago and was teaching at University Washington in Seattle when

he was commissioned by the Institute of Pacific Relations to undertake the study. It was published by the University of Chicago in 1928, as was Mears, *Residential Orientals on the Pacific Coast*. Mears, who taught at the Stanford School of Business, had an MBA from Harvard. Mears specialized in geography and trade and served as commercial attaché to the American High Commission in Turkey during World War I. His first book was *Modern Turkey*.

7. DeWind, "Immigration Studies and the Social Science Research Council," 70–71; Cochrane, *The National Academy of Sciences*, 264; Bowman, "The Pioneer Fringe"; Martin, *Life and Thought of Isaiah Bowman*, 109–121; Smith, *American Empire*, 211–234.

8. Editorial, "A School of Foreign Affairs," *New York Times*, July 26, 1923, 12.

9. Akami, *Internationalizing the Pacific*, 49, 51.

10. H. A. Garfield, "Meet to Develop World Views Here," *New York Times*, July 24, 1921, 9. For the most detailed contemporary account of the first month-long institute, see Abbot, "International Politics in the Berkshire Hills." Garfield was an Ohio lawyer whom Woodrow Wilson brought to Princeton to teach politics. Both Williams College and the Library of Congress hold relevant papers.

11. "The Institute of Politics." The institute published the first *Round-Table Conferences of the Institute of Politics* in 1923, which includes a complete list of attendees, which included Hamilton Fish Armstrong, a writer for the New York *Evening Post* and a future associate editor of *Foreign Affairs*. For Baruch's annual contribution of around $25,000, see Coit, *Mr. Baruch*, 358. Additional details are drawn from Arthur Howland Buffinton's appendix to Harry Augustus Garfield's memoir, *Lost Visions*.

12. Williams, "The Institute of Politics," 645.

13. Akami, *Internationalizing the Pacific*, 49. The roundtable concept was imported from the London pro-imperial organization the Round Table, which was founded in 1909 and began publication of *The Round Table: A Quarterly Review of the Politics of the British Empire* in 1910.

14. Leland Hamilton Jenks was a Canadian who wrote a dissertation under Dunning on the social aspects of the Glorious Revolution. He taught social and economic institutions with Harry Elmer Barnes at Amherst before moving to Wellesley, where he eventually chaired the sociology department. He followed his first book, *The Migration of British Capital to 1875*, with *Our Cuban Colony: A Study in Sugar*. The latter was part of a series on modern imperialism edited by Barnes. On Earle, see Ekbladh, "Present at the Creation."

15. Bryce, *International Relations*. In addition, see Lybyer, Review of *International Relations*; Panaretoff, *Near Eastern Affairs and Conditions*; and Korff, *Russia's Foreign Relations*. Albert Howe Lybyer was Harvard's expert on the Ottoman state.

16. See Lawley, Review of *L'Imperialisme économique*: "There is not much literature on this subject, and students of international politics are therefore to be grateful." He counted Leonard Woolf, a few "minor" and unnamed writers who focused on the oil issue, and journalist and Labour Party MP Edmund D. Morel, leaving Hobson out, presumably because his *Imperialism* was by then over twenty years old. The situation was to change dramatically in the next few years.

17. Culbertson, *International Economic Policies*, viii, and Edward Meade Earle, "The New Mercantilism."

18. Frederic A. Ogg, "Personal and Miscellaneous," *American Political Science Review* 19 (1925): 812–813.

19. "Personal and Miscellaneous," *American Political Science Review* 20 (1926): 414.

20. "Riverside Institute of International Relations," *News Bulletin* (Institute of Pacific Relations), January 1927, 11.

21. "Political Institute to Stress Orient," *New York Times*, June 4, 1928, 7.

22. Russell B. Porter, "Politics Institute Concludes Session," *New York Times*, August 31, 1928, 10.

23. For Logan, see Janken, *Rayford W. Logan*, 74–79. In September 1927, Logan began a two-year MA program at Williams that didn't require residency. He continued to work on U.S.-Caribbean policies and published his MA in 1930 in the *Journal of Negro History*. The *New York Times* identified him ("a Negro") in a story filed on August 12, 1928, about the day's debate on interventions in the Caribbean. Logan had attacked the policy in Haiti. For his address at the institute, see Logan, "Operation of the Mandate System in Africa."

24. For a retrospective account that, among things, confirms Logan's precocious critique, see Bain, "The Idea of Trusteeship in International Society," revised and published as *Between Anarchy and Society*. Unfortunately, Bain does not refer to Logan's scholarship.

25. Smuts, *The League of Nations*, 15.

26. Bain, "The Idea of Trusteeship in International Society," 114.

27. See Manuscript for Buell's Talk to Institute of Politics, Eighth Session, 1928, General Conference no. 9, Problems of Africa, "Africa, Slave or Free," folder 12, and the essay adapted from it, "Is Africa Headed for an Inter-Racial War?" *Register* (New Haven, Conn.), November 25, 1928, box 33, folder 11, Buell Papers LC. Russell Porter provided a brief account in "Charge Exploiting of African Natives," *New York Times* August 28, 1928, 20.

28. Buell, "The Struggle in Africa," 40.

29. See Buell to Locke, May 29, 1928, inviting Locke to speak on the mandate system from the point of view of African Americans; and Locke to Buell, June 4, 1928, recommending Johnson in his place, both in box 18, folder 2, Buell Papers LC.

30. Porter, "Charge of Exploiting African Natives."

31. Ibid.

32. Russell B. Porter, "Sees Imperialism in the Firestone Deal," *New York Times*, August 30, 1928, 12.

33. See Buell, "Mr. Firestone's Liberia"; and Buell, "Liberia's Paradox." Also see Chalk, "The Anatomy of an Investment"; McCoskey, "When Firestone Entered Liberia"; and Sundiata, Brothers and Strangers.

34. "John Franklin Carter, 70, Dies; Wrote Column as Jay Franklin," *New York Times*, November 29, 1967, 47; Coyle, "John Franklin Carter."

35. Duffus, "War Is Hell—But It Is Human," review of *Man Is War*, *New York Times Book Review*, October 17, 1926, 1. Duffus was a novelist and critic who compared Carter to many in the arts who abhorred illusion and sentimentality and who wrote with more sophistication and style "than the majority of those who advance this kind of argument."

36. Carter, *Man Is War*. The same year that Carter published *Man Is War* John Bakeless came out with *The Origin of the Next War: A Study in the Tensions of the Modern World*, five years after publishing his prize-winning undergraduate thesis at Williams, "The Economic Causes of Modern War." Bakeless combined an account of the population pressures and drive for resources that drove countries to wars—a version of the "lateral pressure" analyses of North, Choucri, and others of the 1970s—with a description of the new kind of total war to come: "War will be fought by entire populations with chemistry and bacteriology as well as airplanes and submarines. War will be everywhere. The distinction between soldiers and non-combatants will vanish." Quoted in Frangis Deak, "The Inside and Outside of Diplomacy," *Har-*

vard Crimson, April 10, 1926. http://www.thecrimson.com/article/1926/4/10/
the-inside-and-outside-of-diplomacy/?print=1.

A participant at the Institute of Politics at Williamstown, Bakeless was a brilliant
student who turned down offers of professorships, delayed completion of his dissertation on Marlowe, and taught journalism and literary criticism part time. He served
as assistant chief of the Balkan and Near East Section of the Military Intelligence
Division of the War Department in World War II and was later a consultant for the
CIA while writing popular books on Daniel Boone, Lewis and Clark, and the like.
See the short biography "Bakeless, John Edward," http://pabook.libraries.psu.edu/
palitmap/bios/Bakeless__John_Edwin.html, accessed March 15, 2012. His papers are
at the New York Public Library and deserve study.

37. Carter, *Conquest*, 4.

38. Locke to Melville Herskovits, n.d. [summer of 1925], box 36, folder 10,
Locke Papers. For the longest and best-sourced account of these issues, see Logan,
Howard University, 220–222, 231–242; and Harris and Molesworth, *Alain L. Locke*,
175–178.

39. Harris and Molesworth, *Alain L. Locke*, 226.

40. Helen Howell Moorhead to Buell, n.d. [early May 1927], box 10, folder
13, Buell Papers LC. For the proposal itself, see the handwritten memorandum
"African Mandates Study Project, Foreign Policy Association," May 26, 1927,
box 105/164–105, folder 16, Locke Papers.

41. The Martinique-born Maran won the Prix-Goncourt, France's premier literary award, in 1924 for his novel *Batouala* (1921, English edition 1923), which
outraged many critics. The novel is, among other things, an indictment of the forced
labor regime in French Equatorial Africa. As Brent Edwards discusses, Locke's famous
review of the book in *Opportunity* and Du Bois's discussion in the Harlem number
helped bring him to the attention of African American circles. More famous still
was Maran's open letter to Locke chiding him for his too-rosy view of France and its
putative lack of color prejudice. The colonies and forced slavery there put the lie to
the idea, he said, as Locke would come to see. See Ikonne, "Rene Maran and the New
Negro"; Smith, "Rene Maran's *Batouala* and the Prix-Goncourt"; Edwards, *Practice
of Diaspora*, 104–115 in particular for Locke's exchange with Maran; and Harris and
Molesworth, *Alain L. Locke*, 152–153.

42. Abbe Livingston Warshuis served as a missionary in China for the Reformed
Church of America. After returning to the United States, he played key roles in
many international-oriented and educational associations, including the Foreign
Policy Association, the Institute of Pacific Relations, and the International Institute
of African Languages and Cultures, founded in 1926.

43. See Warshuis to Buell, May 27, 1927, Buell to Warshuis, June 2, 1927, and
Buell to Locke, June 30, 1927, all in box 33, folder 11, Writings, Africa: General
1925–28, Buell Papers LC.

44. For one discussion of the Foreign Policy Association's internal wrangling
about authorship—Buell or Locke—of a future "Bulletin" on native labor, see Paul
Kellogg to Helen Moorhead, December 24, 1927, enclosed in Kellogg to Locke, n.d.,
box 105/164–105, folder 19, Locke Papers.

45. See Harris and Molesworth, *Alain L. Locke*, 220–242, for an accounting.

46. Alain Locke, "The Mandate System: A New Code of Empire," folder 24,
box 116, Locke Papers.

47. "I'm a fairly good bodkin" is how he deprecatingly referred to his
network-building skills. Locke to Paul [Kellogg], n.d. [late in 1928], box 166, folder

15, Rayford Logan Papers, Moorland-Spingarn Research Center, Howard University, Washington, D.C. (hereafter Logan Papers MSRC). A bodkin is a needle used to thread ribbon through eyelets.

48. Alain Locke to Rayford Logan, November 13, 1928, box 166–15, folder 15, Logan Papers MSRC.

49. His biographer, Charles Henry, says that Bunche went to Howard to "establish the political science department." At another point, he says that Bunche created a separate department in 1932 after his return from fieldwork in Africa. See Henry, *Ralph Bunche*, 31, 36. Other recent studies repeat versions of this claim. However, Bunche was not the first person to teach political science at Howard; Rev. William V. Tunnell taught American government, comparative government, and theory for many years. Tunnell had graduated from Howard's law department and was a onetime faculty member, a warden of King Hall (the nearby Divinity School), and a member of Howard's board of trustees who returned to teaching in the history department in the early 1900s. He was then appointed head of what longtime Howard history faculty member Michael Winston called the political science department around 1919. Bunche was hired to replace Tunnell, who retired in 1928. See Winston, "The Howard University Department of History, 1919–1973," note 28, http://www.howard.edu/explore/history-dept.htm#28, accessed August 11, 2010. Winston suggests that Bunche in effect reconstituted and expanded the department (personal communication, April 2, 2012). When Bunche moved to Howard, he had not yet chosen a topic for his PhD, and he wrote a thesis in political theory for his MA. He was clearly interested in race and empire, however, and he first considered writing on the League of Nations and the suppression of slavery. Henry, *Ralph Bunche*, 65.

50. Frederick P. Keppel to Alain Locke, February 1, 1929, box 42, folder 38, Locke Papers; Janken, *Rayford W. Logan*, 79.

51. See John Whitton to Raymond Leslie Buell, December 4, 1929, box 12, Buell Papers LC. Whitton taught politics at Princeton, coached the first rugby team, and in the mid-1930s directed the independent U.S.-organized and Rockefeller-funded Geneva Research Center, which basically studied league matters for U.S. organizations. He also designed the first project to monitor radio propaganda, the Listening Center, at Princeton in 1938, which was also funded by the Rockefeller Foundation, before it was taken over by the FCC. As for "Chinaman," "it worked in the United States as a slur, in a way that, say, 'Frenchman,' or even 'Irishman,' never did." Lepore, "Chan, the Man," 70.

52. William Langer, "Some Recent Books on International Relations," *Foreign Affairs* 10 (July 1932), 702 and 11 (January 1933), 368. The unsigned review of *Lonely America* (1932) in the *Journal of Negro History* notes that his still intact if somewhat subdued Nordic superiority still "stalk through the pages" but "they are the last gasp of this die-hard in a cause that no reputable scientist any longer espouses. *Journal of Negro History*, 18, no. 1 (1933): 85–86. The review's narrow focus only on the chapter dealing with the Negro race in Latin America strongly suggests that Rayford Logan wrote it.

53. Stoddard, *Lonely America*, viii–x.

54. Keith gave the address "Prejudice and Modern Civilization" in 1931 upon his appointment as rector of the University of Abderdeen. He cited it in *Evolution in Ethics*, his essays on war and evolution.

55. Stoddard, *Lonely America*, 296.

56. Nor did the world look any better three years later, to judge from Stoddard's next (and next-to-last) "important" book on western civilization's impact on "other than occidental races," *Clashing Tides of Color*. Neither *Lonely America* nor *Clashing*

Tides of Color sold well. Popular reviews had all but dried up, and, for a while, Stoddard tried political risk consulting for an investment trust. His run as leading analyst of the world white supremacist order also seemed to be coming to an end.

Part III: The North versus the Black Atlantic

1. John Foster Dulles, "The Road to Peace," *Atlantic Monthly*, October 1935), 492-499. For Dulles's relationship to the foundation and the latter's role generally in the period, see Parmar, *Foundations of the American Century*, 48ff.

2. See interviews with R[aymond] B[laine] F[osdick] and S[ydnor] H[arbison] W[alker], November 5, 1936, Mr. John Foster Dulles, box 7, folder 60, Record Group 3, Series 910, Programs and Policy, IR, 1929–1941, Rockefeller Family Archives. Walker headed up the international relations program. The discussion below is based on this memorandum. The list of commitments in international relations is found in Kittridge Memorandum, Future Program in IR, December 19, 1935, box 7, folder 60, Record Group 3, Rockefeller Family Archives.

3. Pruessen, *John Foster Dulles*, 177.

4. For the original rejection of the piece and subsequent wrestling over publication, title, and so forth see Du Bois to Hamilton Fish Armstrong, December 18, 1934, and subsequent correspondence in box 25, folder 5, Armstrong Papers.

5. Anderson, "Pacific Dreams," 62; Akami, *Internationalizing the Pacific*, 217.

6. Mazower, *Hitler's Empire*, xxxviii, 2, 44–45.

7. Ibid., 4.

8. Langer, "Critique of Imperialism"; Bukharin, "Imperialism and Communism." Langer was then coming out with his two-volume *Diplomacy of Imperialism* and the next year would be appointed the first Archibald Cary Coolidge Professor of History at Harvard. Bukharin was destined for arrest, trial, and execution in the course of Stalin's brutal purges.

9. Schuman, "The Dismal Science of World Politics."

10. In the words of left-wing internationalist Schuman, the United States "beat a belated retreat"; ibid., 171–172. Nationalist (or continentalist) historian Samuel Flagg Bemis at Yale argued the same in his *Diplomatic History of the United States*, which Schuman promoted in "The Dismal Science of World Politics," 177.

11. On Schuman, the most detailed account is Bucklin, "The Wilsonian Legacy in Political Science," revised as *Realism and American Foreign Policy*. There is also a recent and extremely useful recovery of his ideas and those of some of his interlocutors in Scheuerman, "The (Classical) Realist Vision of Global Reform." No one to my knowledge has used the Schuman papers at Williams, which were inaccessible during the research for this project.

12. See for example Roger H. Wells, Review of *Nazi Dictatorship*, which judged that Schuman had "unduly minimized the positive (as opposed to the "psychic") achievements of Hitlerism. The resulting picture is, therefore, blacker than it needs to be" (678). For political scientists' cautiously optimistic views of Germany more generally at a key juncture, see Oren, *Our Enemies and US*, which also discusses Schuman.

13. Schuman, *International Politics* xi–xiii, vii. My citations are from the second edition (1937). The book remained in print in updated editions through the 1960s.

14. Most "realist" scholars believe themselves to be objective observers, free of ideological bias. However, see Bell, "Anarchy, Power, and Death."

15. Beard, *The Idea of National Interest*; Beard, *The Open Door at Home*. Philips Bradley of Amherst called *The Idea of National Interest* the most important work on American foreign policy "since the volumes by Mahan on sea power." Bradley, "American Foreign Policy—In Perspective and Cross Section," 145.

16. See Wolfers, "National Foreign Policies and the Strategy of Peace," 141, which rejects the idea that anarchy characterizes the politics of a world "organized along national lines."

17. Fox, *Reinhold Niebuhr*, 185, 193–195.

18. See for example Arthur Dugan's criticism of Edward Mead Earle's departure from the "strategic point of view" in his writing about "the totalitarian menace" and "totalitarian powers" in his tract *Against This Torrent*, although Dugan understood why he did it. It is "easier to work up emotions over slogans than over concrete realities." Dugan, "Needed: A New Balance of Power," 127. Dugan taught political science at the University of the South in Tennessee.

19. Bucklin, "The Wilsonian Legacy in Political Science," 134–135.

20. Ibid., 147–149.

21. Spykman was a specialist in the thought of philosopher Georg Simmel. With Earle he would do much to make the pseudoscience of geopolitics a respectable part of the international relations toolkit; Millikin was one of the best-known academic impresarios of the Cold War.

22. Earle had once described himself as a disillusioned Wilsonian who had voted for Debs in 1920 and was committed to stopping Hoover and his politics of swagger. "Mr. Hoover has personally acted for the greater part of his life as one of the advance agents of that economic imperialism which is one of the principal causes of the war system." Earle, "The Issue Is Tolerance," 28. For Millikan, see Ramos, "The Role of the Yale Institute of International Studies in the Construction of the United States National Security Ideology," 91–92. See also Earle, "Power Politics," for his not-yet-ready-for-war stance and the rapidly shifting terms of debate. A second useful source for the state of the debate is O'Donnell, "American Foreign Policy."

23. Buell tarred with a wide brush. He named New York *Herald Tribune* writer Walter Millis, author of the "isolationist bible" *Road to War* (1935); "Archie" [Archibald] MacLeish, the *Fortune* writer-turned-librarian of Congress; Felix Morley at the *Washington Post*; Spykman at Yale, and Brooks Emeny, an independent international relations scholar who was later president of the Foreign Policy Association. The change in view followed the "new party line," and Buell alleged that many of the same men considered him a "war monger." But Buell had also just undergone treatment for a brain tumor (one that would kill him two years later) and had grown increasingly distressed about the state of intellectuals, American culture, and the country's future. See Buell to Vera Michaels Dean, Foreign Policy Association, July 17, 1944, box 5, Buell Papers LC. Dean had a PhD (1928) in international relations from Radcliffe and rose to the director of research at the Foreign Policy Association just as Buell was stepping down as its president. She remained the director and editor of the association's *Bulletin* until 1961. By that time she was known primarily as an expert in the politics of developing nations. Her papers are at Radcliffe.

24. See Buell, *Isolated America*, six lectures he gave in 1939 at the Fletcher School of Law and Diplomacy, which includes his discussion of the totalitarian trend in the United States and his prescription for a new world order.

25. See also "Why Be a Congressman?," *Time*, August 3, 1942. http://www.time.com/time/magazine/article/0,9171,773317,00.html, accessed February 13, 2013. This is a report on Buell's candidacy for Congress (he lost).

26. Parmar, *Foundations of the American Century*, 68–69.

27. O'Donnell, "American Foreign Policy," 337.

28. Stanfield, *Philanthropy and Jim Crow in American Social Science*, 144.

29. Ekbladh, "Present at the Creation," 119.

30. Schuman, *International Politics*, 219, 234–235, 259.

31. Shils, "Robert Maynard Hutchins," 229. Shils wrote that he knew Schuman "quite well" and that "he was incontestably a fellow traveler."

32. Following the campaign to get him fired, which involved intense pressure on Chicago's president, Schuman took a leave of absence to teach at Williams, where he was offered a permanent position. Although Chicago promoted him from instructor to assistant professor, Schuman informed his mentor, Quincy Wright, he wanted a full professorship and it had been made clear to him he would not get it. Instead, he was advised by both colleagues and the administration to take the Williams job. See Schuman to Wright, January 2, 1936, box 23, Addenda 1, Quincy Wright Papers, Regenstein Library, University of Chicago, Chicago, Illinois (hereafter Wright Papers).

33. See Willey, "The College Training Programs of the Armed Forces." The first of the army occupation schools was set up in Charlottesville, Virginia. The navy had its own programs, including the School of Military Government and Administration created at Columbia to assist in the occupation of the Pacific. See the brief account by one of its architects, Schuyler Wallace, "The Naval School of Military Government and Administration," 29–33. Columbia's School of International Affairs grew out of the naval school, with the same leadership, Professor Schuyler Wallace. See David Horowitz, "Sinews of Empire," Most other universities shut down all these emergency institutes and programs when government funding ceased at the end of the war.

34. In addition to the discussion below, see Parker, "Made-in-America Revolutions."

Chapter 5: Making the World Safe for "Minorities"

1. Du Bois, *Black Reconstruction in America*, 15. For two of the myriad accounts of the writing of the book and its significance for subsequent generations, see Lewis, *W. E. B. Du Bois*, 2:349–387; and Robinson, *Black Marxism*, 195–240.

2. Du Bois, "A Negro Nation within a Nation." For the speech, see Gottheimer, ed., *Ripples of Hope*, 170–173.

3. Bunche, "Reconstruction Reinterpreted"; Harris, "Reconstruction and the Negro"; and Frazier, "The Du Bois Program in the Present Crisis." For a general account of the views and significance of the three "radicals" or self-styled "Young Turks," see Holloway, *Confronting the Veil*.

4. Roediger, *Wages of Whiteness*, is a good place to start.

5. Bunche, "Reconstruction Reinterpreted," 570.

6. Bunche, "Marxism and the Negro Question," box 133, Ralph Bunche Papers, Special Collections, University of California Los Angeles, reprinted in Henry, *Selected Speeches*, 35–48, the version I have relied on in this paragraph. The same argument with some of the identical text appeared five years later in *Workers Age*, an organ of the Communist Party. See Jim Cork, "'Self-Annihilation' in Negro Question: The C. P. and the Theory of Self Determination," *Workers Age*, November 15, 1934, 5, http://archive.org/stream/WorkersAgeVol.320Nov.151934/WA20#page/n3/mode/2up, accessed January 23, 2013.

7. Bunche's 1954 rebuttal to the International Organizations Employees Loyalty Board investigation, quoted in Miller, *Born along the Color Line*, 276.

8. Robinson, *Black Marxism*, 207. In a 1981 lecture, C. L. R. James said that he knew "no finer single-volume history of any episode or any territory." James, "Walter Rodney and the Question of Power."

9. For one of the only efforts to avoid eliding Du Bois's program with the idea of black state building or thinking that self-determination can be realized only through a national state, see Singh, *Black Is a Country*, 58–64. There is also now a much richer appreciation of the push and pull of local and external (Soviet) influence on the communist movement in the development of the Black Belt thesis than in the (still valuable) Cold War era accounts. See Maxwell, *New Negro, Old Left*, including his review of the key contributions by Mark Naison and Robin D. G. Kelley. Draper, *The Rediscovery of Black Nationalism*, is a representative polemic in response to the rise of black studies; and Howe, *Afrocentrism*, to the later Bernalian moment in parts of the discipline.

10. Guterl is the rare scholar who notes the parallels in Du Bois's and Stoddard's proposals; Guterl, *The Color of Race in America*, 149.

11. Buell to Locke, March 11, 1935, box 18, folder 2, Locke Papers. In this letter, Buell notes his worry about the fate of democracy abroad and his premonition of shifts in the southern political landscape in the wake of the New Deal. This was the reason for his interest in autonomy, drawing in part from work in the Caribbean and South Africa. In addition, see Buell to Rayford Logan, May 21, 1935, box 166–8, folder 23, Logan Papers MSRC, where Buell praises Du Bois's "A Nation within a Nation" article and hopes the latter develops a more detailed plan.

12. See Henry, *Ralph Bunche*, 40–47, 174–181; and Miller, *Born along the Color Line*, 172–290. Within the National Negro Conference, Bunche pressed unsuccessfully for a focus on labor issues. He also produced a number of critical assessments, including one for Gunnar Myrdal's Carnegie-funded project. In 1940, he quit what he called in essence, reasonably or not, "a communist cell."

13. No scholarly account of the conferences exists to my knowledge. There is a late revised schedule of speakers in box 50, folder 4 of the E. Franklin Frazier Papers, Mooreland-Spingarn Research Center, Howard University, Washington, D.C. An earlier draft is archived in box 135, folder "Howard University, 1935," Ralph J. Bunche Papers, Special Collections, Charles E. Young Research Library, University of California Los Angeles.

14. See Hatcher, "The World of Inter-Racial Relations," a review of Locke's lectures.

15. My discussion relies on Mazower, "The League of Nations in Interwar Europe"; Mazower, "The Strange Triumph of Human Rights"; and Pedersen, "Back to the League of Nations."

16. Mazower, "The Strange Triumph of Human Rights."

17. This was the working title for Bunche's book when Locke first proposed the project in February and when Bunche formally accepted the commission in June 1935. See Alain Locke to Ralph Bunche, June 4, 1935, box 18, folder 7, Locke Papers. To date, only African American political scientists and intellectual historians have considered Bunche's text worth discussing. See Holloway, *Confronting the Veil*, 163–167; Henry, *Ralph Bunche*, 56–57; Henry, "A World View of Race Revisited"; Kilson, "Ralph Bunche's Analytical Perspective on African Development"; Kilson, "Ralph Bunche: African American Intellectual"; and Waters, "Ralph Bunche and Civil Rights."

18. His biographer, Charles Henry, admires it for being ahead of its time in debunking the scientific status of race, for seeing the idea as a social construction, and for identifying the system of economic exploitation that race buttresses even as belief in its naturalness or reality takes on a life of its own. Henry, "A World View of Race Revisited." These were all arguments that Locke had made twenty years earlier. They needed to be made again—not for the last time—and Bunche was probably unaware of Locke's breakthroughs. What Bunche cared about most, however, was decoupling African American identity and political strategy from the future of colonial rule in Africa.

19. His introductory examples to illustrate the absurdity of typical depictions of the "threats" a politics of (racial) difference projects have lost none of their force today, even if the borders are different ones. "For instance, how can equality be advocated in America when one hundred million members of the 'white race' are constantly 'menaced' by twelve million members of the 'black race?' Can there be equality in Germany when seventy million 'pure' members of the 'Teutonic race' are said to be threatened with 'degeneration and destruction' by half a million members of the 'Jewish race'? The 'Oriental races,' we are often warned, present a constant danger to the pace and unparalleled civilization of the 'white races' of Europe and America." Bunche, *A World View of Race*, 2.

20. Ibid., 25, 1, 41.

21. Henry, "A World View of Race Revisited," 48. He is misleading, however, about a further assertion that the analysis of the relationship between capitalism and slavery "foreshadows" (56) the dissertation published a few years later by Eric Williams and the reworked version of *Capitalism and Slavery* (1944). The problem is that the analysis was Du Bois's from *Reconstruction*, which Bunche read and reviewed prior to writing the essay and cited extensively in the chapter on the United States.

22. Fields and Fields, *Racecraft*.

23. Raymond Leslie Buell to Rayford Logan, May 9, 1935, box 166–8, folder 23, Logan Papers MSRC.

24. Bunche, *A World View of Race*, 96.

25. Ibid., 95. Schuman argued the same thing in *International Politics*, 234–235.

26. Bunche, *A World View of Race*, 2.

27. Bunche, Review of *How Britain Rules Africa*.

28. Henry, *Ralph Bunche*, 75–86.

29. Lewis, *Du Bois*, 424–426, Harris and Molesworth, *Locke*, 298–301, Guy and Brookfield, "W. E. B. Du Bois's Basic American Negro Creed," quote from Locke, 70.

30. See Edwards, *Practice of Diaspora*, 243–244.

31. See Edward Frazier to Alain Locke, December 10, 1921, box 30, folder 27, Logan Papers, MSRC. He did not get the grant. Instead, Frazier traveled to Copenhagen to study cooperative agriculture and folk schools after a controversial award by the American Scandinavian Foundation to its first African American applicant. Platt, *E. Franklin Frazier Reconsidered*, 56–61.

32. Von Eschen, *Race against Empire*, 12–13; Padmore later wrote that three books in particular shaped his understanding of colonialism: Hobson's *Imperialism*, Lenin's *Imperialism: The Highest Stage of Capitalism*, and Parker Moon's *Imperialism and World Politics*. Polsgrove, *Ending British Rule in Africa.*, 10.

33. Edwards, *Practice of Diaspora*, 245.

34. Padmore, *The Life and Struggles of Negro Toilers*, quoting the online version, http://www.marxists.org/archive/padmore/1931/negro-toilers/ch06.htm#s2, accessed February 19, 2013; Hooker, *Black Revolutionary*, 22–32.

35. The discussion below relies on David Henry Anthony III's labor of love, *Max Yergan*, about the enigmatic activist who by the end of his life had become "the point-man for counterrevolution" (275) on the African continent.

36. For biographical information about Van Kleeck, see the finding aid to her papers at Smith College, http://asteria.fivecolleges.edu/findaids/sophiasmith/mnsss 150_bioghist.html, accessed February 20, 2013.

37. See "Carnegie Corporation in South Africa: A Difficult Past Leads to a Commitment to Change," *Carnegie Results*, Winter 2004, http://carnegie.org/file admin/Media/Publications/winter_04southafrica.pdf, accessed February 20, 2013. This is the foundation's own assessment. For a scholarly account, see Bell, "American Philanthropy, the Carnegie Corporation, and Poverty in South Africa."

38. Anthony, *Max Yergan*, 191.

39. Henry, *Ralph Bunche*, 126, 175, 279n22; and Anthony, *Max Yergan*, 208 appear to disagree on the year—1941 or 1943—of Bunche's resignation, with the former less precise on this point. I believe it is 1943. To be clear, other Howard faculty, including Franklin Frazier and Rayford Logan, joined the organization in its most active years during the war. The Council on African Affairs soldiered on in support of African liberation movements until 1955, after Yergan's resignation and refashioning as a cold warrior, but the organization's principals—Robeson, Du Bois and Alphaeus Hunton—faced charges under the McCarran Act before it shut its doors for good. Van Eschen, *Race against Empire*, 143. For an argument that the Council on African Affairs was the forerunner of solidarity organizations that fought apartheid in the United States, see Brock, "The 1950s: Africa Solidarity Rising."

40. Polsgrove, *Ending British Rule in Africa*, 43–44.

41. Padmore to Locke, October 3, 1938, box 76, folder 16, Locke Papers.

42. The other was the St. Lucian economist and future Nobel Prize winner, W. Arthur Lewis, then the first black man to teach at the London School of Economics. Lewis also identified with a less radical (nonrevolutionary) circle of pan-Africanists, the League of Colored Peoples, but Padmore's group published his critique, *The West Indies Today*, as a pamphlet in 1938. See Polsgrove, *Ending British Rule in Africa*, 33–34; and Tignor, *W. Arthur Lewis and the Birth of Development Economics*, 33–38.

43. Polsgrove, *Ending British Rule in Africa*, 67–68. The Anglo-American Caribbean Commission was founded in 1942 to coordinate wartime supplies and ostensibly to pursue economic reform in the region. See Parker, *Brother's Keeper*. For Williams's involvement, see Martin, "Eric Williams and the Anglo-American Caribbean Commission."

44. See, for example, the papers delivered at the Rockefeller Foundation's Bellagio Center's conference in Williams's honor, published as Solow and Engerman, *British Capitalism and Caribbean Slavery*.

45. "There is nothing definite to report yet on the Hull invitation. I am trying to do everything possible, but as you know, things move very slowly here. I will keep trying though, because I think it is an excellent idea." Bunche to Buell, May 22, 1939, box 2, folder 19, Buell Papers LC.

46. Herskovits quoted in Harris, "Segregation and Scholarship," 319, patronizing emphasis mine. Herskovits's paper trail about this kind of gate keeping and behind-the-scenes denigration of scholars is a long one. According to Herskovits, Du Bois, who would soon participate in the first integrated panel on African Americans at the American Historical Association, was "not a scholar" but a "radical" and a "Negrophile." See Janken, *Rayford W. Logan*, 95. Like too many others of this species of scholar, he was also prone to exaggerate his ability to "kill" some project or other. Rayford Logan referred to him in 1943 as the would-be "dictator of Negro studies."

See diary entry for May 24, 1943, box 4, Diaries, 1943–1944, Rayford Whittingham Logan Papers, Library of Congress, Washington, D.C. (hereafter Logan Papers LC).

47. Locke, "In the Setting of World Culture," 5–6.

48. Frazier, Review of *When Peoples Meet*.

49. Ibid., 92.

Chapter 6: The Philanthropy of Masters

1. The title of the chapter is from Du Bois, writing about the outcome of the Dumbarton Oaks discussions, quoted in Anderson, *Eyes off the Prize*, 38.

2. Earle was ill during part of this period, but the truth is that he hadn't published much since he revised his dissertation in 1923. His next book, published in 1941, consisted of three essays totaling seventy-one pages, which he directed at isolationism. It assayed the costs of a German victory for the United States and called for resistance by all means necessary. What was once imperialism was now U.S. expansionism for strategic considerations. And although President Woodrow Wilson himself claimed the opposite, Earle now felt that Wilson's main objective was preservation of the European balance of power. Earle, *Against This Torrent*.

3. Since it apparently didn't look good for the Institute of Advanced Study to be concerned with emergency public policy matters rather than basic research, Carnegie originally designated the American Committee of International Studies as the grantee. Foundation officers also did not want to run the risk of "offending the soul of good old Andrew and the peace of mind of his widow," so the funds were specified for "studies on foreign policy." Earle nonetheless used the cash to run his seminar on the American military. With the dissolution of the American Committee of International Studies the next year, the funds were shifted to the institute. See Conversation between Edward Mead Earle and John Dollard and Frederick Keppel, Notes by W[illiam] W L[ockwood], 1/29/41, marked confidential, box 4, folder ACIS-Correspondence, Rockefeller Foundation, 1939–1941, Edward Mead Earle Papers, Seeley G. Mudd Manuscript Library, Princeton University, Princeton, New Jersey (hereafter Earle Papers). Keppel was then in his last year as president of Carnegie. Dollard, his assistant, became president in 1948.

4. For the Social Science Research Council's courting of Earle and plans for the conference, see Robert Crane to Earle, October 1, 1940, box 4, folder ACIS-Correspondence, SSRC [U.S.-British Dominions-Latin America] 1940, Earle Papers. For the history of the international studies conferences, see Long, "Who Killed the International Studies Conference?"

5. Buell to Earle, April 15, 1941. For the Alpha Phi Alpha press release, see Logan to Buell, April 8, 1941, box 9, folder 19, Buell Papers LC. The fraternity, of which Logan was president, was launching his program for "the Negro in the new world society." The Carnegie Corporation had also allocated funds as part of its national emergency effort to consider what it referred to as problems of Negro morale. See Conversation between Earle and Dollard and Keppel. I have not found any scholarship that deals with this aspect of Carnegie funding. For the general situation see Parmar, "'. . . Another Important Group That Needs More Cultivation.'"

6. Earle to Buell, April 16, 1941, box 6, folder 1, Buell Papers LC.

7. Minutes of meeting of American Committee on International Studies, February 21, 1941, SSRC, box 1, folder ACIS Minutes-General 1932–1941, Earle Papers. Wright and Percy Bidwell, who headed the studies staff of the Council on Foreign

Relations and represented the council on the American Committee on International Studies, were the other members.

8. Wright to Carter, February 14, 1941, box 10, ACIS-CNAR Conference Files General 1941, Earle Papers.

9. Carter to Earle, February 27 1941, box 10, ACIS-CNAR Conference Files General 1941, Earle Papers.

10. Wright to E. C. Carter, March 3, 1941, box 3, folder 2, Wright Papers.

11. Lockwood to Carter, March 4, 1941, box 10, ACIS-CNAR Conference Files General 1941, Earle Papers. It was Buell who had inspired Lockwood's trip to Howard.

12. Lockwood to Buell, April 17, 1941, box 9, folder 26, Buell Papers LC.

13. Quincy Wright to Lockwood, June 2, 1941, box 10, Earle Papers. Wright sought to amend the preliminary agenda invitation: "I do not like the idea that an Anglo-American sea power bloc is to be the permanent foundations for a new order, and do not think it can. It can and should be the initiating nucleus of such an order, however." He also continued to press, without success, for the inclusion of some Latin Americans, Portuguese, Spaniards, and Icelanders.

14. Wheeler-Bennett to Carter, March 3, 1941, box 10, Earle Papers.

15. Earle, "Memorandum Regarding Problems of Morale, Recreation, and Health in Connection with American Naval and Air Bases in the Caribbean," box 25, folder Professional Activities, Consult/Adv.: War Dept-Military Intell. Div. G-2, 1941. Earle Papers. Unfortunately for Earle, matters played out differently. Von Eschen describes the popular calypso Lord Invader wrote following the influx of U.S. troops (Since the Yankees came to Trinidad / They have the young girls going mad, / The young girls say they treat them nice, / And they give them a better price.) Von Eschen, *Race against Empire*, 37. Comedian Morey Amsterdam (later of Dick Van Dyke Show fame) stole the song, changed the most damning of the lyrics, and the Andrews Sisters recorded it. "Rum and Coca-Cola" became the best-selling U.S. single of 1945.

16. Janken, *Rayford W. Logan*, 133–134.

17. Entry for April 15, 1941, Logan diary, box 3, Logan Papers LC.

18. Polsgrove, *Ending British Rule in Africa*, 43; Parmar, "Black Americans"; Chadwin, *Hawks of World War II*, 184–186.

19. Logan eventually got in to see FDR. There is a good discussion of these matters in Janken, *Rayford W. Logan*, 116–125.

20. See Harris, "Racial Equality and the United Nations Charter," 127–128. For the NAACP see Anderson, *Eyes off the Prize*.

21. Headline of the Labor Party's newspaper following Deputy Prime Minister Clement Attlee's appearance before the West African Students' Union. Quoted in Janken, *Rayford W. Logan*, 168.

22. Twelve blacks on a 40-person committee, by Du Bois's count (he was one of them). See his review, "The Future of War."

23. For the drafting of the charter, see Venkataramani, "The United States, the Colonial Issue, and the Atlantic Charter Hoax," 3. Unfortunately, there is no good detailed account of the work of the Africa Committee, but see Plummer, *Rising Wind*, 110–113; and Janken, *Rayford W. Logan*, 171–173. Remarkably, Bunche's biographer and friend imagines him to have been a critic of the "ill-informed, unrealistic, and wooly thinking" of the American Committee, which allegedly was pining for political control by Africans. He clearly had not read the report and was unaware that Bunche wrote it. Urquhart, *Ralph Bunche*, 107. His other biographer repeats the error; see Henry, *Ralph Bunche*.

24. Quotations from the charter found in Committee on Africa, the War, and Peace Aims, *The Atlantic Charter and Africa from an American Standpoint*. For Padmore's reporting and the quotation from Churchill's controversial clarification, see Von Eschen, *Race against Empire*, 26.

25. Smuts, "The Basis of Trusteeship in African Native Policy." Stokes forwarded the "encouraging address" to Buell and drew on it in the introductory section of the conference call. Stokes to Buell, June 3, 1942. Much of the white commentary from the time saw it as heralding the end of race segregation. See Janken, *Rayford W. Logan*, 172–173. For a recent retrospective commentary on Smuts and trusteeship, see Dubow, "Smuts, the United Nations and the Rhetoric of Race and Rights," 65–66.

26. Mazower, *No Enchanted Palace*, 56; African National Congress, "Africans' Claims in Africa," ANC Historical Documents Archive, http://www.marxists.org/subject/africa/anc/1943/claims.htm, accessed March 1, 2013. This was a moment when Smuts was still imagining the creation of a white-ruled pan-African state stretching north to the equator.

27. Committee on Africa, the War, and Peace Aims, *The Atlantic Charter and Africa from an American Standpoint*, 38, 56, 126–127; Walker, *The Cold War*, 30.

28. See Logan's remarkable dissection, "Smuts Speaks of Africa"; and his autobiographical fragment on Smuts in box 166–33, folder 4, Logan Papers MSRC.

29. Du Bois was more blunt. After meeting with the committee on its draft, Du Bois told Logan the next day that "Ralph Bunche is getting to be a white folks' nigger." diary entry for Tuesday Afternoon [September 9, 1941], box 3, folder 1941 Diaries 1941, Logan Papers LC.

30. Williams, "Africa and the Post-War World."

31. For the book's outline and Tate's failed attempt to find funding for the project, see outline, box 23, and William C. Hapwood, Julius Rosenwald Fund, to Merze Tate, December 23, 1942, box 31, Merze Tate Papers, Moorland-Spingarn Research Center, Howard University, Washington, D.C. (hereafter Tate Papers). These papers were unprocessed when I worked in them, and materials in boxes were not in file folders. They have since been processed.

32. Tate, "The War Aims of World War I and II," 523.

33. Entry dated "Thursday Morning [February] 11, [1943?], box 4, Diaries, 1943–1944, Logan Papers LC (although Janken says 1942; *Rayford W. Logan*, 276n21). Nkrumah had just earned his MA (his third master's degree) in philosophy at Penn and was working fitfully on the topic of the philosophy of imperialism in Africa under Glenn Raymond Morrow, a specialist on Plato and a later dean of the college of arts and sciences. His dissertation was never accepted, for reasons that remain a mystery. A detailed outline of the imperialism thesis (one of two he wrote, apparently) remains, however, which develops his critique of the Atlantic Charter and argues that the colonial powers would never give up their possessions without resistance. This is why he believed a revolutionary movement was needed. He called "for independence, the federation of all West African territories, the formation of a constitutional assembly and the return of all expropriated lands and mines." Sherwood, *Kwame Nkrumah*, 65.

34. Janken, *Rayford W. Logan*, 169–170.

35. Ibid., 174.

36. Gerig was a Mennonite who served for years on the League's Information Section in Geneva; taught political science at Haverford; and became a chief official in the state department, where he planned for the future of colonial areas. In 1944, he was made the head of a rechristened Office of Dependent Area Affairs at the

state department. Ralph Bunche began working under him starting in July 1944. See Homan, "Orrie Benjamin Gerig."

37. See Louis, *Imperialism at Bay*; Wolton, *Lord Hailey, the Colonial Office and the Politics of Race and Empire in the Second World War.*

38. Logan to Walter White and Du Bois, June 30, 1945, box 181–8, folder 3, Logan Papers MSRC. For Bunche, see Plummer, *Rising Wind*, 156. On the Manchester meeting, see Adi and Sherwood, *1945 Manchester Pan-African Congress Revisited.* For the competing plans and the eclipse of Du Bois, see Lewis, *W. E. B. Du Bois*, 499–502.

39. See the manuscript of his talk "Race, Colonies and Imperialism" for the YMCA's National Peace Conference, June 15, 1943, box 166–26, folder 42, Logan Papers MSRC.

40. See e.g., entry for October 30, 1944, box 4, Diaries 1943–1944, Logan Papers LC.

41. For the writing of the pamphlet and the search for a publisher, see Polsgrove, *Ending British Rule in Africa*, 56–62. I am referencing the version reprinted in Cunard, *Essays on Race and Empire*, 7–178.

42. Padmore, *The White Man's Duty*, 145, 172, 134–135, 145–146.

43. Ibid., 146. Oxford's expert on colonial administration, Margery Perham (a Leslie Buell on steroids), was one of the frankest voices in the debate with colleagues who saw some merit in even marginal change toward "integration" of the colonial state apparatus. "The political demands of the African intelligentsia 'were rapidly acquiring political consciousness' and, rather than 'give in to them too soon', she proposed 'setting up large regional councils of native administration' which should aim 'to speed up the political education of the native authorities and to head off the intelligentsia from the state system.'" Wolton, *Lord Hailey, the Colonial Office and the Politics of Race and Empire in the Second World War*, 53. Both Padmore and Williams treated her only thinly veiled published positions in particular with scorn.

44. His biographer says that Melville Herskovits originated the idea, but Bunche's early correspondence about possible participants was with Stokes, not Herskovits, and the latter had nothing to do with the American Committee, whose members independently proposed convening a conference. Gershenhorn, *Melville Herskovits*, 182. Anson Phelps Stokes to Bunche, March 4, 1943, box 104, folder African Conference, Bunche Papers

45. Anson Phelps Stokes to Bunche, March 4, 1943, box 104, folder African Conference, Bunche Papers.

46. Marika Sherwood suggests a possible reason: the counsel by both representatives of the State Department and the Colonial Office advised that transportation for an international conference would be impossible. She also notes the dissent by Nkrumah's colleagues in the African Student Association to the paternalism of Stokes and the committee's opposition to African liberation. Sherwood, *Kwame Nkrumah*, 86–88.

47. Entry for Sunday, February 9 [*sic*; 8], 1943, box 3, Diaries 1942, Logan Papers LC.

48. Akami, *Internationalizing the Pacific*, 267–270; Anderson, "Pacific Dreams," 91–118.

49. The description is from "Ethnogeographic Board (Washington, D.C.), Records, 1942–1946," Smithsonian Institution Archives, http://siarchives.si.edu/collections/siris_arc_216694, accessed April 2, 2013.

50. Gershenhorn, *Melville J. Herskovits and the Racial Politics of Knowledge*, 182.

51. Edwin Embree to Bunche, May 12, 1943, box 112, folder labeled Institute of Pacific Relations, Bunche Papers.

52. Which should have been a piece of exculpatory evidence in the later effort to destroy the Institute of Pacific Relations, since Bunche was particularly concerned then to avoid any involvement with "front" organizations. Instead, Bunche's participation at Mont-Tremblant was used to tar him as a communist sympathizer later in the 1950s.

53. Carter to Bunche, March 17, 1943; Bunche to Carter, March 21, 1943; Edwin Embree to Bunche, May 12, 1943, all in box 112, folder Institute of Pacific Relations, Bunche Papers.

54. Reprinted in Henry, ed., *Ralph J. Bunche*, 274.

55. Entry for Tuesday, [February 10?], box 3, folder, Diaries, 1941, Logan Papers LC.

56. See Logan's discussion of Emerson's views at the March 1943 Minorities Workshop at Howard; entry for Thursday, March 4, box 4, Diaries 1943–1944, Logan Papers LC. For Emerson, see "Professor Rupert Emerson Is Appointed to Dept. of Interior: Territories and Possessions to Be in Government Instructor's Jurisdiction," *Harvard Crimson*, May 3, 1940, http://www.thecrimson.com/article/1940/5/3/ professor-rupert-emerson-is-appointed-to/, accessed March 13, 2013.

57. Document headed Mr. [Henry A.] Luce [as author] November 3, 1943, box 17, Luce folder 9, Time, Inc. Memoranda, Buell Papers LC. Not surprisingly, when Du Bois sought a meeting with Luce to discuss Africa's position in the world, Luce refused. Lewis, *W. E. B. Du Bois*, 502.

58. The last discussion of what to do after the American Committee on International Studies shut down can be found in the Minutes of the Problems and Policy Committee, December 7, 1941, box 66, Social Science Research Council Records, Rockefeller Archive Center, Tarrytown, New York (hereafter SSRC Records).

59. Analysis of the sixty or so more or less independent political units into which the world was divided demanded "discussions of race and racial characteristics, of the relations of geographic environment to social development, of group psychology, etc." Lewis Lorwin, "Memorandum on Research in International Relations," n.d., enclosed in Minutes, Committee on Problems and Policy, January 28, 1940, box 66, SSRC Records. This memorandum was likely commissioned by the president, Crane, or by the Committee to provide guidance in the emergency situation the United States confronted.

60. Meeting of American Committee for International Studies, afternoon session, October 4, 1941, box 1, folder ACIS Minutes-General 1932–1941, Earle Papers.

61. Fox, "Geopolitics and International Relations," 18–19.

62. See Fox to Quincy Wright, June 19, 1941, box 14, folder Fox, William, Wright Papers. Fox defended his dissertation, "Some Effects upon International Law of the Govermentalization [*sic*] of Private Enterprise," in 1940. For the date of his move to Yale, see Kaplan, *Wizards of Armageddon*, 21.

63. Strausz-Hupé, Review of *The Super-Powers*. Hans Morgenthau's review underscored how few professors outside the Yale Institute of International Studies and "Mssrs. Lippmann and Welles" shared Fox's "realistic approach"; Morgenthau, Review of *The Super-Powers*. The sole exceptionally critical review called it an exercise in sophistry: "Only the very foolish, for example, are going to be lulled into complacency by the invention of the phrase 'defensive expansionism' . . . to characterize what has long been called imperialism." Hallowell, Review of *The Superpowers*.

64. Fox, "Interwar International Relations Research." Brian Schmidt discusses the tendentiousness of this particular essay and its relationship to the rash of other such accounts in "The Rockefeller Foundation Conference."

65. See Kenneth W. Thompson interview with David Rockefeller, November 20, 1953, box 7, folder 61, IR 1943–1954, RG 3, Series 910, Rockefeller Foundation Archives. Guilhot burdens the fact of the early termination of a committee divided between behavioral-oriented social scientists and "IR scholars" led by Hans Morgenthau with more weight than it can bear. Had the committee not failed, "IR would probably have evolved into an entirely different discipline," Guilhot wrote. Although the Rockefeller Foundation supported the "realists" for the next few years, Guilhot claims that the Social Science Research Council bet instead on the "behavioral approach to international affairs" in the form of its Committee on Comparative Politics in 1954. He was unaware of the Social Science Research Council's support for Fox, Henry Kissinger, and others in the national security policy committee during this same period. See Guilhot, "One Discipline, Many Histories," 16–20.

66. Reinhold Niebuhr, the postwar realists' influential ally, was also considered for the presidency. It is hard to imagine him making the same decision. See Fox, *Reinhold Niebuhr*, 239.

67. Those who left with Dunn were Gabriel Almond, Bernard Cohen, Percy Corbett, Annette B. Fox (Bill's wife), William Kaufmann, and Klaus Knorr, who would take over the Center for International Studies after Dunn in 1961. The *New York Times* ran a front-page story on April 23, 1951, "Six of Faculty Leaving Yale for Princeton in Policy Spilt," but Griswold's motives remained opaque. For what the archival records reveal, see Ramos, "The Role of the Yale Institute of International Studies in the Construction of the United States National Security Ideology," 132–139; and Kuklick, "Rise of Policy Institutes in the United States," 690–691.

68. As for other key Yale Institute of International Studies personnel, Bernard Brodie went to Rand. Arnold Wolfers, who could not get Princeton to match his chair at Yale, remained in New Haven until 1957, when he accepted the directorship of the Foreign Policy Institute at the School of Advanced International Studies in Washington, D.C. Millikan left Yale for MIT in 1949 but then immediately took an extended leave to work for the CIA. On the early days of the Center for International Studies, see Blackmer, *The MIT Center for International Studies*.

69. In 1984, Robert McCaughey defined "international studies" as "serious inquiry by Americans into those parts of the world Americans have traditionally regarded as having histories, cultures, and social arrangements distinctly different from their own" and an enterprise that was different from "international relations, here considered part of political science." McCaughey, *International Studies and Academic Enterprise*, xii–xiii. It may be that McCaughey's reliance on a single native informant for his views on international relations, namely William T. R. Fox, explains the anachronism.

70. Lyons, "The Growth of National Security Research." See also Morton and Lyons, *Schools for Strategy*, which surveyed civilian institutions at great length; and Bock and Berkowitz, "The Emerging Field of National Security," which reinforces the story of the universities lagging behind institutions such as Rand until the 1960s. Finally, see Max Beloff's review of *Schools for Strategy* for the distinction he draws between the relative more scholarly approach of Harvard, MIT, Princeton, and Hopkins and "the very doubtfully useful offerings of the University of Pennsylvania's Foreign Policy Research Institute, the Hoover Institution, and the Georgetown Center for Strategic Studies." Given what to many appeared to be "engaging in what is . . . propaganda for a particular (and some would argue very dangerous) view of the 'Cold War,'" Beloff concluded that one "can understand why a great university like Yale which would have much to offer has preferred to stand aloof."

71. "It is now so frequently employed by the radio and the press communicating in almost any spoken tongue on earth that in February 1960 a frequency account, including the press and radio of America, Europe, Asia, and Africa, showed that imperialism was used at a rate of at least one in every ten political broadcasts. The term was most often used in the Middle East, in Central and North Africa, and in communist countries." Koebner and Schmidt, *Imperialism*, xviii.

72. Lauren, *Power and Prejudice*, 4.

73. Morrison, "Unspeakable Things Unspoken," 24.

Part IV: "The Dark World Goes Free"

1. *New York Times*, July 28, 1958, 1. The title of the chapter is from Du Bois, *Dark Princess*. Toward the end of the novel, the protagonist, Matthew Townes, learns from his ex-lover, an Indian princess, of plans to cement an alliance of colored peoples against imperialism. "The High Command is to be chosen. Ten years of preparation are set. Ten more years of final planning, and then five years of intensive struggle. In 1952 the Dark World goes free—whether in Peace and fostering Friendship with all men, or in blood and storm—it is for Them—the Pale Masters of today—to say" (296–297).

2. Meriwether, *Proudly We Can Be Africans*, 174, quoting a printed copy of Bunche's remarks, Meriwether's emphasis.

3. The attack on Bunche came up in the notorious 1959 documentary by Mike Wallace and Louis Lomax, *The Hate That Hate Produced*, which introduced millions of white viewers to Malcolm X and the Nation of Islam. The main reason for the hostility was his role in Palestine. He was the real "George Washington of Israel," according to one of the interviewees, James R. Lawson, head of the United African Nationalist Movement. See the transcript provided in Memorandum from SAC New York to Director, FBI, July 16, 1959, http://www.columbia.edu/cu/ccbh/mxp/pdf/071659hthp-transcript.pdf, accessed March 18, 2013.

4. Harold R. Isaacs, diary note, New York, January 6, 1959, box 19, file Ralph Bunche, Harold R. Isaacs Papers, Institute Archives and Special Collections, Massachusetts Institute of Technology, Cambridge, Massachusetts (hereafter Isaacs Papers). For the dinner, see "Ghana Honored," *Crisis* (August–September 1958), 407–408. Forty years later, James Meriwether, the only historian I am aware of who discusses the moment, thought that Bunche's sentiments that night reflected a change in the thinking of African American liberals about "increased blending of a racialist nationalism with liberal integrationism." Meriwether, *Proudly We Can Be Africans*, 174.

5. In one sense it foreshadows what international relations scholars in the late 1970s identified as the problem of "the second image reversed," or the international system's effects on domestic politics and society. However, no one working in this area referred to Isaacs, let alone the many African American thinkers who were then discussing the impact of decolonization on the United States, since white supremacy was never a "case" the theorists considered, even as they unselfconsciously resurrected one of its core concepts, "dependency." See Gourevitch, "The Second Image Reversed," 881–912.

6. See Harold Isaacs to Rayford Logan, n.d. [early 1958], enclosing draft "First Notes" on "World Affairs Impact on U.S. Race Relations," dated January 3, 1958, CIS, Communications Program D-58/1, and Isaacs's unpublished paper for the August 1971 meeting of the American Political Science Association, "Group

Identity and Political Change: The House of Muumbi," both in box 166–14, folder 1, Logan Papers MSRC.

7. See "Negro Number Meeting," Survey Library, April 14, [1942], 2:30 pm, box 110, folder 32, Locke Papers; Locke, "Color: The Unfinished Business of Democracy." Molesworth, *Collected Works of Alain Locke*, refashions the text of this and thus possibly other pieces. Seek the originals!

8. The critical exception to this rule is Füredi, *The Silent War.*

9. Myrdal, *An American Dilemma*, 1018.

10. Drake was a member of Padmore's circle. He headed the sociology department at the University College of Ghana in Accra in 1958 and built Stanford's black studies program starting in 1969.

11. Drake, "The International Implications of Race and Race Relations." E. Franklin Frazier developed the same line of analysis while a member of the U.S. delegation to the United Nations Education, Scientific and Cultural Organization (UNESCO). See his "Memorandum Submitted to the Division of the Social Sciences of UNESCO on The Influence of the Negro on the Foreign Policy of the United States, 1951," box 54, folder 23, Frazier Papers. For similar accounts by whites, see Woodward, *The Strange Career of Jim Crow*; and Isaacs, "World Affairs and U.S. Race Relations."

12. The first accounts of the setbacks to the civil rights movement of the 1950s exacted by the Cold War policy of containment are in Roark, "American Black Leaders"; and Cheng, "The Cold War."

13. Lincoln received his PhD in social ethics from Boston University in 1960 for his path-breaking study of black Muslims in America, to which MIT's Harold Isaacs had made two strategic contributions. One was to bring Lincoln to the attention of the Anti-Defamation League, which began to support the work in return for periodic reports from Lincoln to the former FBI agent who handled the league's investigations of "hate groups." Isaacs also intervened with Boston University's dean when Lincoln considered changing topics. Lincoln was uncomfortable with the role of informant for Anti-Defamation League staffer (and later national fact-finding director) Milton Ellerin and looked to Isaacs for advice. Details can be found in Isaacs to Lincoln, November 13, 1959; Isaacs to Oscar Cohen [national program director of the Anti-Defamation League], October 29, 1959; and Lincoln to Milton Ellerin, August 25, 1959. Isaacs also introduced Lincoln to Harvard psychologist Gordon Allport, a member of the editorial board of the international relations journal *International Organization* who later wrote the foreword to C. Eric Lincoln and Aminah Beverly McCloud, *Black Muslims in America* (1961). See Laura [Isaacs's secretary?] to Isaacs, August 18 [probably 1959]. For Isaacs's outreach to Boston University, see Isaacs to Dean Walter Muelder, Boston University School of Theology, March 13, 1959, all in box 2, folder "L," Isaacs Papers.

14. Lincoln, "The Race Problem and International Relations." James Baldwin made the same point toward the end of a famous *New Yorker* essay, "Most of the Negroes I know do not believe that this immense concession [the 1954 Supreme Court decision] would ever have been made if it had not been for the competition of the Cold War, and the fact that Africa was clearly liberating herself and therefore had, for political reasons, to be wooed by the descendants of her former masters." Baldwin, "Letter from a Region in My Mind," 130. A new generation of historians with access to declassified government records revived the tradition in 1980s and early 1990s; see Dudziak, "Desegregation as a Cold War Imperative"; and Dudziak, "Cold War Civil Rights."

15. Vucetic, *The Anglosphere*. For an account of the pervasiveness of talk of race war in this period, see Plummer, *Rising Wind*, 312–315.

16. Füredi, *The Silent War*, 202–221.

17. Sayre, "Quest for Independence," 564, 566–567. Sayre taught government at Williams and international law at Harvard before entering government service as assistant secretary of state and high commissioner of the Philippines under FDR. Also see Perham, "The British Problem in Africa." Perham, who had previously opposed self-government in the colonies, had apparently come around, predicting that most would gain their independence by the end of the twentieth century, although she believed that the second of the two great conflicts of the Cold War, the "division of race, or less inaccurately, of color" might not be contained. See also Huxley, "The Next-to-Last Act in Africa," which imagines Cairo, Conakry, and Accra planning for a widespread anti-white uprising, or what she calls "the racial bomb."

18. "Squeezing A Civil War to Death," *New York Times*, January 27, 1962, 20 ("Algeria, where anarchic race war prevails"); "How to Break Up an Empire," *New York Times*, January 12, 1966, 20 ("Should fighting erupt along the Zambesi line, a brutal and extensive race war might become inevitable"); "Africa's Heart and Horn," *New York Times*, December 9, 1966, 46 ("there is reason to foresee race war along the edges of the white held triangle of Mozambique, Angola, Rhodesia and South Africa. . . . China's neo-colonialism aims at the Congolese heart of darkness and continental dominance"); and "A Sad New Look," *New York Times*, June 15, 1969, E16 ("There is profound worry today about the possibility that the essence of China's revolutionary efforts may lie in a hateful challenge, an attempt encourage race war in the rest of the world. . . . This analysis may help to explain why Peking now regards Moscow as even more of an enemy than Washington. It simply cannot afford to have another and white nation speaking as a legitimate revolutionary power")

19. "'Great Efforts' Have Been Made to Cause Race War, MacArthur Tells Negro Paper," *New York Times*, January 4, 1951, 9. Senator Paul Douglas, a liberal from Illinois who backed losing candidate Estes Kefauver as the Democratic Party nominee in 1952, argued the same in his convention speech, where he counseled against the expansion of the war into China because he believed it would hand the communists "a powerful propaganda weapon to inflame the darker skinned races of Asia and to swing India and Malays against us." *New York Times*, July 22, 1952, 15.

20. Adolph Berle Jr., "Communist Thunder to the South," *New York Times*, July 4, 1954, SM8.

21. Quoted in Jones, *After Hiroshima*, 4.

22. Schelling, "Strategy of Conflict," 203, my emphasis. Schelling would soon publish *The Strategy of Conflict* (1960).

23. Browne, *Race Relations in International Affairs*, iii–iv. Browne had just been forced to quit his position in the U.S. aid administration in Vietnam after authorities learned that he had married a Vietnamese woman. He later founded the *Review of Black Political Economy*. See "Robert S. Browne, 79, Dies; Economist and Advocate," *New York Times*, August 15, 2004; and Wu, "An African-Vietnamese American."

24. In 1952, the Royal Institute of International Affairs appointed Lord Hailey as chair of a new Board of Studies on Race Relations. The board appointed novelist Philip Mason as director of studies of race relations. The president of the Rockefeller Foundation, Dean Rusk, agreed to fund some of the first studies, although his staff advised him that "we should not anticipate an important result either as a solution to the problems or as an addition to knowledge." Mason parted ways with the Royal Institute of International Affairs in 1958 and founded an independent Institute of Race Relations. See the memo from J[oseph] H[.] W[illets] to Rusk, October 30, 1953, box 65, folder 565,

Series 4015, Record Group 1.2, Rockefeller Foundation Archives. For the history of the Institute of Race Relations, see Sivanandan, "Race and Resistance."

25. Hodson, "Race Relations in the Commonwealth."

26. Saxton Bradford, USIA, to Nelson A. Rockefeller, February 9, 1955, Subject: Our Psychological Position in the Far East, box 83, F.635–636, folder "Afro-Asia—Colonialism & Neutralism," Rockefeller Family, Record Group 4 Rockefeller Foundation Archives. For the impossible-to-miss reading by top U.S. officials of Bandung as an anti-white, anti-U.S. gathering see Fraser, "An American Dilemma"; Jones, "A 'Segregated' Asia"; and Parker, "Cold War II."

27. For the problem with this and other myths about the Asian-African Conference, see Vitalis, "The Midnight Ride of Kwame Nkrumah and Other Fables from Bandung."

28. Tate, Review of *The Color Curtain*. Tillman Durdin, the *New York Times* correspondent who wrote some of the first reports on Japanese atrocities in Nanking in the 1930s, challenged Wright and by implication others who imagined Bandung in these terms in "Richard Wright Examines the Meaning of Bandung," *New York Times*, March 18, 1956.

29. Toynbee, "Is a 'Race War' Shaping Up?" 26, 88–90, quotation on 88. Toynbee's answer was a qualified no. The point, however, is the assumptions about the identities that mattered and the contradictions to which these gave rise. For his critic, see Neil Leonard, "Race and Color," *New York Times*, October 11, 1963, 12.

30. Quoted in Isaacs, *The New World of Negro Americans*, 12. How one assesses the extent of threat inflation depends on assumptions about the pace and extent of change toward African American liberation in the period. If one accepts the view that change was slow and prone to setbacks, then the problem is that no one has shown continued resistance to U.S. leadership abroad in response after 1965. Those who are more optimistic about the "civil rights revolution" have to consider the implicit counterfactual, that had Jim Crow remained more or less intact, then key Third World allies (dependencies) such as Saudi Arabia, the Philippines, Taiwan, and so forth would have defected.

31. Memorandum of a Conference with the President, White House, July 31, 1956, Foreign Relations of the United States 1955–1957, Vol. XVI, Suez Crisis, July 26–December 31, 1956, Document 34, http://history.state.gov/historical documents/frus1955-57v16/d34, accessed April 10, 2013. See also Connelly, "Taking off the Cold War Lens."

32. Füredi, *The Silent War*, 217–221.

33. Hoffmann, "Discord in Community," 524.

Chapter 7: The First but Not Last Crisis of a Cold War Profession

1. Vitalis, "Guilhot's Gambit." For the founding of the International Political Science Association, see Boncourt, "Political Science: A Postwar Product."

2. See Harold Sprout to Quincy Wright, January 11, 1949, box 2, folder 21, Wright Papers. Specialists in international relations had a particularly difficult time securing slots at the annual convention. Meetings consisted of only about two dozen panels in those days.

3. Bernard Brodie to Edward Mead Earle, October 5, 1942, box 26, folder "Professional Activities, Prof. Assoc.—American Pol. Sci. Assoc.," Earle Papers.

4. See Memorandum, "Arnold Wolfers, Professor of International Relations, Yale," box 5, folder ACIS-Correspondence W 1940–1942, Earle Papers.

5. Sondermann, "The Merger."

6. Henry Teune, "The International Studies Association," n.d., unpublished revision of a paper originally prepared for the International Studies Association Leadership Meeting, University of South Carolina, 1982, in my possession.

7. Charles McClelland to Quincy Wright, September 30, 1960, box 18, Wright Papers.

8. Quincy Wright to Arthur W. MacMahon, November 25, 1947, box 2, folder 20, Wright Papers. MacMahon, a Columbia University professor of political science, a pioneer in the study of public administration, and, in his own radical days, the lover of Georgia O'Keefe, served as president of the APSA in 1947–1948. http://www.okeeffemuseum.org/chronology.html, accessed March 30, 2015.

9. Wright, "Political Science and World Stabilization," 2.

10. Bunche, "Presidential Address," 970. Hanes Walton Jr. provides a thoroughly misleading gloss on this point by adding words that Bunche never uttered. He imagines Bunche to have raised pointed questions not just about colonialism but about "the fear, intolerance, suspicion and confusion emanating from racial demagogues; and the second-class citizenship emerging from racial segregation, White supremacy, and disenfranchisement." You won't find these ideas expressed on the page Walton erroneously cites or anyplace else. See Walton, "The Political Science Educational Philosophy of Ralph Bunche," 147.

11. Miller, *Born along the Color Line*, 290.

12. Bunche, "Presidential Address," 969.

13. Lilian Sharpley, YWCA National Board, to Bunche, June 30, 1950; and Bunche to Sharpley, July 5, 1950, box 127, folder 60, Bunche Papers.

14. The copy is contained in box 109, folder 13, Locke Papers.

15. Collier, *Political Woman*, 33–35, 67–69; William Chapman, "Scholars Check CIA Activity," *Washington Post*, February 23, 1967, A8; Lowi, "The Politicization of Political Science"; Barrow, "Intellectual Origins of the New Political Science"; and See, "Prophet without Honor." For a complementary account, see Oren, *Our Enemies and US*, 155–164.

16. "The study of exotic areas is necessarily costly, and he who would measure the progress and locate the growing points of international relations research must look elsewhere than to the university's cash box." William T. R. Fox, "Growing Points in the Study of International Relations," address at the dedication of the University of Southern California's Von KleinSmid Center of International Affairs, October 1, 1966, reprinted in Fox, *American Study of International Relations*, 97–116.

17. Rosenau, *International Studies and the Social Sciences*, 29. See also Pye, *Political Science and Area Studies*. Round two of this battle began in the early 1990s. Also see, Wallerstein, "The Unintended Consequences of Cold War Area Studies," 206–210.

18. Stocking, *Race, Culture, and Evolution*, 266. Stocking discusses the transformations in anthropological theory that would exert such a heavy influence on political scientists who pioneered what they called "modernization theory," no more obviously than in the case of early Yale Institute of International Studies member Lucian Pye, who had moved on with the group to Princeton, then joined MIT's Center for International Studies in 1956. Samuels and Weiner, *The Political Culture of Foreign Area and International Studies*.

19. Eisenhower's views as reported in a Memorandum of Conversation, September 3, 1959, quoted in Plummer, *In Search of Power*, 1.

20. Hall, *Area Studies*, as quoted in Wallerstein, "The Unintended Consequences of Cold War Area Studies," 199–200. For Hall's career, see L. A. Peter Gosling and George Kish, "Professor Emeritus Robert B. Hall," University of Michigan

Faculty History Project, http://um2017.org/faculty-history/faculty/robert-b-hall/ memorial, accessed April 17, 2013. In addition to Michigan, Harvard (Regional Program on China and Peripheral Areas), Columbia (Russian Institute), the University of Washington (Far Eastern Institute), and the University of Pennsylvania (Department of South Asian Regional Studies) also founded centers a year or two after the war.

21. Wagley, "Area Research and Training," *Area Research and Training*, 3, both quotations in this paragraph.

22. Although routinely described as the first such African Studies center, Lincoln University's president, Horace Mann Bond, founded an Institute for the Study of African Affairs in 1950. Foundations declined to support it, and Herskovits was kept abreast of efforts to make sure of this outcome. Without external support, Bond, who was an outspoken advocate of African independence, failed in his bid to recruit additional faculty. See Gershenhorn, "African American Scholars and the Development of African Studies," 51–53.

23. Gershenhorn, *Melville J. Herskovits and the Racial Politics of Knowledge*, 184–192, is essential for its detail and its demonstration once more of Herskovits's remarkable willingness to shape his research program in response to donors' preferences (and to undercut his colleagues). Carnegie officials had mixed views about Herskovits and took a while to agree, even after Penn made the decision to narrow its focus to North Africa. Penn eventually shipped one and a half tons of materials on sub-Saharan Africa to Northwestern University. No scholar has explained what led to the decision, although the library's Web site now refers to it as "disastrous." http://www.library.upenn.edu/collections/policies/african.html, accessed March 30, 2015.

24. Janken, *Rayford W. Logan*, 193, calls him a "gadfly . . . challenging government officials and other interested parties . . . over their alleged disregard of African affairs and their procolonial attitude toward trusteeship," although he was also producing position papers for the organization and representing it at State Department conferences and other official and unofficial meetings.

25. Logan Diary entry June, 4, 1949, box 4, Logan LC. He had also witnessed Woodrow Wilson's son-in-law and onetime high commissioner of the Philippines, Francis Sayre, the U.S. representative on the UN Trusteeship Council in 1951, criticize Great Britain for "going too fast in promoting self-government" in the Gold Coast, Nigeria, and Tanganyika. The exchange with Sayre took place at a UNESCO meeting in Paris. box 166–34, folder 1, containing a draft chapter of Logan's unpublished autobiography, Logan Papers MSRC.

26. See Gerri Major, "Society Founder, Eminent Negroes in World Affairs Share Honors at Annual Meeting of History Group," *New York Amsterdam News*, February 24, 1951, reporting on the meeting of the New York branch of the Association for the Study of Negro Life and History, which Logan headed after the passing of the founder and longtime executive director, Carter Woodson.

27. Gershenhorn, "African American Scholars and the Development of African Studies," 53.

28. Frazier's model for African studies mirrored Herskovits's original diasporic vision, although he was also a relentless critic of Herskovits's belief in the significance of African cultural "survivals." Inside Howard, Frazier's proposal was controversial mainly for his refusal to include Leo Hansberry's courses on ancient and medieval African history in the program on the grounds that Hansberry was not a serious scholar. Neither factor explains why Howard fared so poorly.

29. Logan Draft Autobiography, box 5, folder 5, Logan Papers MSRC; Gershenhorn, "Not An Academic Affair," 54–56; Gershenhorn, *Melville J. Herskovits*

and the Racial Politics of Knowledge, 192–195; "Harvard Once Refused Aid to Create Africa Program," *Harvard Crimson*, April 30, 1968, http://www.thecrimson.com/article/1968/4/30/harvard-once-refused-aid-to-create/, accessed April 21, 2013; Robinson, "Area Studies in Search of Africa," 94.

30. Parmar, *Foundations of the American Century*, 158.

31. "Report of First Annual Meeting, September 8–10, 1958," *African Studies Bulletin* 1, no. 2 (1958):12–21; William G. Martin, "1957 Whitewash: Africanist and Black Traditions in the Study of Africa," paper prepared for the conference on Black Liberation and the Spirit of 1957, November 2–3, 2007, draft, http://www2.binghamton.edu/fbc/archive/martin%201957%20whitewash.pdf, accessed April 22, 2013. The African Studies Association was a Carnegie-led initiative put together by program officer (and future president) Alan Pifer and a few insiders who had met periodically with him to draw up plans, which included mechanisms for keeping control of the organization in their hands to protect the association against interference by "action groups, dilettantes, or faddists" through what was called the "College of Fellows." They appointed Herskovits the first president.

32. The unnamed compiler of the African Studies Association *Bulletin's* original list of programs in the United States omitted the programs at Howard University and Roosevelt University. St. Clair Drake, an outspoken defender of African independence, directed the latter program and had been turned down for funding by Ford. See Gershenhorn, "Not an Academic Affair," 58–60.

33. Logan's unpublished autobiography, box 166–35, folder 2, Logan Papers MSRC; Logan diary entry, September 14, 1958, box 6, Logan Papers LC; Gershenhorn, "Not an Academic Affair," 57–58.

34. Quoted in Parmar, *Foundations of the American Century*, 159, but also see the parallel analysis in Martin, "1957 Whitewash."

35. Parmar, *Foundations of the American Century*, 159. Frazier himself had pitched his proposal on these grounds. See Martin, "1957 Whitewash," 20.

36. Parker, "Made-in-America Revolutions."

37. Biondi, *The Black Revolution on Campus*, 202–203.

38. George Shepard Jr., a specialist in African politics and founder of the Institute for International Race Relations at the University of Denver, quoted in Matthews, Gappert, Snyder, and Kornegay, "Washington Task Force Black Paper on Institutional Racism," 27.

39. Parmar, *Foundations of the American Century*, 159. LeMelle received his PhD in international relations from the School of International Studies at the University of Denver in 1963 and taught for two years in the African Studies program at Boston University before joining Ford, serving in the Carter administration, and eventually serving as president of the Phelps-Stokes Fund.

40. Turner and Murapa, "Africa: Conflict in Black and White." Turner received his PhD from Northwestern and was hired to build the Africana Studies and Research Center at Cornell. Murapa received his PhD in 1974 from Northern Illinois University, where he wrote a dissertation on Padmore's role in the African liberation movement.

41. For an early glimpse of the reconsideration of Hansberry's reputation after his 1959 retirement from Howard, see Crawford, "The Scholar Nobody Knows," where one finds possibly the first use of the future cliché about him, "prophet without honor."

42. Urban, *Black Scholar: Horace Mann Bond*, 152–153.

43. See the discussion in Logan's unpublished memoir, box 166–35, folder 2, Logan Papers MSRC.

44. See Isaacs to Ezekiel Mphahlele, June 23, 1958, box 1, Isaacs Papers.

45. See Paris to Washington, May 3, 1956, 54, FBI Files, Richard Nathaniel Wright, part 2 of 2, http://vault.fbi.gov/Richard%20Nathaniel%20Wright/Richard%20Nathaniel%20Wright%20Part%202%20of%202/view, accessed April 29, 2013.

46. Wilford, *The Mighty Wurlitzer*, 198–224, is the most detailed account to date. There is still much to learn, however. For background on Davis, see Kilson, "Political Scientists and the Activist-Technocrat Dichotomy." Kilson's essay does not discuss Davis's extracurricular activities, even though at the time Kilson was a critic of the transformation of the American Society for African Culture from a predominantly African American awareness organization to a Cold War cultural export agency. Davis's name today adorns a diversity center at his alma mater, Williams.

47. Baldwin, "Princes and Powers," 18–19.

48. Entry for August 4, 1958, box 6, Diaries 1958–1959, 1960, Logan Papers LC.

49. See Interview 25/B-6, December 4, 1958, Ralph Ellison, Tivoli, New York, box 21, folder 1/3 Interviews Typed, Isaacs Papers. In 1955, the State Department offered to send Ellison to the Gold Coast and pay him to write a novel about the country that would then be filmed "as a phase of the country's Independence Day's celebrations." Ellison wanted nothing to do with Ghana or the crude propaganda project. See Rampersad, *Ralph Ellison*, 312.

50. Nielsen quoted in Richard Harwood, "O What a Tangled Web the CIA Wove," *Washington Post*, February 26, 1967, E1. For Nielsen's background, see Wolfgang Saxon, "Waldemar Nielsen, Expert on Philanthropy, Dies at 88," *New York Times*, November, 4, 2005. Nielsen insisted on ending the relationship with the CIA as a condition for taking over, an arrangement Harold Hochschild and top officials of both Ford and the Rockefeller Foundations negotiated. Hochschild secured a promise from Special Assistant for National Security Affairs (and later Ford Foundation president) McGeorge Bundy to shift funding from the CIA to the Agency for International Development. See Berman, *The Ideology of Philanthropy*, 132.

51. Wilford, *The Mighty Wurlitzer*, 214.

52. Menand, "Both Sides Now," 193.

53. Kuklick, *Blind Oracles*, 16.

54. Niebuhr, "The Colored Continents"; and Niebuhr, "Power and Ideology in National and International Affairs."

Chapter 8: Hands of Ethiopia

1. Rotter, "In Retrospect: Harold R. Isaacs's *Scratches on Our Minds*."

2. For conservatives' views on decolonization at the time, which the idea men at the Foreign Policy Research Institute reflected quite faithfully, see Staniland, *American Intellectuals and African Nationalists*, 223–236.

3. See, e.g., the summary in Muehlenbeck, *Betting on the Africans*, 3–33.

4. Grunfeld, "Friends of the Revolution," 116; Messmer, *Jewish Wayfarers in Modern China*, 48–55; and Isaacs, *Re-Encounters in China*.

5. Pye, "Harold R. Isaacs"; Wald, *The New York Intellectuals*, 108–109. The Encyclopedia of Trotskyism On-Line lists articles and party resolutions through mid-1941 by Isaacs (sometimes writing as George Stern) in the short-lived theoretical monthly *Fourth International*; see "Harold Isaacs Internet Archive," http://www.marxists.org/history/etol/writers/isaacs/index.htm, accessed May 29, 2013.

6. Isaacs, *No Peace in Asia*, 72. See also "Hurley Hits Books Critical of Chiang," *Washington Post*, April 11, 1948, M11.

7. Freeman, Review of *No Peace in Asia*.

8. See FBI, W[ashington] F[ield] O[ffice] Report, Harold Robert Isaacs, November 12, 1965, enclosing classified information from Isaacs's State Department passport file, Federal Bureau of Investigation, Washington, D.C., released in response to a Freedom of Information Act Request, in my possession (hereafter Isaacs FBI File]. Isaacs had been designated a security threat. He describes the money smuggling in Isaacs, *Re-Encounters in China*, 25.

9. Letter to Boston Re: Harold Robert Isaacs, n.d., declassified April 27, 2010, FBI, Isaacs FBI File.

10. Isaacs, *No Peace in Asia*, xxvii.

11. Collin, "Tragedy of the Chinese Revolution."

12. See United States Civil Service Commission, Report of Investigation, Harold Robert Isaacs, September 27, 1965, in my possession. The quotation in the next sentence is from this document.

13. Blackmer, *The MIT Center for International Studies*, 35–38; Blackmer, e-mail to author, May 10, 2013.

14. Schwoch, *Global TV*, 64–65.

15. Isaacs, *No Peace in Asia*, 1967 reprint, xxv.

16. "Educators Back Vietnam Policy," *New York Times*, December 10, 1965, 1. Isaacs did not recover his critical temper until Kissinger and Nixon took over.

17. Isaacs, "Western Man and the African Crisis," 55.

18. Isaacs, "Back to Africa," 105; Pauli Murray to Harold Isaacs, May 28, 1961, box 21, Isaacs Papers. As Kevin Gaines puts it, "Through Isaacs, Murray inadvertently helped craft a new journalistic image of alienation between African Americans and Africans that debunked notions of pan-African solidarity as illusory and inauthentic." Gaines, "Pauli Murray in Ghana," 258. Polsgrove, *Divided Minds*, 141–146, discusses the article and the controversy it engendered.

19. Russell Warren Howe, "Strangers in Africa," *The Reporter*, June 22, 1961, 34–35.

20. The quotations are from the invaluable archival work in Polsgrove, *Divided Minds*, 145, which documents Howe's anger at the way his article had been reworked, and the *Reporter's* dim view of their own handiwork in comparison to the Isaacs piece. On the UN demonstration, see Woodward, "Amiri Baraka and Black Power Politics," 57–60.

21. Drake "The Negro's Stake in Africa," 42, 44.

22. Rayford Logan to Harold Isaacs, June 26, 1961, box 1, folder "LOGAN, Professor Rayford," Isaacs Papers.

23. Isaacs to Logan, June 29, 1961, box 1, folder "LOGAN, Professor Rayford," Isaacs Papers.

24. For Baldwin see July 27, 1961 Diary Notes, Conversations with James Baldwin, box 19, Isaacs Papers. For Frazier (who said "Despite everything the Negro will not be accepted in American life. We are not going to wipe out the stigma of Negro ancestry and it is a stigma, I say that quite objectively.") 11/A-5 EF Frazier, August 1, 1958, box 21, Isaacs Papers. For Clark, who said the quote was from Thurgood Marshall, re-interview, January 5, 1962, box 19, Isaacs Papers.

25. For Isaacs's disparaging view of Bond, see Isaacs to his children, n.d. [around July 1961], box 37, folder "Back to Africa," New Yorker, 1961, Reviews and Correspondence, Isaacs Papers. For Bond's critique, see Bond, "Howe and Isaacs in the Bush." South African writer and Isaacs's friend Ezekiel Mphahele agreed with and extended his view of the "painful complexes, paradoxes and ironies with which we Negroes related to each other" in Mphahele, "The Blacks: Dialogue across the Seas," 22.

26. "Of course the real point (made neither by Isaacs nor Howe, nor by their Negro critics) is that, as you have pointed out, Negro Americans are generally conservative, if not reactionary, in their social and political thought, and as such will inevitably come into conflict with African states as more of them move along some sort of socialist or radical path as that taking shape in Ghana, Guinea, and Mali, as I believe most will do in due course." Martin Kilson to E. Franklin Frazier, July 3, 1961, box 12, folder 6, Frazier Papers. Kilson came around to Isaacs's views on alienation when he explained Harvard students' romance with black nationalism. See Kilson, "The Black Student Militant."

27. Mel Fox to Harold Isaacs, August 12, 1961, box 37, folder "Back to Africa," New Yorker, 1961, Reviews and Correspondence, Isaacs Papers.

28. Isaacs to his children, n.d. but [around July 1961].

29. Isaacs to Margaret Mead, August 1, 1961, box 37, folder "Back to Africa," New Yorker, 1961, Reviews and Correspondence, Isaacs Papers.

30. For the positioning of Etzioni at the time, see the discussion of his *Hard Way to Peace* (1962) in Sondermann, "Peace Initiatives: The Literature of Possibilities." Sondermann was a founder of the International Studies Association.

31. Etzioni, "Beyond Desegregation," 22.

32. Ibid.

33. Jackson, *Science for Segregation*, 10 (location 321), 148 (location 3074), 150 (location 3113), Kindle edition. Anthony James Gregor, a longtime student of fascism, security studies specialist, and future Berkeley political scientist, was the secretary of its parent organization, the International Association for the Advancement of Ethnology and Eugenics. For his abiding interest in racial science, see "A. James Gregor," Bibliographies: Institute for the Study of Academic Racism, http://www.ferris.edu/isar/bibliography/gregrbib.htm, accessed July 5, 2013.

34. Weyl, Review of *The New World of Negro Americans*. Weyl's story is a variant of the one we now practically know by heart: he was a rebel at Columbia in the early 1930s and a Communist Party member for the rest of the decade (which he denied when investigated during the war). He left the party in the wake of Stalin's pact with the fascists and eventually ended up in the extreme right wing of the Republican Party.

35. Weyl and Possony, *The Geography of Intellect*, 146.

36. Ibid., 226, 283, 248, 288–289.

37. Dunn, Review of *Geography of Intellect*; and Klineberg, Review of *Geography of Intellect*.

38. Strausz-Hupé and Possony, *International Relations in the Age of Conflict between Democracy and Dictatorship*. Strausz-Hupé and his disciples opposed this behavioral revolution in international relations theory and played no role in the new professional association, the International Studies Association. For a unique retrospective account by a onetime partisan, see Plantan, "Multidisciplinary Approaches, Disciplinary Boundaries, and Institutional Response in American Higher Education."

39. Strausz-Hupé, *In My Time*, 193. For the Foreign Policy Research Institute–Hoover Institution–Center for Strategic and International Studies alignment (and their hard-line anticommunist "ideological approach"), see Lyons and Morton, *Schools for Strategy*, 185–192. For the temporary eclipse of Strausz-Hupé (whom Arkansas senator William Fulbright called a threat to world peace) and the Foreign Policy Research Institute's move off the Penn campus after revelations in the *New York Times* of CIA funding, see the account by Harvey Sicherman, an acolyte: "Robert Strausz-Hupé: His Life and Times," which has been reposted on the Foreign Policy Research Institute's Web site, http://www.fpri.org/articles/2003/04/

robert-strausz-hupe-his-life-and-times, accessed March 10, 205. Strausz-Hupé held multiple ambassadorial posts during later Republican administrations. At Hoover, Possony was an early shaper of Governor Ronald Reagan's views on what became the Strategic Defense Initiative (or "Star Wars"), and when Possony died, the hyperbole of Strausz-Hupé's eulogy easily broke through the upper limits of the earth's atmosphere. "The greatest strategist of the twentieth century." See Possony's obituary, *San Francisco Examiner*, May 2, 1995, http://www.sfgate.com/news/article/Stefan-Thomas-Possony-3147535.php, accessed April 1, 2015.

40. Possony and Strausz-Hupé, *International Relations in the Age of Conflict between Democracy and Dictatorship*, 608, 631. All quotations are from the second, revised edition of 1954.

41. Ibid., 631, 623–624.

42. Ibid., 632.

43. Ibid., 621, 603, 635; Possony, "UNESCO and Race."

44. Strausz-Hupé and Hazard, *The Idea of Colonialism.*

45. Possony, "Colonial Problems in Perspective," 36, 17, 40. This polemic fails to cite a single author or text in its catalogue of the "theories" that constitute ideological anticolonialism.

46. See Rhoodie, *Third Africa*, concluding chapter by Possony, 311, 326. When Rhoodie died, the *New York Times* him as "apartheid's chief propagandist" in the 1970s who ran a dirty tricks department in the ministry of information that, when exposed, brought down the presidency of John Vorster. Wolfgang Saxon, "Eschel Rhoodie, a South African at Center of Scandal, Dies at 60," *New York Times*, July 21, 1993.

47. Weyl and Possony, *The Geography of Intellect*, 247–249, 283.

Chapter 9: The Fate of the Howard School

1. Von Eschen, *Race against Empire*, 6; for the discussion of Logan, 145, 148–149.

2. Bunche to Frazier, January 29, 1951, box 127, Bunch Papers; Lewis, *W. E. B. Du Bois, 1919–1963*. For Du Bois and Logan's beliefs about Bunche, see Janken, *Rayford W. Logan*. Logan helped Isaacs get an interview with Du Bois in 1958.

3. Transcript of Logan interview with Ed Bradley, 20, n.d., box 166–7, folder 10, Logan Papers MSRC.

4. Logan's unpublished autobiography, 27, box 166–4, folder 5 WBL-A-V II-"Defiance of McCarthyism"-Chapter II, Logan Papers MSRC.

5. Entry for September 8, 1955, box 6, Diaries 1954–1957, Logan Papers LC. Decades later, Tate used the same word, "coward," to characterize her stance in the 1950s. See the transcript of the oral history interview with Merze Tate, May 2, 1978, Black Women Oral History Project, Tapes 6, 7, 8, p. 54, Black Women Oral History Project, Schlesinger Library. The librarian at Schlesinger would not grant me permission to use the transcripts on the grounds that no one else had been given access. A much more honest and forthcoming scholar, among others who have been allowed to use the transcripts, shared her detailed notes of the tape-recorded interviews, and my quotations are based on those notes.

6. The quote is from Logan's friend and erstwhile colleague, John Hope Franklin, who wrote a powerful essay on the oppressive and alienating conditions of black intellectual production in a still-segregated United States ("Dilemma of the American Negro Scholar"). He wrote it after he was hired at Brooklyn College (after teaching at and being passed over by Wisconsin and Cornell in a quest that his Harvard advisor Arthur Schlesinger criticized as "scattering his energies too much.")

See entry for January 2, 1955, box 6, Dairies 1954–1957, Logan Papers LC. Janken emphasizes the generational differences that determined the likelihood of a black scholar entering the white academy; Janken, *Rayford W. Logan*, 225.

7. Winston, "Through the Back Door," 708.

8. Entry for December 16, 1960, box 6, Diaries 1960, Logan Papers LC; Janken, *Rayford W. Logan*, 213–214. Also see Michael R. Winston, "The Howard University Department of History, 1913–1973," 1998, http://www.howard.edu/explore/history-dept.htm, accessed August 8, 2013.

9. Winston, "Through the Back Door," 708.

10. See "John H. Herz, 97, Howard U. Scholar," *Washington Post*, January 25, 2006. Herz's papers are at the State University of New York at Albany.

11. See Fall, *Bernard Fall*, 139–172. For Tate's role in bringing Fall to the attention of the Rockefeller Foundation, see Merze Tate to Kenneth Thompson, January 9, 1961, box 522, folder 4459, Series 200S, Record Group 1.2, Rockefeller Foundation Archives.

12. Eric Williams to Alain Locke, n.d. [presumably summer of 1942], box 93, folder 23, Locke Papers.

13. Entry for September 5, 1942, box 3, Dairy 1942, Logan Papers LC.

14. Atwater, Review of *The Disarmament Illusion*; Logan, "No Peace for the Pacifists."

15. Morgenthau, Review of *Disarmament Illusion*; Frei, *Hans J. Morgenthau*, 123–125.

16. Arnold-Foster, Review of *The Disarmament Illusion*; Du Bois, "Scholarly Delusion." Contrast these with the Pitman B. Potter's patronizing review in the *American Political Science Review*. Potter, a leading interwar-era international relations scholar who was obviously incensed by her implicit critique of the disarmament movement, didn't bother to summarize the argument and instead mocked Tate's style and the publisher's choice of an overly generalized title.

17. Theresa Danley, interview of Merze Tate, 205, April 24, 1978, personal files of Ruth Hill; Jean E. Busch, Princeton University Press, to Merze Tate, February 19, 1958, box 31, Tate Papers; C. E. Carrington to Gerald Freund, March 24, 1961, and Payson Wild to Gerald Freund, March 24, 1961, box 522, folder 4459, RG 1.2, Series 200S, RFA; Merze Tate, "Extracts from a New Zealand Scholar's Report on Australia and New Zealand from the Tropics to the Poles," 1969), box 20, Tate Papers. Two other facts emerged from the fragmentary correspondence on fate of the Australia–New Zealand book in the unprocessed mass of Tate's papers at Howard. An editor and friend at Yale University Press who had been working with her on it left the press and his successor declined to continue. Her exhaustively detailed narrative style had also fallen out of fashion ("not sufficiently penetrating and interpretative for a scholar"). See Merze Tate to Edward Tripp, Yale University Press, July 19, 1972, and R. Miriam Brokaw (the editor who disparaged the manuscript), Princeton Box, University Press, to Tate, March 13, 1973, 9, Tate Papers.

18. Tate, *The United States and the Hawaiian Kingdom*; and Tate, *Hawaii: Reciprocity or Annexation?*. She produced a third manuscript from her research on Hawaii on the life and short reign of its fourth king, Kamehameha, who attempted to resist the encroachment of American interests. Tate imagined the long, novelistic history being optioned for the screen and even shopped it for a while under the pseudonym Lelia Kaliokalani, but she failed to sell it.

19. See, for example, Lilley and Hunt, "On Social History, the State and Foreign Relations."

20. Transcript of the oral history interview with Merze Tate, May 3, 1978, Black Women Oral History Project, Tape 9, p. 14, Schlesinger Library; Merze Tate, Review of *Warning to the West*. The topics of Tate's subsequent reviews ranged widely, from U.S. society and foreign policy to South Africa, India, and China.

21. See, for instance, Tate's embittered letter of protest to Dean Frank Snowden, a Logan ally, September 1, 1960, box 31, Tate Papers: "Under the discriminatory treatment which has existed for years I have suffered a tremendous financial loss not only in compensation but in retirement benefits . . . and trust some rectification will be made to cover my remaining years."

22. Entry for September 24, box 6, Diaries 1954–1955, Logan Papers, LC.

23. Entry for Thanksgiving Day, November 28, [1957], box 6, Diaries 1956–1957, Logan Papers LC.

24. Logan's unpublished autobiography, Chapter VII, box 5, folder 8, WBL-A-Vol II–"Seven Distressing and Productive Years, 1960–1967," Logan Papers MSRC; Tate to Logan, February 9, 1964, box 166–21, file 2, Logan Papers MSRC; *Washington Post*, January 25, 1964. See also *Washington Afro-American*, November 21, 1964, for the luncheon Tate held to thank her supporters, including Radcliffe president and friend Mary Bunting, who was then on leave while serving on the Atomic Energy Commission. Both clippings in box 26, Tate Papers.

25. Tate never forgave Logan. When his biographer approached Tate about him, she closed the door in his face; Kenneth Janken, personal communication. Janken also chose not to write about it directly but instead discussed Logan's penchant for rewarding friends and punishing rivals "and colleagues with whom he did not get on well." Janken, *Rayford W. Logan*, 208. One would be hard pressed to name a colleague whom Logan treated worse, however.

26. Harris, "Professor Merze Tate."

27. See Woodard and Preston, "Black Political Scientists," 81, Table 1, which identifies Jewel Prestage wrongly as the first black woman to obtain a PhD (in 1954), based on information Prestage had provided. The record was not corrected until 2005.

28. Shepherd, "The Center on International Race Relations"; Shepherd and LeMelle, *Race among Nations*, xvi. See also Shepherd, *Racial Influences on American Foreign Policy*; LeMelle and Shepherd, "Race in the Future of International Relations"; and LeMelle, "Race, International Relations, U.S. Foreign Policy, and the African Liberation Struggle."

29. See Donald S. Will, "Paradigm of the Scholar/Activist: Reflections on the Life of George W. Shepherd, Jr.," 12, unpublished paper written for a panel honoring Shepherd at the International Studies Association annual meeting, Los Angeles, March 2010, in my possession.

30. Details on the centers story come from George Shepherd Jr., to whom I am grateful. Edmonson, one of the earliest commentators on Fanon's role in the black power movement, wrote two influential early articles as part of this challenge to international relations theory: "Internationalization of Black Power" and "The Challenge of Race." By 1974, Edmonson was engaging Eric Williams via a rediscovered idea in international relations from Joseph Nye (Harvard) and Robert Keohane (Swarthmore) and was analyzing both racism and slavery as transnational processes. See Edmonson, "Transatlantic Slavery and the Internationalization of Race."

31. Preston and Woodard, "The Rise and Decline of Black Political Scientists in the Profession"; Wilson, "Why Political Scientists Don't Study Black Politics."

32. Doty, "Bounds of 'Race' in International Relations."

33. Doyle, *Empires*, 10–11.

34. Ibid., 11.

Conclusion: The High Plane of Dignity and Discipline

1. Lindblom, "Political Science in the 1940s and 1950s," 261. As George Steinmetz writes about political science's close relative, "Sociology can never aspire to be a cumulative science in which earlier work can be safely discarded. Ongoing social research always remains connected to its own past in ways that distinguish the human sciences from the natural sciences. The much vaunted reflexivity of social science requires historical self-analysis. Intellectual history or the historical sociology of social science is an integral part of all social science." Steinmetz, *Sociology and Empire*, xi.

2. Barnes, Review of *Empire and Commerce in Africa*, 130–131, quotation from Woolf in this paragraph from 131.

3. Quoted in Woolf, "International Morality."

4. Woolf quoted in Bain, *Between Anarchy and Society*, 84.

5. White House, Office of the Press Secretary, "Remarks by the President at the US-Africa Business Forum," August 5, 2014, http://www.whitehouse.gov/the-press-office/2014/08/05/remarks-president-us-africa-business-forum, accessed August 20, 2014.

6. In *Imperialism* (1902), John A. Hobson, another supporter of the mandates, sought a strategy, as his great grandson puts it, for bringing the "*practice* of the benign civilizing mission into line with the theory." Hobson, *The Eurocentric Conception of World Politics*, 47.

7. For a discussion of the key differences, based on Bunche's analysis of one mandate and one non-mandate French possession, see Crawford, "Decolonization through Trusteeship," 93–114.

8. Abbott, "A Re-Examination of the 1929 Colonial Development Act," 68–81; Hinds, *Britain's Sterling Colonial Policy and Decolonization*.

9. Perham, "African Facts and American Criticisms," 444–457. Equally reliably, the first postmortem of the amended Colonial Development and Welfare Acts showed that local British colonial administrations had no planning mechanisms in place and that the earmarked funds went unused. See Wicker, "Colonial Development and Welfare, 1929–1957," 170–192.

10. Isaacs, *The New World of Negro Americans*, ix, xiv.

11. The quote is from Jackson, "Surrogate Sovereignty?," 9. Support for this point can also be found in Bain, *Between Anarchy and Society*, 121–124; and Lyon, "The Rise and Fall and Possible Revival of Trusteeship," 96–110.

12. Crawford, "Decolonization through Trusteeship"; Fearon and Laitin, "Neotrusteeship and the Problem of Weak States," 5–43. See also Pugh, "Whose Brother's Keeper?," 321–343, both for following the state of debate and for the author's fanciful account of the "flexible" UN Trusteeship "system," which Pugh claims the designers intended to apply to any and all "weak, postcolonial, post-conflict or fractured states" that might be "administered under the aegis of the UN, a great power state, or group of states" (324). Bunche would be rolling over in his grave if he saw that. Pugh also explains the logic behind trusteeship in the way that his international relations ancestors once explained imperialism: "a parent (or foster parent) teaches a child how to take care of herself during the first two decades of her life before allowing herself to take responsibility for herself in the world" (328).

13. For the powerful hold of this idea, see Mazower, *No Enchanted Palace*; and Throntveit, "The Fable of the Fourteen Points," 445–481.

14. Contrast the idea of the Wilsonian moment with St. Croix-born, Harlem-based writer and orator Hubert Harrison's dissection of the white race at war and the prospects for independence in India and Egypt following its end. Harrison, "The White War and the Colored World," 202–203.

15. For the radical revisioning of Germany in the imagination of political scientists, see Oren, *Our Enemies and US*.

16. See Guilhot, "Imperial Realism."

17. Dobbin, Jones, Crane, and DeGrasse, *Beginner's Guide to Nation-Building*.

18. Kuklick, *Blind Oracles*, 160–161. For May's continued disdain for the revisionists, see Ruth Glushien, "Profile Ernest R. May," *Harvard Crimson*, October 18, 1969, http://www.thecrimson.com/article/1969/10/18/profile-ernest-r-may-ptwo-years/, accessed August 23, 2014.

19. Vitalis, "The Democratization Industry and the Limits of the New Interventionism," 46–50.

20. Brownlee, *Democracy Prevention*.

21. Quoted in Hazbun, "The Geopolitics of Knowledge and the Challenge of Postcolonial Agency," 217.

22. Faust, "The Scholar Who Shaped History."

23. For example, Howe, *Afrocentrism*.

24. Marable, *Malcolm X*.

25. For example, Gaddis, *George F. Kennan*, which has no index entries for race, racism, African Americans, eugenics, and so forth, and a one-sentence explanation, in the course of explaining Kennan's defense of separate development and of the incapacity of "Bantus" to govern themselves, for his long held belief that "race shaped culture" (603). Kennan was a throwback to John W. Burgess.

26. H. R. Haldeman diary entry for April 28, 1969, quote in Plummer, *In Search of Power*, 251. Nixon (and doubtless others) distinguished between personal feelings of enmity ("prejudice") and the truth of sociobiology. "I have the greatest affection for them [blacks], but I know they're not going to make it for 500 years. They aren't. You know it, too. I mean, all, this, uh, Julie [Nixon Eisenhower], I asked her about the black studies program at Smith. You know . . . and she said, the trouble [is], they didn't find anything to study. . . . The Mexicans are a different cup of tea. They have a heritage, but at the present time they steal, they're dishonest, but they do have some concept of family life at least. They don't live like a bunch of dogs, which the Negroes do live like." Nixon in conversation with John Erlichman and H. R. Haldeman, May 13, 1971, Conversation No. 498–005, Presidential Recordings Program, Miller Center, University of Virginia, http://whitehousetapes.net/clip/richard-nixon-john-erlichman-hr-haldeman-nixon-race.

27. Kaplan, "Looking the World in the Eye," 68–82.

28. Huntington, "Clash of Civilizations," 25.

29. Ikenberry, "Illusions of Empire," 144–154, my emphasis.

30. Vucetic, *The Anglosphere*.

31. Biersteker, "The Parochialism of Hegemony."

32. Oren, "A Sociological Analysis of the Decline of American IR Theory"; and Whitley, *The Intellectual and Social Organization of the Sciences*.

33. Holsti, "The Study of Strange Bedfellows," 217–242; and Pfaltzgraff, Holsti, Riley, Kennington, Marenin, Eckstein, Bloom, and Allen, "Communications."

34. On the histories of internationalism (of which the discipline of international relations forms a part) and the beginnings of engagement with worldwide liberation struggles see Mazower, *Governing the World*; Sluga, *Internationalism in the Age of Nationalism*; Parmar, *Foundations of the American Century*; Rietzler, "Experts for Peace"; Pedersen, *The Guardians*; Zimmerman, *Alabama in Africa*; and Anderson, "Pacific Dreams."

35. Including Douglas, "Periodizing the American Century"; Gines, *Hannah Arendt and the Negro Question*; Gordon, *Creolizing Political Theory*; Kaplan, *The Anarchy of Empire in the Making of U.S. Culture*; and Singh, *Exceptional Empire*.

36. Menand, *The Marketplace of Ideas*; Jenny Blair, "Louis Menand Challenges Humanities Colleagues to 'Take No Hostages,'" *Alcalde*, April 26, 2013, http://alcalde.texasexes.org/2013/04/louis-menand-challenges-humanities-colleagues-to-take-no-hostages/, accessed March 1, 2014.

37. Including Tarek Barkawi, Branwen Gruffydd Jones, John Hobson, Naeem Inayatullah, Lily Ling, Richard Seymour, Robbie Shilliam, Christine Sylvester, and J. Ann Tickner. Their work will lead readers to others who have been left off the reading lists of intro courses and grad seminars.

Bibliography

Archival Collections

Archives and Special Collections, Massachusetts Institute of Technology, Cambridge, Massachusetts
 Harold Isaacs Papers
Goddard Library, Clark University, Worcester, Massachusetts
 George Hubbard Blakeslee Papers
George Kahin Papers, Ithaca, New York (courtesy of Audrey Kahin)
Houghton Library, Harvard University, Cambridge, Massachusetts
 Raymond Leslie Buell Papers
 Carl Joachim Friedrich Papers
Library of Congress, Washington, D.C.
 Raymond Leslie Buell Papers
 Rayford Whittingham Logan Papers
Moorland-Spingarn Research Center, Howard University, Washington, D.C.
 E. Franklin Frazier Papers
 Alain LeRoy Locke Papers
 Rayford Whittingham Logan Papers
 Kwame Nkrumah Papers
 Merze Tate Papers
Rare Book and Manuscript Library, Columbia University, New York
 John William Burgess Papers
Regenstein Library, University of Chicago, Chicago, Illinois
 Charles E. Merriam Papers
 Quincy Wright Papers
Rockefeller Archive Center, Tarrytown, New York
 Rockefeller Foundation Archives
 Laura Spelman Rockefeller Memorial Series
 Social Science Research Council Records
Seeley G. Mudd Manuscript Library, Princeton University, Princeton, New Jersey
 Hamilton Fish Armstrong Papers
 Edward S. Corwin Papers
 Edward Mead Earle Papers
 Foreign Policy Association Papers
Special Collections, Charles E. Young Research Library, University of California Los Angeles
 Ralph J. Bunche Papers
Wisconsin Historical Society, Madison, Wisconsin
 Merle Curti Papers
 Paul Reinsch Papers

Works Cited

Abbott, George C. "A Re-Examination of the 1929 Colonial Development Act." *Economic History Review*, n.s. 24 (1971): 68–81.

Abbot, Willis J. "International Politics in the Berkshire Hills." *Outlook*, September 14, 1921, 51–55.

Adi, Hakim, and Marika Sherwood. *The 1945 Manchester Pan-African Congress Revisited*. Edited by George Padmore. London: New Beacon Books, 1995.

Alker, Hayward, Jr., and Thomas Biersteker. "The Dialectics of World Order: Notes for a Future Archeologist of International Savoir Faire." *International Studies Quarterly* 28 (1984): 121–142.

Anderson, Lisa. *Pursuing Truth, Exercising Power: Social Science and Public Policy in the 21st Century*. New York: Columbia University Press, 2003.

Anderson, Michael Richard. "Pacific Dreams: The Institute of Pacific Relations and the Struggle for the Mind of Asia." PhD diss., University of Texas at Austin, 2009.

Anderson, Perry. "Consilium." *New Left Review* 83 (2013): 113–167.

Andrews, Charles M. "Boston Meeting of the American Historical Association." *American Historical Review* 5 (1900): 423–439.

Anievas, Alexander, ed. *Marxism and World Politics: Contesting Global Capitalism*. London: Routledge, 2010.

Anthony, David Henry, III. *Max Yergan: Race Man, Internationalist, Cold Warrior*. New York: New York University Press, 2006.

Akami, Tomoko. *Internationalizing the Pacific: The United States, Japan, and the Institute of Pacific Relations in War and Peace, 1919–1945*. London: Routledge, 2002.

Anderson, Carol. *Eyes off the Prize: The United Nations and the African American Struggle for Human Rights, 1944–1955*. Cambridge: Cambridge University Press, 2003.

Arnold-Foster, W. Review of *The Disarmament Illusion: The Movement for a Limitation of Armaments to 1907*, by Merze Tate. *International Affairs Review Supplement* 19 (1942): 532–533.

Atwater, Elton. Review of *The Disarmament Illusion: The Movement for a Limitation of Armaments to 1907*, by Merze Tate. *American Journal of International Law* 36 (1942): 742–743.

Bachman, James Robert. "Theodore Lothrop Stoddard: The Bio-Sociological Battle for Civilization." PhD diss., University of Rochester, 1967.

Bagby, Laurie M. Johnson. "The Use and Abuse of Thucydides in International Relations." *International Organization* 48 (1994): 131–153.

Bain, William. *Between Anarchy and Society: Trusteeship and the Obligation of Power*. Oxford: Oxford University Press, 2003.

——. "The Idea of Trusteeship in International Society: Unity, Progress, and the Perfection of Humankind." PhD diss., University of British Columbia, 2001.

Bakeless, John. *Origin of the Next War*. New York: Viking, 1926.

Baker, Lee. *From Savage to Negro: Anthropology and the Construction of Race, 1896–1940*. Berkeley: University of California Press, 1998.

Baldwin, James. *The Fire Next Time*. New York: Dial Press, 1963.

——. "Letter from a Region in My Mind." *New Yorker*, November 17, 1962, 59–144.

Bannister, Robert. *Social Darwinism: Science and Myth in Anglo-American Social Thought*. Philadelphia: Temple University Press, 1979.

Barkawi, Tarak. "Empire and Order in International Relations and Security Studies." In *The International Studies Encyclopedia*, vol. 3, edited by Robert Denemark, 1360–1379. Chichester: Wiley-Blackwell, 2010.

Barkan, Elazar. *The Retreat of Scientific Racism: Changing Concepts of Race in Britain and the United States between the World Wars*. Cambridge: Cambridge University Press, 1992.

Barkawi, Tarak, and Mark Laffey. "The Postcolonial Moment in Security Studies." *Review of International Studies* 32 (2006): 329–352.

Barnes, Carleton P. Review of *Re-Forging America*, by T. Lothrop Stoddard. *Economic Geography* 4, 2 (1928): 211–212.

Barnes, Harry Elmer. Review of *Empire and Commerce in Africa*, by Leonard Woolf. *Journal of International Relations* 12 (1921): 130–131.

Barrow, Clyde. "Intellectual Origins of the New Political Science." *New Political Science* 30 (2008): 215–244.

Bay, Mia. "'The World Was Thinking Wrong about Race': *The Philadelphia Negro* and Nineteenth-Century Science." In *W. E. B. Du Bois, Race, and the City*, edited by Michael Katz and Tom Sugrue, 41–60. Philadelphia: University of Pennsylvania Press, 1998.

Beard, Charles. *The Idea of National Interest*. New York: Macmillan, 1934.

——. *The Open Door At Home*. New York: Macmillan, 1934.

Bell, Duncan. "Anarchy, Power, and Death: Political Realism as Ideology." *Journal of Political Ideologies* 7 (2002): 221–239.

——. "Writing the World: Disciplinary History and Beyond." *International Affairs* 85 (2009): 3–22.

Bell, Morag. "American Philanthropy, the Carnegie Corporation and Poverty in South Africa." *Journal of Southern Africa Studies* 26 (2000): 481–504.

Beloff, Max. Review of *Schools for Strategy*, by Louis Morton and Gene Lyons. *International Journal* 20 (1965): 540.

Bemis, Samuel Flagg. *A Diplomatic History of the United States*. New York: Holt, 1936.

Bennett, Andrew, and G. John Ikenberry. "The Review's Evolving Relevance for U.S. Foreign Policy, 1906–2006." *American Political Science Review* 100 (2006): 651–658.

Berman, Edward H. *The Ideology of Philanthropy: The Influence of the Carnegie, Ford and Rockefeller Foundations on American Foreign Policy*. Albany: State University of New York Press, 1986.

Bierstecker, Thomas. "The Parochialism of Hegemony: Challenges for "American" International Relations." In *International Relations Scholarship Around the World*, edited by Arlene Tickner and Ole Waever, 308–327. London: Routledge, 2009.

Biondi, Martha. *The Black Revolution on Campus*. Berkeley: University of California Press, 2012.

Blackmer, Donald L. M. *The MIT Center for International Studies: The Founding Years*. Cambridge: MIT CENIS, 2002.

Blatt, Jessica. "'To Bring Out the Best That Is in Their Blood': Race, Reform, and Civilization in the Journal of Race Development." *Ethnic and Racial Studies* 27 (2004): 691–709.

Bock, P. G., and Morton Berkowitz. "The Emerging Field of National Security." *World Politics* 19 (1966): 122–136.

Boncourt, Thibaud. "Political Science: A Postwar Product (1947–1949)." *IPSA/ AISP Participation* 33 (2009): 4–7.

Bond, Horace Mann. "Howe and Isaacs in the Bush: the Ram in the Thicket." *Negro History Bulletin* 25 (1961): 72, 67–70.

Bowman, Isaiah. "The Pioneer Fringe." *Foreign Affairs* 6 (1927): 49–66.

Bradley, Philips. "American Foreign Policy—In Perspective and Cross Section." *Social Forces* 14 (1935): 143–147.

Brock, Lisa. "The 1950s: Africa Solidarity Rising." In *No Easy Victories: African Liberation and American Activists over a Half-Century, 1950–2000*, edited by William Minter, Gail Hovey, and Charles Cobb Jr., 59–72. Trenton, N.J.: Africa World Press, 2008.

Browne, Robert S. *Race Relations in International Affairs.* Washington, D.C.: Public Affairs Press, 1961.

Brownlee, Jason. *Democracy Prevention: The Politics of the US-Egyptian Alliance.* Cambridge: Cambridge University Press, 2012.

Bryce, James. *International Relations.* New York: Macmillan, 1922.

——. *The Relations of the Advanced and the Backward Races of Mankind.* Oxford: Clarendon Press, 1903.

Bucklin, Steven. *Realism and American Foreign Policy: Wilsonians and the Kennan-Morgenthau Thesis.* Westport, Conn.: Praeger, 2001.

——. "The Wilsonian Legacy in Political Science: Dennis F. Fleming, Frederick L. Schuman, and Quincy Wright." PhD diss., University of Iowa, 1993.

Buell, Raymond Leslie. "Again the Yellow Peril." *Foreign Affairs* 2 (1923): 295–309.

——. "'Backward' Peoples under the Mandate System." *Current History* 20 (1924): 386–395.

——. "The Development of the Anti-Japanese Agitation in the United States." *Political Science Quarterly* 37 (1922): 605–638.

——. *International Relations.* 1925. Reprint, New York: Henry Holt, 1929.

——. *Isolated America.* New York: Alfred Knopf, 1940.

——. "Liberia's Paradox." *Virginia Quarterly Review* 7 (1931): 161–175.

——. "Mr. Firestone's Liberia." *The Nation,* May 2, 1928, 524.

——. *The Native Problem in Africa.* 2 vols. New York: Macmillan, 1928.

——. "Some Legal Aspects of the Japanese Question." *American Journal of International Law* 17 (1923): 29–49.

——. "The Struggle in Africa." *Foreign Affairs* 6 (1927), 22–40.

Bukharin, N. "Imperialism and Communism." *Foreign Affairs* 14 (1936): 563–577.

Bunche, Ralph. "Presidential Address." *American Political Science Review* 48 (1954): 961–971.

——. "Reconstruction Reinterpreted." *Journal of Negro Education* 4 (1935): 568–570.

——. Review of *How Britain Rules Africa,* by George Padmore. *Journal of Negro Education* 6 (1937): 75–76.

——. *Selected Speeches and Writings.* Edited by Charles P. Henry. Ann Arbor: University of Michigan Press, 1995.

——. *A World View of Race.* Washington, D.C.: Associates in Negro Folk Education, 1936.

Burgess, John W. "The Decision of the Supreme Court in the Insular Cases." *Political Science Quarterly* 16 (1901): 486–504.

——. *Foundations of Political Science.* New York: Columbia University Press, 1933.

——. "How May the United States Govern Its Extra-Continental Territory?" *Political Science Quarterly* 14 (1899): 1–18.

——. "The Ideal of the American Commonwealth." *Political Science Quarterly* 10 (1985): 404–425.

——. *Political Science and Comparative Constitutional Law.* Vol. 1, *Sovereignty and Liberty.* Boston: Ginn and Company, 1890.

——. *Recent Changes in American Constitutional Theory.* New York: Columbia University Press, 1923.

——. "The Recent Pseudo-Monroeism." *Political Science Quarterly* 11 (1896): 44–67.

——. *Reconciliation of Government with Liberty.* New York: Charles Scriber's Sons, 1915.

——. *Reminiscences of an American Scholar: The Beginnings of Columbia University.* New York: Columbia University Press, 1934.

Burgess, W. Randolph. "Introductory Remarks." *Proceedings of the Academy of Political Science* 14 (1931): 213–214.

Buzas, Zoltan. "Race and International Politics: How Racial Prejudice Can Shape Discord and Cooperation among Great Powers. PhD diss., Ohio State University, 2012.

Carr, Edward Hallett. *The Twenty Years' Crisis: An Introduction to the Study of International Relations.* 1939; repr., Hampshire: Palgrave, 2001.

Carter, John Franklin. *Conquest: America's Painless Imperialism.* New York: Harcourt Brace, 1928.

——. *Man Is War.* Indianapolis: Bobbs-Merrill, 1926

Chadwin, Mark Lincoln. *The Hawks of World War II.* Chapel Hill: The University of North Carolina Press, 1968.

Chalk, Frank. "The Anatomy of an Investment: Firestone's 1927 Loan to Liberia." *Canadian Journal of African Studies* 1 (1967): 12–32.

Cheng, Charles W. "The Cold War: Its Impact on the Black Liberation Struggle within the United States." *Freedomways* 13 (1973): 281–293.

Child, Clifton J. Review of *United States and Armaments,* by Merze Tate. *International Affairs* 25 (1949): 114–115.

Chomsky, Noam. *American Power and the New Mandarins: Historical and Political Essays.* New York: Pantheon, 1969.

Cochrane, Rexmond. *National Academy of Sciences: The First Hundred Years 1863–1963.* Washington, D.C.: National Academy of Sciences, 1978.

Coit, Margaret. *Mr. Baruch.* Boston: Houghton Mifflin, 1957.

Collier, Peter. *Political Woman: The Big Little Life of Jeane Kirkpatrick.* New York: Encounter Books, 2012.

Collin, Paul. "The Tragedy of the Chinese Revolution: An Essay on the Different Editions of that Work." *Revolutionary History* 2 (1990).

Collings, Harry T. Review of *Conquest: America's Painless Imperialism,* by John Franklin Carter. *Annals of the American Academy of Political and Social Science* 141 (1929): 272–273.

Committee on Africa, the War, and Peace Aims. *The Atlantic Charter and Africa from an American Standpoint.* New York, n.p., 1942.

Connelly, Matthew. "Taking Off the Cold War Lens: Visions of North-South Conflict during the Algerian War for Independence." *American Historical Review* 105 (2000): 739–769.

Coolidge, Harold Jefferson, and Robert Howard Lord. *Archibald Cary Coolidge: Life and Letters.* Freeport, N.Y.: 1932. Reprint, Books for Libraries Press, 1971.

Coombs, Orde, ed., *Is Massa Day Dead?: Black Moods in the Caribbean.* Garden City: Anchor Press, 1974.

Cork, Jim. "'Self-Annihilation' in Negro Question: The C. P. and the Theory of Self Determination," *Workers Age* November 15, 1934, 5. http://archive.org/stream/WorkersAgeVol.320Nov.151934/WA20#page/n3/mode/2up. Accessed January 23, 2013.

Cox, Michael. "Introduction." In *The Twenty Years' Crisis: An Introduction to the Study of International Relations,* by Edward Hallett Carr, 1939; repr., Hampshire: Palgrave, 2001, ix–lviii.

Coyle, Gene. "John Franklin Carter: Journalist, FDR's Secret Investigator, Soviet Agent?" *International Journal of Intelligence and Counterintelligence* 24 (2010): 148–172.

Crawford, Marc. "The Scholar Nobody Knows." *Ebony,* February 1961, 59–68.

Crawford, Neta. "Decolonization through Trusteeship: The Legacy of Ralph Bunche," In *Trustee for the Human Community: Ralph J. Bunche, the United Nations, and the Decolonization of Africa,* edited by Robert Hill and Edmond Keller, 93–114. Athens: Ohio University Press, 2010.

Culbertson, William Smith. *International Economic Policies: A Survey of the Economics of Diplomacy.* New York: Appleton, 1925.

Cunard, Nancy. *Essays on Race and Empire.* Edited by Maureen Moynagh. Ontario: Broadview Press, 2002.

——, and George Padmore. "The White Man's Duty." In *Essays on Race and Empire,* by Nancy Cunard, edited by Maureen Moynagh, 127–178. Ontario: Broadview Press, 2002.

Daniels, Roger. *The Politics of Prejudice: The Anti-Japanese Movement in California and the Struggle for Japanese Exclusion.* Berkeley: University of California Press, 1966.

Degler, Carl. *In Search of Human Nature.* New York: Oxford University Press, 1991.

Dennis, Donald Philips. *Foreign Policy in a Democracy: The Role of the Foreign Policy Association.* New York: Foreign Policy Association, 2003.

DeWind, Josh. "Immigration Studies and the Social Science Research Foundation." In *Immigration Research for a New Century: Multidisciplinary Perspectives,* edited by Nancy Foner, Ruben Rumbaut, and Steven Gold, 63–75. New York: Russell Sage Foundation, 2003.

Dobbin, James, Seth Jones, Keith Crane, and Beth Cole DeGrassee. *The Beginner's Guide to Nation-Building.* Santa Monica, Calif.: RAND Corporation 2007.

Doty, Roxanne Lynn. "The Bounds of 'Race' in International Relations." *Millennium* 22 (1993): 443–463.

Douglas, Ann. "Periodizing the American Century: Modernism, Postmodernism, and Postcolonialism in the Cold War Context." *Modernism/modernity* 5 (1998): 71–98.

——. *Terrible Honesty: Mongrel Manhattan in the 1920s.* New York: Farrar, Straus & Giroux, 1995.

Doyle, Michael. *Empires*. Ithaca, N.Y.: Cornell University Press, 1986.

Drake, St. Clair. "The International Implications of Race and Race Relations." *Journal of Negro Education* 20 (1951): 261–278.

———. "The Negro's Stake in Africa." *Negro Digest*, June 1964, 33–48.

Draper, Theodore. *The Rediscovery of Black Nationalism*. London: Becker and Warburg, 1971.

Dryzek, John, and Stephen T. Leonard. "History and Discipline in Political Science." *American Political Science Review* 82 (1988): 1245–1260.

Du Bois, W. E. B. "The African Roots of War." *Atlantic Monthly* 115 (1915): 707–14.

———. *The Autobiography of W. E. B. Du Bois: A Soliloquy on Viewing My Life from the Last Decade of Its First Century*. New York: International Publishers, 1968.

———. *Black Reconstruction in America*. Introduction by David Levering Lewis. 1935. Reprint, New York: Free Press, 1998.

———. *Dark Princess: A Romance*. Introduction by Claudia Tate. 1928. Reprint, Jackson: University Press of Mississippi, 1995.

———. *Darkwater: Voices from within the Well*. New York: Harcourt, Brace, and Howe, 1920.

———. "The Development of a People." *International Journal of Ethics* 14 (1904): 292–311.

———. "The Future of War." Review of *The Atlantic Charter and Africa from an American Standpoint*, by Ralph Bunche. *Phylon* 3 (1942): 435–437.

———. "A Negro Nation within the Nation." *Current History* 42 (1935): 265–270.

———. "The Present Outlook for the Dark Races of Mankind." *A.M.E. Church Review* 17 (1900): 95–110.

———. "The Relation of the Negroes to the Whites in the South." *Annals* 18 (1901): 121–140.

———. "Scholarly Delusion." Review of *The Disarmament Illusion: The Movement for a Limitation of Armaments to 1907*, by Merze Tate. *Phylon* 2 (1943): 189–191.

———. *The Souls of Black Folk: Essays and Sketches*. Chicago: A. C. McClurg, 1903.

———. "Worlds of Color." *Foreign Affairs* 3 (1925): 423–444.

Dubow, Saul. "Smuts, the United Nations and the Rhetoric of Race and Rights." *Journal of Contemporary History* 43 (2008): 45–74.

Dudziak, Mary L. "Cold War Civil Rights: The Relationship between Civil Rights and Foreign Affairs in the Truman Administration." PhD diss., Yale University, 1992.

———. *Cold War Civil Rights: Race and the Image of American Democracy*. Princeton, N.J.: Princeton University Press, 2000.

———. "Desegregation as a Cold War Imperative." *Stanford Law Review* 41 (1988): 61–120.

Dunn, L. C. Review of *Geography of Intellect*, by Nathaniel Weyl and Stefan Possony. *Political Science Quarterly* 79 (1964): 287–290.

Dugan, Arthur. "Needed: A New Balance of Power." *Sewanee Review* 50 (1942): 124–127.

Duster, Troy. "Race and Reification in Science." *Science* 307 (2005): 1050–1051.

Earle, Edward Mead. *Against This Torrent*. Princeton, N.J.: Princeton University Press, 1941.

———. "The Issue Is Tolerance." Letter to the Editor. *The Nation*, September 26, 1928, 28–29.

———. "The New Mercantilism." *Political Science Quarterly* 40, 4 (1925): 594–600.

———. "Power Politics." *New Republic*, May 31, 1939, 106–108.

Edmonson, Locksley. "The Challenge of Race: From Entrenched White Power to Rising Black Power." *International Journal* 24 (1969): 693–716.

———. "Internationalization of Black Power: Historical and Contemporary Perspectives." *Mawazo* 1 (1968): 16–30.

———. "Transatlantic Slavery and the Internationalization of Race." *Caribbean Quarterly* 22 (1976): 5–25.

Edwards, Brent. *Practice of Diaspora: Literature, Translation, and the Rise of Black Internationalism*. Cambridge, Mass.: Harvard University Press, 2003.

Ekbladh, David. "Present at the Creation: Edward Mead Earle and the Depression-Era Origins of Security Studies." *International Security* 36 (Winter 2011/12): 107–141.

Elison, Ralph. "The American Dilemma: A Review." In *Shadow and Act*, 303–317. New York: Random House, 1964.

Elliott, William Yale. Review of *The Indestructible Union*, by William McDougall. *American Political Science Review* 20 (1926): 195–198.

Etzioni, Amitai. "Beyond Desegregation, What Is Needed Is a Change in Heart." Review of *The New World of Negro Americans*, by Harold Isaacs. *New York Times*, July 14, 1963, 165.

Fairlie, John A. "Politics and Science." *Scientific Monthly* 18 (January 1924): 18–37.

Fall, Dorothy. *Bernard Fall: Memories of a Soldier-Scholar*. Washington, D.C.: Potomac Books, 2006.

Farr, James. "The Historical Science(s) of Politics: The Principles, Association, and Fate of an American Discipline." In *Modern Political Science: Anglo-American Exchanges since 1880*, edited by Robert Adcock, Mark Bevir, and Shannon Stimson, 66–96. Princeton, N.J.: Princeton University Press, 2007.

Faust, Drew Gilpin. "The Scholar Who Shaped History." Review of *The Problem of Slavery in the Age of Emancipation*, by David Brion Davis. *New York Review of Books*, March 20, 2014. http://www.nybooks.com/articles/archives/2014/mar/20/scholar-who-shaped-history/.

Fearon, James, and David Laitin. "Neotrusteeship and the Problem of Weak States." *International Security* 28 (2004): 5–43.

Fields, Karen, and Barbara Fields. *Racecraft: The Soul of Inequality in American Life*. New York: Verso, 2012.

Fitzgerald, F. Scott. *The Great Gatsby*. New York: Scribner's, 1925.

Foley, Barbara. *Spectres of 1919: Class and Nation in the Making of the New Negro*. Urbana: University of Illinois Press, 2003.

Fox, Richard Wightman. *Reinhold Niebuhr: A Biography*. New York: Pantheon, 1985.

Fox, William T. R. *The American Study of International Relations*. Columbia: University of South Carolina Press, 1968.

———. "Geopolitics and International Relations." In *On Geopolitics: Classical and Nuclear*, edited by Ciro Zoppo and Charles Zorgbibe, 15–44. Dordrecht: Martinus Nijhoff, 1985.

———. "Interwar International Relations Research: The American Experience." *World Politics* 2 (1949): 67–79.

Franklin, John Hope. "The Dilemma of the American Negro Scholar." In *Soon, One Morning: New Writing by American Negroes 1940–1962*, edited by Herbert Hill, 60–76. New York: Knopf. 1963.

Fraser, Cary. "An American Dilemma: Race and Realpolitik in the American Response to the Bandung Conference, 1955." In *Window on Freedom: Race, Civil Rights, and Foreign Affairs, 1945–1988*, edited by Brenda Plummer, 115–140. Chapel Hill: University of North Carolina Press, 2003.

Frazier, E. Franklin. "The Du Bois Program in the Present Crisis." *Race* 1 (Winter 1935–1936): 11–13.

———. *Race and Culture Contacts in the Modern World*. Boston: Beacon Press, 1957.

———. Review of *When Peoples Meet: A Study of Race and Culture Contacts*, edited by Alain Locke and Bernhard J. Stern. *Science and Society* 6 (1942): 92–94.

Freeman, Harrop A. Review of *No Peace in Asia*, by Harold Isaacs. *Annals of the American Academy of Political and Social Science* 255 (1948): 192–193.

Frei, Christoph. *Hans J. Morgenthau: An Intellectual Biography*. Baton Rouge: Louisiana State University Press, 2001.

Frieden, Jeffry, and David Lake. "International Relations as a Social Science: Rigor and Relevance." *Annals of the American Academy of Political and Social Science* 600 (2005): 136–156.

Füredi, Frank. *The Silent War: Imperialism and the Changing Perception of Race*. London: Pluto Press, 1998.

Furner, Mary. *Advocacy and Objectivity: A Crisis in the Professionalization of American Social Science, 1865–1905*. Lexington: University Press of Kentucky, 1975.

Gaddis, John Lewis. *George F. Kennan: An American Life*. New York: Penguin, 2011.

Gaines, Kevin. "Pauli Murray in Ghana: The Congo Crisis and an African American Woman's Dilemma." In *Race, Nation, and Empire in American History*, edited by James Campbell, Matthew Pratt Guterl, and Robert G. Lee, 250–276. Chapel Hill: University of North Carolina Press, 2007.

Garfield, Harry Augustus. *Lost Visions*. Boston: Thomas Todd Printers, 1944.

Garst, Daniel. "Thucydides and Neorealism." *International Studies Quarterly* 33 (1989): 3–27.

Germain, Randall D., and Michael Kenny. "Engaging Gramsci: International Relations Theory and the New Gramscians." *Review of International Studies* 24 (1998): 3–21.

Gershenhorn, Jerry. "'Not an Academic Affair': African American Scholars and the Development of African Studies." *Journal of African American History* 94 (2009): 63–68.

———. *Melville Herskovits and the Racial Politics of Knowledge*. Lincoln: University of Nebraska Press, 2004.

Gibb, Paul. "Unmasterly Inactivity? Sir Julian Pauncefote, Lord Salisbury, and the Venezuela Boundary Dispute." *Diplomacy and Statecraft* 16 (2005): 23–55.

Giddings, Franklin. *Democracy and Empire, with Studies of Their Psychological, Economic and Moral Foundations*. New York: Macmillan, 1900.

———. "Imperialism?" *Political Science Quarterly* 13 (1898): 585–605.

Gill, Stephen. "Epistemology, Ontology, and the 'Italian School.'" In *Gramsci, Historical Materialism, and International Relations*, edited by Stephen Gill, 21–48. Cambridge: Cambridge University Press, 1993,

———. "Gramsci and Global Politics: Towards a Post-Hegemonic Research Agenda." In *Gramsci, Historical Materialism, and International Relations*, edited by Stephen Gill, 1–20. Cambridge: Cambridge University Press, 1993.

Gilman, Nils. *Mandarins of the Future: Modernization Theory in Cold War America*. Baltimore, Md.: Johns Hopkins University Press, 2003.

Gines, Kathryn. *Hannah Arendt and the Negro Question*. Bloomington: Indiana University Press, 2014.

Go, Julian. *Patterns of Empire: The British and American Empires, 1688 to the Present*. New York: Cambridge University Press, 2011.

———. "Sociology's Imperial Unconscious: The Emergence of American Sociology in the Context of Empire." *In Sociology and Empire: The Imperial Entanglements of a Discipline*. Edited by George Steinmetz, 83–105. Durham, N.C.: Duke University Press, 2013.

Gordon, Jane. *Creolizing Political Theory: Reading Rousseau through Frantz Fanon*. New York: Fordham University Press, 2014.

Gore, Dayo. *Radicalism at the Crossroads: African American Activists in the Cold War*. New York: New York University Press, 2011.

Gottheimer, Josh. Ed. *Ripples of Hope: Great American Civil Rights Speeches*. Cambridge, MA: Basic *Civitas* Books, 2003.

Gourevitch, Peter. "The Second Image Reversed: The International Sources of Domestic Politics." *International Organization* 32 (1978): 881–912.

Grunfeld, Adalebert Tomasz. "Friends of the Revolution: American Supporters of China's Communists" PhD diss., New York University, 1985.

Guilhot, Nicolas. "Imperial Realism: Post-War IR Theory and Decolonization." *International History Review*, October 18, 2013. Published online.

———, ed. *The Invention of International Relations Theory: Realism, the Rockefeller Foundation and the 1954 Conference on Theory*. New York: Columbia University Press, 2011.

———. "One Discipline, Many Histories." In *Invention of International Relations Theory*, edited by Nicolas Guilhot, 16–20. New York: Columbia University Press, 2011.

Gunnell, John. "The Founding of the American Political Science Association: Discipline, Profession, Political Theory, and Politics." *American Political Science Review* 100 (2006): 479–486.

Guterl, Matthew Pratt. *The Color of Race in America, 1900–1940*. Cambridge, Mass.: Harvard University Press, 2001.

Guy, Talmadge, and Stephen Brookfield. "W. E. B. Du Bois's Basic American Negro Creed and the Associates in Negro Folk Education: A Case of Repressive Tolerance in the Censorship of Radical Black Discourse on Adult Education." *Adult Education Quarterly* 60 (2009): 65–76.

Guyer, Jane. "Perspectives on the Beginning." *PAS News Events* 8 (1998): 2–4.

Hagedorn, Ann. *Savage Peace: Hope and Fear in America 1919*. New York: Simon and Schuster, 2007.

Hall, Robert B. *Area Studies with Special Reference to Their Implications for Research in the Social Sciences*. New York: Social Science Research Council, 1947.

Hallowell, John. Review of *The Super-Powers*, by William T. R. Fox. *Journal of Politics* 7 (1945): 441–442.

Harris, Abram. "Reconstruction and the Negro." *New Republic*, August 7, 1935, 367–368.

Harris, Joseph E. "Professor Merze Tate—A Profile, 1905–1996." *Negro History Bulletin*, July–December 1998, 77–93.

Harris, Leonard, ed. *The Critical Pragmatism of Alain Locke*. Lanham, Md.: Rowman and Littlefield, 1999.

Harris, Leonard, and Charles Molesworth. *Alain L. Locke: The Biography of a Philosopher*. Chicago: University of Chicago Press, 2009.

Harris, Robert L. "Racial Equality and the United Nations Charter." In *New Directions in Civil Rights Studies*, edited by Armstead Robinson and Patricia Sullivan, 126–148. Charlotte: University Press of Virginia, 1991.

———. "Segregation and Scholarship: The American Council of Learned Societies' Committee on Negro Studies, 1941–1950" *Journal of Black Studies* 12 (1982): 315–331.

Harrison, Hubert. "The White War and the Colored World." In *A Hubert Harrison Reader*, edited by Jeffrey Perry, 202–203. Wesleyan, CT: Wesleyan University Press, 2001.

Hart, Albert Bushnell. *Actual Government as Applied Under American Conditions*. 4th revised edition. 1903. Reprint, New York: Longmans, Green and Co., 1919.

Hatcher, J. Wesley. "The World of Inter-Racial Relations." *The Berea Alumnus* 6 (1931): 252–257.

Hattam, Victoria. *In the Shadow of Race: Immigrant Politics in the United States*. Chicago: University of Chicago Press, 2007.

Hazbun, Waleed. "The Geopolitics of Knowledge and the Challenge of Postcolonial Agency: International Relations, US Policy, and the Arab World." In *The Oxford Handbook of Postcolonial Studies*, edited by Graham Huggan, 217–234. Oxford: Oxford University Press, 2013.

Helbling, Mark. "African Art and the Harlem Renaissance: Alain Locke, Melville Herskovits, Roger Fry, and Albert C. Barnes." In *The Critical Pragmatism of Alain Locke: A Reader on Value Theory, Aesthetics, Community, Culture, Race, and Education*, edited by Leonard Harris, 53–84. Lanham, Md.: Rowman and Littlefield, 1999.

———. "Albert C. Barnes and Alain Locke." *Phylon* 43 (1982): 57–67.

Henderson, Errol. "Navigating the Muddy Waters of the Mainstream: Facing the Mystification of Racism in International Relations." In *African American Perspectives on Political Science*, edited by Wilber C. Rich, 325–363. Philadelphia: Temple University Press. 2007.

Henry, Charles. "Abram Harris, E. Franklin Frazier, and Ralph Bunche: The Howard School of Thought on the Problem of Race." In *The Changing Racial Regime*, edited by Matthew Holden, 18–35. New Brunswick, N.J.: Transaction Publishers, 1995.

———. *Ralph Bunche: Model Negro or American Other?* New York: New York University Press, 1999.

———. ed. *Ralph J. Bunche: Selected Speeches and Writings*. Ann Arbor: University of Michigan Press, 1995.

———. "A World View of Race Revisited." *Journal of Negro Education* 73 (2004): 137–146.

Herbert, Hilary. "The Race Problem of the South." *Annals of the American Academy of Political and Social Science* 18 (1901): 95–101.

Higham, John. *Strangers in the Land.* Rutgers, N.J.: State University Press, 1955.

Hill, Robert, and Edmond Keller. *Ralph J. Bunche, the United Nations, and the Decolonization of Africa.* Athens: Ohio University Press, 2010.

Hinds, Allister. *Britain's Sterling Colonial Policy and Decolonization.* Westport, Conn: Greenwood Press, 2001.

Hobson, J. A. *Imperialism: A Study.* London: James Nisbet, 1902.

———. "The Scientific Basis of Imperialism." *Political Science Quarterly* 17 (1902): 460–489.

Hobson, John. *The Eurocentric Conception of World Politics: Western International Theory, 1760–2010.* Cambridge: Cambridge University Press, 2012.

———. "Is Critical Theory Always for the White West and For Western Imperialism? Beyond Westphalian, Towards a Post-Racist, International Relations." *Review of International Studies* 33 (2007): 91–116.

Hodson, H. V. "Race Relations in the Commonwealth." *International Affairs* 26 (1950): 305–315.

Hoffmann, Stanley. "An American Social Science: International Relations," *Daedalus* 106 (1977): 41–60.

———. "Discord in Community: The North Atlantic Area as a Partial International System." *International Organization* 17 (1963): 521–549.

Holloway, Jonathan Scott. *Confronting the Veil: Abram Harris Jr., E. Franklin Frazier, and Ralph Bunche, 1919–1941.* Chapel Hill: University of North Carolina Press, 2002.

Holloway, Jonathan Scott, and Ben Keppel. *Black Scholars on the Line: Race, Social Science, and American Thought in the Twentieth Century.* Notre Dame, Ind.: University of Notre Dame Press, 2007.

Holsti, Ole R. "The Study of Strange Bedfellows: Theories of the Radical Right and the Radical Left." *American Political Science Review* 68 (1974): 217–242.

Holt, Thomas. "W. E. B. Du Bois's Archaeology of Race: Re-Reading 'The Conservation of Races.'" In *W. E. B. Du Bois, Race, and the City,* edited by Michael Katz and Tom Sugrue, 61–76. Philadelphia: University of Pennsylvania Press, 1998.

Homan, Gerlof D. "Orrie Benjamin Gerig: Mennonite Rebel, Peace Activist, International Civil Servant and American Diplomat, 1894–1976." *Mennonite Quarterly Review* 73 (October 1999). https://www.goshen.edu/mqr/past issues/oct99homan.html. Accessed March 2, 2013.

Hooker, James R. *Black Revolutionary: George Padmore's Path from Communism to Pan-Africanism.* New York: Praeger, 1967.

Hooper, Paul. "A Brief History of the Institute of Pacific Relations." In *Rediscovering the IPR: Proceedings of the First International Research Conference on the Institute of Pacific Relations,* edited by Paul Hooper, 110–142. Manoa: Department of American Studies, University of Hawaii at Manoa, 1994.

Horowitz, David. "Sinews of Empire." *Ramparts Magazine* (October 1969): 32–42.

Howe, Stephen. *Afrocentrism: Mythical Pasts and Imagined Homes.* London: Verso, 1998.

Huggins, Nathan. "Afro-American Studies: A Report to the Ford Foundation." In *Inclusive Scholarship: Developing Black Studies in the United States: A 25th Anniversary Retrospective of Ford Foundation Grant Making, 1982–2007*, edited by Farah Jasmine Griffin, 11–78. New York: Ford Foundation, 2007.

———. *Harlem Renaissance*. London: Oxford University Press, 1971.

Huntington, Ellsworth. Review of *Rising Tide of Color*, by T. Lothrop Stoddard. *Geographical Review* 12 (1922): 145–146.

Huntington, Samuel. "The Clash of Civilizations." Foreign Affairs (Summer 1993): 22-48.

———. *The Clash of Civilizations and the Remaking of World Order*. New York: Simon and Schuster, 1996.

———. *Who Are We: The Challenges to American National Identity*. New York: Simon and Schuster, 2004.

Huxley, Elspeth. "The Next-to-Last Act in Africa." *Foreign Affairs* 39 (1961): 655–669.

Ikenberry, G. John. "Illusions of Empire: Defining the New American Order." *Foreign Affairs* 84 (March–April 2004): 144–154.

Ikonne, Chidi. "Rene Maran and the New Negro." *Colby Quarterly* 15 (1979): 224–239.

——— "The Institute of Politics." *American Journal of International Law* 15 (1921): i–iv.

Ireland, Alleyne. *The Far Eastern Tropics: Studies in the Administration of Tropical Dependencies: Hong Kong, British North Borneo, Sarawak, Burma, the Federated Malay States, the Straits Settlements, French Indo-China, Java, the Philippine Islands*. Boston: Houghton, Mifflin, 1905.

———. "On the Need for a Scientific Study of Colonial Administration." *Proceedings of the American Political Science Association* 3 (1906): 210–221.

———. *Province of Burma: A Report Prepared for the University of Chicago*. Boston: Houghton, Mifflin. 1907.

Isaacs, Harold. "Back to Africa." *New Yorker*, May 13, 1961, 105–143.

———. *The New World of Negro Americans*. New York: Viking Press, 1964.

———. *No Peace in Asia*. 1947. Reprint, Cambridge, Mass.: MIT Press, 1967.

———. *Re-Encounters in China: Notes of a Journey in a Time Capsule*. New York: M. E. Sharpe, 1985.

———. *Scratches on Our Minds: American Images of China and India*. New York: J. Day Co., 1958.

———. "Western Man and the African Crisis." *The Saturday Review*, May 2, 1953, 10–11, 55–56.

———. "World Affairs and U.S. Race Relations: A Note on Little Rock." *Public Opinion Quarterly* 22 (1958): 364–370.

Jackson, John P., Jr. *Science for Segregation: Race, Law, and the Case against Brown v Board of Education*. New York: New York University Press, 2005.

Jackson, Robert H. "Surrogate Sovereignty? Great Power Responsibility and 'Failed States.'" Working Paper No. 25, Institute of International Relations, University of British Columbia, November 1988.

James, C. L. R. "Walter Rodney and the Question of Power." Talk given on January 30, 1981. C. L. R. James Archive. https://www.marxists.org/archive/james-clr/works/1981/01/rodney.htm. Accessed March 7, 2015.

James, Leslie. *George Padmore and Decolonization from Below*. London: Palgrave, 2014.

Janken, Kenneth Robert. *Rayford W. Logan and the Dilemma of the African-American Intellectual*. Amherst: University of Massachusetts Press, 1993.

Jenks, Leland Hamilton. *The Migration of British Capital to 1875*. New York: Knopf, 1927.

———. *Our Cuban Colony: A Study in Sugar*. New York: Vanguard Press, 1928.

Jones, Branwen Gruffydd, ed. *Decolonizing International Relations*. Lanham, Md.: Rowman and Littlefield, 2006.

Jones, Matthew. *After Hiroshima: The United States, Race and Nuclear Weapons in Asia, 1945–1965*. Cambridge: Cambridge University Press, 2010.

———. "A "Segregated" Asia?: Race, the Bandung Conference and Pan-Asianist Fears in American Thought and Policy, 1954–1955." *Diplomatic History* 29 (2005): 841–868.

Kaiser, Ernest. ed. *A Freedomways Reader*. New York: International Publishers, 1977.

Kaplan, Amy. *The Anarchy of Empire in the Making of U.S. Culture*. Cambridge, Mass.: Harvard University Press, 2005.

Kaplan, Fred. *Wizards of Armageddon*. 1983. Reprint, Palo Alto: Stanford University Press, 1991.

Kaplan, Robert. "Looking the World in the Eye: Profile of a Harvard Professor." *The Atlantic*, December 1, 2001, 68–82.

Katz, Michael, and Thomas Sugrue, eds. *W. E. B. Du Bois, Race, and the City*. Philadelphia: University of Pennsylvania Press, 1998.

Kelley, Robin D. G. "'But a Local Phase of a World Problem': Black History's Global Vision, 1883–1950." *Journal of American History* 86 (1999): 1045–1077.

———. *Race Rebels: Culture, Politics, and the Black Working Class*. New York: The Free Press, 1994.

Kelsey, Carl. "Comments on D. Collin Wells, 'Social Darwinism.'" *American Journal of Sociology* 12 (1907): 71.

———. "The Evolution of Negro Labor." *Annals of the American Academy of Political and Social Science* 21 (1903): 55–76.

———. "The Negro Farmer." PhD diss., University of Pennsylvania, 1903.

———. Review of *Souls of Black Folk*, by W. E. B. Du Bois. *Annals of the American Academy of Political and Social Science* 22 (1903): 230–232.

Keppel, Ben. *The Work of Democracy: Ralph Bunche, Kenneth B. Clark, Lorraine Hansberry, and the Cultural Politics of Race*. Cambridge, Mass.: Harvard University Press, 1995.

Kilson, Martin. "The Black Student Militant." *Encounter*, September 1971, 83–90.

———. "Political Scientists and the Activist-Technocrat Dichotomy: The Case of John Aubrey Davis." In *African American Perspectives on Political Science*, edited by Wilbur Rich, 167–192. Philadelphia: Temple University Press, 2007.

———. "Ralph Bunche: African American Intellectual." In *Trustee for the Human Community: Ralph J. Bunche, the United Nations, and the Decolonization of Africa*, edited by Robert Hill and Edmond Keller, 3–18. Athens: Ohio University Press, 2010.

———. "Ralph Bunche's Analytical Perspective on African Development." In *Ralph Bunche: The Man and His Times*, edited by Benjamin Rivlin, 83–95. New York: Holmes and Meier, 1990.

King, Desmond. *Making Americans: Immigration, Race, and the Origins of the Diverse Democracy*. Cambridge, Mass.: Harvard University Press, 2000.

Klineberg, Otto. Review of *Geography of Intellect*, by Nathaniel Weyl and Stefan Possony. *Harvard Educational Review* 34 (1964): 607–610.

Koebner, Richard, and Helmut Dan Schmidt. *Imperialism: The Story and Significance of a Political Word, 1840–1960*. Cambridge: Cambridge University Press, 1964.

Koelsch, William. *Clark University 1887–1987: A Narrative History*. Worcester, Mass.: Clark University Press, 1987.

Korff, S. A. *Russia's Foreign Relations During the Last Half Century*. New York: Macmillan, 1922.

Kramer, Paul. *Blood of Government: Race, Empire, the United States and the Philippines*. Chapel Hill: University of North Carolina Press, 2006.

——. "The Pragmatic Empire: U.S. Anthropology and Colonial Politics in the Occupied Philippines, 1898–1916." PhD diss., Princeton University, 1998.

Kuklick, Bruce. *Blind Oracles: Intellectuals and War from Kennan to Kissinger*. Princeton, N.J.: Princeton University Press, 2006.

——. "The Rise of Policy Institutes in the United States, 1943–1971." *Orbis* 55 (2011): 685–699.

Lake, David. *Hierarchy in International Relations*. Ithaca, N.Y.: Cornell University Press, 2011.

Lake, Marilyn, and Henry Reynolds. *Drawing the Global Color Line: White Men's Countries and the International Challenge of Racial Equality*. Cambridge: Cambridge University Press, 2008.

Langer, William. "A Critique of Imperialism." *Foreign Affairs* 14 (1935): 102–119.

——. *The Diplomacy of Imperialism*. 2 vols. New York: Knopf, 1935.

——. *In and Out of the Ivory Tower: The Autobiography of William L. Langer*. New York: Neale Watsun Academic Publications, 1977.

——. Review of *Re-Forging America* by T. Lothrop Stoddard. *Foreign Affairs* 5, 4 (1927): 684.

Lasswell, Harold. Review of *Social Class in Post-War Europe*, by T. Lothrop Stoddard. *American Journal of Sociology* 31 (1926): 701.

Lauren, Paul Gordon. *Power and Prejudice: The Politics and Diplomacy of Racial Discrimination*. 2nd edition. Boulder: Westview, 1996 [1988].

Lawley, Francis D. Review of *L'Imperialisme économique et les relations internationles pendant le dernier demi-siècle (1870–1920)*, by Achille Villate. *The Economic Journal* 34 (1924): 123–125.

Lederman, Rena. "Anthropological Regionalism." In *A New History of Anthropology*, edited by Henrika Kuklick, 311–325. London: Blackwell, 2007.

LeMelle, Tilden. "Race, International Relations, US Foreign Policy, and the African Liberation Struggle." *Journal of Black Studies* 3 (1972): 95–109.

LeMelle, Tilden, and George Shepherd, Jr. "Race in the Future of International Relations." *Journal of International Affairs* 25 (1971): 97–109.

Lepore, Jill. "Chan, the Man: On the Trail of the Honorable Detective." Review of *Charlie Chan: The Untold Story of the Honorable Detective and His Rendezvous with American History*, by Yunte Huang. *New Yorker*, August 9, 2010, 70.

Lewis, David Levering. *W. E. B. Du Bois: Biography of a Race, 1868–1919*. New York: Henry Holt, 1993.

Lewis, George Cornwall. *An Essay on the Government of Dependencies.* London: John Murray, 1841.

Levy, David. *University of Oklahoma: A History.* Vol. 1, *1890–1917.* Norman: University of Oklahoma Press, 2005.

Lilley, Charles R., and Michael H. Hunt. "On Social History, the State and Foreign Relations: Commentary on the 'Cosmopolitan Connection.'" *Diplomatic History* 11 (1987): 243–250.

Lincoln, C. Eric. "The Race Problem and International Relations." *New South* 21 (1966): 2–14.

Lindblom, Charles. "Political Science in the 1940s and 1950s." In *American Academic Culture in Transformation: Fifty Years, Four Disciplines*, edited by Thomas Bender and Carl Schorske, 243–269. Princeton, N.J.: Princeton University Press, 1998.

Liss, Julia. "Diasporic Identities: The Science and Politics of Race in the Work of Franz Boas and W. E. B. Du Bois, 1894–1919," *Cultural Anthropology* 13 (1998): 127–166.

Locke, Alain. "Apropos of Africa." *Opportunity*, February 1924, 37–40.

——. *Collected Works of Alain Locke*, edited by Charles Molesworth. Oxford: Oxford University Press, 2012.

——. "The Concept of Race as Applied to Social Culture." *Howard Review* 1 (1924): 290-299.

——. "Color: The Unfinished Business of Democracy." *Survey Graphic*, November 1942: 455-459.

——. "Enter the New Negro." *Survey Graphic* 6 (March 1925): 631-634.

——. "Foreword." In *The New Negro*, edited by Alain Locke. 1925. Reprint, New York: Atheneum, 1992, xxv–xxvii.

——. "The High Cost of Prejudice." *Forum* 78 (1927): 500–510.

——. "In the Setting of World Culture." In *When Peoples Meet: A Study in Race and Culture Contacts*, edited by Alain Locke and Bernard Joseph Stern, 3–11. New York: Committee on Workshops, Progressive Education Association, 1942.

——. *Race Contacts and International Relations.* Edited and with an introduction by Jeffrey Stewart. Washington, D.C.: Howard University Press, 1992.

——, ed. "Harlem: Mecca of the New Negro." *Survey Graphic* 6 (March 1925).

——. *The New Negro.* 1925. Reprint, New York: Atheneum, 1992.

Logan, Rayford. *Howard University: The First Hundred Years, 1867–1967.* New York: New York University Press, 1969.

——. "The Operation of the Mandate System in Africa." *Journal of Negro History* 13 (1928): 423–477.

——. "No Peace for the Pacifists." Review of *The Disarmament Illusion: The Movement for a Limitation of Armaments to 1907*, by Merze Tate. *Journal of Negro Education* 12 (1943): 92–93.

——. "Smuts Speaks of Africa, 1917–1942." *The Crisis* 50 (September 1943): 264–267.

Long, David. "Paternalism and the Internationalization of Imperialism: J.A. Hobson on the International Government of the 'Lower Races.'" In *Imperialism and Internationalism in the Discipline of International Relations*, edited by David Long and Brian Schmidt, 71–92. Albany: State University of New York Press, 2005.

——. "Who Killed the International Studies Conference?" *Review of International Studies* 32 (2006): 603–622.

Long, David, and Brian Schmidt, eds. *Imperialism and Internationalism in the Discipline of International Relations.* Albany: State University of New York Press, 2005.

Louis, William Roger. *Imperialism at Bay, 1941–1945: The United States and the Decolonization of the British Empire.* Oxford: Oxford University Press, 1977.

Lowell, Albert Lawrence. *Colonial Civil Service: The Selection and Training of Colonial Officials in England, Holland, and France.* New York: Macmillan, 1900.

——. "The Colonial Expansion of the United States." *Atlantic Monthly*, February 1899, 145–154.

——. "The Status of Our New Possessions—A Third View." *Harvard Law Review* 13 (1899): 155–176.

Lowi, Ted. "The Politicization of Political Science." *American Politics Quarterly* 1 (1973): 43–71.

Lowndes, Joe, Julie Novkov, and Dorian Warren. eds., *Race and American Political Development.* New York: Routledge, 2008.

Ly, Son-Thierry, and Patrick Weil. "The Antiracist Origin of the Quota System." *Social Research* 77 (2010): 45–78.

Lybyer, Albert Howe. Review of *International Relations*, by James Bryce; *Near Eastern Affairs and Conditions*, by Stephen Panaretoff; and *Russia's Foreign Relations During the Last Half Century*, by Sergius A. Korff. *American Political Science Review* 16 (1922): 695–699.

——. Review of *The New World of Islam*, by T. Lothrop Stoddard. *American Historical Review* 27 (1922): 322–324.

Lyon, Peter. "The Rise and Fall and Possible Revival of Trusteeship." *Journal of Commonwealth and Comparative Politics* 31 (1993): 96–110.

Lyons, Gene. "The Growth of National Security Research." *Journal of Politics* 25 (1963): 489–508.

Lyons, Gene and Louis Morton. *Schools for Strategy: Education and Research in National Security Affairs.* New York: Praeger, 1965.

Makalani, Minhah. *In the Cause of Freedom: Radical Black Internationalism from Harlem to London, 1917–1939.* Chapel Hill: University of North Carolina Press, 2011.

Maliniak, Daniel, Susan Peterson, and Michael J. Tierney. "Trip around the World: Teaching, Research, and Policy Views of International Relations Faculty in 20 Countries." Williamsburg, VA: Institute for the Theory and Practice of International Relations at the College of William and Mary, 2012. http://www.wm.edu/offices/itpir/_documents/trip/trip_around_the_world_2011.pdf, accessed July 17, 2014.

Manela, Erez. *The Wilsonian Moment: Self Determination and the International Origins of Anticolonial Nationalism.* New York: Oxford University Press, 2007.

Marable, Manning. *Malcolm X: A Life of Reinvention.* New York: Viking, 2011.

Martin, Geoffrey. *The Life and Thought of Isaiah Bowman.* Hamden, Conn.: Archon Books, 1980.

Martin, Tony. "Eric Williams and the Anglo-American Caribbean Commission: Trinidad's Future Nationalist Leader as Aspiring Imperial Bureaucrat." *Journal of African American History* 88 (2003): 274–290.

Martin, William G. "1957 Whitewash: Africanist and Black Traditions in the Study of Africa." Paper prepared for the conference Black Liberation and the Spirit of 1957, November 2–3, 2007, http://www2.binghamton.edu/fbc/archive/martin%201957%20whitewash.pdf.

Mason, Ernest. "Alain Locke on Race and Race Relations." *Phylon* 40 (1979): 342–350.

Matthews, Daniel, Gary Gappert, Margaret Snyder, and Francis A. Kornegay Jr. "Washington Task Force Black Paper on Institutional Racism." *Africa Today* 16 (1969): 25–31.

Maxwell, William. *New Negro, Old Left: African-American Writing and Communism between the Wars.* New York: Columbia University Press, 1999.

Mazower, Mark. *No Enchanted Palace: The End of Empire and the Ideological Origins of the United Nations.* Princeton, N.J.: Princeton University Press, 2009.

——. *Hitler's Empire: How the Nazis Ruled Europe.* New York: Penguin Press, 2008.

——. *Governing the World: The History of an Idea.* New York: Penguin, 2013.

——. "The League of Nations in Interwar Europe." *Daedalus* 126 (1997): 47–63.

——. "Paved Intentions: Civilization and Imperialism." *World Affairs* (Fall 2008): 72–84.

——. "The Strange Triumph of Human Rights." *Historical Journal* 47 (2004): 379–398.

McAfee, Cleland Boyd. "Studies in the American Race Problem." *Journal of the Royal African Society* 8 (1909): 145–153.

McCarthy, Thomas. *Race, Empire, and the Idea of Human Development.* Cambridge: Cambridge University Press, 2009.

McCaughey, Robert. *International Studies and Academic Enterprise: A Chapter in the Enclosure of American Learning.* New York: Columbia University Press, 1984.

McCoskey, Suzanne Kathleen. "When Firestone Entered Liberia: Constructing the American Tropical Capitalists of the 1920s." Unpublished, n.d.

McDougall, William. *The Indestructible Union: Rudiments of Political Science for the American Citizen.* Boston: Little Brown, 1925.

——. *Is America Safe for Democracy?* New York: Scribner's 1921.

——. "Stoddard's The Revolt Against Civilization—The Menace of the Underman; Desmond's Labour, The Giant With the Feet of Clay." *Quarterly Journal of Economics* 36 (1922): 666–682.

McDuffie, Erik. *Sojourning for Freedom: Black Women, American Communism, and the Making of Black Left Feminism.* Durham: Duke University Press, 2011.

McKee, James. *Sociology and the Race Problem: A Failure of Perspective.* Champaign: University of Illinois Press, 1993.

McKenzie, Roderick. *Oriental Exclusion: The Effect of American Immigration Laws, Regulations and Judicial Decisions upon the Chinese and Japanese on the American Pacific Coast.* Preliminary Report for the July 1927 Conference of the Institute of Pacific Relations. New York: American Group of the IPR, 1927.

Mears, Eliot. *Modern Turkey: A Politico-Economic Interpretation, 1908–1923.* New York: Macmillan, 1924.

——. *Residential Orientals on the American Pacific Coast: Their Legal and Economic Status.* New York: American Group, Institute of Pacific Relations, 1927.

Menand, Louis. "Both Sides Now: Doris Lessing's Sixties." Review of *The Sweetest Dream*, by Doris Lessing. *New Yorker*, February 18 and 25, 2002, 193–194.

———. *The Marketplace of Ideas: Reform and Resistance in the American University.* New York: W. W. Norton, 2010.

Meriwether, James H. *Proudly We Can Be Africans: Black Americans and Africa, 1935–1961.* Chapel Hill: University of North Carolina Press, 2002.

Merriam, Charles. "Masters of Social Science: William Archibald Dunning." *Social Forces* 5 (1926): 1–8.

———. "Recent Tendencies in Political Thought." In *History of Political Theories—Recent Times*, edited by Charles Merriam and Harry Elmer Barnes, 1–45. New York: Macmillan, 1924.

Merriam, Charles, and Harry Elmer Barnes, eds. *History of Political Theories—Recent Times.* New York: Macmillan, 1924.

Messmer, Mathias. *Jewish Wayfarers in Modern China: Tragedy and Splendor.* Plymouth, UK: Lexington Books, 2012.

Miller, Eben. *Born along the Color Line: The 1933 Amenia Conference and the Rise of a National Civil Rights Movement.* Oxford: Oxford University Press, 2012.

Millis, Walter. *Road to War: America 1914-1917.* Boston: Houghton Mifflin, 1935.

Mills, C. Wright. "Crackpot Realism." *Fellowship: The Journal of the Fellowship of Reconciliation* 25 (1959): 3–8.

Minter, William, Gail Hovey, and Charles Cobb Jr. *No Easy Victories: African Liberation and American Activists over a Half Century.* Trenton, N.J.: Africa World Press, 2007.

Moon, Parker T. *Imperialism and World Politics.* New York: Macmillan, 1926.

———. *Syllabus on International Relations.* New York: Macmillan, 1925.

Morgenthau, Hans. Review of *The Disarmament Illusion: The Movement for a Limitation of Armaments to 1907*, by Merze Tate. *Russian Review* 2 (1943): 104–105.

———. Review of *The Super-Powers*, by William T. R. Fox. *Ethics* 55 (1945): 227–228.

Morrison, Toni. *Playing in the Dark: Whiteness and the Literary Imagination.* New York: Random House, 1992.

———. "Unspeakable Things Unspoken: The Afro-American Presences in American Literature." *Michigan Quarterly Review* 28 (1989): 1–34.

Morton, Louis, and Gene Lyons. *Schools for Strategy: Education and Research in National Security Affairs.* New York: Praeger, 1965.

Mphahele, Ezekiel. "The Blacks: Dialogue across the Seas." *Africa Today* 14 (1967): 22–25.

Muehlenbeck, Philip. *Betting on the Africans: John F. Kennedy's Courting of African Nationalist Leaders.* London: Oxford University Press, 2012.

Myers, Denys P. Review of *The Washington Conference*, by Raymond Leslie Buell. *Harvard Law Review* 36 (1922): 237–239.

Myrdal, Gunnar. *An American Dilemma: The Negro Problem and Modern Democracy.* New York: Harper Brothers, 1944.

Nexon, Daniel H., and Thomas Wright. "What's at Stake in the Empire Debate." *American Political Science Review* 101 (2007): 253–271.

Ngai, Mai. *Impossible Subjects: Illegal Aliens and the Making of Modern America.* Princeton, N.J.: Princeton University Press, 2003.

Nicols, Christopher. *Promise and Peril: America at the Dawn of a Global Age.* Cambridge, Mass.: Harvard University Press, 2010.

Niebuhr, Reinhold. "The Colored Continents." In *Reinhold Niebuhr on Politics*, by Harry Davis and Robert Good, 308–312. 1960. Reprint, Eugene, Ore.: Wipf and Stack, 2007.

———. "Power and Ideology in National and International Affairs." In *Theoretical Aspects of International Relations*, edited by William T. R. Fox, 107–118. Notre Dame: University of Notre Dame Press, 1959.

Norton, Anne. "Political Science as a Vocation." In *Problems and Methods in the Study of Politics*, edited by Ian Shapiro, Rogers Smith, and Tarek Masoud, 67–82. Cambridge: Cambridge University Press, 2004.

Nye, Joseph. *Bound to Lead: The Changing Nature of American Power.* New York: Basic Books, 1990.

———. *Soft Power: The Means to Success in World Politics.* New York: Public Affairs, 2004.

O'Donnell, Charles. "American Foreign Policy: A Review of Some Recent Literature on Isolation and Collective Security." *Review of Politics* 1 (1939): 333–347.

Olson, William C., and A. J. R. Groom. *International Relations Then & Now: Origins and Trends in Interpretation.* London: Harper Collins, 1991.

Oren, Ido. "The Enduring Relationship between the American (National Security) State and the State of the Discipline." *PS* 37 (2004): 51–55.

———. *Our Enemies and US: America's Rivalries and the Making of Political Science.* Ithaca, N.Y.: Cornell University Press, 2003.

———. "A Sociological Analysis of the Decline of American IR Theory." Unpublished, 2014.

———. "The Unrealism of Contemporary Realism: The Tension between Realist Theory and Realist Practice." *Perspectives on Politics* 7 (2009): 283–301.

Padmore, George. *The Life and Struggles of Negro Toilers.* London: Red International of Labor Unions, 1931.

Page, Arthur Wilson and Walter Hines Page, *The World's Work . . . : A History of Our Time*, Vol. 1 (New York: Doubleday, 1900).

Page, William Tyler. *The American's Creed: Summary of American Civic Faith.* Washington, D.C.: Government Printing Office, 1926.

Painter, Nell. "Jim Crow at Harvard: 1923." *New England Quarterly* 44 (1971): 627–634.

———. *The History of White People.* New York: Norton, 2010.

Panaretoff, Stephen. *Near Eastern Affairs and Conditions.* New York: Macmillan, 1922.

Parker, Jason. *Brother's Keeper: The United States, Race, and Empire in the British Caribbean, 1937–1962.* New York: Oxford University Press, 2008.

———. "Cold War II: The Eisenhower Administration, the Bandung Conference, and the Reperiodization of the Postwar Era." *Diplomatic History* 30 (2006): 1–26.

———. "'Made-in-America Revolutions'? The 'Black University' and the American Role in the Decolonization of the Black Atlantic." *Journal of American History* 96 (2009): 727–750.

Parmar, Inderjeet. "'. . . Another Important Group that Needs More Cultivation': The Council on Foreign Relations and the Mobilization of Black Americans for Interventionism, 1939–1941." *Ethnic and Racial Studies* 27 (2004): 710–731.

——. *Foundations of the American Century: The Ford, Carnegie, and Rockefeller Foundations in the Rise of American Power.* New York: Columbia University Press, 2012.

Pedersen, Susan. "Back to the League of Nations." *American Historical Review* 112 (2007): 1091–1117.

——. *The Guardians: The League of Nations and the Crisis of Empire.* New York: Oxford University Press, 2015.

Perham, Margery. "African Facts and American Criticisms." *Foreign Affairs* 22 (1944): 444–457.

——. "The British Problem in Africa." *Foreign Affairs* 29 (1951): 637–650.

Pfaltzgraff, Robert Jr., Ole Holsti, Patrick Riley, Richard Kennington, Otwin Marenin, Harry Eckstein, Allan Bloom and R. E. Allen. "Communications." *American Political Science Review* 69 (1975): 186–198.

Plantan, Frank. "Multidisciplinary Approaches, Disciplinary Boundaries, and Institutional Response in American Higher Education: A History of International Relations as a Field of Study." PhD diss., University of Pennsylvania, 2002.

Platt, Anthony. *E. Franklin Frazier Reconsidered.* New Brunswick, N.J.: Rutgers University Press, 1991.

Plummer, Brenda Gayle. *In Search of Power: African Americans in the Era of Decolonization, 1956–1974.* Cambridge: Cambridge University Press, 2013.

——. *Rising Wind: Black Americans and U.S. Foreign Affairs, 1935–1960.* Chapel Hill: University of North Carolina Press, 1996.

Polsgrove, Carol. *Divided Minds: Intellectuals and the Civil Rights Movement.* New York: W. W. Norton, 2001.

——. *Ending British Rule in Africa: Writers in a Common Cause.* Manchester: Manchester University Press, 2009.

Possony, Stefan. "Colonial Problems in Perspective." In *The Idea of Colonialism*, by Robert Strausz-Hupé and Harry Hazard, 17–44. New York: Praeger, 1958.

——. "UNESCO and Race: A Study in Intellectual Oppression." *Mankind Quarterly* 8 (1968): 115–146.

Potter, Pitman B. Review of *The Disarmament Illusion: The Movement for a Limitation of Armaments to 1907*, by Merze Tate. *American Political Science Review* 36 (1942): 973.

Pratt, Julius W. "The 'Large Policy' of 1898." *Mississippi Valley Historical Review* 19 (1932): 219–242.

Preston, Michael, and Maurice Woodard. "The Rise and Decline of Black Political Scientists in the Profession." *PS* 17 (1984): 787–792.

Prideaux, Simon. "From Organizational Theory to the New Communitarianism of Amitai Etzioni." *Canadian Journal of Sociology* 27 (2002): 69–81.

Pruessen, Ronald W. *John Foster Dulles: The Road to Power.* New York: Free Press, 1982.

Pugh, Jeffrey T. "Whose Brother's Keeper? International Trusteeship and the Search for Peace in the Palestinian Territories." *International Studies Perspective* 13 (2012): 321–343.

Pye, Lucian. "Harold R. Isaacs (1910–86)." *China Quarterly* 111 (1987): 469–470.

——, ed. *Political Science and Area Studies: Rivals or Partners?* Bloomington: Indiana University Press, 1975.

Ramos, Paul. "The Role of the Yale Institute of International Studies in the Construction of the United States National Security Ideology, 1935–1951." PhD diss., University of Manchester, 2003.

Rampersad, Arnold. "Introduction." In *The New Negro*, edited by Alain Locke, ix–xxiii. 1925. Reprint, New York: Atheneum, 1992.

——. *Ralph Ellison: A Biography*. New York: Knopf, 2007.

Reinsch, Paul. "Influence of Geographic, Economic and Political Conditions," in Papers on Inter-Racial Problems Communicated to the First Universal Races Congress, edited by Gustav Spiller, 49–57. London: P. S. King and Son, 1911.

——"The Negro Race and European Civilization." *American Journal of Sociology* 11 (1905): 145–167.

Rhoodie, Eschel. *The Third Africa*. New York: Twin Circle, 1968.

Rice, Margaret F. "What Shall We Do For Armistice Day?" *The English Journal* 17 (1928): 757–760.

Rietzler, Katharina. "Experts for Peace: Structures and Motivations of Philanthropic Internationalism in the Interwar Years." In *Internationalism Reconfigured: Transnational Ideas and Movements between the World Wars*, edited by Daniel Laqua, 45–66. London: I. B. Tauris, 2011.

Roark, James L. "American Black Leaders: The Response to Colonialism and the Cold War, 1943–1953." *African Historical Studies* 4 (1971): 253–270.

Roberts, Priscilla. "'The Council Has Been Your Creation': Hamilton Fish Armstrong, Paradigm of the American Foreign Policy Establishment?" *Journal of American Studies* 35 (2001): 65–94.

Robinson, Cedric. *Black Marxism: The Making of the Black Radical Tradition*. 1983. Reprint, Chapel Hill: University of North Carolina Press, 2000.

Robinson, Pearl. "Area Studies in Search of Africa." In *The Politics of Knowledge: Area Studies and the Disciplines*, edited by David Szanton, 119–183. Berkeley: University of California Press, 2004.

——. "Ralph Bunche and African Studies: Reflections on the Politics of Knowledge." *African Studies Review* 51 (2008): 1–16.

——. "Ralph Bunche the Africanist: Revisiting Paradigms Lost." In *Trustee for the Human Community: Ralph J. Bunche and the Decolonization of Africa*, edited by Robert A. Hill and Edmond J. Keller, 69–90. Athens: Ohio University Press, 2010.

Roediger, David. *The Wages of Whiteness: Race and the Making of the Working Class*. London: Verso, 1999.

Rogers, Howard J., ed. *Congress of Arts and Sciences*. Vol. 7, *Economics, Politics, Jurisprudence, and Social Sciences*. Boston: Houghton Mifflin, 1906.

Rojas, Fabio. *From Black Power to Black Studies: How a Radical Social Movement Became an Academic Discipline*. Baltimore, Md.: Johns Hopkins University Press, 2007.

Rooks, Noliwe. *White Money, Black Power: The Surprising History of African American Studies and the Crisis of Race in Higher Education*. Boston: Beacon Press, 2006.

Roosevelt, Theodore. "The Monroe Doctrine." In *American Ideals and Other Essays, Social and Political*, Vol. 4, by Theodore Roosevelt, 220–237. New York: G. P. Putnam's Sons, 1897.

Rosenau, James. *International Studies and the Social Sciences: Problems, Priorities and Prospects in the United States*. Beverly Hills: Sage Publications, 1973.

Ross, Edward. "The Causes of Race Superiority." *Annals of the American Academy of Political and Social Science* 18 (1901): 67–89.

Ross, Dorothy. *G. Stanley Hall: The Psychologist as Prophet.* Chicago: University of Chicago Press, 1972.

——. *The Origins of American Social Science.* Cambridge: Cambridge University Press, 1988.

Rotter, Andrew J. "In Retrospect: Harold R. Isaacs's *Scratches on Our Minds.*" *Reviews in American History* 24 (1996): 177–188.

Samuels, Richard, and Myron Weiner, eds. *The Political Culture of Foreign Area and International Studies: Essays in Honor of Lucian W. Pye.* Washington, D.C.: Brassey's, 1992.

Sayre, Francis B. "The Quest for Independence." *Foreign Affairs* 30 (1952): 564–579.

Schelling, Thomas. "The Strategy of Conflict: Prospectus for a Reorientation of Game Theory." *Journal of Conflict Resolution* 2 (1958): 203–264.

Scheuerman, William E. "The (Classical) Realist Vision of Global Reform." *International Theory* 2 (2010): 246–282.

Schmidt, Brian. *The Political Discourse of Anarchy: A Disciplinary History of International Relations.* New York: State University of New York Press, 1998.

——. "The Rockefeller Foundation Conference and the Long Road to a Theory of International Politics." In *Invention of International Relations Theory*, edited by Nicolas Guilhot, 79–96. New York: Columbia University Press, 2011.

Schuman, Frederick L. "The Dismal Science of World Politics: The Year's Books on International Affairs." *American Scholar* 6 (1937): 170–179.

——. *International Politics: An Introduction to the Western State System.* 2nd ed. 1933. Reprint, New York: McGraw-Hill, 1937.

Schwoch, James. *Global TV: New Media and the Cold War, 1946–69.* Carbondale: University of Illinois Press, 2008.

See, Jennifer. "Prophet without Honor: Hans Morgenthau and the War in Vietnam, 1955–1965." *Pacific Historical Review* 70 (2001): 419–448.

Shambaugh, Benjamin. Review of *Reconstruction and the Constitution, 1866–1876*, by John W. Burgess. *Annals of the American Academy of Political and Social Science* 20 (1902): 127–130.

Shepherd, George W. "The Center on International Race Relations, University of Denver." *Race and Class* 11 (1969): 228–229.

——. *Racial Influences on American Foreign Policy.* New York: Basic Books, 1970.

Shepherd, George, Jr., and Tilden Lemelle. *Race among Nations: A Conceptual Approach.* Lexington, Mass.: D. C. Heath, 1970.

Sherman, Richard. "The Harding Administration and the Negro: An Opportunity Lost." *Journal of Negro History* 49 (1964): 151–168.

Sherwood, Marika. *Kwame Nkrumah: The Years Abroad, 1935–1947.* Legon, Ghana: Freedom Publications, 1996.

Shils, Edward. "Robert Maynard Hutchins." *American Scholar* 59 (1990): 211–235.

Shimazu, Naoko. *Japan, Race, and Equality: The Racial Equality Proposal of 1919.* London: Routledge, 1998.

Sicherman, Harvey. "Robert Strausz-Hupé: His Life and Times." *Orbis* 47 (2003): 195–215.

Silva, Edward, and Sheila Slaughter. "Prometheus Bound: The Limits of Social Science Professionalization in the Progressive Period." *Theory and Society* 9 (1980): 781–819.

Singh, Nikhil. *Black Is a Country: Race and the Unfinished Struggle for Democracy.* Cambridge, Mass.: Harvard University Press, 2004.

———. *Exceptional Empire: Race and War in US Globalism.* Cambridge, Mass.: Harvard University Press, 2015.

Sivanandan, A. "Race and Resistance: The IRR Story." *Race and Class* 50 (2008): 1–30.

Sluga, Glenda. *Internationalism in the Age of Nationalism.* Philadelphia: University of Pennsylvania Press, 2013.

Smith, Alice J. "Rene Maran's Batouala and the Prix-Goncourt." *Contributions in Black Studies* 4 (1980): 17–34.

Smith, Edwin W. "The Book of the Quarter: Africa Emergent." *Journal of the Royal African Society* 38 (1939): 75.

Smith, Neil. *American Empire: Roosevelt's Geographer and the Prelude to Globalization.* Berkeley: University of California Press, 2003.

Smith, Rogers M. "Beyond Tocqueville, Myrdal, and Hartz: The Multiple Traditions in America." *American Political Science Review* 87 (1993): 549–566.

———. *Civic Ideals: Conflicting Visions of Citizenship in U.S. History.* New Haven, Conn.: Yale University Press, 1997.

Smuts, Jan Christian. "The Basis of Trusteeship in African Native Policy." An address to the South African Institute of Race Relations in Cape Town, January 21, 1942. Johannesburg: R. L. Esson, 1942.

———. *The League of Nations: A Practical Suggestion.* London: Hodder and Stoughten, 1918.

Solow, Barbara Lewis, and Stanley Engerman, eds. *British Capitalism and Caribbean Slavery: The Legacy of Eric Williams.* Cambridge: Cambridge University Press, 1987.

Somit. Albert, and Joseph Tanenhaus. *The Development of Political Science: From Burgess to Behavioralism.* Boston: Allyn and Bacon, 1967.

Sondermann, Fred. "The Merger." *Background* 6 (1962): 3–4.

———. "Peace Initiatives: The Literature of Possibilities." *Journal of Conflict Revolution* 7 (1963): 141–149.

Solovey, Mark. *Shaky Foundations: The Politics-Patronage-Social Science Nexus in Cold War America.* New Brunswick, N.J.: Rutgers University Press, 2013.

Spiller, Gustav, ed. *Papers on Inter-Racial Problems.* London: P. S. King, 1911.

Spiro, Jonathan Peter. *Defending the Master Race: Conservation, Eugenics, and the Legacy of Madison Grant.* Burlington: University of Vermont Press, 2009.

Stalker, Nancy. "Suicide, Boycotts, and Embracing Tagore: The Japanese Popular Response to the 1924 US Immigration Exclusion Law." *Japanese Studies* 26 (2006): 153–170.

Stanfield, John H. *Philanthropy and Jim Crow in American Social Science.* Westport, Conn.: Greenwood Press, 1985.

Staniland, Martin. *American Intellectuals and African Nationalists, 1955–1970.* New Haven, Conn.: Yale University Press, 1991.

Steinmetz, George, ed. *Sociology and Empire: The Imperial Entanglements of a Discipline.* Durham, N.C.: Duke University Press, 2013.

Stewart, Jeffrey C. Ed. *The Critical Temper of Alain Locke: A Selection of his Essays on Art and Culture.* New York: Garland, 1983.

Stocking, George. *Race, Culture, and Evolution: Essays in the History of Anthropology.* 1968. Reprint, Chicago: University of Chicago Press, 1982.

Stoddard, T. Lothrop. *Clashing Tides of Color.* New York: Scribner's, 1935.

——. "The Impasse at the Color-Line." *Forum* 78 (1927): 510–519.

——. *Lonely America.* New York: Doubleday, 1932.

——. "Pan-Turanism." *American Political Science Review* 11 (1917): 12–23.

——. *The New World of Islam.* New York: Scribner's, 1921.

——. *Present-Day Europe: Its National States of Mind.* New York: The Century Company, 1917.

——. *Racial Realities in Europe.* New York: Scribners, 1924.

——. *Re-Forging America: The Story of Our Nationhood.* New York: Scribners, 1927.

——. *Revolt against Civilization: The Menace of the Under Man.* New York: Scribner's, 1922.

——. *Revolution in San Domingo.* Boston: Houghton-Mifflin, 1914.

——. *Rising Tide of Color: The Threat against White World Supremacy.* New York: Scribner's, 1920.

——. "Santo Domingo: Our Unruly Ward." *American Review of Reviews* 49 (1914): 726–731.

——. *Social Class in Post-War Europe.* New York: Scribners, 1925.

Stoddard, T. Lothrop, and Glenn Frank. *Stakes of the War.* New York: The Century Co., 1918.

Stone, Alfred Holt. *Studies in the American Race Problem.* New York: Doubleday, 1908.

Strausz-Hupé, Robert. *In My Time: An Eclectic Autobiography.* New York: Norton, 1965.

——. Review of *The Super-Powers*, by William T. R. Fox. *Annals of the American Academy of Political and Social Science* 238 (March 1945): 204.

Strausz-Hupé, Robert and Harry Hazard. *The Idea of Colonialism.* New York: Praeger, 1958.

Strausz-Hupé, Robert, and Stefan Possony. *International Relations in the Age of the Conflict between Democracy and Dictatorship.* New York: McGraw Hill 1950.

Sumner, William Graham. *The Conquest of the United States by Spain.* Boston: D. Estes, 1899.

Sundiata, Ibrahim. *Brothers and Strangers: Black Zion, Black Slavery, 1914–1940.* Durham: University of North Carolina Press, 2003.

Tate, Merze. *The Disarmament Illusion: The Movement for a Limitation of Armaments to 1907.* New York: Macmillan, 1942.

——. *Hawaii: Reciprocity or Annexation.* East Lansing: Michigan State University Press, 1968.

——. *The United States and the Hawaiian Kingdom.* New Haven, Conn.: Yale University Press, 1965.

——. "The War Aims of World War I and II and Their Relation to the Darker Peoples of the World." *Journal of Negro Education* 12 (Summer 1943): 521–532.

———. Review of *The Color Curtain*, by Richard Wright. *Journal of Negro History* 41 (1956): 263–265.

———. Review of *Warning to the West*, by Krishnalal Shridharani. *Journal of Negro Education* 12 (1943): 654–655.

Thomas, Ebony Elizabeth. "'We're Saying the Same Thing': How English Teachers Negotiated Solidarity, Identity, and Ethics Through Talk and Interaction." PhD diss., University of Michigan, 2010.

Thompson, Lanny. "The Imperial Republic: A Comparison of the Insular Territories under U.S. Dominion after 1898." *Pacific Historical Review* 71 (2002): 535–574.

Throntveit, Trygve. "The Fable of the Fourteen Points: Woodrow Wilson and National Self-Determination." *Diplomatic History* 35 (2011): 445–481.

Tickner, J. Ann. *A Feminist Voyage through International Relations*. New York: Oxford University Press, 2014.

Tignor, Robert. *W. Arthur Lewis and the Birth of Development Economics*. Princeton, N.J.: Princeton University Press, 2006.

Toynbee, Arnold. "Is a 'Race War' Shaping Up?" *New York Times Magazine*, September 29, 1963.

Turner, James, and Rukudzo Murapa. "Africa: Conflict in Black and White." *Africa Today* 16 (1969): 13–14.

Urban, Wayne J. *Black Scholar: Horace Mann Bond, 1904–1972*. Athens: University of Georgia Press, 1992.

Urquhart, Brian. *Ralph Bunche: An American Life*. New York: Norton, 1993.

Van Wienan, Mark, ed. *Rendezvous with Death: American Poems of the Great War*. Chicago: University of Illinois Press, 2002.

Venkataramani, M. S. "The United States, the Colonial Issue, and the Atlantic Charter Hoax." *International Studies* 13 (1974): 1–28.

Vitalis, Robert. "A Great-Grandson Breaks New Ground in Critical IR Thought." *Millennium* 42 (2014): 480–484.

———. *America's Kingdom: Mythmaking on the Saudi Oil Frontier*. Palo Alto, Calif.: Stanford University Press, 2007.

———. "Birth of a Discipline." In *Imperialism and Internationalism in the Discipline of International Relations*, edited by David Long and Brian Schmidt, 159–182. Albany: State University of New York Press, 2005.

———. "The Democratization Industry and the Limits of the New Interventionism." *Middle East Report* 187–188 (1994): 46–50.

———. "The Graceful and Liberal Gesture: Marking Racism Invisible in American International Relations." *Millennium* 29 (2000): 331–356.

———. "Guilhot's Gambit." Review of *The Invention of International Relations Theory*," edited by Nicolas Guilhot. HDiplo/ISSF Roundtable 3 (2011). http://www.h-net.org/~diplo/ISSF | http://www.issforum.org.

———. "International Studies in America." *Social Science Research Council Items and Issues* 3 (2002): 1–2, 12–16.

———. "Midnight Ride of Kwame Nkrumah and Other Fables from Bandung." *Humanity* 4 (2013): 261–288.

———. "The Noble American Science of Imperial Relations and Its Laws of Race Development." *Comparative Studies in Society and History* 52 (2010): 909–938.

Von Eschen, Penny. *Race against Empire: Black Americans and Anticolonialism, 1937–1957*. Ithaca, N.Y.: Cornell University Press, 1997.

Vucetic, Srdjan. *The Anglosphere: A Genealogy of a Racialized Identity in International Relations*. Stanford, Calif.: Stanford University Press, 2011.

Waever, Ole. "The Sociology of a Not So International Discipline: American and European Developments in International Relations." *International Organization* 52 (1998): 687–728.

Wagley, Charles. *Area Research and Training: A Conference Report on the Study of World Areas*. Social Science Research Council Pamphlet, no. 6, June 1948.

Wald, Alan. *The New York Intellectuals: The Rise and Decline of the Anti-Stalinist Left*. Chapel Hill: University of North Carolina Press, 1987.

Walker, Martin. *The Cold War: A History*. New York: Henry Holt, 1993.

Wallace, Schuyler. "The Naval School of Military Government and Administration." *Annals of the American Academy of Political and Social Science* 231 (1944): 29-33.

Wallerstein, Immanuel. "The Unintended Consequences of Cold War Area Studies." *The Cold War and the University*, edited by André Schiffrin, 195–232. New York: Free Press, 1997.

Walton, Hanes, Jr. "The Political Science Educational Philosophy of Ralph Bunche: Theory and Practice." *Journal of Negro Education* 73 (2004): 147–158.

Walton, Hanes, Jr., Cheryl M. Miller, and Joseph P. McCormick II. "Race and Political Science: The Dual Traditions of Race Relations, Politics and African-American Politics." In *Political Science in History: Research Programs and Political Traditions*, edited by James Farr, John Dryzek, and Stephen Leonard, 145–174. London: Cambridge University Press. 1995.

Ware, Edith E. *The Study of International Relations in the United States*. New York: Columbia University Press, 1934.

Waters, Ronald. "Ralph Bunche and Civil Rights." Unpublished, 2004.

Watson, James. "Bernard Moses: Pioneer in Latin American Scholarship." *Hispanic American Historical Review* 42 (1962): 212–216.

Welch, David. "Why International Relations Theorists Should Stop Reading Thucydides." *Review of International Studies* 29 (2003): 301–319.

Wells, Roger H. Review of *International Politics: An Introduction to the Western State System*, by Frederick Schuman. *American Political Science Review* 29 (1935): 677–678.

Weyl, Nathaniel. Review of *The New World of Negro Americans*, by Harold Isaacs. *Mankind Quarterly* 5 (1964): 50–51.

Weyl, Nathaniel, and Stefan Possony. *The Geography of Intellect*. Chicago: Henry Regnery, 1963.

Whitley, Richard. *The Intellectual and Social Organization of the Sciences*. Oxford: Oxford University Press, 1984.

"Why Be a Congressman?" *Time*, August 3, 1942. http://www.time.com/time/magazine/article/0,9171,773317,00.html. Accessed February 13, 2013.

Wicker, E. R. "Colonial Development and Welfare, 1929–1957: The Evolution of a Policy." *Social and Economic Studies* 7 (1958): 170–192.

Wilbur, Ray Lyman. *The Memoirs of Ray Lyman Wilbur, 1875–1949*. Palo Alto: Stanford University Press, 1960.

Wilford, Hugh. The *Mighty Wurlitzer: How the CIA Played America*. Cambridge, Mass.: Harvard University Press, 2008.

Willey, Malcolm. "The College Training Programs of the Armed Forces." *Annals of the American Academy of Political and Social Science* 231 (1944): 14–28.

Willkie, Wendell L. *One World*. New York: Simon and Schuster, 1943.

Williams, Bruce. "The Institute of Politics." *American Political Science Review* 17 (1923): 643–649.

Williams, Eric. "Africa and the Post-War World," *Journal of Negro Education* 11 (1942): 534–536.

Willoughby, Westel W. "Report of the Secretary for the Year 1904." *Proceedings of the American Political Science Association* 1 (1904): 27–32.

Wilson, Ernest III. "Why Political Scientists Don't Study Black Politics, but Historians and Sociologists Do." *PS* 18 (1985): 600–607.

Wilson, Peter. *The International Theory of Leonard Woolf: A Study in Twentieth Century Idealism*. New York: Palgrave Macmillan, 2003.

Wilson, Woodrow. "A System of Political Science and Constitutional Law." In *The Papers of Woodrow Wilson*, Vol. 7, *1890–1892*, edited by Arthur S. Link, 195–203. Princeton, N.J.: Princeton University Press. 1969.

Wimmer, Andreas, and Nina Glick Schiller. "Methodological Nationalism and Beyond: Nation-State Building, Migration, and the Social Sciences." *Global Networks* 2 (2002): 301–334.

Winston, Michael. "Through the Back Door: Academic Racism and the Negro Scholar in Historical Perspective." *Daedalus* 100 (1971): 678–719.

Wolfers, Arnold. "National Foreign Policies and the Strategy of Peace." *Pacific Affairs* 7 (1934): 139–152.

Wolton, Suke. *Lord Hailey, the Colonial Office and the Politics of Race and Empire in the Second World War: The Loss of White Prestige*. New York: St. Martins, 2000.

Wonham, Henry B., ed. *Criticism and the Color Line: Desegregating American Literary Studies*. New Brunswick, N.J.: Rutgers University Press, 1996.

Woodward, C. Vann. *The Strange Career of Jim Crow*. Oxford: Oxford University Press, 1955.

Woodward, Komozi. "Amiri Baraka and Black Power Politics." In *The Black Power Movement: Re-thinking the Civil Rights—Black Power Era*, edited by Peniel E. Joseph, 55–78. London: Routledge, 2006.

Woodard, Maurice, and Michael Preston. "Black Political Scientists: Where Are the new PhDs?" *PS* 81 (1985): 80–88.

Woolf, Leonard. *Imperialism and Civilization*. New York: Harcourt, Brace, 1928.

———. "International Morality." *International Journal of Ethics* 26 (1915): 11–22.

Worcester, Donald. *A River Running West: The Life of John Wesley Powell*. New York: Oxford, 2001.

Wright, Quincy. "Political Science and World Stabilization." *American Political Science Review* 44 (1950): 1–13.

Wriston, Walter. *Prepare for Peace*. New York: Harper and Brothers, 1941.

Wu, Judy Tzu-Chun. "An African-Vietnamese American: Robert S. Browne, the Antiwar Movement and the Personal/Political Dimensions of Black Internationalism." *Journal of African American History* 92 (2007): 491–515.

Yoder, Stephen, and Brittany Bramlett. "What Happens at the Journal Office Stays at the Journal Office: Assessing Journal Transparency and Record-Keeping Practices." *PS* (April 2013): 363–373.

Zakaria, Fareed Rafiq, "The Rise of a Great Power: National Strength, State Structure, and American Foreign Policy." PhD diss., Harvard, 1993.

Zimmerman, Andrew. *Alabama in Africa: Booker T. Washington, the German Empire and the Globalization of the New South.* Princeton, N.J.: Princeton University Press, 2010.

INDEX